EYE *to* I

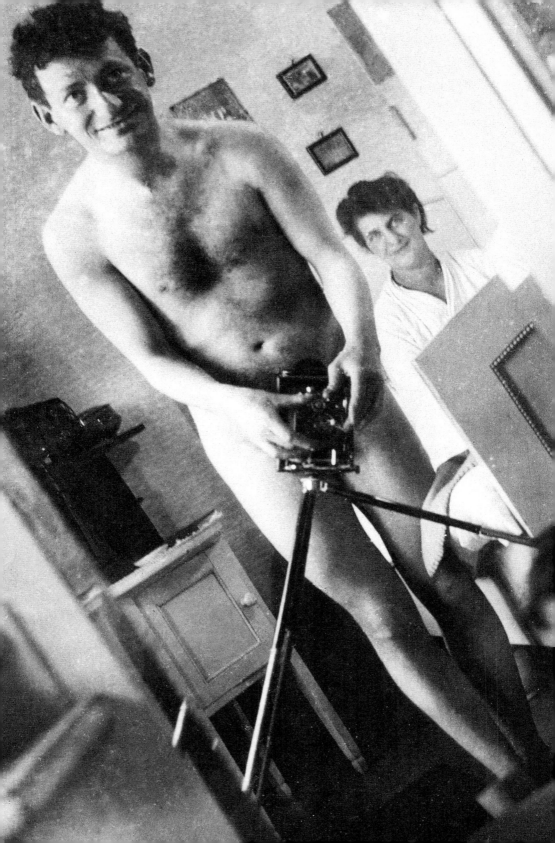

EYE *to* I

The Autobiography of a Photographer

Erwin Blumenfeld

Translated by
Mike Mitchell and Brian Murdoch

with 70 illustrations

THAMES AND HUDSON

Title page: Self-portrait with wife Lena, daughter Lisette
(in mirror), and son Henry (below right). Zandvoort, c. 1930.

This translation by Mike Mitchell and Brian Murdoch is from the German *Durch tausendjährige Zeit* (first published in 1976). They benefited from an unpublished draft translation of Blumenfeld's manuscript by Nora Hodges, to whom they and the publishers extend gracious acknowledgment.

The 1998 edition published by Eichborn Verlag, Germany, carries Blumenfeld's own choice of title, *Einbildungsroman*.

First published in hardcover in the United States of America in 1999 by Thames and Hudson Inc., 500 Fifth Avenue, New York, New York 10110

Library of Congress Catalog Card Number 98-75140
ISBN 0-500-01907-X

Designed by Maggi Smith

Printed and bound in Slovenia

CONTENTS

PART ONE

1 Prenatal Education

Once upon a time, far too long ago, when man could still more or less understand the language of the birds, a cabbie with his homespun little rhyme, 'Giddy-up, horsey, don't you stop, keep on goin' clippety-clop', was trotting my parents-to-be from Berlin's Royal Opera House in Unter den Linden to their apartment in Wilhelmstrasse. They were having an animated row behind the drawn blinds of the hackney. Papa, condemned yet again to Tristan's interminable 'Liebestod', had struggled in vain not to nod off, in spite of his brand-new tails. (At high school I used to boast I was an anti-Wagnerian even before I was a lecherous gleam in my father's eye.)

Whatever the precise details, on 5 May 1896, at the midnight hour, I was unceremoniously thrust into my first concentration camp. Doubled up and tethered in solitary confinement for nine months and condemned to death under the most inhumane living conditions, I began learning how to die. (In the Twenties people used to ask, 'Prenatal education, does that mean anything to you?') The Mamasbelly Concentration Camp: a subtropical dark-room, unpleasantly damp, poorly ventilated. Facilities for development: unsatisfactory, could do better – fail. My fate: from dark-room to dark-room. In other words, I'm a bellyacher.

My memory, which I tend to brag about, has let me down in the matter of my conception: am I one of Onan's offspring, an illegal immigrant, or maybe even planned? Of course, I was only partially there, and the fact that I share that experience with the rest of humanity is small comfort. ('Our Erwin is usually only half there, he lets himself go, up in the clouds, tends to be silly.') The procreative act becomes so much our own flesh and blood that it is not surprising we tend to forget it. All that is left are variants of subconscious primal memories: *cadenza ad libidum*, we know the variations. We only have *one* thing to live out: our life, and it is spent searching for the theme that is concealed from us. Once begotten, that's the end of our free will. ('The freedom I sing – ain't no such thing.' Ringelnatz)

Even while I'm vainly trying to feather my nest in Manhattan, that Isle of the Dead in the Augean stables that is New York, old age, the Stone Guest, is stealthily creeping up on me. Even if I had been able to foresee the predicament, nothing could have stopped it. I was always too young, too timid, too conventional. The road to heaven is paved with lame excuses. Not even my vanity could visualize me dying 'young, in beauty, with vine leaves in my hair' (Ibsen was *the* chic disease before appendicitis). I have spent my whole life letting off suicidal steam, which some might call vitality. To date, everyone has had to die, yet immortality is just around the corner. It's every man for himself. Will I still manage to shuffle off this mortal coil?

Mother cleverly managed to combine a restless fidgetiness with an irritating habit of unpredictably jerky movements. My prison was getting more and more cramped by the minute. I had played at being a foetus for too long. One fine evening we both lost patience and something snapped. I tried to kick my way out. But there was no other way out of the frying pan and into the firing line than by being squeezed traumatically through the Bearing Straits out into the light of day. Mothers don't like separation, especially from their sons. Had she had her way, I'd still be stuck in there even now. I was bored to death with her everlasting 'An intelligent person is never bored'. Besides, her heart was so off-beat that I resolved to go my own way as quickly as possible and get my ticker going at a metronomic sixty a minute. To date, it has done its bounding duty over two hundred million times. I became a pathological counter and recounter. Only towards the end of this book, at the age of sixty-seven, did I have my first heart attack.

The midwife, Frau Ladislawa Kuhlmai, standing by on the alert, went into action. She gave me a nasty little nip in my soft cerebellum. This made me so furious that my mother responded with contractions which poisoned my life for good: labour began.

I got my own back on Frau Kuhlmai. Two years later, when my mother was expecting my younger brother, she went to consult the wise woman at her place in the milk market. Whilst the ladies were whispering about the mysteries of birth, I watered some imaginary roses in a dark corner of the room. Revenge is sweet. That particular piece of poetic licence got me a smack on the posterior, for all sins shall be paid for Here Below. Mostly.

2 THE MEDICINE MAN

As the waters broke into a promising trickle (inside it was more like the thunder of the Rhine Falls, threatening to drop me in it from a great height), merry jingle bells accompanied by muffled hoofbeats were heard in the snow outside. Our family doctor, put together from designs by Etc. Hoffmann, emerged in funereal solemnity from his rented coal-black sleigh, with the bearskin-coated cabbie at his heels carrying the bag with the instruments of torture (force-ceps and crowbar). It would have been beneath the dignity of a professional gentleman to carry it himself.

Dr Ludwig Grunwald: black stovepipe hat, dark-green Tyrolean loden cape, black frock coat, yellow kid gloves, reddish beard, bits of everything. Like all other Berlin medicine men, he spent the summer with rucksack and alpenstock – in high spirits despite having a poor head for heights – merrily yodelling his way from peak to peak. Just thinking of it made me feel peaky. His fondest ambition was to be in an avalanche, to fall just once from the Piz Palu via Grindelwald straight onto the front page of the newspaper. The long winter nights he spent fiddling his way through quartets – Brahms, Beethoven, Schubert – with three colleagues, or as a trio con brio when there were just two others.

His motto was 'Prevention's the thing'. His prescriptions he wrote in hiero-glyphics, something for everyone, to each his own. With extreme unction, he regularized our bowel movements in no time at all with herbal teas and luke-warm enemas. There was unsweetened cocoa made with water to block you up, rhubarbara and castor oil to get you going again. He was poor at taking one's pulse, while I, on the other hand, was good at thermometering. Even before I could count, I was able to produce any desired temperature. In those days fevers were exclusively rectal.

Belching, bowel disorders and heartburn he bombarded with balsam, bi-carbonate of soda and bromide. Slight stomach aches were soothed by an infusion of camomileucalyptusmentholpeppermint with a few of Dr Hoffmann's drops, more serious ones by the removal of the appendix. Haemorrhoids he throttled with bismuth suppositories, which I, presumably under the highly infectious influence of Wilhelm Busch's urchins Max and Moritz, fed to horses in the street. Chapped hands he massaged with nitroglycerine (just add sugar and – bang!), lumbago and mumps he cured by the laying on of hands combined with boiling-hot mustard plasters and blancmange compresses. For loss of appetite and listlessness, three drops of hydrochloric acid were put in our raspberry juice; the way they hissed on Mama's marble-topped table showed how strong they were. For debility there was either pigeon soup, or thin porridge with half an egg beaten up with sugar in it. If the debility increased and the patient's strength decreased there was Somatose and Sanatogen in powder form. For chronic anaemia there was cod-liver *oi weh*, followed by iron-rich spinach. For sore (saw) throats he prescribed frequent gargling with Ems salts, but only after he had pressed your furry tongue down so painfully with the handle of a silver spoon that you couldn't say AAAAAH. For whooping coughs there was Pertussin, for colds the modern germ-killer Formamint, for bronchial catarrh half a lemon in lukewarm water with a teaspoon of honey and a half tablet each of aspirin, antipyrin and pyramidon followed by being trussed up in a cold, wet sheet. In cases of double pneumonia the patient was given up for dead. Headaches he drove away – unfortunately only temporarily – with cream puffs and mild migraine powders, styes with ichthyol ointment and Goulard water, serious eye troubles with that oh-so-expensive distilled water mixed with an equal amount of boric acid lotion. If all that did not work then that priceless specialist, Professor Silex, had to be called in. He would turn a blind eye – Dr Grunwald at a loss was his gain. For the fainting fits that were so popular at the time, or if you were only slightly dead, it was spirit of ammonia. How its pungent smell brought the tears to your eyes. Now I understood why the dear departed stank so: when they gave up the ghost they were still with us in spirit of ammonia. Scruffulous children were bathed in brine, and that stings! Warts were gobbled up by lunar caustic or charmed away. For boils and freckles there was yeast. For any kind of agitation, first there was a spoonful of sugared water, then a couple of sharp clips round the ear. If neither worked, you were made to stand in the corner then popped into bed, still quivering. The purpose of the Goulard water was unclear. If you claimed to have ringing in the ears you were sent straight away to stand in a corner and The Nice Doctor would whisper, with his hand in front of his mouth so you couldn't hear, 'Little numbskull, artillery, chocolate.' If you didn't hear anything, then you had septic inflammation of the middle ear, which he treated by pouring boiling oil into it, though not before threatening to puncture your eardrum if necessary. Before we were taken to the proper dentist, Dr Walschock, who drilled, extracted and limped (his left leg was ten centimetres too short, but his right leg – fortunately!

– ten centimetres longer), they rubbed oil of myrrh or tincture of idiotine on our swollen gums at home. Mother loved pulling the wrong tooth with passion and a piece of string. Instead of 'piss' The Nice Doctor – a supreme piss-artist himself – said 'urinate'; I heard this as 'you're in it', and, having thus grasped how the bladder functioned, promptly wet my bed.

For – or against – a flat fee of 150 marks per annum The Nice Doctor inspected the whole family, servants included, from top to bottom, back and front, inside and out, once a fortnight. Like all antisemitic assimilated Jews he was an anti-vivisectionist. By way of a bonus, twice a year we were allowed to sit at the doctor's window at the corner of Kochstrasse and Friedrichstrasse to cheer His Majesty the Emperor and his seven sons (I know, I know, he only had five, but they looked much more numerous) as they rode back in triumph to the castle from the grand autumn or spring parades at the head of black-red-and-white betasselled Guards regiments.

3 DELIVERY

That day our dear old Hippocrates fortified himself, as usual, with a glass of fiery Tokay accompanied by a Leibniz biscuit. At the same time he tried to reassure my agitated father, who was nervously chewing his cigar. Papa was trotting up and down the smoking room, reciting Schiller's 'The Lay of the Bell': 'Passion departs,/ But love must remain./ The flower fades,/ The fruit must sprout.' (In high school I was sent out of the class because this verse made me laugh.) The next lines – 'The man must go out/ Into a hostile world' – our Aesculapius took personally. Armed only with his stethoscope, he slipped into the labour room to diagnose acute pregnancy, for which the only cure was immediate delivery. Without hesitation he peeled off his suede gloves (snug as a bug in a rug) to reveal his hairy hands. In those days every delivery was a life and death struggle at knife-point. The Nice Doctor rarely washed his hands; that discovery was only made a generation later by Dr Knox.

My final hour approached in fear and trembling. For the first time in my life I groaned Balzac's 'Seulement Bianchon pourrait me sauver' – 'only Bianchon could save me'. I was propelled into this bloody life in quite an amateur fashion. By the time I had read the invitation over the exit, 'Lasciate ogni speranza, voi ch'entrate', 'Abandon all hope, you who enter', it was too late to turn back. Until that moment

I had blindly gone along with everything, utterly dependent on the usual Umbilical Cord Convention. Amazing how painless the severance was! Later, when my ideological umbilical cord was cut, that really did hurt! And now I had to fend for myself, a self-sufficient plaything of nature, of *my* nature. A man, a slave, a moral howler monkey, a degenerate beast of prey: homo sapiens. My eyes opened in amazement. Everything was upside down, blurred, out of focus, just as inside a camera: female movements in flesh-tints, in bright dreamy greys, in greyish blues, all without rhyme or reason. That I only discovered later: Mama!

Thus on 26 January 1897, a Tuesday morning I shall never forget, half-squashed, speechless, at the end of my tether, stark naked and sincerely yours, I was sent out into the fresh air. They thought I ought to breathe so they slapped me on the back. What I inhaled was the carbolic-enriched stench of lysol gutter-blended with the steam of fresh horse droppings – the celebrated Berlin air:

Oh the balmy Berlin air, air, air,
It's scent is something rare, rare, rare!

The bloodthirsty medieval midwife joyously trumpeted to the world at large: 'A man!' Papa countered with the quotation, 'Voilà un homme!' which the doctor, clumsily pulling out the afterbirth, translated into Latin: 'Ecce homo!' 'Doesn't he just look like a little wrinkled old man,' Mama cooed with delight, adding, with her talent for getting proverbs wrong, 'Just like a sheep in wolf's clothing'.

I was just happy that I was free of my mother and that my parents liked me. That, I knew, would not last long. Instead of feeling like a new man in a new fatherland, the Inferno, I was completely shattered. Was I perhaps a prince who could feel a pea through twelve mattresses? I decided not to show it. I, who was so determined to love all humanity, was repelled by this superfluous assembly. Can't one even be born in peace?

In the beginning everything is ugly. Beauty is something that has to be learned the hard way. Could that be the Sermon on the Mount of Venus that little Casanovalis had been dreaming of for nine months? They bathed me in boiling water, scrubbed me clean, plonked me on the changing table, oiled me, dusted me down with Pech's Patent Antiseptic Baby Powder ('Only the genuine article has the trade mark!'), smeared some rock-hard Lazaar's zinc ointment over my delicate baby's bottom, wrapped me up too tightly in my swaddling clothes and popped me into the white iron cradle: art nouveau hygiene.

Moaning softly, my birth trauma hardly behind me, I sought refuge in dreams from the new objectivity that was creeping up on me: through angst and trauma to Ångström. Alone at last, all all alone, I tried to kick and scream myself to sleep, to that thousand-year sleep from which I have never quite awakened: through all the wonderfully horrible stations of a cosmopolitan life, to and fro through languages, countries, wars, women, labyrinths, adventures, books, beauty, crap, wisdom, stupidity, truths, lies, keyholes – *à voir n'est-ce pas l'avoir? Savoir?* Like Lynceus in *Faust*, 'Born to see, employed to watch', a blind voyeur, a deaf eavesdropper: eavesdroppers hear no good of themselves. *Photographe par excellence: veni*, I came; *vidi*, I saw; I *never* conquered. My defeat coincided with the various ends of the world.

Whooping with joy, Papa came galloping in from the smoking room to disturb my first rest and to place a sloppy kiss on the forehead of his heir now apparent. He wheezed an admiring '*Shnowtisayowton!*' It was supposed to be Greek, with a Lower Saxony accent. In those days every town spoke its own Greek – the purest was spoken in Lehrte near Hanover. My father suffered an inferiority complex from the fact that he spoke no Greek at all. *Shnowtisayowton* was supposed to mean 'Know thyself'. To hear those words was to heed them, so I touched my body to get the feel of it. Just as Adam knew his Eve, I came to know my little soul, my fate: condemned to death. Why, why, why? And, above all, when? Long before the days of Freud and Fraud, of Jung and Old, I had started my own relentless process of self-anal-assess, *sine ira et studio*: Blumenfeld Studio Inc., 222, Central Park South, New York NY 10019. What I wanted was to live, to infect the world with my spirit. My situation was already starting to get precarious.

4 EPITAPHS

Pour tuer le temps I looked for epitaphs for my black marble catafalque. Shakespeare's farewell to life's tempest:

> *Now my Charmes are all ore-throwne*
> *and what strength I have's mine owne*
> *which is most faint ...*

*… Now I want
Spirits to enforce: Art to inchant,
and my ending is despaire,
Unlesse …*

– or Pascal's 'Les hommes sont si nécessairement fous, que ce serait fou par un autre tour de folie de n'être pas fou!' – or Voltaire's 'écrlinf – écraser l'Infâme!' Crush the vile thing! In vain I tried to shake myself free from my mother tongue.

I was driven by an encyclopaedic mania: since I could not know everything, I wanted to know *about* everything. Blumenfeld's own personal *Mein Kampf*: should I search for truth à la Montaigne, Voltaire, Rousseau, Schopenhauer, Nietzsche and expose fraud, or, following my own miracle-rabbi tendency towards mysticism and mystification, become a charlatan, illusionist, magician, medicine-man and card-sharp like Cagliostro, Casanova, St Simon, Houdini?

While Oscar Wilde was in Reading Gaol composing his bitter love-letter (castrated by his publisher to *De Profundis*) to his Bosie, while Elisabeth Förster Nietzsche and Isabelle Rimbaud, like the good sisters they were, were busy adulterating the unpublished manuscripts of their brothers who had escaped into madness (the age of adultery, in any sense of the word) I, *à la recherche de l'absolu, de l'absolution*, entered that public convenience, the *World* (please adjust your dress before leaving) and became engrossed in my cardinal problem: isolation in the cosmos. A lonely star in the seemingly overpopulated sky. I sank my teeth into myself and into my little fingernails that were still so appetizing.

Time is pressing. I have to capture all this end-of-the-world stuff in words for posterity – if any. The course of history = the course of disease = the fabrication of legends = a web of lies from which no fly can escape.

'Tout finit par les commencements.'

5 NOMINA SUNT OMINA

Without my consent they named me after a friend of the family, a manufacturer of mourning hats. That pushy smoothy Erwin Mühlberg, had, as I was forever being told, been top of every class at the Graues Kloster, a rival school. Because of that model pupil, I have been condemned for life to the embarrassing name of Erwin

(how earnest!). The fact that, in honour of grandfather Blumenfeld, I was also baptised Moses (Mausche) was kept secret from me and the world. On the other hand
the Blessed Erwin of Steinbach, the architect of Strasbourg cathedral, seems to
have been in part responsible for my excessive interest in cathedrals, organs, church
windows, rosettes, wafers, hosts, incense, holy water, pets-de-nonne, martyrs,
relics, prayer wheels, rosaries, confessionals, rude screens and assorted stools,
sarabandes and toccatas – with or without fugues – (Gothic, Fizzygothic, Doric,
Ionic, Ironic), baroque passacaglias, pavanes and similar cadaveresque flummery,
folderols, gewgaws and mumbo-jumbo.

My birth had taken place according to plan under a favourable horoscope
(Aquarius, the Water Bearer) on the eve of the Kaiser's birthday. I can thank my
lucky stars I wasn't called Wilhelm. Wilhelm II, by the grace of God Emperor *in*
Germany and King *of* Prussia (those ins and ofs were questions of provincial pro-
tocol) ruled absolutely everything, including my youth. A moustachioed Majesty
(Court barber Haby marketed his patent moustache-trainer under the name
'Mission Accomplished') with the permanent expression of a child in a huff. In
those days the whole world was in a permanent huff. A ham with a passion for
dressing up, a partial cripple with the historic mission of brandishing his gilded
field marshal's baton and leading the world towards the glorious days of Herr
Hitler: *mission accomplished!*

6 MAMA

My mother, Frau Emma, née Cohn, was born on 11 December 1869 in Stettin,
Pomerania (as it then was; after Herr Hitler's glorious days it had a consonant
transplant and became Szczecin, Poland). She was very narrowly built: rachitic
spinal scrofulosis, the English disease. The Nice Doctor prescribed Bleuel's iron
pills and rusty ship's nails washed down with red wine and followed by brine-
baths: for an iron constitution, you need blood and iron. The ABC of vitamins was
still a thing of the future.

Because of her outstanding flatchestedness (look for the brooch, that's the
front) a contract was signed with the 'Professional Wet Nurse Agency' on Belle
Alliance Square a good five months before I came into the world. For a deposit of
fifteen marks they undertook to have a 'good milker' from the Spree Woods on call
from January 1897. After a fruitless search for milk on mama's frontage, I yelled,

'Je meurs de faim auprès de la fontaine', and was plugged in to a wet nurse's some-what overblown breast. More content, less form. Aluminium acetate mixed with stout – milk! I have only retained one word of my wet nurse's gin-and-slavonic mother tongue, 'Oblüschmerüsch' – meaning not 'my little bundle of joy' but 'kiss my arse'.

Not even while performing the most difficult manoeuvres during labour would Mama condescend to remove her pince-nez on its dainty gold chain from her bright red nose with its bluish-white powder. From the very beginning this highly intelligent, highly interested, highly intellectual lady of high standing and a most excellent olfactory organ did all she could to guard me from the dangers of a mother complex. I never saw her in the altogether, not even through the keyhole, thank God. She hardly had a body at all and attached no importance to it. Instead of becoming a mama's boy I did deep-sea diving investigations into her underwear in the laundry basket and became a knicker fetishist. Unfortunately women's knickers have lost their mystery. Yesterday's perversion is today's norm. As Seneca said not long ago, 'Quae fuerant vitiae, mores sunt'.

In spite of a constantly mentioned dowry of 100,000 'emmies' ('m' for mark), which in 1893 had marked my mother down (also called Emmie, which could lead to confusion) as a fine catch, my parents' marriage was never presented as a finan-cial transaction but as a marriage of two souls. Mother was not exactly athletic. She did have a tennis racket and two balls, but she could neither serve nor return. Her only sport consisted of weekly visits to the poor. She descended upon them armed with a wicker basket containing a quarter bottle of red wine, a quarter of a boiling fowl and half a cake of soap tastefully wrapped in an acrid-smelling super-annuated dishcloth. All the well-to-do ladies of my youth soothed their sentimental consciences with such charitable activities. It was the proper thing to do, absolutely *comme il faut*, my dear.

She was also a stickler for principles. No one I knew could stickle as she could. As a matter of principle, she was *for* the ultra-modern three-child-system (I was furious about having to serve as one-third evidence for it), *for* progressive Pee-eff-aitch (Pestalozzi-Fröbel House) education by means of games and puzzles. Even more as a matter of principle she was *against* 'free love' and its fatal consequences. With an unshakeable belief in education through proverbs she taught us, always with a touch of *schadenfreude*:

Hoist with his own petard! The way to Hell is paved with good intentions, the Devil finds work for idle hands and your sins will find you out. Look before you leap, weeds want no sowing, learn from your mistakes and you'll have the last laugh on the other side of your face, people who live in glass houses shouldn't throw sticks and stones may break my bones but words will never hurt me. The early worm makes a man healthy, wealthy and wise, time is money, silence is golden, all that glitters is not as good as gold, and a fool and his money talks, put your money where your mouth is, wash your mouth out, don't count your chickens and never put off till tomorrow is another day, poverty is no disgrace and hard work never did no one no harm. How to get rich quick? Honesty is the best Polly, see, but virtue is its own reward and charity begins at home. One swallow doesn't make a summer pudding, one man's meat is another man's *poisson*, what's sauce for the goose is sauce for the gander, hunger is the best sauce. Quality's what counts, count the cost, count yourself lucky, know yourself, to each his own, on your own head be it if the cap fits, fit to bust, fit and well, in sickness and in health, *maladie est sans T, mais santé n'est pas sans T*, the flesh is weak but the spirit is willing to make allowances, a monthly allowance, the child is father of the man, you can't teach an old dog new tricks and only time will tell, nothing ventured, nothing gained, fortune favours the brave, where there's a will there's a way, more haste less speed, patience is a virtue and they also serve who only stand and wait till the cows come home sweet home, your time is up, don't blow your own trumpet, handsome is as handsome does and when in Rome do as you would be done by (categorical imperative for older children), a man's a man for all that, the lady doth protest too much, *qui s'excuse s'accuse* (always in reproachful tones), children should be seen and not heard, spare the rod and spoil the child, all work and no play makes Jack a dull boy, boys will be boys, all for one and one for all, God bless us all's well that ends well, and so on and so forth.

Any corny expression was grist to her mill, which ground exceeding small. As an adherent of the Gilded Mean, she liked to clothe her platitudes in high-falutin fancy phraseology. Instead of 'My children are growing up', she would point her nose in the air and say, 'My progeny is involved in the difficult process of growth'.

Whenever she discussed me with one of my teachers (for which occasions she would dress in half-mourning) she would speak of her 'problem child'. To my intense annoyance she studied Förster's psychopaedagogic masterpiece, *How Should I Bring Up My Son Benjamin?* which was pointless, since my name was Erwin.

Not for one second was she idle, above all in the house. She was against any kind of slapdashery and a person of decided taste – the most exquisite bad taste, which reached its acme in the decoration she chose for her hats, whose still lifes of fruit draped with grotesque arrangements of ostrich feathers reduced nature's rich harvest to a lifeless image of its true self. She had a penchant for thick-cut salami, Quillaja bark, Soxhlet's milk sterilizing machines, callisthenics, suburban villas (*real estate* put her in a real state), dressmaking patterns, jellied goose liver, knickerbockers, pumpernickel and buttermilk, dark-brown velvet suits, white sailor suits, woollen stockings with tourniquet-tight elastic garters that made life a misery, salsify that she served up as fresh asparagus, spoiling my taste for the real thing, Eton collars, itchy woollen Jaeger underwear, false hairpieces (it was her hairdresser's daily sisyphean task to attach these chignons artistically while she whinged), dress-shields, whalebone corsets, aspidistras and aurecalias that inevitably died, long-stemmed crystal glasses that spent their lives sparkling in the corner cabinet until they, equally inevitably, broke. She was decidedly against throwing anything away. Every scrap of paper was stored in the lumber room and sold, under her personal supervision, for a few pennies to a rag-and-bone man who came by regularly with his dog-cart. Most of all she was against twilight.

From time to time – but never when she was on her own – Mama as an authentic bluestocking (Bluebeard's wife?) would attempt, coughing and spluttering, to puff her way through a lady's cigarette (Manoli Gibson Girl 'with the guaranteed genuine twenty-two-carat-gold tip'). This type of emancipation annoyed me. What delighted me were the complicated pieces of needlework she conjured up at her sewing table: broderie anglaise, macramé, crochet work from which she fashioned so-called breeze-blockers (*brise-bise*), delightfully hideous drapes which rendered our drawing-room window viewless. I would sit on a footstool, snuggling up to her skirts, and she would dribble forth fairytales – my introduction to world literature.

Whenever she felt a pronouncement of some significance coming on – both on social occasions and just before, with her war-cry of 'Less-of-your-lip!' she gave me, obnoxious little brat that I was, a 'clip round the ear' – her mouth would go crooked. Tightly pressed together on the left, her bloodless lips narrowed, sending the right corner of her mouth shooting up towards her pierced earlobe. I witnessed the same spectacle when she ordered a roast from Frankenstein's the butchers, or when, in a flutter of stuttering, she attempted to introduce two people. A richness of embarrassment, which she blushingly called her 'dilemna'. 'Missa Dilemna', was Papa's response.

Like any practical Berlin lady of the period after the founding of the Empire, she was a fully paid-up back-to-nature freak and considered herself, with some justification, as one of the inventors of fresh air. No holiday could end without us hearing her say, 'Now, children, one last deep breath.' Accordingly, all our double windows had to be left wide open at night, even in the iciest depths of winter.

We had to be hardened. She swore by pine baths, bicarbonate of soda, castor oil, and was fond of quoting a nature fiend by the name of Nail who used to trot through the Grünewald woods in a hair shirt. 'She hits the Nail on the head', as Papa put it. What that had to do with Mama's reply of, 'Lay down your arms', I have no idea. She turned our Saturday-night bath – always much too hot – followed by a shower – always much too cold and without a rub-down afterwards – into a ritual celebration of German Culture.

Faced with a sunset, nothing and no one could stop her from poking fun at her own nose: 'Hail to thee, my mountain with its ruby-tipped peak.' That was the summit of her humour. She exulted modestly in her position as deputy vice-chairwoman of the 'Housewives League for Womens' Suffrage, Gentlewomen of the Hallesches Tor District Branch'. Even Papa admired her for that, though with the irony of male superiority. With her caustic pen she wrote exemplary family epistles, uplifted by the knowledge that they were read aloud from Essen to Stettin. Her movingly humorous letters of condolence were learnt by heart. From her I have my ability to condemn with a quick wit and a quicker tongue, without having any idea what it is about. Before I was even three years old she decided I was clinging too affectionately to her skirts. In order to cure me of excessive dependence before it was too late she attached me to her, following a patent peddergogickle remedy, with a safety pin. Being shortsighted, she pricked me with the pin. Well meant.

7 PAPA

In spite of the fundamental differences between them, I found my parents as like as two peas, presumably because they had the three of us in common. Perhaps, though, I just thought that was the way it had to be.

My father, Albert Blumenfeld, was born in Essen on 1 December 1860. Like most worthy paterfamiliases of the day, he smeared himself with horribly ineffective quack ointments (arsenic and bitsaglass) for the French disease which meant he spent his short life forever trembling under a blackmailing cloud. An impressive sea lion with a philosopher's brow, omnipotent, omniscient, he made it clear to me from the very beginning that I owed my life to him. As principal partner in the firm of Jordan & Blumenfeld, Wholesale & Export, Kommandantenstrasse 12/13, Berlin SW19, tel: 1/13133, one of the leading suppliers of umbrellas, parasols and walking sticks in the German Empire if not the world (the most leading was called Victor), he sheltered us from life's storms under the slogan 'Rain Brings Gain'. Despite his constant efforts to be regarded as an industrial magnate he barely managed to make it as a sound businessman. As his visiting card proudly stated, he was 'Honorary Justice of Commerce and Expert Witness for Umbrella Affairs at the Royal Prussian District Courts I and II and the High Court'. In reality he suffered from chronic disappointment at never having been appointed Commercial Judge, as which he could have given full vent to his eloquent sense of justice. Honorary posts came expensive, especially for Jews. Even a crummy little commercial counsellor's title cost thousands.

In the Prussian three-class franchise (not to be confused with the three-draw lottery) one had, depending on income and residence, one, two or three votes – or none at all. Papa was in the second class, and unfortunately he stuck to that for railway journeys as well. Among the close friends with whom he played skat (heart of my hearts, diamonds are a girl's best friend, let's see the colour of them, then!) he was a two-vote liberal-monarchist democrat, decidedly a man of the progressive middle ground, neither left nor right. As soon as a uniform appeared he brought the conversation round to the ultramontanist party, the current scapegoats. I have never got over this fear of uniforms and informers. One of his skat cronies, his old skittles and cycling partner and fellow Freemason, Comrade Lissenheim, a cardboard manufacturer, was the first socialist I came across. He read *Vorwärts* and they made fun of him for being a 'red'. I couldn't see anything red about him, nor about the maids for that matter, who cried when they had the red curse, and cried when they didn't.

As punctual as his good Saxon pocket watch, a timepiece with pedigree that popped open when I blew on it, at half past seven sharp every morning Papa would clamber clumsily onto his bicycle, held for him by our manservant, Hermann. Clothed in authority and rolled-up trousers, a full beard and a sense of duty, he would pedal to work, where he strove with unremitting industry and tireless energy to earn sufficient daily pumpernickel to keep his poor wife and darling children from starvation. Instead of admitting to himself that he was in the wrong job, he used to compensate by indulging in fits of temper. Whenever I went to call for him, he would be in the middle of yelling at someone and giving them the sack. 'You'll have to get up very early before you can pull the wool over my eyes, you peasant, just you wait, I'll teach you to tangle with me, you'd better watch out, jackass, or I'll break every bone in your body' (he never hurt a fly), 'there's the door, get the hell out of here, buffoon, and don't let me see you ever again, you blockhead.' Why the blockheaded jackass was being fired I never understood. After he had whined for long enough Papa would relent and allow him to stay. Every employee was thrown out twice a month on average, even the ones who had worked for Jordan & Blumenfeld for the twenty-five years that qualified them for a silver pocket watch or an umbrella with a silver tip. Although I realized it was all an act, I was still afraid that one day I too might be thrown out as a blockheaded jackass. It never came to that. Papa died when I was sixteen. The fine art of bawling people out has been lost in world wars and atomic explosions.

From Papa I learnt that physical labour should be respected because it brought in the money, but that we brain-workers should look down on those who worked with their hands. The mind stood higher than the body in public esteem. Goethe's *Goetz with the Iron Hand* wearing Schiller's *Glove*. It was a sign of education to behave as if you were clumsy, so that was what people did. Papa never bent down except in direst need. He was unsupple, stiff; never in his life did he so much as hammer in a nail, and he had to be waited on hand and foot like a helpless baby. The more he was spoilt, the more spoilt he became. We children were proud of his privileges. *He* had two eggs with his morning coffee ('Every man an egg; two for the man with the wooden leg'), we only half each; *he* had all the cream off the milk every morning, we only a teaspoonful on Sundays; *he* had poppy-seed breakfast rolls and croissants, we had plain rolls; *he* spread the butter on thick and took whatever he wanted without asking, we were not even allowed to ask. Even in the lavatory there was cotton wool for him, hard newspaper for us. On Sunday mornings there was a starched shirt, stiff as a board, standing to attention on his chair into which he had to be helped by Mama, all deftness and dexterity. With her help he changed collars and cuffs twice a week. Trying to tie his elaborate cravat she would mutter about inanimate objects having a mind of their own. Underneath everything Papa wore one-piece close-fitting, greyish-beige, flecked Jaeger underwear. The lower classes wore washable synthetic collars mounted on cardboard dickeys. The machine age approaching from the New World did away with moustache-trainers and the daily visit from the barber. Papa kept up with the times; his beard disappeared amid tears. Flushed with victory, Mama brandished Gillette's safety razor in preparation for the massacre. She started as an absolute beginner, like Niobe all tears; she never did become any good at it.

The most distinctive thing about my father was his gait. He managed to limp with both legs ('Because the earth is round', he explained), which did give it a certain symmetry. Like a drunken sailor, he reeled ponderously from side to side, all the while twisting his hands in indefinable gestures. It was all connected with the arch-supports for his flat feet. My Sunday-morning walk with him in his top hat and fitted overcoat with velvet collar was torture. He walked much too slowly for me and clutched my hand in a painfully tight grip to stop me from running away. For business reasons he felt he had to behave like a walking-stick fetishist and carried a different one each day. The pride of his collection, a walking stick made from a rhinoceros horn, was too heavy to carry and was kept at home, wrapped in cotton wool. Publicity demanded that I too should enjoy the blessing of a little walking stick, which I managed to break by tripping over it. I broke a record number of walking sticks.

Papa's habits were sacrosanct. No one but he ever sat in his upholstered armchair with the turned wooden armrests, not even post mortem. Her virgin folds intact, Auntie Voss (the *Vossische Zeitung*) was waiting for him beside his morning coffee cup. Who would have dared to touch it before him? This 'Newspaper for Public and Scientific Affairs, Published by Royal Patent' overshadowed everything. We looked down in scorn on readers of the *Berliner Tageblatt*. Papa studied the *Voss* with its editorials, reviews, parliamentary reports, features, births, marriages and deaths, and mysterious stock market quotations whose figures influenced his moods as if by magic. Not a single letter remained unread, and afterwards he would read between the lines. After lunch he would retire to the smoking room with the midday edition of the *Berliner Zeitung* for his quarter-hour nap from 2.30 to 3.50. Before dropping off he filled the room with clouds of pale blue smoke from a genuine Hamburg Leuchtegold Perfecto Claro Havana with a Sumatra broadleaf wrapper. We had to creep round on tiptoe. Silence was golden.

Within the family circle, whose sole centre he was, Papa was considered an outstanding intellectual. He read. And not just Auntie Voss – he was a man of culture, he read Schiller! He had an *Encyclopaedia of Schiller's Works* full of coloured maps which brought alive Theseusville, Aulis-on-Sea, Phocis, the land of the Spartans. He was constantly studying Bismarck's drunken *Reflections and Reminiscences*, Bebel's speeches, Carl Schurz, Eugen Richter, Sven Hedin's *Adventures in Tibet*, Heine's *Harzreise* and the first three pages of Zola's *Germinal* in French (the rest remained uncut). Now and then he would complain, with a sigh and a reproachful look in our direction, that *his* parents had not had the means to send him, the only son among seven children, to high schools and universities. Instead, at fourteen he had been apprenticed to Katz Brothers, haberdashers in Elberfeld. He had a craving for higher education, more specifically the highest: classical languages; to be able to discuss economic problems in the rarified company of privy councillors, versed in both civil and ecclesiastical law, *in Latin*! His unfulfilled dream: student fraternity life. That's enough swotting over rulings and precedents! Show your colours! No chickening out, you idle layabouts! A fraternity Old Boy takes no nonsense from townees! To array yourself in full fig after a lunchtime beer and stand your ground without flinching on the duelling floor of the scarred elite of the Bonn *Borussia* (!). Papa disapproved of the Berlin Jewish duelling (!!) fraternities (!), *Sprevia* (!!!) and *Barkochba* (!!!!). (The exclamation marks stand for duels.) After a bloodsoaked compulsory duel with sabres (tierce, quarte, quinte – music to his ears), the Fraternity President rises: to the strains of the solemn hymn 'Silent now, our heads we bow ...' the Honours Men raise high their cockaded caps onto their bared blades while the lowly Freshmen rattle foaming tankards of the brewer's finest together in strict tempo beneath crossed rapiers for the 'Salamander', the great toast: '*Ad exercitium salamandri salamandrorum salamander incipitur!*' As a finale, the assembled topers quaff an extra-special toast to my Papa, the Famous Old Boy, 'Here's to your Beeriness! O great Beer-belly! The Beer-all and end-all! Beer and Skittles! O Alcohol! O Alma Mater! O Varsity rags! O jolly student days of yore! O gaudeamus Isidore! Where are those days so free from care, when all the world was bright and fair?'

In the absence of such splendid experiences, Papa would indulge in first-class dog-Latin: *Caesar'adsomejamfortea*. But he also spoke proper Latin: *Mens sauna in corpore sano*. Or *Sic transit gloria mundi* – Gloria leaves on Monday.

And then he kept on picking up some unusual word or other which he would suddenly bring into the conversation – or silence – at a completely inappropriate point. After a few weeks, when even he was fed up with it, he would trot out another, even more incomprehensible jawbreaker such as 'Kuropatkin', 'parallelepiped ', 'Ons Wilhelmientje', 'Caltha palustris' (marsh marigold), 'rumen and abomasum', 'Tasmania, alias Van Diemen's Land', 'Bab el Mandeb', *'carte blanche'*. This regular Roget, a Brewer of phrase if not fable, got high on sayings and quotations. It was the way things were at the time. Whole tribes communicated exclusively by means of saws and adages, believing it was a mark of culture. Everything came with saw or adage attached until an age came that realized their futility. Never-understood maxims taken too seriously at too early an age guided my generation through a life full of sayings straight to a hero's grave. *Dulce et decorum est pro patria mori*, several times if possible. That I managed; 'it is finished'. Papa quoted often and wrongly. He liked combining different quotations to produce new effects. He was impressed by the fact that his favourite genius, Schiller, had the nerve to contradict himself. He would trumpet in stentorian voice: 'Give honour to women, they weave and entwine/ Round our earthly existence sweet roses divine', he went on, 'For woman is treacherous and loves what is new.'

'Figures prove it' and 'figures prove nothing' were followed by *quod erat demonstrandum*. He made connections that were clear to him, unclear to me. 'Jews have quick tongues' was coupled with 'Quick as the ravenous shark/ Tearing the waters apart'. Morning, noon and night we were subjected to the Schiller's 'Siegesfest':

> *Whate'er our earthly goods, of all*
> *The greatest and the best is fame.*
> *For though to dust frail bodies fall*
> *For ever lives a glorious name.*

We were never in any doubt that the name he meant was the glorious name of Blumenfeld. We were idealists.

One Sunday Papa revealed himself as a poet of genius before our very eyes. The veins in his forehead swelled as the poetry flowed from his gold fountain pen:

Father bears the picnic hamper,
Mother, kids behind him scamper,
Auntie, bringing up the rear,
Carries Heinz, the little dear.

Papa had a sense of humour. He wasn't a comedian, but a highly serious man who garnished his seriousness with jokes. He would often laugh until he was helpless with laughter, at other people's weaknesses, sometimes even at his own. But woe to anyone who had the audacity to laugh at him! Even Mama had to take extreme precautions and disguise it as a compliment. Then we all trembled, including Papa.

Jokes, the manna of my childhood, were the private property of Jews. A goy could not understand them, little Morrie knew them already. Only Jews knew how to tell jokes. Only Jews had the art of laughing at the right moment. Only Jews had the ability to formulate, in a few words, a punch-line that tickled your subconscious. The short story as a Jewish art: Kerr, Kraus, Kafka; aphoristic thought: Heine, Freud. With ghetto humour they tried to laugh off the spectre of the pogrom. To show how well assimilated you were, you made jokes mocking the Eastern Jews. (A drowning Eastern Jew: 'So I'm swimming downwards already.') My favourite jokes were the ones about the miracle rabbi. Whenever Papa brought a new one home we would talk of hardly anything else for weeks. The same old stories did the rounds for years, growing with the retelling. It was Papa's jokes that made us laugh most, especially his frequent flatulence, which he would refer to as 'telegrams from Darmstadt' (literally Boweltown):

Father farts,
The children laugh.
How nice that such a little thing
So much happiness can bring.

There were many jokes I only understood after I had been laughing at them for several decades. 'Do asses marry, too? – *Only* asses.' Riddles that played on words delighted me and spoiled me. 'What is the difference between a cat and a comma? A cat has claws at the end of its paws and a comma has a pause at the end of its clause.' We were asked the same riddles again and again, some at least twice a week.

Just as with laughing, Papa was a past master at groaning. After devouring too much of his favourite dish, cucumber salad, in the course of a champagne breakfast at the Traube, or after a lively night out with the boys at Mayer's Oyster Bar, the inevitable colic would ensue and he would spend days with curtains drawn and specialists in attendance, moaning and groaning as though his end were nigh. It would develop into a competition between The Nice Doctor and Mama, who turned into a Bridge of Sighs, to ply him with camomile tea, laudanum, ice packs, hot-water bottles and bed-pans. Even when he was well, Papa used to moan himself to sleep, 'Poor, poor dear father.'

I knew Papa's childhood memories backwards and forwards, so often did he regale us with them. Unfortunately he only had two: firstly how they were given a half-holiday to celebrate the victory of Sedan and he ran home, his trousers stuffed into his boots, freed at last from plucking lint for dressings; secondly that there was a boy in his class called Karl Genauer which, when pronounced with the Rhineland accent, sounded like Karlchen Auer, a diminutive that made everyone laugh. Mama had no childhood memories because at that time they were not yet in fashion. In idolizing their own parents both of mine outdid each other. Of their grandparents they knew nothing.

8 Parental Dreams

They had great plans for me. Papa had set his mind on his son-and-heir becoming a journalist so that he could impress the world with an editorial every morning. That one day thousands of Blumenfeld photos would be published was beyond the scope of his imagination. It was my duty to live up to parental dreams, to be exceptionally intelligent, articulate, well read, knowledgeable about literature, of excellent taste, highly musical, tactful, highly educated, not conceited, famous, not infamous, neither arrogant nor obsequious, a likable noble spotlessly clean affable athletic model modest modern Jew, a worthy descendant of Heinrich Heine, no starry-eyed visionary, but a highly interesting slightly dreamy inwardly agonizing fillanfropist, an idealist not a nihilist, a deep thinker (Rodin), an optimist not a pessimist, no yes-man, a winner not a loser, a lover of the arts but not an artist (they live from hand to mouth, a painter is a pain), not messy, not grubby, no sleepyhead, no slowpoke, no namby-pamby nincompoop, neither superhuman nor subhuman, and above all not common-or-garden variety, run-of-the-mill, but my own man, a man of the world, *sans peur et sans reproche*, neat and tidy, never slovenly, a sharp-witted man of honour with his heart in the right place, an apostle of truth, ready to be willing to die a martyr's death for his deeply held convictions (without ever letting it come to that), a liberal free-thinker of the golden mean, a thorough sceptic (Mama said 'keptic') through and through who knows what to say and what not to say without always having to have the last word, a personality, incorruptible, his salary as high as his principles, a man of outstanding integrity, a self-made man, every last penny earned, by marrying money if necessary, by the sweat of his brow like Papa, a financial genius, director of gigantic concerns, a pillar of society, of high society, the highest even, Grand Master of countless lodges, Nobel etc prizewinner with an honorary doctorate from every university, highly respected by contemporaries and future generations, for he who is accounted by the beasts of his day the best, his fame will live forever in the human breast! But above all it was my duty to be an eternally grateful son of my dearly beloved parents whose sole desire was respectfully to be permitted to gild their twilight years. In other words, a cretin.

In return Papa promised me the twenty-four volume, gilt-edged, half-leather luxury edition of Brehm's *Encyclopaedia of Natural History*. A promise often given and never kept, no more than the one to have me do a PhD in economics and business administration at the Geneva Business School, for which I am eternally grateful, just as I am that he never made me become a lawyer or an archdeacon, or an inspector of mines and foundries.

9 GRANDPAPA MOSES AND GRANDMAMA LISETTE

Grandfather Moses Blumenfeld, often, though in vain, called Matthias or even Mattatias, was an old-German, all-German Jew, born on 21 December 1821 (Flaubert's birthday) in Schwerte on the Ruhr. His family tree reached proudly back to the seventeenth century and to Fürth in Bavaria. He lived for many decades in Essen, the city of the homosexual arms magnate, Krupp, where, as a worthy Jewish schoolteacher and preacher, he anointed, taught and circumcised. During the 1848 revolution, although not one of the heroes who fell for the cause, he was at least imprisoned with Carl Schurz and Friedrich Hammacher. This, it was emphasized, was not 'dishonourable', and so he could be venerated by family and pupils as a fighter and martyr in the cause of freedom. His true fame came from his ban in 1846, way ahead of his time, on spitting out chewing tobacco on the synagogue floor. Fifty years later Schützenstrasse was renamed Blumenfeldstrasse, the highest honour to come to our name. Under Hitler it became Streicherstrasse, today it's Blumenfeldstrasse once more.

After Grandpapa's death, Mama displayed his four medals on red velvet in a gilt-lined glass case in her drawing room. I had seen them proudly bouncing up and down on his chest while he was still alive: the Iron Cross Second Class for civilians with the red-and-white ribbon, the Order of the Red Eagle Fourth Class and two smaller gilt medals. My most vivid memory of this grandpapa was of the time when we were on holiday in Eisenach in 1901 and I put caterpillars into his grey beard while he was peacefully sleeping on the grass. I thought they were silkworms and was already visualizing Grandmama in a self-spun silk dress, but all I reaped was ingratitude in the form of a box on the ears. Grandpapa wore a dignified, dark-grey frock coat that always had greasy spots, despite the constant attentions of loving hands. He died on 9 January 1902, when I was five, of prostate trouble, bequeathing me his weak bladder. After that Papa constantly went on about 'late-lamented-father', quoting Matthias Claudius in plaintive tones, 'Alas, they have buried a good man; he was even more to me.' One of my favourite occupations was to try to console his widow, Grandmama Lisette (I named my daughter after her), with kisses and caresses. Everyone, herself included, considered her a venerable matriarch. She adorned herself with old lace and smelled of lavender, patchouli, oranges, rose-water and camphor. (Perfumes are veiled memories of urine, urine stinks of your instincts, says old Father Uranus, your anus.) Grandmama's chief accomplishments were matzo balls and shortbread ('I'll still be eating shortbread when the hearse comes to fetch me'), the secret recipes for which she took with her to the grave. Lovingly warding off my kisses, she would giggle, 'Oh please don't, Uncle Leeser' (a kissing uncle of her childhood). She had been born around 1825 in Bonn on the Rhine and given a Catholic education by nuns in a convent school.

Grandmother's mother, Fanny van Geldern, was the youngest sister of Heine's mother, Elisabeth (Betty) van Geldern, a source of family pride that did not spare even me, even though I share this childless great grand-uncle who died of syphilis with thousands of other Jewish-German offspring of the textile trade.

10 GRANDPAPA HENRY

Chajim Cohn was born around 1830 (he himself was not certain of the year) in Dobrzyn on the Drina, between Golub and Rypin, now in Poland, but in those days on the border between Russia and East Prussia. His father, Itsche, was a Talmud scholar in the synagogue. His grandfather was a miracle rabbi, thus explaining my gift of intuition. At the age of thirteen Grandpapa Chajim ran away, to avoid having to serve in the Russian army, and sailed to America, a journey which took sixty days. There he changed his name to Henry and started out as a peddlar and 'self-made man' in New York, doubling his initial capital of one dollar in the very first week. He became rich in the gold rush as owner of a gambling saloon with the splendid name of 'Pokerflat', even richer as owner of a department store in the Mormon stronghold of Salt Lake City and returned to 'good old Europe' in 1855 to marry his childhood sweetheart, his cousin Rosa Cohn, a great grand-niece of Meyerbeer and just as unmusical. This listless, parchment-skinned, tight-lipped, little mouse with an ear-trumpet and distrust to match, guaranteed non-erotic, presented him with six complex-laden children. Grandpapa bought a wine-merchant's, I. Mentzel & Co, in Stettin, only two hours by rail from Berlin but deep in the provinces and today, as Szczecin, even deeper in Poland.

From Grandpapa Henry I inherited my passion for climbing towers, Worcester sauce ('shake before taking', my first English words), brewing up punch, losing money on the stock market and nibbling my nails. Until *I* arrived, *he* was champion nail-biter and his three sons were equally devoted adherents of the art. My mother, fearing the worst, lost no time in smearing galling wormwood oil on my fingers. Wormwood became my favourite delicacy. She went on too often, too earnestly, too insistently and at too great length about my vice; she tried bribery, blackmail, withdrawal of pocket money, of goodnight kisses, of apple pie with whipped cream, physical violence. She was becoming a nuisance. Nothing worked. Finally she started nibbling her own nails in a desperate attempt to deter me. Today, in all due modesty, I can proudly claim to have surpassed Grandpapa in this art, though not in his other functions. With stately *shabbes* dignity he several times served as honorary chairman of the Jewish community of Stettin, Pasekow and Heringsdorf, and, with self-important secretiveness, as Grand Master of a masonic lodge. He took snuff, chewed tobacco and possessed a phial of gold dust he had found in California; from his watch chain dangled an ivory spoon for removing ear wax and a piece of genuine rock-crystal. He wrote a charmingly naive little book about his early years in America which his sons had printed for his eightieth birthday. I inherited as little of his innocence as I did of all the money he left to his fifteen grandchildren, to be paid out ten years after his death. He died peacefully in 1916, in the middle of the war. His inheritance was completely swept away by inflation and his sons, who were models of ineptitude when it came to business. When a billion marks reached the value of one cent, I had to acknowledge with thanks a cheque for three million marks.

Grandpapa Henry subscribed to a complete edition of the classics, together with Becker's *History of the World*, which filled his bookshelves to overflowing with exceptionally ugly, entirely unread volumes bound in brownish red cloth with 'Henry Cohn' embossed on the spine in gold. His lavatory paper had quotations from the classics printed on it, thus providing an appropriate outlet for his interest in literature: 'He sinks into the depths with bubbling groan', 'For this relief much thanks', 'Paper will put up with a lot of things', 'A foul and pestilent congregation of vapours', 'It droppeth as the gentle rain from heaven upon the place beneath', 'Along this narrow passage must he come', 'O! my offence is rank, it smells to heaven', 'An open mouth and an open heart are two great gifts, but a man must also have open bowels', 'Why is a man's life like a mushroom's? Both are kept in the dark and covered in shit', 'Why is life like a child's vest? Because they are both short and shitty', 'What is the difference between a poor marksman and a constipated owl? One shoots and can't hit', 'All the perfumes of Arabia will not sweeten this little hand'.

The family never tired of repeating that he had still been chasing the ladies right up to his death at the ripe old age of eighty-seven. I certainly – with the help of my first torch, which he had given me the previous day – caught him masturbating one night in his eightieth year. He was the ideal white-bearded grandfather with beautifully oiled hair, who brought me a handsome present every time he came. On leaving he would give me one mark to console me. 'A small insult', he would say, referring to the time I had asked him 'not to insult me' as he pressed the coin into my hand. He couldn't leave often enough for me, even if it did hurt to say 'adieu' (almost as much as 'yes' and 'thank you'), since I needed the money to pursue my various passions. At one time it was my collection of notebooks, at another seeds for my botanical garden, later postage stamps.

On the occasion of his seventieth birthday, when I was three years old, I got blind drunk for the first (and almost only) time in my life. The ladies' choir of the synagogue had assembled, every last one of them, to sing a birthday anthem, proclaiming the glory of the heavens in forty-two voices. In return they were liberally plied with sherry, port, Tokay and sickly-sweet liqueurs. To demonstrate their love of children, the ladies allowed me to sip from their glasses. While the gallant host was escorting his guests down the stairs, I finished off what was left in each glass. Then I tumbled down the stairs, howling, and was put to bed to sleep it off. Jack London – a *goy* has more style – would have turned it into the start of a glorious alcoholic career. I was congenitally unsuited to the role of dipsomaniac.

Grandpapa and I loved each other dearly, until the occasion when I insisted on going out with him bareheaded, like all the other boys in my class. This offence against American manners so displeased him that it brought the first great friendship of my life to an end, leaving me with an aversion to hats, friends, family, society, America.

11 HEINZ

I remember clearly the night when the twentieth century was born. On 22 December 1899 I had been presented with a little brother, whose circumcision ceremony took place, as did Christ's, on the afternoon of New Year's Eve. The nursery had been promoted to pantry for the occasion and standing up in my cot I marvelled at the chaos and confusion: candles and aunts and ices and tears and grandfathers and laughter, all washed down with German champagne, Kupferberg Gold and Henkell Trocken. Cooks in tall white hats carved pheasants trimmed with their own feathers and stuffed with truffles, while rabbis in tall black hats honed circumcision knives. As if in a dream, I climbed down from my observation post and tiptoed my way, more invisible than a Red Indian, behind the black rabbi along the dark back corridor into the dark-green smoking room, from there through the red 'Berlin' room and into the drawing room with its silk-covered walls, where I hid behind the almond-green velvet curtains. All these earnest men in their top hats were muttering mysterious incantations in secret languages. They all seemed familiar to me, but on that afternoon each one looked different and behaved differently. I was too small, one or other of them kept blocking my view. What little I did manage to see became jumbled up in a bloody dream. It was only sixty years later that I found an explanation in Montaigne's diary of his Italian journey (30 January 1581): the man with the knife was cutting my little brother while all the others were singing. Grandpapa gargled with wine, dark red wine in a silver chalice, then licked blood from my brother; after that he wafted incense round the new little Jew's nose so that he might partake of the holy spirit. This mystery play under the supervision of the rabbinate was the very first theatrical performance I attended. For a long time I believed the stories of ritual murder. A gift to interpreters of dreams! Scarcely was I back in my beloved cot than I fell asleep, to be picked up at midnight by my favourite aunt, Bronja (Bronislawa), to look out of the window. To celebrate the turn of the century she was wearing a particularly low-cut dress and as the rockets fizzed and popped in the snow-covered street I stared down into the unfathomable depths of my young aunt's décolletage. All the bells started ringing and I burst into tears. As always, I understood everything and nothing. And that's the way it has stayed my whole life through: nothing and everything. All the best for 1900.

My brand-new baby brother was made of pink marzipan. It was not yet the age when penis envy and Oedipus complexes were on everyone's lips and I enjoyed him until, in August 1918 during the last weeks of the First World War, he was killed in action at Jaulgonne on the Marne, sacrificing his eighteen-year-old life for the German Fatherland, Jewish family life and a world gone mad. The most grievous loss of my life. Whom the gods love die young. Nowadays they seem to love mankind rather less, since, despite hydrogen bombs and a multiplicity of cancers, they let them live longer and longer.

My brother Heinz combined an irrepressible sense of humour with a primitive interest in money and money-making. He was less interested in school than in life, so that he was given bad reports and thrice-weekly private tuition. After his death I read in his diary how right at the start he had told the tutor that his lessons were poor and not worth three marks. Heinz suggested he should make better use of his time and share the sum with him. If he didn't agree, Heinz went on, he would lose a pupil and one and a half marks three times a week. He succeeded in convincing the tutor and thus earned four marks fifty per week, together with sufficient free time to squander this hard-earned money on the movies. His sense of humour also came out in verse. He thought up a surprise for Uncle Georg's fiftieth birthday, a poem that no one else was allowed to see beforehand. This sealed surprise was sent by post to Stettin, resulting in a family feud that lasted for years. The poem ran, 'Uncle George, you hairy-chested old sinner, be glad you don't have shit for dinner.' Short and sweet (well maybe not sweet) for a ten-year-old. A mischievous little smart-arse. To see whether Papa really was omniscient, he devised a simple experiment. In the bathroom Papa had two cloths, one for up top and one, with a knot in it, for down below. Heinz changed the knot, watched, and discovered Papa's omnignorance. Unlike me, Heinzi loved to go a-wandering and that was partly responsible for his early death. At five o'clock on a Sunday morning he would disguise himself as a boy-scout and march off in formation to the Grunewald woods. As an apprentice with the button-makers Seliger & Co he showed great ability, especially at getting promoted. Buttons quite often went missing.

12 ANNIE

My late sister Annie started out as a sweet little girl, sometimes cute, sometimes cheeky, the apple of Papa's eye. Unfortunately her sweetness diminished daily until by the age of thirteen she had turned into an unbearably sharp-tongued sourpuss, a bossy old bitch with buckteeth and freckles, a green-eyed crosspatch I had come to hate. She was the cause of my first conflict with the fair sex. She made a great fuss of the fact that she was eighteen months older than I, throwing out her chest and boasting that she was a woman, which supposedly gave her mystically mythological rights and attractions. It was my duty to obey her, to dance attendance on her like a gallant courtier, especially when her friends were there to see. Her reward was to play me false, to betray me whenever she could, to worm her way into the good graces of parents, nannies, servants, friends and enemies. Whenever she started losing she would change the rules of the game retrospectively. I never did figure out whether she was really horrid or awfully nice (the word for it nowadays is ambivalence). I usually managed to give as good as I got. When I was four she steadfastly refused to get off the chamber pot to let me have my turn. She just stayed sitting on it: passive resistance. So, after warning her twice, I was quite within my rights when I peed on her head. Foaming with rage, she hissed, 'You'll pay for that!' Our parents were both out. By the time they came back her hair had long since dried out but, in typical female fashion, the poisonous little snitch quickly dunked her head in the still full chamber pot, as evidence of my heinous crime. Our parents believed her howls of accusation and I was severely punished: no whipped cream on my apple cake for two whole weeks. It was a joy to hate Annie.

In her teens Annie and her friends started a club with the motto, 'Follow Duty – Love Beauty'. Annie took on the task of decorating little wooden panels with that motto in pokerwork and I helped her. How gloriously, scorchingly hideous they were! The club had a saccharine foretaste of the well known Thirties film, *Girls in Uniform*. Just as every German boy was born in Arcadia, so every German maiden came from Lesbos. I observed this with breathless interest through a slightly enlarged knothole in the door of a wardrobe where I had hidden before the girls' secret meeting. After carefully locking the door, the young ladies tenderly undressed each other and went round in lacy underwear (some done up, some undone), displaying with pride – or envy – their budding little breasts. The one who possessed the largest (that was Gerti Jacobi) was kissed by each of the other girls. It was all part of the club's ritual. And they sang songs such as 'How doth the busy little bee' or 'My pretty maid'. Once I was caught because the mothballs in the wardrobe made me sneeze. A summary court was convened. My punishment was to stand before Annie, Grete Manes, Gerti Jacobi, Lotte Seliger, Edith Lewin and Marga Kühn in turn and on the command 'On thy knees, slave', to bow down low then fall to my knees and say 'I humbly beg your forgiveness, my lady', after which my life was spared. How humiliating! Thus was I initiated into the mysteries of Lesbos, Samos, Chios and Cos, fell in love with young lesbians and became a voyeur.

Laughing (she laughed all the time), Gerti Jacobi invited me round on Thursday afternoons after my religious instruction when her parents would certainly not be at home. Her father was a corset salesman. We played dressing up. She got me to try on corsets while she wore my boy's clothes, which were rather tight on her and produced some odd effects. She enjoyed it more than I did and kept bursting out of my clothes and into peals of laughter. I was embarrassed, but Gerti got such glowing cheeks and shining eyes that I was happy to do her the favour every Thursday. Hercules and Omphale.

Although they were much older than I (two years at that age is a whole generation), at one time or another I did some platonic courting with all the girls, with the exception of Margot Kühn, the only non-Jew. I loved them and I hated them, just as I hated my sister Annie. Annie's best friend was the beautiful Grete Manes, whose father, Uncle Willy, was Papa's best friend, and whose mother was the best friend of Grandmother Lisette.

There was a boring story that was told over and over again. Grete's mother, Aunt Marie, fat, short and ugly, used to play up to me. Her nanny Eulalie Hoffmann, an oldish spinster usually referred to as Hoppi, was caught in bed with her and kicked out, which fascinated me, even though I had no idea what it was all about.

Later Annie became a shorthand typist and worked as a private secretary. Her first employer was an admiral of the fleet by the name of Schräder who put his hand up her skirt, at which she was flattered and insulted, both in equal measure. After that she worked for the renowned skin specialist (venereal diseases), Dr Blaschko, and was obnoxiously pompous about rescuing fallen women, which activity she called 'the abolition of slavery'. She was working as a police auxiliary in Hamburg when she died on 24 June 1925, not yet thirty years old, hopelessly consumptive and still more or less demivirgo intacta. May her ashes rest in peace. They may even still be lying in the left-luggage office at Zoo Station in Berlin. In one of her many last-wills-and-testaments Annie had asked me, since I lived by the North Sea, to scatter her ashes in the sea with my own fair hand, all the while singing lieder from Heine's Nordsee. It was during the inflation, and after the funeral I bought a tin with my sister's ashes under the counter for ten billion marks from the crematorium (were they really her ashes?). Before taking the train back to Holland I decided to wet my whistle at Kantorowitz's Bar in Joachimsthalerstrasse and deposited the package in the left-luggage at Bahnhof Zoo. When I went to collect it, at the last moment before the train was due to leave, it was nowhere to be found. I had to get my train. To this day Annie's ashes are still waiting for me or, rather, for the North Sea.

13 CHILDREN'S GAMES

I preferred children's tricks to any games: standing on your head, doing somersaults, fooling around, pulling faces, sticking your tongue up your nose, rolling on your belly, belly dancing, belly laughs, writing your name in yellow on the snow, holding your breath for hours (and cheating), producing weird noises (I wanted to talk with my bottom, but all that came were sounds full of fury, signifying nothing), stammering, squinting, stinking, staggering, pretending to be deaf, dumb, dead, rising from the grave. I was master of all these arts. The usual party games I despised: Here we go gathering nuts in May, Piggy in the middle, Grandmother's footsteps, What time is it Mr Wolf? Postman's knock, pass the parcel, musical chairs, blind-man's buff, Simon says, *tableaux vivants*, charades – all soppy kids' stuff.

My birthday was on 26 January, the Kaiser's on the 27th, which meant that every year the dress rehearsal for the gala illuminations to celebrate the Kaiser's birthday was held on the evening of my birthday. In token of our delight in His Majesty all the windows of Berlin were lit up with candles, which dutifully burnt down sadly. The carnivals I saw were never jolly, nor even sad, and it wasn't *just* my fault. I learnt at an early age to avoid festivities. For children's parties I was thoroughly scrubbed and squeezed into a white sailor suit, only to play a stupid card game where I was always left with the Old Maid which meant I had my face blackened with burnt cork. It hurt and, anyway, they always cheated and made sure I was the one who got the unlucky card and was exposed to the the laughter of the other children. Oh, the sweet sound of childish laughter! I kept a sharp needle carefully concealed in my pocket in order to puncture the most expensive of the birthday presents, the gas-inflated rubber ball, with tiny, invisible holes, so it would slowly expire. If you do it cleverly enough nothing comes out, apart from the gas. The hardest part is to look bored during the inevitable interrogation, and not to blush. Concentrating your thoughts on your own death is the best way. Never once was I suspected. Puncturing gasbags, though by less drastic means, remains my favourite party game to this day.

My creative urge found its outlet in smashing up toys. The 'destructive mania' of the Blumenfeld children became a by-word. As soon as we got our presents on Christmas Eve I slit open the belly of the rocking horse to see what it looked like inside. Didn't Mama always say its what's inside that counts? It turned out that rocking horses didn't have souls; instead of blood it was straw that came out. With the precision of an expert I took apart Mama's new mother-of-pearl opera glasses from Paris. When they refused to fit back together again, I chucked the whole lot in desperation out of the window into the back yard, which resulted in a good spanking and a new nickname: Erwin the Screwdriver. To console myself I invented a real Blumenfeld game, 'Onto the wardrobe', followed by a break-in. All the children had to climb up onto Mama's big wardrobe together and jump up and down until the top gave way and we landed in a heap among the clothes. Mama had a yellow evening dress by Drécoll of Paris, the others were from Herpich, Gerson, Israel, Kersten & Toodear of Berlin, or by Mama's own dressmaker, old Frau Geballe. Every child then put on the dress which he or she had fallen on top of. It was a lot of fun, especially since I had double-locked the doors beforehand so that they had to be broken open from inside. When the game was over the wardrobe was ruined and Mama's clothes and nerves in tatters.

Just as fanatically as I hated party games, I loved games I could play by myself. With my Anker-brand building blocks I constructed romantic medieval fortresses and castles in the air where tin soldiers paraded and fought to my command. With a couple of candles I achieved light effects which I vainly try to reproduce today with too many lamps. Where are the shades of yesteryear? Mais où sont les neiges d'antan? The spirit-powered steam engine with its steam whistle sent me into a trance, the magic lantern with its smoky paraffin lamp projected mirages onto the wall and chemistry experiments used the four elements to transform the nursery into an alchemical pigsty. The ultimate was the medicine chest, fixed to the wall above Mama's bedside table, placed so high that she had no qualms about leaving the key in the lock. All I had to do was climb up onto a chair balanced precariously on the bed to find, among colourful packets filled with lethal powders, phials with enticing skulls over crossed bones: Poison! Pills were dissolved in acid so that 'It seethed and foamed and boiled and hissed/ Like fire and water mixed/ Till it rose to Heav'n, a reeking mist' that was collected and poured into little bottles which were already labelled as laxatives for anaemia. No one found out about my clandestine experiments and no one died. Through my youthful flirtations with belladonna, lysol, almond-eyed prussic acid, ether and arsenic, I was mithridatized, which stood me in good stead for gas warfare and darkrooms. I was intoxicated by aromatic names and smells which still lead me into temptation, even today. It is probably due to the fact that I was born intoxicated that my guardian angel has managed to keep me out of the labyrinth of drugs all my life.

Every time a black-tasselled funeral procession came trotting along the street our nannies would drag us into the nearest dark, musty hallway in order to protect us little ones from confrontation with the plain unvarnished fact of death. On the other hand, from the drawing-room window we were allowed to feast our eyes on the magnificent funeral processions of Theodor Mommsen, Anton von Werner and Adolf von Menzel as they crawled their way down Wilhelmstrasse. Playing 'funerals' became our passion. It usually began with brain surgery which I, Professor B., in my nightgown done up back-to-front, performed on my poor little brother Heinz using the whole range of my drawing instruments. I stuffed cotton wool into every orifice and stuck corn-plasters over his eyes, ears and mouths, wielding my tweezers, probes, whalebone stays, douches and curling tongs with practised hand. Heinz had such a thick skull that for trepanation I had to resort to the hammer. Nurse Annie, wearing a white petticoat, stood by with wet towels. Red-ink blood flowed in torrents. Proudly I announced, 'Operation successful. Patient dead', at which Heinz would groan and expire. Then came a thorough washing of the corpse – a ticklish job – followed by embalming. A preparation of green soap, Vaseline and mustard gave the corpse a yellowish shine. The black sofa-cover was thrown over it, the packaged corpse laid out on the ironing board and lovingly strewn with dried flowers, preferably immortelles. Since the corpse had no further function to perform, Heinz was allowed to get up and make himself useful as a mourner. His mortal remains were tipped into an open grave, three handfuls of soil from a flowerpot sprinkled on top and Annie, in deepest mourning, restrained from jumping in after them, whereupon I, now taking the part of the rabbi in a winter coat buttoned up from behind, delivered a deeply moving funeral oration until the handkerchiefs, previously soaked under the tap, could bring no more tears to the mourners' eyes and, as we made our condolences – 'Sincerest sympanties' – we burst out into uncontrollable laughter. The funeral meal consisted of thickly spread blood-pudding sandwiches.

Rituals of death are older than the circus. The clown came after the priest. The hygienic disposal of stinking remains, once a tragi-comic necessity, has developed into a multi-million-dollar business. Like so many fine old customs, the cremation of the merry widow is the invention of medical court jesters. Relicts should be left in peace to rest in peace in their own good time. How they choose to clear away my remains is a matter that leaves me cold.

14 FEARS

Herr Adolph Mühlberg, manufacturer of mourning hats, father of the other Erwin and a loathsome, primeval beast with the bronze skin of a sufferer from Addison's disease, used to find it amusing to creep up behind me and, in the tones of a fire-breathing dragon, whisper in my ear that he was going to devour me, toenails and all, though only after he had chopped me up into neat little pieces first. If my parents happened to look, he would pretend to be ever so nice and shower me with chocolates and caresses. If he caught me alone he would threaten the worst. And once the worst almost did happen. Promising to show me some pretty things he lured me into his cellar. There, in the candlelight, was a butcher's block surrounded by cleavers, saws and other instruments of murder and torture. The monster was sharpening his handsaw, tooth by tooth, all the while bawling out the grisly words of 'My dear little daughter lies dead in her grave'. He was a virtuoso on the barrel organ. Murder to music, a German melodrama. When I saw the blood dripping from his mouth I wriggled out of the ogre's grip, crawled to the door, raced for dear life up the cellar steps and ran, ran, ran through the dark snowy night from the old Jakobstrasse, down Kommandantenstrasse, along Lindenstrasse and round Bel-lealliance platz to Wilhelmstrasse and home – saved! Unnoticed and shivering with cold, I crept into my favourite hiding place under my bed and, vowing never to come out again, fell fast asleep.

They looked for me everywhere. When they finally found their little lost child Papa granted me safe conduct and immunity from punishment. As soon as I was out he broke his promise and beat me for having so bravely saved my life. Mama added insult to injury. 'The boy's psychopathological. First he plays the savage, then he feigns persecution mania. We should get a strict disciplinarian to sort him out, the violent brute. The little brat should be in a home for problem children.' Afterwards Papa brought me a box of chocolate cigars from Herr Mühlberg. A modern upbringing. Proudly, I refused to accept them and then ate them all the same. When I refused to thank him you should have seen my parents' fury. If the cigars hadn't already been safely in my tummy they would have taken them away from me. I'm not just against modern upbringing, I'm against upbringing *per se*.

The long winters in Berlin had freezing nights with all kinds of snow and double-septic chilblains which hurt poor little Erwin something awful. In addition he was compelled to go skating in shoes that were always too tight and with skates that were always too loose on the never-quite-completely-frozen-over New Lake in the Tiergarten. We must get our exercize, mustn't we? *Navigare necesse est, vivere non.*

Another torture was having my hair cut. There was no getting out of it. They dragged me down Friedrichstrasse to a barber by the name of Backofen (which means furnace) who repeatedly assured me he would shove me into the furnace if I didn't sit there quiet as a mouse while he cut off my curly locks. However much I struggled, I was tied to a high chair with a white shroud. All around me were wild men with razors and scissors slapping foam onto lifeless heads, each one trussed up in its shroud. I had to wait until it was my turn. Should I sit there quietly like the others and let them cut my throat without protest? When no one was looking, the sly Furnace, a skeleton with wild, greying blond locks, sidled up to me in a little danse macabre, a long, gleaming dagger in his hand, and whispered in my ear, 'If you dare to scream I'll cut off your head instead of your hair.' That was just what I was expecting. Now nothing in the world could stop me yelling with all my might until it was all over and I found myself, to my surprise, out in the street and still alive, proud of having once again saved my life by screaming. From then onwards I screamed all the way to the barber's.

Later, when I could read, I discovered beside the entrance to a *German* tavern opposite, on the corner of Friedrichstrasse and Kochstrasse, the invitation 'Jews out!' (a neon sign in Florida in 1943: 'No dogs! No Jews! No niggers!') I had learnt to take pride in the fact that we are the chosen people who had been hated for thousands of years because we had always been able to read and write. Jehova and Eliahu, the ineffable, sacred names of the Jewish God, contain all the vowels. I am proud to be a reading, writing Jew.

In those days Berlin was plagued by policemen, aunts, pederasts (in German the word is *Urning*, the most beautiful in the language!), rapists, murderers, sex offenders, vagrants, blockheads, Krautheads, poets, thinkers and all the other riff-raff of the German underworld that became the overworld in 1932. As a whippersnapper of four I found it child's play to learn the alphabet and reading together with my six-year-old sister (shortly before I started school I managed to unlearn it again). The first word I deciphered on a poster in the street was 'Murder!' In Heine's words, I knew not what it meant, nor why I felt so sad.

I spent my childhood in thrall to fears that sent thrills and chills up my spine. Alone in the street it was impossible to walk normally, I had to run, run, run. And I had to make sure nobody noticed I was scared to death, I had to seem happy and carefree, since murderers loved sad children, and all grown-ups were murderers.

All of them. Thus I learned to run faster than any other hunted animal through the sadistic German fairytale forest of Grimm, Bechstein, Hauff, Etcetera Hoffmann and Struwwelpeter (by loony doctor Heinrich Hoffmann), past Gudrun washing clothes barefoot in the March snows and Griselda patiently suffering, past Schmidt's Easter eggs and the rather dubious oath of the Nibelungen on the banks of the Rhine. The name of Xanten, Siegfried's home on the lower Rhine, still enchants my dreams, even today.

Breathless, I managed to hide from witches, murderers, gypsies and magicians in cupboards and cracks in the wall. With the help of a magic cloak I was rendered invisible on the back stairs that reeked of bugs and that were poorly lit by flickering, bluish-yellow gas will-o'-the-wisps. I held my breath, but how my heart was beating with creative angst, since I knew the black man over there, the rat-catcher, carried a sack beneath his long black coat. In the sack was his handsaw with the long, sharp teeth. 'You come along o' me, me little one', commanded the bogeyman in a peremptory whisper. When he had caught me, he gagged me and stuffed me in the sack which he trundled along on a handcart to a dark cellar, all the time whistling, 'On a tree there hangs a plum. I'll have that plum, that plum's for me.' If my parents didn't deposit two thousand marks ransom (in gold) behind the churchyard wall in Bellealliancestrasse within nine hours (they always waited until it was too late; understandable really – was I worth two thousand marks?) he would saw off my little head, which I am so fond of I can't live without it.

No one but me could understand all this. Don't breathe! Be quiet! Be invisible! simply in order to stay alive. It was from 'French' Bertha, a brunette nanny who could say 'oui', that I got my fear of the black bogeyman. She also used to sing, 'There's a corpse floating down the canal' in touchingly sweet tones. At night I didn't dare close my eyes, in case I might miss the first signs of impending danger. When, exhausted by fear, I finally did fall asleep I was assailed by dreams more gory than the terrors of the day. Every sound in the house, every memory was translated into a ghastly nightmare. Added to that, I was being devoured from inside by the slow, sharp pricking of mysterious, tiny, pale greyish-white wriggling things. The Nice Doctor's diagnosis: worms! I was given horrid, greyish-brown worming chocolate, disgusting and ineffective. I was thin, pale, distressed, full of worries and worms, a bag of nerves. Mama had expressed her great desire too often and too soon that I should not do my 'number ones' in my bed. So when I was five I was still waking up every morning in mortal terror and a wet bed. I was despised as a bedwetter. As punishment – and as protection! – they put a humiliatingly smelly rubber sheet over my mattress, and told everyone about it. I was even threatened with the latest thing, that curse of childhood, the child psychologist. I had such a healthy atavistic horror of these medicine-men that I invented a secret method (not to be revealed, to this day) of drying sheets without leaving telltale yellowish-green rings. At the same time I learned to keep my worries to myself, and withdrew into a cocoon of reserve.

In the beginning, even before I wore pants, I was so worried about dirtying my pants that I did dirty my pants. I was terrified of people and things, of things that might happen and did happen, things visible and invisible, of sounds and of silence. Language, even one tiny little word, bred fear, fear of remaining illiterate all my life, whilst all the rest could read, fear of remaining a child for ever, fear of growing old and childish, fear of dying young, fear of dying old, a groundless fear of bottomless depths, fear of attracting attention, fear of craving attention: praise brought tears to my eyes. (When I was nine I cried when Mrs Fliegel, the mother of one of my school friends – her bosom is ever lodged in my memory – said to her husband, pointing at me, 'Ce garçon est un génie', little knowing I could understand French.) 'Une louange est une injure à l'orgueil' (a word of praise injures one's pride – Valéry). If I was reprimanded I cried for fear of falling into disfavour (falling over backwards was Erwin's downfall), fear of falling behind, by the wayside, flat on my face, fear of pitfalls, nightfall, anything that might befall me (all a fallacy?); fear of becoming known, of knowing people, of knowing looks, of the unknown, of remaining unknown, of being misunderstood, of being understood, sweetest of fears, since true genius is always misunderstood; fear of being left out, left on the shelf like a leftover leper, of floundering in the mire (Erwin's just a stick-in-the-mud!), of sinking into quicksand, of drowning while swimming against the tide, of being downcast, cast off, an outcast, left in the lurch, sold into slavery (Joseph by his brothers); fear of wasting away, wracked by incurable disease (softening of the brain, 'Mother, give me the sun'), then having to beg my way from door to door, all on my own, blind, lame, deaf and dumb, a hunchbacked, despised orphan living from hand to mouth, filling my belly with the husks the swine didn't eat, mocked and misunderstood, humiliated, insulted, compelled humbly to beg pardon for uncommitted misdeeds (original sin); fear of being hounded by bloodhounds, bitten, torn limb from limb (this since Waldmann, our dachshund, had taken a snap at my hand as I tried to pull its tail off); fear of the dog-catcher, black as the dreaded chimney-sweep, casually swinging his lasso from the back of his cart as if he were after mad dogs when in reality he was after ME! Fear of professional runners in their striped bathing suits, kicking up trouble; even today I twitch when-ever one of those runners runs past. Fear of the army: having to be a soldier, examined, conscripted, kitted out, deployed, withdrawn, drilled and degraded, running the gauntlet; to the sound of muffled drums (beating funeral marches to the grave), the deserter is stripped of his epaulettes; fear of having one's eyes put out, condemned, an innocent man, by a drumhead court-martial to lifelong death for high treason, to be hung, drawn and three-quartered alive, broken on the wheel, autodaféed by the rope, killotined (King Gillette), crucified (King Jesus!) because one is a Jew, then buried alive in a coma (it happened all the time in those days) with no one to hear my screaming and knocking when I awoke, in my coffin and out of my mind; fear of going raving mad and being punished by being tied up in a strait-jacket to make escape difficult (people are never discharged from lunatic asylums); fear of speeding to death, bleeding to death, drop by drop: the human condition. If you manage to survive it in good health, it starts all over again. Life: 'the eternal recurrence of the ever-same', 'a tale told by an idiot, full of sound and fury, signify-ing nothing.' At least it gives people something to write books about. Is not all literature, are not all the arts nothing more than a modest compendium of our childhood terrors?

I was forever trying to figure out ways of avoiding all this. They felt I was pre-cocious and blessed with too vivid an imagination ('his imagination runs away with him'). They poked fun at their quaint little melancholic boy. They spoke of *Weltschmerz*, *Werther* and *Wurst*; the word masochism was mentioned. By means of painstaking experiments I discovered the sophisticated techniques of the art of getting to sleep, which have kept me out of the clutches of doctors and sleeping pills all my life. In this I was helped by my first mistress, who would snuggle up to me, soft and gentle, devoted and trusting, without much will of her own: my pillow. Only rarely (on cold winter nights) was I unfaithful to her with the eiderdown. Every evening I caressed my beloved until we both fell into a blissful sleep. Faith-fully she accompanied me through the First World War, all quiet on the western front, and equally faithfully deserted with me to Holland in December 1918, discreetly changing her sex when I married and became 'kaptijntje' (little captain). Only in 1940 in Le Vernet d'Ariège, that most inhumane of French concentration camps, was it stolen from under my very head by some Devil's Island convict.

The irresistible magic of 'Hush-a-bye baby' returns again and again in the constant loving motion of the waves, back and forth, up and down, until there is no escaping their rhythmic spell and you have gently fallen asleep. Counting, counting, counting, slowly counting countless numbers until you lose count, reciting row upon row of numbers, slowly writing huge numbers with a huge piece of chalk on a huge blackboard until you fall into the embrace of Dream, the master of Sleep. Sleep, never without a dream, became the better half of my existence. Not a day goes by but I marvel at how the beggar who dreams every night that he is a king leads the same life as the king who dreams every night that he is a beggar. The true beggar is the true king, except, unfortunately, there are neither true beggars nor true kings. 'Au plus élevé thrône du monde, si ne sommes nous assis, que sur notre cul' ('On the highest throne in the world, what we sit on is still our arse') – Montaigne. In my dreams, freed from the shackles of reason, I have ideas, I invent, I see connections, I am a poet. 'We are such stuffe as dreams are made on.' If there's no way out, I fly *ad astra*, up to the sky: flight in flight. *Sursum corda*. Lift up your hearts. Technically not all that easy; even in water we're too heavy. Icarus fell because of a design fault. You have to know your own angle (it changes with the years), master your own parallelogram of forces, breathe slowly and deeply, slowly and steadily tread the heavy air with the tips of your toes, and up you rise, floating away from the earth. You become a free spirit, every night astounded by breathtakingly beautiful dreams, labyrinths that leave their mark on you. When you wake they vanish into thin air. There are many wonderful things in this world, but none as wonderful as dreams. Never in my waking moments have I managed to match its creative power.

15 Taboos and Totems

The official taboos had not yet been classified and ratified. Instead, everything in my parents' house was simply totem and verbotem. My parents had no end of fun forbidding things. It was the childrens' duty to obey without demur. Grown-ups abused their authority and made laws just to assert their superiority. If that did not suffice, they threatened to call the police. That did the trick. I was scared shitless. The policeman ruled the world (his black Maria appeared on the blue paper wrapping of a laxative). To this day the memory works as an effective morning laxative.

In any case, parents were much more ignorant than we children. The things they had learnt at school were no longer true, and they'd forgotten it all anyway; born dumb, nothing learned since. But to doubt a parent's word was a mortal sin. This axiom remained intact despite their daily 'little white lies' – did *they* ever tell the truth? But woe betide us poor little children if *we* should try to deviate from the truth – what was our imagination for? – woe to us if *we* ever sinned against whichever commandment (I never managed to remember the numbers). By the age of six we had to be able to reel off the Ten Commandments backwards and forwards. While the Christian numbers were different from the Jewish ones the commandments, confusingly, remained the same. Before I could understand the difference between lying and stealing, I knew that I should not commit adultery. I felt a bit young for that, anyway. Our brains were scrambled at an early age.

Bread was endowed with a mystical sacredness. Papa flew into a rage when he asked me to pass him a halfpenny roll and I playfully lobbed it across the table.

Religion led complicated double lives. My parents thought they were free-thinkers, believing atheists, modern Jews, above primitive superstition. We children, on the other hand, had to accept unbelievable nonsense as eternal truth. I have never yet met anyone who was able to convince me that he believed in God, though there were many who tried. Religion as a conjuring trick, a way of maintaining lucrative relations with higher powers, of bribing Providence to turn a blind eye, religion as an equation containing the unknown, as the *perfect crime* for the God squad.

Everyone knows that the same God who makes the stronger army win only helps those who help themselves. I refused to leave things to this senile, bigoted God of the Jews, who had chosen us to be murdered, and by stupid goyim at that! I wanted to unmask that deranged criminal and unthrone him, make him abdicate, along with his precious son, since he was clearly not up to the job; his Creation is a professional error. With his highly dubious omniscience, this sadist, who has every perversion to answer for, makes mankind suffer. Were I omnipotent, omniscient and omnibenevolent, I would never have invented hunchbacks or sex killers. This eternal, cruel Stepfather-who-art-in-Heaven treats us, his chosen people, like dirt.

How does he behave towards unchosen peoples? Should we fall down on our knees before him for fear that he might treat us even worse?

We children had to pray of course, no use protesting. The blessing we rattled off in one single breath, 'Thank-you-dear-God-who-has-sent-this-our-daily-nourishment'. Our bedtime prayer, on the other hand, we spun out for as long as possible with folded hands, reverent whispers and feigned humility – 'Now I lay me down to sleep, I pray the Lord my soul to keep' – anything to make the day last just a little longer and get a goodnight kiss. After that, for some obscure reason we were not allowed to put our hands under the blankets. 'Why?' 'Because the good Lord doesn't like it.' 'Why?' 'Because. Children should be seen and not heard. Ask no questions, hear no lies.'

What fascinated me about the holy services to which I was dragged by grandparents and servants was the business aspect: the jingling collection bag and letters of indulgence. Later on, at the cash desk of the brothel in the rue Chabanais, the elective affinity between love and money was revealed to me by the ringing of the till. 'Religion is a fortune.' A heaven-sent business opportunity, an unholy holy alliance to con the simple-minded, to blackmail the blessed poor in spirit. The pope lives in splendour, the faithful creditor lives off the millions of the credulous faithful. Amen.

The real holy images of my youth were not pictures of saints, but the gold coins bearing the Kaiser's profile. Gold ruled the world. Money was unspeakably holy. As a matter of principle, when the little ones were present they never – that is always – talked about money. They regularly mentioned a mysterious business friend called Balance whom I never met. In cases of emergency, and that was every day at table, my parents used Jordan & Blumenfeld's secret code, 'Utvorzichd' (U = 1, T = 2 etc.), which I soon had figured out. 'Aaaliss, the lazy cow, treated herself to a Persian lamb coat from Herpich for T grand. Who's behind it? Who'd stand her something like that? Who's her admirer? Who's the affair with?' Confusing double meanings! Although I couldn't stand her myself, I also liked to admire her from behind. And I was always being told things weren't my affair. – 'Is she engaged? To whom? What's the dowry? A love match? How did they meet? Through a matchmaker? *Mazl un Broche* (Luck and blessings)!'. – Aaaliss, the lazy cow, was manageress of a clandestine umbrella shop of Papa's in Tauentzienstrasse. Aaaliss, full-bosomed and wasp-waisted, was almost the only divorcee (the innocent party, of course) of my youth. People smirked when her name was mentioned. This witch of Endor smelled of cinnamon, cloves, Egyptian cigarettes, scented dress-preservers and all the other shameless perfumes of Arabia. In her musty little room at the back of the shop there was a wrinkled red plush sofa that looked so visibly put-upon that I felt sorry for it. The shop was open on Sunday mornings, even though no one ever buys an umbrella on a Sunday. Papa used to go then to collect Saturday's takings. Mama's housekeeping came from that; it annoyed me that we had to eat out of the hand of the lazy cow. Besides, I had to wait for ages at the front of the shop. Papa thought it proper to have his son take an interest in umbrellas. He took hours going through the accounts with the lazy cow behind locked doors. When he finally emerged, breathless and irritated, moaning about the unsatisfactory state of his affairs, Aaaliss, the lazy cow, looked somewhat the worse for wear, as if they had been fighting.

My parents' hypocrisy took refuge in the phallusy that they were the innocent victims of the Fall, and they hid their shame behind a rampart of secrets. Secrets mean power, which is why children are not allowed to have any, why they have to tell their parents everything immediately, giving *them* something to gossip about and enabling *them* to sound off about their deep insight into children's psyche. Before you are ready for your own secrets, you have to discover those of grown-ups. You have to hide behind curtains, listen at walls, peep through keyholes ('Looking through the keyhole shows/ Mum and Dad without their clothes' – Ringelnatz) and deduce from the movements of flickering shadows what is actually going on in the parental bedroom. At the first suspicious noise I would glue my ear to the keyhole, only to discover that night has its own acoustics. Or were there more other, more profound reasons why at night Mama whispered an octave higher, Papa an octave lower? *Coloratura contra basso buffo*. They were probably using some secret code. (Long before I could write I was interested in invisible inks: wee-wee plus sugar appears brown on paper when heated, excellent for smuggling secret messages, so-called palimpsests, out of dungeons.)

Six – *sechs* – was more than just a number for me, it was a torture: sex + 6 = 12. I knew that sex life consisted of an excremental piece of smuttiness, a cunning trick of Mother Nature's to keep humanity, the dirty swine, alive *à tort et à travers*. Existence as the lowest form of being. The body between navel and knee was particularly obscene. Hair was dubious stuff, women's breasts were (de)pendant, men's pointless. Digestion was so disgusting as to put you off your food, and immoral to boot. Sexual intercourse was for dogs and the lower classes. It was self-evident to me that my parents could never have descended to such perversions, so incompatible with Jewish family life. They were beings from a higher plane, sexless like angels. The bidet in their bedroom, that stood on a somewhat lower plane, they passed off as a footbath, and that is what it has remained for the rest of my life. Truth will out.

Mama considered herself a sexual educator without equal. When I refused to believe in the stork any longer, she promised me the whole truth and nothing but the truth as a present for my ninth birthday. She kept her word. From the top of my birthday cake – as usual shaped like a tree and, as even more usual, too dry – dangled, written out in gothic calligraphy in her own fair hand, Ludwig Fulda's informative verses:

> *We know not whence we come.*
> *We know not whither we go.*
> *Our life on earth is short —*
> *And that is all we know.*

Underneath was, 'To be continued next year. Mama.' Next year she put off removing the seventh veil with the hated anti-encyclopaedic Grail motif from *Lohengrin,* 'These questions ask me never'. Knowledge about sex was for sexologists, Professor Magnus Hirschfeld or Professor Krafft-Ebing, and not for the general public, let alone children. Fortunately, that very same summer on the beach at Ahlbeck I saw a woman rise from the waves with a terrible scar on her back and knew at once 'whence we come'.

Every year Papa went to Paris to buy umbrellas and brought back with him – apart from grotesque lace parasols with which Mama, to her great embarrassment, had to parade up and down the streets – light-green body lotion by Roger & Gallet and 'Quatre Fleurs' perfume by Houbigant (it smelled of 'I know something you don't know', a parlour game of knowledge, possession and love). With it came matching mother-of-pearl opera glasses. Behind it all lurked new mysteries: tears, scenes, reconciliations. At table sexual matters were discreetly veiled in French. Without understanding each other, my parents spoke terrible French, after a fashion, and felt terribly fashionable and sophisticatedly 'riskay'. I very quickly came to the conclusion that sex was a smutty secret somehow connected, like body lotion, with Paris. Accentaigu smiles at accentcîrcônflêxe double entendres, chiefly for men, since, when you look closely, women have no sexual organs.

So I had to learn the language of love. For that purpose I fell in love three afternoons a week with Annie's French governess, Mademoiselle Réséda Ansermier. She had the fragrance of a plump lily of the valley with dimples all over (some hidden, some exposed) and coquettishly concealed a delightfully mobile bosom behind lace frills which I loved to straighten out for her. Learning French was child's play. She also taught me how to find the *racine de la vie* in her neck. I had to be very careful not to break it, and not to tickle. In no time at all I was speaking French as it is spoken in Lausanne. Madamoiselle Réséda Ansermier said it was better than the Paris variety. Hunger is the best sauce, they say, and love certainly spices lessons, and not only language lessons. The day Mademoiselle left us, my French left me too.

As a ten-year-old revolutionary I manfully quoted Nietzsche all over the place. Mama's regular periods when we were enjoined to show her respect made me disrespectful. When her monthly migraine had once more reduced her to tears I declaimed, 'When you go to a woman, don't forget your whip', whereupon she seized an inoffensive cane to beat the sauce out of the bumptious little brat. Once I drew myself up before Papa, finger in the air, and demanded he should not procreate but create. He goggled at me from his kindly protuberant eyes, laughed, tapped his forehead and said, 'Idio-ot!' I could never tell whether my smart-aleck Berlin tongue would bring me a tender kiss or a good spanking. My parents' inconsistency was one of their attractive features. They rarely beat me, but when they did, it was always unfairly and at the wrong moment, on the principle of 'If you won't listen, you'll have to feel it'.

Once a year folk custom decreed that I was allowed to beat Mama and Papa. On the morning of 1 May we crept into our parents' warm nest. The evening before our servant, Hermann, had brought twigs with tender green leaves, tied into little bundles, with which we were allowed to thrash our parents. For me it was too symbolic. The twigs were too small.

Why do parents have to break their word? Why do parents have such awful friends? Why do parents have to be so boring, always harping on about things they've harped on about before? Why do parents always belong to the older generation? Why are they old-fashioned, out-of-date, excruciatingly senile? My children ask themselves the same questions.

It never struck me that my parents associated exclusively with Jews. They were probably not even aware of it themselves. Not, of course, with the filthy Jews from eastern Europe, Polacks and Galicians, but with people like ourselves, urban, cosmopolitan, civilized German Israelites (an Israelite is a Jew who's ashamed of it, a Jew is an Israelite who is without shame), who wanted to have nothing to do with religion. For all that, they despised every renegade Jew who had acquired his 'ticket to European culture' (certificate of baptism). It was very rarely that a stray goy happened to find his way into our house. When one did we had no idea how to behave. Foreigners were curiosities whom we showered with grotesque courtesies, since we were unable to communicate with them. In order to speed up communication between nations, Mama took up Volapük, a kind of Esperanto you could learn to speak fluently in six hours. Unfortunately no one could understand it. Between 1897 and 1913 the following foreigners graced our humble home: (a) one genuine Belgian, Eujeentje Paradis from Brussels (née Wolf from Cologne), (b) one genuine Frenchwoman, Rosa Lion from Lille (née Cohn from Essen), who had cataracts and wore glasses, and a son, André, also with glasses. Uncle Louis Cohn, our genuine American uncle, Salt Lake City, Utah (born in Dobrzyn on the Drina), Grandpapa's spitting image, came 'across the big pond' every five years with his wife, Aunt Harriet (complete with false teeth, removable, 'made in USA'), and daughter Edna, six feet tall and unmarried, who sang in the Mormon Tabernacle Choir. Such was our international world. All around us were invisible walls; the world is a ghetto: *borghetto*. Contented pariahs in 'splendid isolation'. My parents lulled themselves into a false sense of security. A century of emancipation had forever driven the stench of the ghetto and the spectre of the pogrom from Germany to the East, where it belonged. Blind to the true situation, we were slumbering in the darkest of Dark Ages. In his long poem 'Germany. A Winter's Tale', written in 1844, Heine had portrayed Germany's future as a miasma, 'As if they had piled up the dung/ From six-and-thirty privies.' In 1850 Grillparzer prophesied, 'The course of modern culture goes from humanism via nationalism to bestialism.' I was no prophet. Even with the advantage of hindsight I did not claim to have foreseen that the annihilation of six million Jews in the name of the German people could become a large-scale industrial undertaking. Nothing was wasted: gold teeth, women's hair, children's brains; soap from corpses. Six million that I cannot forget, nor want to, not for one second, even when I am gazing into the eyes of the most beautiful German girl. The nightmares of my childhood in which the Germans were torturing me to death were not my persecution mania, as my parents soothingly tried to persuade me, but German reality.

16 IWAN

Russia had a nice line in pogroms, even in those days. Iwan, a distant cousin (several times removed, if he was ever there in the first place, he was the son of a sister of Grandpapa Henry's stepbrother Itsche from his second marriage with the cousin of an aunt), had fled from Dobrzyn on the Drina to Berlin in 1906, and the whole *mishpokhe* had no choice but to take him in, which we did with friendly disdain. On Sundays he was allowed to eat his fill in our house and with every mouthful he was made to feel how much more refined we Berlin Jews were than the grubby *tefilim*-wearers from the east (he didn't wear *tefilim*). Did he realize how lucky he was that we allowed a *schnorrer* with a funny Jewish accent like him (he didn't have a funny accent and he didn't beg, though he did have an odd smell) to sit with us at table instead of eating with the servants in the kitchen? I was shocked at the submissiveness with which this fourteen-year-old boy accepted everything. He got a pittance from Papa's umbrella factory for drawing walking sticks in the pattern book. He would lay a stick on a sheet of paper, draw the outline and colour it in freehand. The result was a work of art, more beautiful by far than the stick itself, for Ivan was an artist. We spent the Sunday afternoons doing watercolours together. What fun! I had the ideas, he the talent: mountains reflected in an alpine lake, the chalk cliffs of Rügen, with the Königsstuhl at twilight reflected in the waters of the Baltic. While he was painting Ivan would tell me how the cossacks used to lean down from the saddle and whip the Jews with their *nagaika. Kunst* (art) and *Knute* (lash) were almost anagrams and definitely opposites; I opted for art. Soon I could paint the cliffs mirrored in the water myself.

When he reached the age of fifteen Iwan was automatically sent a deportation order as an 'undesirable alien'. He emigrated to America and today lives in Liverpool, a wealthy, miserly Englishman: Sir Irving Sommerfield, formerly Irving Saturday, formerly Iwan Sonnabend, formerly Jitzrock Schabbes. Every few years he comes to New York, as servile as he was sixty years ago and with a slightly pained air besides. In him I observe myself in my primordial state, a gorilla clambering its way through cultures between one Great Flood and the next.

17   140 WILHELMSTRASSE

The building where we lived was the ideal setting for wild games: robbery, murder, assassination. There were two houses, built together in a horseshoe shape around a courtyard. The front yard went with the house at the front, the back yard with the house at the back. Each house assumed *it* was the front house. Across the courtyard we played at being courtiers, courteously paid court, courted each other – and despised each other, a microcosm of society. Each courtyard had its own courtly language, its own court jesters. The front yard had the pump, so it justifiably looked down its nose on the back yard. Alfried Rektor's father, for example, was an agent and we had a deaf-mute, Otto Jakobi, who could almost speak and was very strong, whilst all the rear courtyard had to show was a hunchback with a nasty disposition, although Admiral von Tirpitz frequently came secretly to visit Admiral von Holle. Fairhaven and Foulstrand from Strindberg's *Dream Play*, separated and joined by the garden, surrounded by a paling fence on which you were sure to tear every pair of trousers, old or new. The garden was made even smaller by a summerhouse leaning against the front house. The garden itself consisted of half a walnut tree, the better half of which had rotted and fallen down. Its roots formed the roots of the front house. A sparse elm provided those of the rear house.

It was our janitor, Herr Hermann Sendtke, who taught me all this, since I was his favourite (Papa used to tip him accordingly). Herr Sendtke had a charming repertoire of songs that he would bawl out loud: 'Such a lovely dress, so pure, so white, and all down the back it's covered in shite'; 'Man has reason, man has wit, man has an arse that's full of shit'; 'My darling's a lovely young thing, I love her with all my might, she's just like a beautiful rose, a-growing up out of the shi…ning earth' and others with a similar rhyme scheme. His songs were as full of shit as the soul of the German *Volk*. From a basement hole at the gate of the rear house, 17 Königgrätzerstrasse, he tyrannized the whole building in his felt slippers, aided and abetted by his lady wife, Frau Sendtke. They lived on meatloaf and smelly cheese. He had a little skylight through which he could see who was ringing the bell. The passage was a short cut, and he would only open up for those who purchased his favour by greasing his greasy palm. I loved to take over the office of Cerberus, and I was strict and just. Apart from me, no one was allowed to enter the garden. In the autumn there were some rare walnuts, the tastiest morsels I have ever eaten. Herr Sendtke tried to induce me to eat earthworms with them, but even though he called me a coward, I couldn't bring myself to do it. He showed me how the blood squirts out when you squash them and how each piece goes on living when you cut them up: eternal life.

The summer-house consisted of one single room. Every quarter, when the rent was due, the owner, young Herr Püschel, used to come and stay in it. He was a pastor in Prenzlau, a member of the Moravian Brethren and a knight of the Order of St John of Jerusalem. He was large and obese, with a permanently lugubrious expression; I was the only one who was favoured with a friendly, inviting smile. I was allowed to play in the summer-house room while he wrote out the receipts. The curtains were always drawn. Hanging on the wall in the murky room was a thin, black rapier with a handle in the shape of a cross which fascinated me. Once, when I was in the garden looking for a walnut, he called me into his room. He was standing there in a voluminous black velvet cloak with a white cross sewn on, wearing a large black broad-rimmed hat with an ostrich feather dangling down, as magnificent as any knight in a fairy tale. 'Why', I asked, 'should one of the Brethren wear a lady's hat?' At that he gave a funny laugh and let me hold his rapier. When I shyly asked if he would give it to me, he threw open his cloak and stood there in fancy dress, in a corset and lace panties like Mama. It made me laugh, but at the same time it alarmed me. 'If you want my sword, you must come here and take it out of its sheath.' He didn't look friendly any more. I was getting bored and said that Mama had tea waiting for me. He shook his finger threateningly at me. 'If you start telling tales about the games we've been playing you'll be a liar and you'll be stabbed to death with this sword.' Ever after there was something about young Herr Püschel that gave me the creeps.

In the passage there were two rubbish bins which during the day were filled to overflowing with stinking garbage and smoking cinders. In the morning, after they had been emptied by two ash-coloured mythological giants, huge dustmen in heroic leather aprons, my idol, Sendtke, Warden of the Portal, taught me the noble art of the hunt. With the same professionalism he showed in everything he did, he emptied the previous night's catch of rats and mice out of the traps into the tall, round metal bins. With great ceremony he armed me with an iron bar that was much too heavy and hoisted me up onto the rim of the tall bin, from where I was supposed to crush the poor beasts with my heavy crowbar. It wasn't as easy as it looked. They ran for dear life, and I was too weak and clumsy to handle my murder weapon properly. To punish me for my botched handiwork, the bleeding vermin would drag their mashed intestines round and round behind them, squeaking horribly. Herr Sendtke was furious and I had to beg his forgiveness. Then he would smugly tip a pinch of snuff into his nostrils, let me have a snort too, and, guiding my hand, expertly split each animal through the middle, laughing as he did so, 'That's the way we should exterminate those Jew rats, the vermin of humanity. And you, Erwin, you'll grow up to be a proper German.' I didn't dare tell my parents about that. They would have either been angry with Herr Sendtke, or not believed me, or punished me. It was better to keep my mouth shut. I found this German virility fascinatingly revolting: my first insight into the sport of genocide. Once, when he was particularly merry, Herr Sendtke even tried to kill me with the crowbar. In the front house was a schnapps shop, where he frequently repaired to drown his sorrows. When he came at me with the iron bar I thought he was joking, but when he tried to throw me into the rubbish bin I ran away.

Standing like gallows beside the rubbish bins were the frames on which the servant girls, scarves wrapped tightly round their hair, would beat clouds of smelly dust out of ancient Persian rugs with their carpet-beaters. I once organized a peeing competition over the frames for the boys of both houses; the girls were allowed to be the referees (to save them from getting inferiority complexes). An hour before the contest we boys had tanked up on fizzy lemonade (if nothing goes in, nothing comes out). I was just about to break the world record when Mama arrived and attacked me (from behind, the coward), beating a brand-new parasol to tatters on my bottom. I turned round and, challenging her in front of all the children, asked her, 'Please do beat me again if you enjoy it so much.' Blushing with shame, Mama withdrew. What a humiliation for Jordan & Blumenfeld! Mama had a collection of over a hundred umbrellas and parasols.

In the courtyard we practised class distinctions: tinker, tailor, soldier, sailor, rich man, poor man, beggarman, thief, played at cops and robbers, secret police, master and slave, tag, hide and seek, marbles, tops, hoops, Flying Dutchman and Indians. My interest in cap pistols, stink bombs, itching and sneezing powder was less than minimal, but I will admit to a passion for bows and arrows. We high-born children of the upper classes naturally went to high school. Young ladies went to Academies for Young Ladies. Coeducation had not yet arrived. Young gentlemen who completed six years at high school were allowed to do their military service as one-year volunteer cadets, could become officers and command. The plebs went to council schools, after which they had to spend three years in the army as common soldiers in the poor bloody infantry. When they came out they became, at best, postmen, servants, carters, street-sweepers, factory workers, criminals or beggars. The world was their oyster.

The front stairs were only for the tenants and their guests: 'Servants and tradesmen use the rear stairs.' At the front door you pressed the electric bell, the door sprang open and there was the front entrance, resplendent in all its extravagant cleanliness, the stair carpet taut beneath its gleaming brass rods. At the back door you pulled a string and a bell jangled. The rear stairs were dark and covered in filth. We children had to go round the back, we were driven into the open arms of the maids. At the front there was roast veal, pork in the kitchen at the back. Ever since my earliest days I had a liking for the kitchen staff ('Young men have a liking, truth to tell, for the charms of the kitchen personnel' as Wilhelm Busch revealed) who rebelled against the tyranny of my parents, and a dislike for nursemaids and nannies who always had one eye on the possibility of rising in the world and becoming mistresses in their own homes themselves. Maids had no future: they got it from gypsies who read it in their palms.

At two and a half Mama left me at home by myself for the first time and calmly went off on a trip. She was going to regret it! The servants indoctrinated me. When Mama came back a week later I was sent to receive her at the front door in my Sunday best. I pretended not to know her. 'Clear off, old girl, you're daft.' My Mama, struck down with migraine and remorse, swore she would never leave me alone again.

One fine morning when I was four the postman who delivered money orders died of a stroke in the bed of our cook, Olga Ziem. The poor man did not even have his trousers on. Our three maids slept together in a hanging loft – a kind of dog-kennel with a skylight, made by inserting a false ceiling – to which you climbed up from the kitchen on a ladder. (I thought it was called a hanging loft because people went there to hang themselves.) As the space was not high enough for a grown-up to stand up in, they were forced to lie down all the time. It was hard to imagine how those three hefty things managed to sleep on the two iron bedsteads. It was always nice and warm up there, though; there were always full chamber pots standing around and it stank unashamedly of human livestock. Schulz the money-order postman had an imposing beard (painted by Van Gogh) and steel-rimmed spectacles. He liked me and used to let me play ride-a-cock-horse on his knee, using his beard as reins. The excitement was terrific: people were going round shouting and screaming, and I was there when the police came and put their official seal on the mailbag with the money. Dr Saatz was called in. Health Councillor Dr Saatz lived opposite us on the upper ground floor, right-hand side (the right was more elegant than the left!), and was having an affair with the most celebrated actress, Amanda Lindner, which made his wife cry continuously into a lace handkerchief, while telling me, in strictest confidence, exciting stories of floods with cradles floating on the waters. There was a constant coming and going of ambulances and curious neighbours. On top of it all, Olga, as if she had not been through enough already, was dismissed on the spot. Mama surpassed herself. Leaving Papa in the shade, she swelled to mythical proportions and, with outstretched finger, severe and final, the very image of Eternal Justice, pointed at the door and declared, 'There is the door!' It was generally agreed that the dead postman made a fine corpse. He looked so serious, and everybody in the house was grinning, which mystified me: true puzzles are those that have no answer.

I tried to improve the lot of the poor housemaids by telling them what my parents said about them at table. If there was not enough to report, then I made it up, since I knew exactly what my parents could have said. I made things up, I lied, I suffered from the stress of these breathtakingly dangerous intrigues. And I loved it. It was stronger than I was. I just had to support the oppressed against the ruling class, and like a journalist, I had to have something new to report each day. I loved the girls who had the bosoms Mama lacked and the courage to be cheeky to Mama that I lacked. In order to soothe my conscience I occasionally felt I had to tell my mother what they thought of her in the kitchen. Thus I became a double agent provocateur. This back-stairs culture bred a thrilling back-stairs eroticism. Irresistible hawkers came round to the back door selling back-stairs novels in weekly instalments that the maids devoured. It was a dung-heap on which German literature of the turn of the century flourished.

Ella Tiersch (only Papa was allowed to say, 'Tiersch – it's a nice name') had the most marvellously bouncy, bobbling blancmange of a bosom, and a bobbling, bouncy bottom to match. As a reward for passing on secret items of news, she taught me a game which could only be played in the loft, and only when my parents were both out. Amalia would stay in the kitchen, a singing look-out: when she stopped it meant danger was approaching. The rules of the game were that I had to find a small coin that Ella had hidden in some very secret place on her body, in her bun for example. We called it 'spend-a-penny'. She would lie down on her unmade bed (since no one else ever made the ascent to this Olympus, they never bothered to make the beds with the red-checked sheets that were changed once a month). When I finally found the coin I got a kiss and was allowed to keep the copper. Naturally I always knew exactly where it was hidden, but since it was more blessed to search than to find, I would spend a long time searching, I would search thoroughly and I would search everywhere. In the course of my searches I made the interesting discovery that a woman has more nooks and crannies than a man. Then we changed roles: I lay on the bed and Ella searched. She could never find anything. It often tickled, and laughing or speaking was against the rules; anyone who spoke had lost. After we had played spend-a-penny non-stop until we were both exhausted, Ella invented a variant that made the game more difficult. We had to start by undressing each other, since it is obviously much more difficult to hide a coin on a naked body, and once well hidden it is almost impossible to find it. As it was not a game of chance, but demanded nimble fingers and a sharp mind, I always found the coin. Filled with the desire to be dexterous, I almost managed to become so. There is often a serious purpose behind children's games.

18   GIERITZ THE CLOCKMAKER

Gustav Gieritz the clockmaker had a pointed, black-waxed beard (like Robert le Diable), a glass eye (like all clockmakers), a wooden leg and two crutches to go with it. (It's not true that I hid those crutches in the cellar!) I liked to watch him as he sat repairing clocks at the open window that gave onto the street. He didn't say very much, but once, suddenly, unexpectedly and without the slightest reason, he smeared the slimy black snot out of his nose over my hand. I went home to tell my parents the tearful tale. When the doorbell rang next Sunday morning I knew it must be Satan himself: Gustav Gieritz in his well-brushed black frock coat and goatee, with his wooden leg and crutches. He earnestly declared that I was a liar and gave his sacred word of honour that he had not smeared his snot over my hand. Then he beat his breast with his fist and asked, 'I am a man of honour. Do I look like someone who would smear the snot from my nose on the hand of some cheeky little Jew brat?' My parents left me in the lurch and agreed that he didn't. I thought he did look like somebody who would do just that, but his voice was so vibrant with sincerity that even I began to have my doubts. After he had left, my parents laughed themselves silly at this Sunday farce, and were not in the least interested in whether they should believe him or me. I saw nothing funny in it at all and spent a long time in philosophical reflection, trying to work out whether truth was a credible lie, or a lie twisted truth, or whether they were both the same, reversed mirror images of each other. Why should little Erwin think up such a snotty lie? But also: why should Herr Gieritz the clockmaker behave in such a loathsome manner? The truth was that he did smear his snot over my hand. Even at the time there was no way of proving it; today, sixty years later, there is no one apart from me left who knew Gieritz. I swear the story is true.

19 SCHOOL

In the beginning was the word. Which word? I knew that was not the case. In the beginning was play. A lovely word: play. I loved word-play. 'Rats live on no evil star.' The same backwards as forwards, pure poetry! (Schopenhauer is said to have worked out the first German example.) Did it all begin with some slip of the tongue? Or with a play on words? In the beginning was the miracle of the alphabet, A + B = C. At lastbutnotleast came the word. I found thtarting to thpeak difficult. I had a lithp and everyone laughed at me. And there were questions nobody answered. They pretended they weren't interested, but in reality they couldn't answer them. Who needs bread? Who kneads bread? What's a Grecian urn? Five drachmas a day? Should I bare my soul or bear my sole? At first I felt I would never find the thread to guide me through this linguistic maze, this amazing wordplay-ground. Why did I have to speak like the others who never listened to me anyway? Why shouldn't I lithp, it made the wordth thlip tho thweetly off the tongue? Why shouldn't I have a language of my own? Languages are secret languages that nobody understands, unspeakably dangerous, never saying what I want them to say, just a rough approximation. How can I express myself? Am I really 'I'? Quite often I am also 'me my mine', never 'yours'. Am I always the selfsame self? Who is that crying in the hall of mirrors? Not me! Who's behind it? I'm here, in front. Am I unique, one-off, all of a piece? Or doubly redoubled toil and trouble? Singular or plural? Animal, vegetable or mineral? Was language just a guessing game? Would Master Erwin ever master it?

In the beginning the word, that threatening sphinx, set me insoluble riddles from which I had to learn to think. Think or thwim. The word forced itself into the straitjacket of convention, taught me to lie, laugh, live. It was a long time before it managed to teach me to thpeak, and even longer before I learnt to keep my trap shut. Lacking a gift for languages, I have remained faithful to my mother tongue: turn-of-the-century middle-class-Berlin standard German (the jargon in which these chapters are supposed to be written). When I started to read, letters and words were hieroglyphics. Where was the meaning? That I had to learn at school. My thirst for knowledge was so great I found the wait unbearable before I was sent, at the age of six, to the preparatory school of the Askanisches Gymnasium. Despite Mama's urging, I was never able to swallow a single bite in the morning before school, for fear of being chucked out for lateness.

Our school was of the classical and Prussian (Russian with a P in front) persuasion. Teachers and pupils put on a sanctimonious show of believing in a reformed-Lutheran-protestant Lord Jesus. In reality the only things they believed in were the Kaiser and success. The Virgin Mary was ridiculed as a joke figure, and a Catholic to boot. The only true national religion was patriotism. Merely to hum the *Marseillaise* would have been high treason, the *Internationale* unthinkable. An all-consuming hatred between teachers and pupils prepared us for life and death for the Fatherland. Pupils and teachers drove each other to suicide. When the First World War broke out everyone was ready for the worst. Pleasantly ruthless, fanatical German hero-fodder marched singing to the grave, first of all for Wilhelm, then – *Siegheil!* – for Adolf. Apart from my best friend, Ravel, I have never seen any of my classmates again. They're probably stone-cold-dead, all of them. At least for me they are: Albrecht, Allner, Arnold, Artz, Berendt, Bersau, Bissing, Blumenfeld, Davidson, Diederichs, Gerbode, Hagen, Hauss, Harvard, Heinrich, Herbst, Jakobson, Joseph, Kirsch, Klauer, Lademann, von Ledebour, Lebrun, Lilienthal, Makowsky, Nost, Niering, Orlt, von Papart, Rahm, Roelofsz, Schattschneider, Schultze I, Schultze II (redheaded twins), Seidenschnur, Storm, Völker, Warnatsch, Wolfheim and Zimmer.

The reason the names of those forty oafish bullies are for ever engraved on my memory is that at the time I had a passion for notebooks. My entire pocket money went on little cloth-bound jotters. I could not get enough of them. For each of my classmates I kept a notebook in which I recorded every one of his answers, followed by a plus or minus. Likewise I noted down, in red ink, every grade for every piece of written work by every pupil. That was my main occupation at school. Studying was incidental.

I suspected that the injustices which I learned from fairy tales, and from my sister Annie, also happened in real life, and I tried to work out why some pupils were favoured, others not. In my first year at school I was the best in the class. Conduct: Excellent; Attention and Diligence: Very Good; everything else: Very Good, apart from Neatness, unfortunately only: Good. Twelve commendations and no black marks, no absences, no lateness – a model pupil. In spite of that I did not come top of the class, only third. Jews should not be pushy. I came to see justice as a game society played by arbitrary rules.

After that my morale went downhill. With every year my grades got worse. Conduct: not without reproach. A letter from my class teacher to my father: 'Erwin, who used to be so obedient, is now repeatedly trying to disrupt the class by *hissing*. May this little reminder serve as a warning and save him from further black marks. Your most obedient servant, Brauer.' When I was in my third year at the preparatory school that selfsame Brauer had written in my autograph book:

Strive ever to obey
Duty's stern command.
Keep the narrow way
With Virtue's happy band.

To little Erwin, with best wishes
from his affectionate primary school teacher, Brauer.

I got my first reprimand in the second year at the senior school. Up to then nothing but commendations, with perhaps one little black mark. Three black marks added up to a reprimand, three reprimands meant you had to stay behind in school; two 'punishment schools' brought you a *consilium abeundi*, 'advice to leave': in other words you were chucked out. A reprimand was entered in the class book, and also in my homework notebook, which Papa had to sign – no problem since I am good at imitating handwriting. I got my first reprimand for not doing my Latin prep. In principle I was against homework, but in practice the awful reality of a reprimand was too much for me. Two days earlier Hauss's crocodile tears had got him off a reprimand (his father was president of the Royal Prussian Patent Office). The unjust teacher let me cry until the whole class was laughing at me, but he didn't let me off. How could I bring such disgrace on my parents? Suicide seemed the obvious solution. When I arrived home three-quarters of an hour late for dinner, I got such a scolding for being late that the reprimand was somehow completely ignored.

Class-consciousness was drummed into us with our daily lessons. Even at home I was ashamed to see the way my parents pandered to wealthy friends, while they themselves basked in the exaggerated respect of poorer acquaintances. In school were learnt the ground rules of social relationships: 'YOU have to greet ME first because I'm on familiar terms with people who wouldn't ever bother to cut you and therefore I'm going to go farther than you.' On Monday mornings, after the prayer, 'In the name of the Lord maker of heaven and earth, amen', the personal particulars of every boy were read out. Niering's father was a bus conductor and catholic, which was plain for everyone to see; there is such a thing as a popish face. You could also see that he was a scholarship boy, too poor to pay the school fees, for which he was despised. Raucous laughter greeted the name of Rudolf Herbst, sending the blood rushing to his cheeks, for he was illegitimate and had to suffer the public humiliation of it every week. Ernst Albert Behrendt on the other hand we gazed at in awe. His father was president of the Royal Prussian State Railways and they had an official apartment in Potsdam Station in the middle of Berlin, the dining-room window of which looked out over the cemetery for those who had died in the 1848 revolution. Behrendt's grandfather, a baptised Jew, had donated the money to build Trinity Church in Königgrätzerstrasse and had been accepted at court. I was invited to Behrendt's seventh birthday party. His mama stood me on the table and introduced me to the adults, 'One of us'. They all applauded and I was so moved I burst into tears.

In order to keep existing anti-semitic feelings alive our director, Professor Dr Busse, had dug up the most grotesque caricature of an Eastern European Jew to take our religious instruction. Dr Jizrock Jannowitz spoke with an accent that made him sound like a caricature stage Jew. He branded our Christian classmates as 'followers of one of the offshoots of our religion'. When, before saying the closing prayer, this almost blind, doddery old man with the whining voice put on his worn-out top hat, into which one of us had poured a bottle of 'Kaiser' ink (flows blue, dries deepest black), we peed ourselves laughing as the ink slowly dribbled down his white goatee.

After religion the most important subject was gym, to toughen us up. We wore brownish gym-suits, beltless straitjackets with armbands on which there shone that precursor of the swastika, the four Fs: *Frisch, Froh, Fromm, Frei* (bright, happy, god-fearing, free). Gym lessons in the period between the founder of the German gymnastics movement, *Turnvater* Jahn, and the Nazi youth leader, Baldur von Schirach, were wreathed in all sorts of nationalistic, German-male-voice-choir clap-trap with a descant of queer overtones: souls seeking the land of the Greeks. The place where that sort of thing went on was the stinking privy in the school yard; in 1903 Marquart, the gymnastics supervisor, paid for it with four years in jail. We prep-school kids pretended we knew why and would smirk knowingly when doing our pull-ups, climbing the pole or swinging clubs. I was only average at javelin-throwing, shot-putting, vaulting and the parallel bars; free exercizes and team gymnastics didn't appeal to me, but I was all the more keen on the high and long jump, any variant of tag, long-distance running and the unofficial games we organized on Saturday afternoons on Tempelhof heath. We learnt to swim in the public swimming baths in Dennewitzstrasse which stank like a monkey-house. The trick was to pee in the pool without the attendant noticing. Daredevils managed even worse. And always we sang: marching in step, in the howling storm and the clash of waves, keeping the Watch on the Rhine, riding with Lützow's wild daredevil hunt, all with echo effect. When we sang my favourite song, 'Nice and slowly, my lads, we're not in a race, poor old Dad's Army can't keep up the pace', I laughed so much I couldn't keep in step.

I was derisively small, with a head that was slightly too large. Since I was light as a feather, I could run very fast. Just for fun I would throw myself at full speed onto the sharp cobbles. During my childhood I was always bleeding from some cut or other, and I laughed at my wounds in proud anticipation of picking at the itchy scabs. During class fights I would throw myself into the middle of the fray out of sheer terror simply in order to forget everything, especially myself: a cowardly hero. I overdid everything. No game was wild enough for me. In the course of a snowball fight an icy snowball hit me full in the eye. Since then, scaredy-cat that I am, I have been incapable of catching or throwing a ball.

My navigational talents notwithstanding, the school rowing club was closed to me; Jews were not allowed to join the officer cadets either. For the same reason, and despite my outstanding ability on the horizontal bar (I once almost managed a full circle) I never made it beyond number two in the gymnastics fourth team. Humiliating, when we put on public demonstrations and my parents were watching.

Though in constant fear that we would never manage it, we did learn to read German, and to write it, beautifully neatly, in Gothic script. We memorized little rhymes to teach us the rules of spelling:

After L, N and R, we say
Don't put TZ or CK.

We learnt axioms, tenets, definitions, nonsense: Walking is the constant avoidance of falling down. (Is living the constant avoidance of dying?) I was infatuated with linguistic oddities and grammatical hair-splitting. Subject, predicate, object, attribute, adverbial modifiers of time, place and manner. Reading Schiller's ballads aloud with the parts given out, we learnt to declaim a role. We learnt to memorize by heart, mostly poems set as punishment. To this day I have not dared forget the least little word. 'We learn in order to forget', without learning how to forget. One thing I did learn: how to learn. We learnt that German is the richest, most beautiful, most unique language in the world:

O mother tongue, o blissful sound,
Sweet music of this hallowed ground.

We learnt to write boring essays, at least four pages long, on boring subjects. We learnt history, which consisted almost entirely of dates: 333, punch-up at Issos; 768–814, Charlemagne; 1618–1648, Thirty Years War; 1870–1871, War of Eighteen-Seventy-to-Eighteen-Seventy-One. We got stuck in the depths of the Middle Ages – the modern period was not quite politically *comme il faut*. For seven long years we sweated over Latin, seven long hours every week. Caesar's *De Bello Gallico* to send us to sleep. We translated words without ever getting the meaning. We learnt all the unforgettable rules of Latin grammar.

At the same time we had no problems at all learning the ABC of love: Alberto Bedded Clarissa During Evening Festivities, Grand Hotel, In January. Kissed, Laid Maiden Nude On Parquet. Quickly Ravished, Screwed, Terrifically, Urgently, Vigorously. Wailed Xstatically YEEES! Zzzzzz…

They were just as successful at spoiling Greek for us. Two years of Xenophon's Anabasis had us screaming, 'Thalassa! Thalassa! H_2O! H_2O!' The unexpected result of all this is that forty years on I have a profound interest – without a great deal of knowledge – in classical languages. I wish the 'Little Bastard' could hear that: Professor Dahms ('The little pelican, that's me, in trousers white as white can be'), a dwarf of truly millennial viciousness who had tried to fill us with enthusiasm for the beauties of the ablative absolute, the gerund and the gerundive (acc. and inf. was easy) through liberal use of the cane. French we learnt with a Berlin accent and that envious disdain which every honest German Tellheim feels for every slimy, cheating Frenchman from Lessing's *Minna von Barnhelm*, that most boring of comedies which German teachers have managed to get hailed as a masterpiece of German humour). English was optional, since English was not a language but a medium of trade. The marks you got for English did not count towards your overall average. It was only of interest to those poor unfortunates who, on leaving school, would have to dirty their hands in trade. We were taught that Shakespeare was unreadable and only reached his true significance in the masterly German translation of Schlegel and Tieck.

In our long years at school we learnt false enthusiasms, but no foreign languages. We learnt that 'mountains divide, oceans unite' (blood is thicker than water), but we did not learn that languages unite even better. That was something I learnt out in the world, during all those dumb, stumm years spent in foreign lands.

I tried to understand the peculiarities of my own intellectual equipment. Why was I good at physics, poor at chemistry, good at geometry, poor at algebra? Why did I find even numbers easier than odd ones, why is one simpler than two, why was I better at adding than subtracting, better at multiplying than dividing, good at mental arithmetic, poor at fractions? I could just about do powers, extracting roots hurt and I gave up on logarithms, not to mention sines, cosines, tangents and cotangents. The indicative was easier than the subjunctive, active easier than passive, perfect easier than future perfect, major easier than minor. North and south I could find in my sleep, with east and west I still have problems today, even when I'm wide awake. We were helped in this by an excellent geography teacher, Professor Kraetsch (known as Krikrakrae) who warned us, 'Anyone who mixes up east and west will get a black mark first time, be kept behind after school the second and chucked out the third!' As a result, none of us ever dared to err. ('Tc purr is human' I once wrote in a dictation; I thought it was one of the traps Herr Brauer was famous for.)

The aim of our education was to make officers, civil servants, idiots and heroes out of us. We were Germans, Germans *über alles*; we were Prussians, by our colours ye shall know us; we were Brandenburgers of the Mark: our holy Trinity. Bullshit. I was never a German. I was a Berliner, and a Berliner I have stayed, nothing but a Berliner. To be more precise, a Southwestberliner and a Westwestberliner. The other parts of the city were foreign countries. I never became a Dutchman; in all my seventeen years there I hardly even became an Amsterdamer. I was never a Frenchman, just one of the *Montparnos de la rive gauche*. I am not an American, only a passionate New Yorker, Midtown-Manhattan. I am a citizen of certain parts of certain big cities. I know nothing of fatherlands or mother countries. Love of nature, though, was de rigueur, even though at best our only contact with nature was on Sunday excursions. ('Picnicking permitted here, but leave the grass of litter clear.')

In the study of local history and topography that passed for geography at primary school we were taught that Berlin was by far the most beautiful of the world's great cities. We were taken to the Museum of the Mark Brandenburg to stand in awe before the old symbol of the city's jurisdiction, the column with the statue of Roland (the city phallus). We learnt a little story to memorize the names of the streets that crossed Friedrichstrasse in the city centre: '*Under the lime trees* (Unter den Linden) the *bears* (Behrenstrasse) were dancing and speaking *French* (Französischestrasse). Along came the *huntsmen* (Jägerstrasse), shot the *pigeons* (Taubenstrasse) and gave the *moor* (Mohrenstrasse) the *crown* (Kronenstrasse). At that the *Leipzigers* (Leipzigerstrasse) became *confused* (Krausenstrasse) and drove the *cook* (Kochstrasse) down the *Puttkamerstrasse* and out through the *gate* (the Hallesches Tor).' Although we already knew it by heart, we learnt how superior we Berliners were, and what a terrible affliction it was to be born a small-town dweller, let alone a peasant! Provincials and Austrian yokels were to be laughed at, especially because of the way they spoke. Dialects were defects for which the speaker was responsible. Saxon, Bavarian or East Prussian were hideous, but the worst of all was talking using your hands. A Berlin accent, on the other hand, had an irresistible charm. We were superior. We even learnt to look down on skyscrapers as ludicrous bombast, since in Berlin no buildings were permitted to be higher than seventy feet because the water pressure and the length of the Fire Department's ladders were insufficient.

Germany I only knew from geography lessons and our annual holidays. Even the shortest trip swelled to a catastrophe of immense proportions, with weeks of incomprehensibly difficult preparations. Mama was transformed into an even bigger fusspot than usual, and spent days practising packing far too many cases, trunks, cardboard boxes, travelling rugs, thermos flasks, etcetera. She would pack, unpack and repack, weighing and measuring all the time; there were complicated reservations, ticket offices, transport arrangements, all in consultation with the family doctor. There was her constant fear of the strain of changing trains, forgetting hand luggage and missing connections; fear of getting off the wrong train. No trip without tears.

Twice a year, for the Easter and Michaelmas holidays, I went to Stettin to be spoiled by my grandparents. Grandpapa spared no effort to have something special for me to do every day. Near the port was a forbidden street called *Lasterdie* (Vice Alley). When the Eucharistic Conference was held there I saw a notice on the gate to the forbidden quarter: 'Come along Catholics, you're in luck, for three marks here you can have a fuck.'

Every year there were the *Summer Holidays!!!* We spent them in Berlin's overcrowded resorts on the Baltic: Binz, Heringsdorf, Misdroy, Sellin. During our first day in Nordeney on the North Sea I got lost and the town crier went round calling out my name. I managed to get seasick on the mudflats. In Müritz there were millions of midges, it was before the days of DDT. In Kösen by the 'bright banks of the Saale', where Annie went to take saline baths, I almost beat Cousin Werner, a hated degenerate, to death with my spade because he refused to get down from my sandbank. In Friedrichroda in the Harz the hill was called 'Thank God' and Annie won a prize at diabolo because I was one of the judges and fiddled it. The King of Bulgaria was watching. Also, through lack of skill I managed accidentally to hit Papa right in the middle of the forehead with my diabolo top while he was asleep. It was terribly painful and I was terribly sorry. A diabolical year. In Weimar I admired Goethe's house and decided that when I grew up I would also have light-brown furniture with green upholstery. The longer the train ride, the happier I was. At first I thought we were going through Lilliput, all the people looked so small from the carriage window, particularly in Bückeburg. Foreign countries were dream worlds. On the Danish island of Bornholm I saw someone saved from drowning by a brave nobleman. The young woman whom he had saved thanked him with a kiss. There were also patent lavatories with removable bowls and ruby-red velvet seats that I have never ever seen again. In Zandvoort in Holland the North Sea cured my disgusting boils (Papa's syphilis?), and I had a rosy foretaste of my Dutch future. I was thrilled by the canals in Amsterdam, Rembrandt's Night Watch, Gerard Dou's candles, and fell in love with the clouds in the Dutch sky.

A much later vacation in the gloriously rainy May of 1960, over fifty years after my schooldays, took me back to Berlin, which in the meantime had risen (even more than I) to become the undisputedly ugliest ruin in the world. As on my honeymoon, I stayed in the Hotel am Zoo on the Kurfürstendamm, generally referred to as the Ku'-damm. *Kuh* means 'cow', and it was a standard Berlin joke at the time that while the princes (*Fürsten*) had been slung out, the Nazi cows had been left in. For my first breakfast (counterpart to the Last Supper) I was treated to a complimentary 'freshly squeezed, ice-cool orange juice in a silver goblet' ('Oranges from Israel, *of course*, Mr Blumenfeld'), 'genuine ground coffee' (I had forgotten the existence of ersatz coffee) with fresh cream, poppy-seed croissants and various types of rolls, Westphalian ham and assorted cheeses.

In a gentle drizzle I set off to walk from Berlin WW (the new West) *à rebours* to Berlin SW (southwest, where I was born). Just around the corner from the hotel one pillar left standing bore silent witness to the departed splendour of the ugly Fasanenstrasse synagogue. Surviving Berlin Jews had affixed a memorial tablet to it, in Hebrew with the German below, 'Thou shalt love thy neighbour as thyself' (Leviticus 19, 18). As I was photographing it, a father with two little boys came past and one asked, 'What's that man taking a picture of?' The father came over, read the inscription out loud and announced in self-satisfied tones, 'I like 'em when they know their place.' I was seized by a sentimental hangover as I, the vanquished victor, stumbled my way through the ruins of the shattered idols of my imperial years, above all the Kaiser Wilhelm Memorial Church (bomb-damage suits it!). Café Megalomania – gone. The Tauentzienstrasse, the resplendent setting of my adolescent love-life, had been reduced to a provincial fairground. The KDW, the Kaufhaus des Westens department store, unchanged in style since 1910, had lost all its glamour. (When it opened I went to admire the flying machine in which Blériot had made the first crossing of the Channel the previous year in twenty-seven minutes.) The spot where 56 Ansbacherstrasse used to stand, the house in which Papa died in 1913, is where I used to set off for school. I knew every stone. Where are the stones? The great sea of houses there used to be, wave upon wave of them, is now nothing more than a field of parched grass with a chaos of mounds. Even the sky seemed gnawed at the edges. A sudden panic: the homing-pigeon instinct I am so proud of appeared to have deserted me. The Victory Column, of which I had an unobstructed view from here for the first time in my life, stood, with its freshly gilded goddess of victory on top, 45 degrees farther to the west than I remembered. It was as if the Arc de Triomphe were suddenly to be found on Montmartre. It was only two years later that I learnt that Hitler had transplanted the Victory Column to the Grosser Stern roundabout. The next morning I completed my sentimental pilgrimage to my old school: along the Landwehr Canal, beneath chestnuts in bloom. The Spree barges had been motorized; they were no longer propelled by wild men with long poles. Past the lugubrious harbour square, formerly the haunt of derelicts. At the gigantic yellowish ruin of Anhalt Station the world came to an end. In the open ground beside it, steadfast and firm, untouched by the ravages of time, stood my old school, the Askanisches Gymnasium. The ivy where sparrows chirped had been burnt away, leaving a brick barracks in all its hideous, ochre-yellow glory, gleaming in the sunlight like baby shit. The surrounding area had gone back to nature, except there was none for it to go to. There was not a single building left; even the 'Corrugated-Iron Café', as we used to call the urinal on the corner of Grossbeerenstrasse and Halleschestrasse, was no more. On the wrong corner there was a new advertising column staring out forlornly over a moonscape with dandelions.

The Askanisches Gymnasium stood alone, frighteningly severe, boring, authoritarian, like the soul of its director. I had just plucked up the courage to photograph the buildings when the face of a young lady seemed to look down invitingly at me from the window of the lower-third classroom on the second floor. Forgetting all inhibitions and my advancing years, I raced up the granite stairs to investigate the unprecedented fact of a female in my classroom. In reply to my timid knock a surly, schoolmasterish voice shouted 'Come in!' Thirty twenty-year-old Berlin girls, transformed into American cowgirls in their blue jeans and turtlenecks, grinned at me vacantly. The classroom glowered, unchanged; only the plaster bust of the Kaiser had gone and the gas lamps had been changed to electric. The same teacher's desk dominated the room from the same dais beneath the same slate blackboard on which the young teacher was writing, 'German artificial silks conquer the world through their outstanding quality'. The quality of my reception, however, was anything but outstanding. 'Wellwhatd'youwant?' he bellowed at me. I tried the human-interest touch. 'I used to sit at one of these desks in the lower third here fifty years ago.' Derisive laughter from the assembled maenads. The teacher raised his arms in a contemptuous gesture. 'As you may have noticed, my dear world-war victim, this is not a boys' high school, but is, as it has been for many years, the 'Commercial College for Female Apprentices in the Textile Trade of the Mehringplatz District.' (My old Belleallianceplatz!) When I tried to protest, he asked Fräulein Schulz to fetch the janitor to throw out the intruder. He illustrated his intention with a symbolic kick. Did I lack the presence of mind to leave of my own accord, or was I secretly determined to see another of my childhood nightmares come true? Whichever was the case, a little man in a red stationmaster's cap came and showed me the door.

20 JADIS ET DAGUERRE

When I was ten and had once again not done my Latin prep (Caesar crossing the Rhine with fiendish vocabulary) I pretended, so as to skip school, to have awful belly pains. There was nothing wrong with me, but without further ado The Nice Doctor diagnosed a potentially fatal, and very fashionable, appendicitis. An authority on the appendix, Professor Roetter, was promptly called in and less than three hours later my *appendix vermiformis* had been removed. It was rumoured that the operation had cost three hundred marks. It taught me the value of a diagnosis, and I resolved to stay healthy for the rest of my life, something which, for fear of doctors, I have managed to do. When I came round from the anaesthetic in St Hedwig's Infirmary Sister Bonaventura, a medieval nun dressed in black and white, bent down and kissed me on the forehead. In all the excitement they had packed one of my sister's lacy nightdresses in my overnight case. When the nun leant over me lovingly and put her hand under my nightgown to see if I really was a girl, a black-and-white lesbian thrill ran through me. This passion was soon replaced and repressed, sublimely sublimated by a folding camera, to re-emerge later on as an element in my photo-eroticism. That camera – nine by twelve with ultra-rapid anastigmatic lens, ground-glass screen, red rubber bulb, metal plate-holders and a tripod – was a present from Uncle Carl, a skilled amateur photographer, as a reward for my heroic suffering without complaint. Since time immemorial I had been fascinated by photographic paraphernalia. The nine-by-twelve format got into my blood to such an extent that it was as if I was wedded to it. Thirty years later in the USA I had to start thinking in four-by-five and I suffered more from that change than from the summer heat in New York.

My real life started with the discovery of chemical magic, the play of light and shade, the two-edged problem of negative and positive. I had a good photographer's eye right from the start. In order to test out the little device straight away, to see if it really was capable of capturing everything that was placed in front of the lens, I composed the most elaborate still life imaginable: Michelangelo's Moses with a half-peeled potato – into which I had stuck a toothbrush – in his lap. Moses was standing on our open de luxe edition of Doré's Bible. Above it was brother Heinz, resting his head on an upturned chamber pot, wearing Mama's pince-nez and Papa's moustache-trainer, and clutching Mama's rolled-up corset in his fist. It was only a short step from that experiment to advertising pictures for which, forty years later, American companies paid me $2500 per photo.

I developed that first picture straight away in my parents' bathroom by red candlelight. My hands were shaking as I rocked the glass plate up and down in a soup bowl filled to overflowing with pyrogallol. Their new white lavatory seat ever after bore a brown stain, and I was punished accordingly, but the negative was perfection itself. I made a print by sunlight on Celloidine paper with a Goldtone fixer. I was a photographer.

In those days taking snaps was not yet a profession, more a hobby in fancy dress like cycling, mountaineering, playing tennis or driving cars. A professional photographer with his shabby velvet jacket, greasy Lavallière cravat and dirty intentions was a pitiful nebbichthyosaurus, like Hjalmar Ekdal in Ibsen's *Wild Duck*. He would spend ages clumsily pushing small blinds around with a rod to regulate the light, then twist your head back and forwards with his clammy hands, finally immobilizing it in a painful head-clamp so that when he disappeared behind his black cloth and asked you to smile ('Say cheese'), the most you could do was wink. Result: blurred pictures. The incredible miracle of the New World was that one day I was to earn my living there in this miserable profession.

21 MY BEST FRIEND

Nothing so becomes a man
As trust and friendship true.
No finer soul than one who can
Keep faith his whole life through.
(Simon Dach)

Until my first day at school the moon was my only companion, she was the one I loved, without being moonstruck, even though it was fashionable at the time. If I stopped, she would stop too, like a well-trained dog, until I set off again. I flirted with other heavenly bodies, and even knew a few of the beauties by name: Arcturus Boötis, Betelgeuse, Orion, Sirius, Cassiopeia, Vega Lyrae, Altair Aquilae and the Pleiades. On my first day at school, however, after six years of privation I luxuriated in the delusion that I had finally found a fitting partner for eternal friendship. Nothing could ever tear us apart, neither Erwin Seidenschnur with his long, blond locks falling down over his shoulders, nor even Walter Lebrun, speaking fluent French with his elegant *maman* (they were Huguenots). Ravel Roelofsz was Dutch. His name alone attracted an enormous amount of interest. He was the only Ravel in the school, being named after a rich French cousin Raoul. Not a day passed without long discussions as to why the 'oe' in Roelofsz had to be pronounced as 'oo'. Thus right from the start Ravel was marked out as an expert in Dutch pronunciation and Dutch art: Fon Ache! (Van Eyck.) Ravel, born in Berlin like the rest of us, was the sole Dutch boy among the 579 Ascanians. He couldn't speak Dutch. Foreigners were rare, which made people overlook the fact that he was Jewish. Arrogantly modest (a Dutch virtue), he basked in the admiration of his unique status.

The Roelofszs had arrogated to themselves the privilege of making the final judgment as to what was genuine, what was honest, what was art and what was kitsch. At home I had only been exposed to relatively mild levels of family affectation. Now, with the Roelofsz family, I sailed full-speed ahead and all flags flying straight into the ambush of unprecedented pretentiousness. I was like the fabled horseman who dropped dead from his steed when he was told that during the night he had ridden across the frozen surface of Lake Constance; even today I shudder to think how unsuspectingly I was swept into that maelstrom of sham, into that school of humbuggery with its borrowed ideals and stolen ideas.

Ravel was a little hypocrite, a moral coward with a loyal smile, as honest as a German history book. He knew how to fake brilliance, to be original *à tout prix*, to impress, and I fell for it. I idolized him. An artist's quiff fluttered in the breeze over his strikingly pale pug face. Something had gone wrong at his circumcision, apparently, and he had traded his foreskin for a pale, greenish Matthias-Grünewald complexion. His eyes were pale grey. They all, especially his parents and he himself, thought he was the ultimate handsome genius, and they let everyone know it, me in particular. Although I was not at all bad looking, I was allotted the flattering role of the ugly friend, at first in his family, and then among our wider circle of acquaintances. My function was to be repulsively ugly and at the same time immensely witty with a touch of malice, all at their command. My bitten fingernails were shown around for all to see. They even teased me for not having a hunchback. When puberty arrived and my cute little nose started to grow into a big nose, attracting corny jokes I could have done without, I had to play the parts of Cyrano de Bergerac, Red Itzig, Dwarf Nose and Abner the Jew. This role of the Hunchback of Notre Dame would have been unbearable if my mirror, mirror on the wall had not assured me that the family were simply exaggerating my ugliness to enhance their own beauty. Playing the clown in a farce performed in a flea-pit: life. A marvellous part, made to measure for me, the great actor. Oddly enough, such manipulation of the facts can have a lasting effect: fifty years later descendants of the Roelofszs, who had it from their parents, were still telling me how notoriously ugly I had been as a child. Photos prove the opposite.

To seal our blood-brotherhood, we mixed our blood by candlelight, a deed that was to have a decisive bearing on the later chapters of my life. (You wet the back of your hand, hit it as hard as possible with Mama's stiffest hair-brush, swing your arms round furiously and mix the blood that comes trickling out with maraschino from Papa's liqueur cabinet.) Using this 'blood' Ravel illuminated a document with multiple seals. Our motto: 'Through thick and thin.' I swore a perjurious oath (I assumed that was the holiest of oaths) to keep it secret. Since this took place on the anniversary of Caesar's assassination, we took to greeting each other by raising our right arms, at which one would shout 'Iduuus!' whereupon the other had to shout back, 'Martiae!' Oh, the benefits of a classical education! 'Beware the Ides of March.'

In the Roelofsz household there was an insatiable demand for witticisms, even more for jokes that they could retell: wit that could be shown round to visitors. The younger members of the family – there were two older and two younger ones to show round – were expected to deliver ready-made bon mots almost as soon as they could talk and any childish prattling was twisted into a profound statement. Witty in the cradle, perfidious in life. To my amazement I found here an appreciative audience for any nonsense that came out of my mouth. 'Thank goodness, young fellow, you have no idea how witty you are.' I felt equally flattered and humiliated when I heard my own bullshit, still freshly steaming, served up, botched and garbled, diluted and misunderstood, as a genuine original product of the Roelofsz family. They had forgotten I was the author. A nasty world of bogus values. They could never persuade me to repeat my own stories, it would have been an insult to my artistic pride. I was amazed to discover that, for people who were not too particular, any nonsense could be made to sound like the most profound sense. I was particular, and was criticized for quibbling. I found myself coming out with pearls of wisdom without realizing it and became the family improviser, one word giving parthenogenetic birth to the next. Without ever having had a lesson in philosophy – I was only ten! – I was capable, as the celebrated epissedemologist, Professor Fuctum Pregnatus, of holding forth for a whole hour on the subject of 'the world is deep, but negative'. The whole family listened in amused astonishment, convinced I had no inkling of how obscene the name I had chosen sounded (children are born pornographers). Amid a storm of applause, I concluded, 'Death is the most beautiful way to die!' Panting with the effort, Ravel wrote down every word. I had already had cause to admire him as the inventor of creative moaning. That was when, with coloured chalks and much moaning, he had conjured up a Christmas tree on the classroom blackboard and, with exaggerated modesty, accepted the plaudits of teachers and pupils (even from other classes!) as part-co-inventor of the Christmas tree.

Thus I became comedian and court jester, by appointment to the Roelofsz family, who admitted me to their roast-beef circle, while at the same time trying to make out that I was a plebeian whom they could not possibly put before people of refinement. In addition I was expected to be grateful for having been demoted to the position of trust of family clown.

Ravel's father, Roelof Roelofsz, was a fur dealer with the highly respected firm of Roelofsz & Roelofsz. As well as the most exquisite quality furs, he also dealt in religious devotions and imitation furs. He was part-co-inventor of a fake-fur trimming, 'Kolinsky polecat' (half bunny rabbit, half Kandinsky), which was sold by the mile to the women's garment industry. One of the consequences of this was that the whole family lived in part from decking out other people – and themselves – in fake plumes. Almost everything about them was fake except their pretensions. Ravel's furrier father had to provide daily proof to his adored wife (who despised him), his marvellously gifted children, his competitors and the world in general that, although he was a Dutchman and an Israelite into the bargain, he was equal to everyone in everything in Berlin. The Dutch Jews attributed the fact that they had not been persecuted for centuries to their superiority over all other Jews, who were were neither patriotic-honest-modest-adaptable, nor did they know how to behave in respectable company. Dutch Jews on the other hand were accepted throughout the world as model citizens. *Leve de koningin!* Long live the Queen!

Once a year this fur hunter, dressed up in check cap and pipe as a globe-trotting John Bull, travelled via Amsterdam *first class* to London. From there he always brought home the latest operetta hits (*The Mikado*), which he hummed slightly off-key, and the same anecdote, namely how his friend, Captain Bigsby, had galloped on his steed up the house stairs into the dining room. Whenever he told this story, he would purse his lips, and all the members of the family who were listening did the same, as if they were all about to say 'prune'. I just loved watching them. It is a family trait which has survived to this day.

Ravel's mother 'Meeli' (his father was 'Peeli'), Ellinor, Eleanora, Nora, saw herself as one in a long line of eternally misunderstood, great little women: Nora from *A Doll's House* plus Theodor Fontane's Effi Briest, the fictional idol of end-of-the-bourgeois-century Berlin, and Rebekka West minus Hedda Gabler, equals Irene Triesch, a Jewish actress and the Eleanora Duse of Jewish family life. The daughter of a bankrupt property speculator, her line was social self-importance. Uneducated, arrogant and well-read in romantic fiction alone, she would go into sentimental raptures about the spirit of art, by which she meant that all artists should go into raptures about her. She would wait impatiently for trembling piano-teachers to kiss her hand reverently, and then give them an indignant slap for their presumption. She took it for granted that every creature, be it man, woman, child or dog, should be filled with hopelessly unrequited devotion for her, in her black velvet gown and long white kid gloves (with which Ravel used to masturbate) the ideal woman *par excellence*, the dream of all artists from Sacher-Masoch to the specialist in idealized nudes, Jean-Jacques Henner. When I was eleven she caught me checking out the books in her bedside cabinet: Casanova, Maupassant's *Yvette* (in German, she couldn't speak French), *Justine* by the Marquis de Sade, *The Kreutzer Sonata* by Tolstoy, *Sappho* by Daudet, *Mrs Warren's Profession* by Shaw, *A Story of Cadet Life* by Wildenbruch and sentimental novels by a bevy of lady novelists. Half pouting, half scolding, her voice trembling with excitement, she ordered me into the bedroom where I had committed this shocking indiscretion. To atone for it, I had to kiss her silk-stockinged foot. For this scene she was in her underwear: tight-fitting black directoire knickers (Mozart panties, *haute nouveauté* – pronounced 'hoat noovoatay'). Mrs Potiphar cunningly combined flattery with insult: as she was kissing me on the forehead as a sign of forgiveness (during which, duly admiring herself in the mirror, she whispered the opening lines of Goethe's *Torquato Tasso*, 'You eye me with a smile, Eleonore, then eye yourself and smile once more. What is it? Surely you can tell a friend...') she slapped me, symbolically of course, with one of her kid gloves, at the same time wrinkling her nose. 'I was very hurt, Erwin. The question is, can you ever make up for it? The whole matter must remain between ourselves of course. You're not a child any more, with that little Moses Mendelssohn head of yours. From now on you really ought to call me Madame.' I was too ignorant of pornography to appreciate the charm of the situation, deaf to its erotic undertones. I just thought it was silly and grinned.

No virginal mother ever wore her halo with more shamelessly sanctimonious sham saintliness. With a sickly sweet, submissive smile and eyes lowered in exemplary fashion (that's where the children got it from), she would accept her mawkishly devoted husband's blessing as 'Princess Sabbath' every Friday (*shabbes*) evening before the roast beef with provocative modesty. And all the time she kept an eye on me to see if I could manage to keep a serious expression on my face. I bit my lip. The Roelofszs outdid us in piety. At home we did not eat ham on Yom Kippur because we would feel guilty about it. The Roelofszs went so far as not to eat it on Saturday. Also, they called the synagogue the 'temple' which sounded holier. At Christmas they had a resplendent Chanukkamas tree. In contrast to women of the people, who just got pregnant, Ravel's mother became 'with child'.

On the most recent occasion her husband had given her a plain double string of pearls (from the court jeweller's, of course) and I asked at table whether they were genuine. For reply I received a barrage of indignant looks. Afterwards Ravel explained to me, 'Everything we have is genuine. Mama would immediately come out in a rash if she wore imitation anything. My mother's a lady!'

One morning when we were fourteen Ravel came to school trembling with excitement. During the first break he summoned me to the 'Corrugated-Iron Café' to confide a state secret to me, a matter of life and death. The previous day, he told me, his Mama had gone skating on the New Lake and the ice had broken and she had almost drowned (impossible in that puddle). A policeman had rescued her and brought her home in a cab. The family doctor had ordered her to stay in bed. Since Peeli was away on business, Meeli had asked Ravel to spend the night with her in her bed. When I asked him what it was like, Ravel said it stank. Ten years later he claimed not to remember a thing. As usual, he said, it was all pure fabrication on my part.

Naturally Ravel also had a favourite aunt, Làlà, who preened herself on the fact that she was his mother's elder twin sister. Instead of flesh and blood, these two parallel phenomena were made of silk and satin, black, with pearl chokers round their slightly wrinkled necks. Both wore the same Persian lamb coat, the same kid gloves and thought they were irresistible; both were unbearable. To her intimate friends Aunt Làlà was known simply as Làlà. Uncle Fritz, who was famous for one, regularly repeated joke, often called her Olàlà. No one dared to laugh. The divorced (innocent party, of course) widow of a bankrupt banker, she had no children of her own and vented the whole unbridled force of her maternal instincts on the children of her hated sister. She even included me. She lived close to the Askanisches Gymnasium and would pick us up after school to regale us with apple cake, lemonade and serious conversation in her cramped apartment, where we were all on top of each other. There we could complain about our parents to our hearts' content and be sure of an understanding reception. There, too, we often met an imposing young male friend with frock coat, top hat and splendid moustache. We were sure Herr Dr Bortz enjoyed her favours. Ravel's mother was also well-disposed towards him, he belonged to the Roelofszs' roast-beef circle. This dandy took a fancy to me, which I was rather pleased about. On our way home after the *shabbes* performance at the Roelofszs' he told me about life. He refused to believe that my sharp eye had missed the tragi-comedies in the House of Roelofsz, the rivalry between the sisters, the father's limited intelligence, the idolization of the children. I had noticed none of it. He opened my eyes and I was filled with grateful admiration.

Bortz died at the age of thirty-six, during the first months of the war, carried off in three days by pneumonia. I wrote Làlà the first letter of condolence of my life, four whole pages that brought me praise, appreciation and a terrifying kiss of thanks on the forehead. I began to fancy myself in the role of widow's comforter, even flirted with the idea of becoming Bortz's successor, but only with the idea. I was not the least bit interested in Làlà herself, in fact I was afraid of her. After the good doctor's death we once saw Ravel's father and Làlà arm in arm in the street. When they noticed us there was a quick, embarrassed unlinking of arms. Ravel and I considered the possibility that his father felt he had to perform certain Biblical duties.

Ravel's precociousness confirmed Karl Kraus's aphorism, 'Wide-awake at ten, too tired to think at twenty'. By the age of twelve he was already making his first cute little experiments in perversion. At dusk he would sneak into the Tiergarten park and chase after filthy old beggarwomen (he called them 'hags') to slap them across the breasts with his Mama's kid gloves. He could not explain to me what sense that made, but just gave himself mystical airs. Around that time his mother rang up mine to complain that I had talked to her little Ravel about reproduction. Such obscenities had to stop once and for all, she declared, otherwise she would be compelled to forbid her son any further association with me. She would, she said, take care of delicate questions such as the sexual instruction of her eldest herself.

After finishing school Ravel fulfilled the dreams of his fame-obsessed parents and became a painter. He dabbled in every style, brilliant but without talent. The purpose of pictures was to look pretty, garner praise and prizes. *L'art pour l'admiration* – a mutual admiration society. His creative groans and the soulful eyes of his female sitters grew in proportion to the social standing of the client and his own fee. He clung like a limpet to big names and worshipped anything that enabled him to bask in the shadow of the great. A big name for his own band of nonentities, he laid down the law about art in lectures to his disciples: 'Impressionism — external impressions; Expressionism – internal expression.' (Wasn't it Herwarth Walden who coined that in *Der Sturm*?)

Unfortunately for a painter who worshipped success, Ravel was as colour-blind as he was lacking in ideas. He created nothing original, everything was borrowed, stolen: subtle recreations of someone else's style. Searching in vain for a personal style, he dealt in imitation. Twenty years after Chagall he had cows cavorting through the air; twenty-five years after Van Gogh his cabbage fields billowed in the breeze; thirty years after Modigliani he pulled long faces. 'Art only begins where imitation ends' (Oscar Wilde). When even Müller's little manual on landscape had run out of motifs, Ravel took up abstraction. After every Ism had denied him thrice, he tried sensationalism and painted an open lavatory bowl, complete with contents, for an Amsterdam art exhibition. Thus he could be regarded as part-co-inventor of pop art, just as, when he was fifty, he modestly described himself in one of the little booklets he published at his own expense as part-co-inventor of photomontage.

It was characteristic of his craving for prestige that he should turn the blemish of his pale skin and colourless eyes into the marks of a superior race. It could just as well be German as Jewish as Dutch (three chosen peoples). Similar atavistic tendencies and false analogies drove him to nature mysticism. With a saccharine smile he began to see himself as Christ – flowing garb and flowing beard. Nowadays people wear their pubic hair on their face just in order to be on everyone's lips. When the provocative obscenity of an all-embracing full beard proved beyond Ravel, he gave up the pursuit of hairiness in a huff, shaved himself, after a fashion, and as an open-neck-shirted Bauhaus student plunged into a hocus-bogus religion from the Orient: *Mazdaznaan*. A con-man and sex offender by the name of Zaraduscht Hanisch was the high priest of these blond master-racers. Breathing exercizes in a hair shirt, sanctified by drops of menstrual blood from a Basle virgin, Lotti W., and cloven garlic fumes produced ecstatic visions in the morning dew. Next, like the blindman's-buffoon he was, Ravel threw himself fanatically into the arms of the latest fashion, the Blackshirts. He flattered himself that he looked like Benito and even managed to learn one verse of the *Giovinezza*, a remarkable achievement given his absolute lack of talent for languages. He was even in favour of Adolf Schicklgruber until the latter started to get at him personally. My best friend, together with our vow of eternal friendship, sank into the morass of the Netherlands. A few years ago, groaning all the time, he did a final sketch of me as a repulsively degenerate old Jew, just the way he would have liked to see me as a child.

Papa, Mama, my sister Annie and I on the beach at Ahlbeck, 1900

My portrait of Papa on his fiftieth
birthday, 1910

Mama, 1905

Erwin, Annie and Heinz, 1904

First self-portrait as Pierrot, 1911

At the Gymnasium, 1913

Lena, 1922

With Lena (left) and friends in Paul Citroen's room, Berlin, *c.* 1916

Paul Citroen in the dog kennel

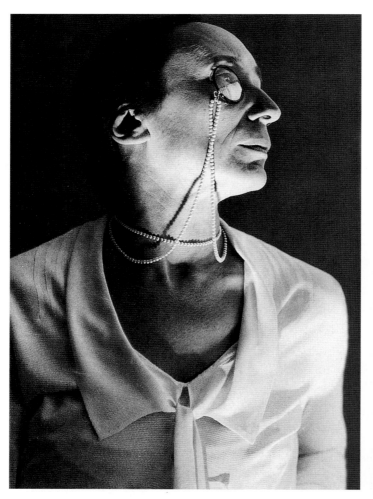

Clem, our *postillon d'amour*

Driving school at Zwickau in Saxony, 1916

France 1917

With my company near Laon, early 1917

The newly weds, 1921

My first son. Zandvoort, 1925

Drawing of man/woman, *c*. 1921

Invitation to a masked ball, 1921

Dadamontage, Amsterdam 1920

Collage postcard to Tristan Tzara, 1921

PART TWO

22 L'Education sentimentale

Prior to my birth I had, as ordained by German Romanticism, dreamt of heavenly love. I started life as a sexless sexual maniac. With all my love I loved only Love, loved all women, not just one. As soon as things started getting personal they started to go wrong. Out of fear of actual females, I took refuge in the Eternal Feminine. SHE, my platonic idea of woman, was a slim fairy-tale princess with almond eyes dark with yearning, long, free-flowing hair, delicate fingers, rosebud bosom – and chaste unto the grave. In moments of profoundest understanding, past any possibility of misunderstandings, we communicated without words, we knew a truth beyond saying. We suffered beauty and died fleshless spirits, à la art nouveau. I believed that love was necessarily coupled with beauty and exclusively reserved for young, noble beings who were good from sheer beauty. *Kaloikagathoi.* That old lechers (over thirty!) might fall under the spell of love was perverse.

As a photographer, I reluctantly made the discovery that sparkling pale-blue eyes are usually myopic. A classically proportioned bosom does not necessarily produce the best milk. It was only when I eventually read Ovid's *Echo and Narcissus* that I came to understand the tragic interrelation between beauty and love: the youth of perfect beauty who is incapable of giving, and his counterpart, the nymph Echo, is only capable of reciprocating: two emotional cripples.

1.   Before I ventured out into the world, I practised in the nursery on our nanny, Aunt Trude, our beloved Tittymouse, who was no longer that young (twenty-eight). If you like your nanny, it is perfectly all right to fondle and cuddle her, which I enjoyed doing. Her father was a talcum-powder manufacturer, and she smelt of it. She had tiny pock-marks, which I tried to kiss away. In return she taught me the butterfly kiss and how to glue together cardboard cut-out models. When Mama's youngest brother, Uncle Bruno, came back from America, where

he had been on a 'study trip' (he brought with him a photo that we children were not allowed to see, showing him standing between two bare-breasted hula-hula beauties), he sat down in a corner of the room and kept staring at my Tittymouse until she married him. I was nine years old and against the marriage. I have never forgiven him for making my beloved Aunt Trude desperately unhappy. He never forgave me either and during the First World War he denounced me for attempted desertion and tried to get me court-martialled.

2.   I secretly longed not only for naked women, but for an artist's *atelier* (it was not until much later that I thrilled to the word 'studio'). It was when I was nine that, clutching the seductive hand of my nanny, I first visited an *atelier* (of the painter Leo Prochownik), where naked flesh hastily disappeared behind a screen. Outlines suggested Trude Borgzinna, a cousin of my nanny who was rumoured to be an artist's model, to 'sit' in the nude. Whenever I met her afterwards we both blushed. She could hardly have guessed that I had no problem dressing and undressing her with my eyes, nor that I knew she was a naughty girl, since I had seen her crumpled underwear shamelessly sprawled out over the studio couch. Over it she wore a summer dress of sprigged muslin that was even more transparent. Especially when seen against the light. Thus was born my delight in seeing through anything transparent.

3.   In the summer of 1908, when Wabash defaulted on the New York stock exchange, we were spending a long summer holiday in Gremsmühlen in Schleswig-Holstein, and it was my task to go to the station every morning to collect the newspaper so that Papa and Grandpapa could work out how much they had lost. That was how I came to meet Trude Rosenbaum from Essen, who was doing the same for her father. We felt a mutual attraction. She had her blond hair done up in a sky-blue satin ribbon and was astonishingly mature for her nine years. I could have talked to her about anything, only I lacked the courage. We exchanged experiences. She had dancing lessons, perhaps even a lover. My programme for the holidays dictated that I should fall in love with her. I rowed her across the lake in a frail bark. With one daring blow of my oar I drove off a poisonous water-snake (an eel?) that was threatening to bite her. Out of gratitude she sang the latest hit, 'You're my sweetie, you're the apple of my eye',

every single verse. Her eyes were moist with tears. Ought I to be overcome with emotion and cry too? No! Incapable of looking each other in the eye, we both looked away. We trembled, closed our eyes and almost fell into the water. The next day she left. In farewell she silently shook my hand. It was too much. From then on I rowed alone, thinking of her. When we got back from the holiday, I had a hundred visiting cards printed, just for her. My idea was to write 'p.f.c.' (*pour faire connaissance*) on one and 'p.p.c.' (*pour prendre congé*) on the other, and to have both handed in at her door in Essen by a liveried footman. When, two years later, I did go to Essen, I never managed to find a footman, liveried or unliveried, and I never saw Trude again. Sometimes when a fat *émigrée* waddles past me on Columbus Circle in the evening the thought flashes through my mind, 'Could that be Trude Rosenbaum?'

4.   There was so much written and said about love that I set my platonic heart on falling in love. I found Paula Levy's mother bewitching: chic, elegant, rich, Russian. Since, however, I didn't dare fall in love with a married woman of thirty-two, I went head-over-heels for her daughter who, though not beautiful, had a certain something. Unfortunately Paula was already being courted by my friend Walter Seliger, so that was that.

> *Love is like an omnibus,*
> *You wait ages for a ride,*
> *And when one comes along at last,*
> *It's 'Full right up inside!'*

5.   My next love I shared with my best friend Ravel. A love shared seemed to be a love doubled. The object of our affections was Hilde, a genteel young lady who was as beautiful as she was rich. We had once bowled hoops together with her in the Tiergarten park (she had worn a straw bonnet), and we decided to fall in love with her. From then on we spent hours every day walking up and down the Lützow Embankment beneath her window, hoping to catch a glimpse of her silhouette. We were soon well acquainted with the silhouettes of all the family and loved them: Hilde, her charming little sister Ilse, and even her brother Fritz, in spite of the fact that he went to a rival high school. We saw ourselves as a pair

of Dantes. Every week I sent her two anonymous letters consisting of quotations from a play by Kleist: on Mondays, 'In death yet will my swan sing: Penthesilea', and on Thursdays, 'Was this the feast of roses that you promised?' After months of preparation we went over to the attack. One of us had to speak to Hilde on the way to school. I drew the short straw.

Jointly we concocted a question, which I desperately memorized. Blushing, I stood in her path. 'Do you think or do you imagine we are in love with you?' She answered, 'No.' Struck dumb by such quick-wittedness, I withdrew and never exchanged another word with our great love.

6.   Ravel's sister Carola, two years older than us and blonde with cornflower-blue eyes, was pretty as a picture, and I loved her as one can only love at fourteen, or at seventy-five. She was a genius, as was de rigueur in the family, and wrote anaemic Pre-Raphaelite poetry. She died, just before sunrise, of a heart-breakingly botched operation on a brain tumour. She was so innocent and so young that there were whispers of 'the sins of the fathers', meaning her father. As she lay paralysed on her deathbed, I played my star role of court jester, trying to elicit a contorted smile from her lips. To love a dying girl seemed the height of bliss. Ravel and I listened in the next room while the doctor performing the autopsy sawed her head off ('The sound of the flute is moonlight to the ear' – Jean Paul). We had planned to recite from *Tasso* but couldn't. What are the sorrows of young Herr Werther compared with the sufferings of a fourteen-year-old schoolboy?

7.   My first funeral: *Spring Awakening*. Over Carola's freshly dug grave her best friend embraced me in great sorrow, sticking her little tongue into my mouth. I assumed this was a Jewish mourning ritual and responded in kind. This venerable custom soothed my pain – oh, that I had a thousand tongues! In order to find out more about such religious rites, and at the same time to desentimentalize myself, I starting going to all sorts of funerals of people I didn't know, without, however, ever coming across that archaic practice again.

8.   The place where we used to meet the girls from Charlotte High School was the Mengel cake-shop on Magdeburger Platz where we went almost every day

to feast on chocolate eclairs, cream puffs, chocolate marshmallows, cream meringues, fruit drops and liquorice.

> *Oh, darling, where's your cream meringue?*
> *What is tea without a cream meringue?*
> *Life seems like a pointless trick*
> *Without my cream meringue to lick.*

It was there that I met Lottchen; she was twelve, I was fifteen. She was an old maid who, without ever having read Dostoyevsky, could simulate hysterical-epileptic fits in the course of which she would would fall down flat on the floor of the crowded cake-shop. I was planning an essay on 'The inner life of ugly people' and fell for her rectangular construction. She, however, loved my best friend Ravel alone. To console me she wrote 'Let us be brother and sister' in my autograph album. When I met her again in New York last year she had become a monumental inverted Pythagorean letter (Y). Hardly had we said hello than she threw her 235 pounds flat on the carpet in front of my whole family. Beware the sweethearts of your youth!

9.   We spent the last summer holidays before the collapse of the family in Johannisbad in Bohemia. In the course of a confetti battle there I got carried away and stuffed a handful of confetti deep inside the low neckline of the tight-fitting black satin dress of the provocative Gertrud Samosch, discovering in the process that she did not have a corset, like Mama, but a warm bosom with saucy little points. Instead of the expected slap, I got the first uninhibited kiss of my life, of which I was reminded every time I saw pictures of the famous dancer, Valeska Gert. I told this story in 1937, sitting outside the Café du Dôme in Paris, to one of the former greats of Café Megalomania, Pavel Barchan, after he had leapt up with true old-fashioned Berlin gallantry to kiss the hand of the somewhat ravaged virago, Valeska Gert. The solution to the riddle: Valeska Gert was Gertrud Samosch. In 1943, during the war, I photographed her in New York where, gone to rack and ruin, she was dancing her old hits in a gay bar called The Beggar's Cellar on the Bowery. When I saw her once again in 1965 as an old medium in Fellini's *Giulietta degli spiriti* I almost had a heart attack.

10.   I fell for Lilly's thick braids. After an endless conversation on a bench in the Tiergarten park, I thought I would try my luck. As she raised her arms to embrace me I saw, through the hole in her sleeveless blouse, the hairs in her armpit stuck together with sweat. Quite natural, but too much for me. Repelled, and angry with nature for allowing it, I left Lilly there, went home and dashed off these lines in the manner of Heine:

> *Drunk with joy, I would declare*
> *All the love I felt for her.*
> *But alas, before I had*
> *Spoken words both sweet and sad,*
> *I stopped short – her breath was bad!*

I thought that in poetry rhyme mattered more than truth. Forgive me, all you Lillys.

23   KITTY-CAT

Basking beneath the gas lamps, lit by a ragged lamplighter with a long pole, were the harlots, done up in the classic whore's costume, as if modelled on figurines by Félicien Rops. On every street corner death lurked in depraved disguise. Berlin was teeming with these provocatively tottery pros in black silk fishnet stockings (only whores wore them), high-heeled, tightly laced patent leather boots (out of a masochist's dream), and even more tightly laced corsets. The prostitutes of 1910 appealed to the mother-complexes of our fathers by arousing memories of the ladies of 1870, just as the wasp waists of 1947 reminded me of the prostitutes of 1910. I succumbed to the charm of the perverse, seeing myself as a reincarnation of Baudelaire, of whom I only knew the name. These creatures were incapable of walking, they minced. They were so constricted they could barely stand. They balanced their tightly padded cotton-wool bosoms by sticking out their fleshy bottoms behind them, with their elbows jutting out at either side. The badge of their profession was a huge, greasy, black patent-leather handbag (a defensive weapon) dangling down beside their umbrella. Faces powdered white, eyes lined in black above cheeks daubed in blazing red, they did not speak like human beings, but chirped in sibilants, like love-witches from some classical

Walpurgisnacht. They would nudge men, clicking their tongues and making strange gestures. Lust! They feared nothing except the vice squad, their 'Louis' (pimp), and the French disease (syphilis). They usually walked the streets in twos and arranged themselves in picturesque groups on street corners, under the surveillance of their Louis, the vice squad and the syph. Street prostitution seemed to me like unearthly, heavenly love. Frank Wedekind confessed,

I'd rather be an honest whore
Than a man with fame and wealth galore.

At the age of twelve I developed a passionate longing to make the conquest of such a lady just once with declarations of love and to be loved by her in return. At fifteen, after heroic struggles, I plucked up three marks (saved from my pocket money) and the courage to whisper to a well-built blonde on the corner of Schillstrasse, whom I had been observing for a long time (you have to know your women), 'Fräulein, I love you.' I blushed violently; the strength drained out of me and all I could do was stare at her. She responded with impassive disdain, 'Cut the crap. Yer got five marks?' I had only three! Unfeeling, businesslike, she demanded, 'Come on dearie, show us the colour of yer dough, moola, money, an' make it snappy.' I took the three-mark coin out of my pocket, but kept hold of it. She softened a bit. 'Wotcher want me to do? A hand job? Let yer come on me tits? 'Ow abaht a balloon-ride? Yer'll feel like you were flyin'.' Without paying attention to her menu, I answered passionately, 'I love you, Fräulein!' She said, 'Bollocks. Who gives a damn about that?' took me by the arm and led me straight to 22 Nettelbeckstrasse. An unexpected blow: it was the house where the Lewins lived, revolting card-partners of my parents, with whose revolting children we were expected to be friends. If they caught me on the stairs here with this girlfriend there would be nothing for it but to kill myself on the spot (*A Story of Cadet Life*). How terrible that love and respectable citizens should live under the same roof. There was no going back. My career as a roué had already sunk too deep in the morass of depravity. At fifteen I was no longer a child, I was a man, a man of the world. Kitty-cat despised me because I still looked like a schoolboy, and I wanted to show her that at fifteen a boy is a man. I had to seduce her with craft and cunning – by force if necessary. Afterwards I would help her back onto the straight and narrow. 'For I am accustomed to saving people's lives' (Bismarck). Nothing was further from my mind than immorality; I wanted to uplift her (it's just the same today). She would embrace me with gratitude.

She thought Erwin was a nice name. Was it dangerous for her to know my name? She took ages unlocking the front door, an eternity. Warily I climbed the dark stairs behind her up into the underworld. One indiscretion could cost me my life. The Lewins! Like a child at its mother's skirt, I clung to her coat. Once we were safely past the Lewins' third-floor apartment floor I felt I had to break the silence and asked her what she read. 'Put a sock in it', she said. 'I'll read yer fortune in yer arsehole if yer like.' Clumsily she opened the door of the fourth-floor apartment. The air was foul! She tapped mysterious signals on various doors, thrust me into a lightless attic and went out again without a word, leaving me alone in the darkness of a strange room. Not nice! Where was the little god of love with his sweet little wings? Was sex so sad? She spent ages talking to some men in the next room, as if I wasn't there. Her dialect was incomprehensible. She came back smoking and lit an oil lamp, much more naturally than in all the Naturalist dramas of Gerhart Hauptmann, Max Halbe and Arno Holz, or in Gorky's *Lower Depths*. The word 'surrealism' had not yet been coined. Unfamiliar, enchanting desolation: the world of prostitution. There was a birdcage, without a bird. It seemed she didn't like birds. On the buckled brass bedstead was a tumbled mattress with straw welling out of its slashed, distended belly. An overturned water jug lay behind a brimming witches' cauldron from which pungent miasmas rose. 'We do it in the bucket', she explained, and she did it, entirely without shame and alarmingly naturally, as I had never seen it done before. When she demanded her three marks I was determined not to be done. 'Would you please be so good as to undress first?' 'Why?' she snapped. 'Because I would very much like to examine the inside of a female *pudendum*.' In order to enhance the erotic experience, I had brought my five-power magnifying glass with me. I also wanted to gain deeper insight into animal salts. 'I know it all fairly well from Meyer's Encyclopaedia, only I can't quite get a clear idea of the clitoris. The difference between the upper and lower labia is equally unclear to me. I probably know more about the sequence of pregnancy than you do, since I always get an A in biology.' I then asked her how her uterus was doing. Her jaw dropped in astonishment. She must have been impressed by my knowledge. "And over them free marks now or I'll call me boyfriend an' 'e'll straighten out yer partin' wiv a meat-cleaver.' I handed over three weeks' pocket money, disappointed because I had hoped she would give herself to me for love. On the spot I decided to buy myself some roller-skates and to skate to school from now on, thus saving the fare for the tram, the ninety-six. 'Joy thou source of light immortal' costs money, especially with a daughter from Elysium.

'Nah wot?' she yawned, as if I were boring. I insisted she get undressed, with my help. Then, after profound discussions, we would be able to love one another, despite the differences in social status. 'You must tell me in as much detail as possible how you lost your virginity and why you became a prostitute. In return I will recite Goethe's ballad *The God and the Bayadère* for you; you can read the lines of the bayadère, if you like. I'm a great actor, only you mustn't say anything about it.' And I launched straight into it: 'For the sixth time Mahadevah / Came to earth in human form.' 'Don't be stupid', she said, 'Gimme anuvver two marks an' I'll get undressed an' you can 'ave a peek at my twat. There's a nice boy.' When I admitted that I hadn't another copper on me, she quickly unbuttoned her coat, twitched her shoulders so it fell to the floor and stood there before me, without a blouse and trussed up in a flesh-coloured corset and a greasy black sateen petticoat. Could she be pregnant? O horrors of nature and art! I was flabbergasted. 'Tulle on top and nuffink underneath', she said as, to my horror, she cautiously, as if it were hurting, removed balls of cotton wool which she had stuffed, apparently for protection, between bosom and corset. Were her breasts swollen? They looked so immense. It was all too much for me. Red blotches shone out in the darkness, red for danger! Everywhere I could see red spots dancing before my eyes. I was scared stiff. Syphilis! Was I already infected? Terrified, I tried to run away, but she refused to allow me premature evacuation, locked the door, slipped the key into her patent-leather handbag and turned into a tiger, stretching her limbs wearily on the bed, sticking her tongue out invitingly, licking her lips and starting, in all her loathesomeness, to look dangerously beautiful. Too late! Three times I said no, my right hand clasping my left in a sacred vow. I was a man, and said, politely but firmly, 'Please let me go. You only want to seduce me for fun.' 'None o' yer lip, sonny.' 'Once again, please let me go.' When she did not react, I went to the window as if I were going to shout for help. I knew very well it was impossible: the Lewins' house! The school! My good name! Was I a sex offender? 'You take yer cloze orf, I'll take mine orf', she said. I remained silent, but was already faltering when I heard an impatient, 'If-yer-don't-want-ter, yer-don't-'ave-ter'. She got up and started to dress in front of the mirror as if she were alone in the room. She brushed her filthy, straw-like hair, splashed powder underneath her armpits, over her face, everywhere, smeared rouge on her cheeks and was a marketable commodity once more, as she had been when I saw her on the street corner. A half-dressed woman is so much more attractive than a dressed one, than an undressed one! She went back into the adjoining room, leaving me alone for ages again. I heard laughter. At me? After that we crept down the stairs, past the Lewins'. Kitty opened the front door and gave me a contemptuous shove. 'Scram, titch.' And off I ran, a guilty innocent little child, back into the world, home, without even having dared to touch the lady. The whole affair had lasted less than half an hour.

Thus ended the most magnificent adventure of my childhood. In actual fact, it never ended. All too often I would cruise round Kitty's harlot beat, hoping to see her again and become her friend. She, however, who meant so much to me, did not recognize me. She hissed the same to me as she did to every male passer-by, 'Hey! Sonny! Wanna nice time?'

24 THE ARTS

What was it that drove me, an upper-*juste-milieu*-class boy, to that *rive gauche* from which all roads climb towards Montparnasse? It cannot have been the influence of my nurse's breasts alone which led to the development of this addiction to golden sections. ('Our first perception of the distance between nipples determines our sense of proportion for life.') I had a sophisticated predilection for artful tricks, an enjoyment of recounting anecdotes, an urge to shape things, further stimulated by the Jew-God's commandment not to make any graven image or any likeness of any thing etc. And then there was the anxiety about whether I would ever develop a personal taste of my own. I imagined good taste to be a constant, a standard platinum bar in an underground vault in Paris, watched over by a secretive clique of intellectual snobs. The only means of penetrating this exclusive world was a letter of recommendation from a wealthy female patron. I fell in love with Paris when I was a child, sight unseen, as is ever my way, and when I finally got there at the age of forty I realized that taste is merely foretaste. Taste comes from tasting. Americans have none; as babies they are fattened up on tasteless 'formulas', which turn them into babies without taste. Taste cannot be learnt from books, not even from cookbooks. From the very beginning I had favourite dishes and I have remained true to them: cold beer soup, liver sausage, smoked breast of goose, smoked salmon, cranberries, goose crackling, pumpernickel, Worcester sauce, *Berliner Weisse mit Schuss* (light beer with a shot of raspberry juice), stewed cherries, potato fritters with apple sauce, Dutch rumpsteak with fried potatoes, toasted almonds, mocha. I have always detested rice, Roquefort, noodles, meat balls, calf's liver, meat loaf, lentil soup, Gorgonzola, buttermilk, peanuts and tea. My taste not only has aberrations, but whims as well: today I like spinach, tomorrow I can't stand it, and it's not just the fault of the spinach.

I have always believed that the creative urge is dependent on latitude and longitude, that temperatures beget temperaments, that no genius was ever born south of the equator, that watercolours freeze at the North Pole and that the Sahara produces very few ice-skaters. I knew that art had to earn its keep. Early on I felt there were cultural connections between the Cheops and Mayan pyramids; I looked for and found similarities everywhere. I was talented, but not in any specific direction. I wavered between fireman, philosopher, dustman, doctor, rabbi and actor. I knew, although I was not a hundred per cent sure about it, that I was not a genius, and I agreed with Papa that genius was reserved for men. Men invent, fight, earn, worry; women, on the other hand, give birth, cook, keep house and do needlework without knowing what they do – like Mama, for example. Learning to speak, sing, rhyme, think is child's play; you gather impressions and imitate before you venture to produce something original. Style comes later – or never.

25 MUSIC

In the beginning there was no word without sound, no song without words. Piano practice: the tinkle of scales pursuing you everywhere in the apartment. Nurses' fairy tales lurked like enchanted toads in the bottomless well of primal feeling. Note. Melody. Word. From the depths – folk song – profundity.

In the courtyards Julie the Harp croaked pathetically, quivering with cold, itinerant boys' choirs dressed in black capes sang heart-rendingly off-key chorales, and wooden-legged war-veterans came hobbling along with hurdy-gurdies on which little monkeys dressed as Turks waltzed to the Blue Danube until you threw a pfennig crumpled up in a bit of newspaper down to them. Day and night the servants bawled out sentimental songs of love and sex:

All my desire,
All my bliss:
Two dark eyes
And a bum to kiss.

(It really went, 'And a burning kiss'; I was close to becoming a bum-fetishist.) From those enviable street urchins who were beyond good and evil and could do as they liked, I learnt forbidden ditties:

My old girl loves jellied eels,
And if she don't get none, she squeals.

When my old woman goes to bed
It's like a rag-and-bone man's shed:
Glass eye, a wig and false teeth
On the table, and underneath
A second-hand wooden leg.

She's got a flea, she's got a flea,
She's got a fleecy coat.
She's just a bitch, she's just a bitch,
She's just a bit cheerier today.

You're mad as a hatter, but that don't matter,
Your dad's a fruitcake too.
Off you both go to Loony Hall,
That's just the place for you.

My dearest Mrs Titmouse,
Where is the nearest shithouse?
My guts are in such a state
I can't even stand up straight.

Anyone seen Izzy Green?
Anyone know where 'e's been?
The back of 'is shirt
Is all covered in dirt.
And 'e stinks like an army latrine.

First on the left, second on the right
You'll see the bog come into sight.

We were not allowed to sing songs like that, though when we did, every-one laughed.

Every morning the Cockchafers (the First Guards Infantry Regiment) on their way to the parade ground goose-stepped past our windows to the sound of a last-trump *tuba mirum*. We Prussians had not lost a war for a hundred years, and we let the whole world know it. I admired the hussars, the uhlans, the dragoons, but above all the Pasewalk Cuirassiers with the gilded eagles on their silver helmets, riding behind their bearded drum major on his prancing dapple grey. I became a militarist with a cardboard helmet on my ride-a-cock-hobby-horse.

In contrast to the maids, who let strange men smooch with them on benches on the Kreuzberg, the nannies used to meet their gentlemen secretly in the cool seclusion of churches. Whilst they whispered *pianissimo* the organists would practise *fortissimo* the same pieces over and over again, which later in life I found strangely familiar, like the primal memories of a prior existence. The C-major scale, with uncomplicated one-dimensionality in four-four time, was my favourite tune. To this day I doubt the right of D major to exist, not to mention minor-key perversions. Even in music I remain a voyeur. My favourite instrument was, of course, the kettledrum, though even in those days I had no sense of rhythm. My parents too were models of tone-deafness. Mama played the piano with two fingers and still hit the wrong notes; Papa would bellow out 'Toréador, prends gaaaarde' on the lavatory.

Every other Sunday, when the servants had their afternoon off, our parents, because they could not leave us at home alone, would take us to the Philharmonic Sunday afternoon subscription concerts. People sat at tables, drinking bock beer to Bach, Beethoven and Brahms. The musicians were dressed as waiters. I would stand below the conductor's podium, admiring the uninhibited way the timpanist thrashed about with his drum-sticks. Why are there no toccatas for solo kettledrum? My second favourite instrument was the zither. When I went to meet my sister Annie after school (the Burtin School, one of the most ladylike schools for young ladies; the special senior class would sit on the assembly-hall dais with dazed expressions on their faces) we would pass the windows of Lechleitner's, Purveyors of Toys to His Majesty the Kaiser, where His Majesty was always buying rocking horses for his sons (Friedrich Wilhelm, August Wilhelm, Eitelfritz, Waldemar, Sigismund, Oskar). There I fell in love at first sight with an Appenzell zither, I could already see myself in *Lederhosen* dancing the 'Schuhplattler' to my own music. As Christmas approached I went on and on in a feverish babble about zithers until Mama finally capitulated. And now I have an awful confession to make: one hour before the presents were to be handed out on Christmas Eve, I peeked through the keyhole and saw the zither lying beneath the Christmas Tree. Trembling, I sidled up to Mama and heard myself saying that I would much rather have a steam engine with a horizontal boiler, water-level indicator, safety valve and steam whistle. Goods could not be exchanged in those days, so Santa Claus's assistant, Knecht Ruprecht (bearing a remarkable likeness to my cousin Ada), brought me the magnificent instrument, not without a prior threat that he would carry me off in his sack for biting my nails, which I resisted with a vigorous outburst of bawling. It took me only a few minutes to turn the highly strung instrument into a permanent wreck. I never did learn to play the zither.

Piano lessons were arranged in order to further my personal musical education. Our piano teacher, Herr Ziehlesch, charged fifty pfennigs less than the average (he did it for two marks), had a split nose and sour breath. With his yellow pencil he would beat out time mercilessly on my frozen fingers, without improving my touch at all. After three years of unsuccessful torture, he was relieved by Fräulein Liebmann, who had a velvety black moustache, not the faintest feeling for music and acrid breath. Her lessons consisted of systematic drill, the sole purpose of which was to enable my sister and me to move my parents to tears with four-handed pieces on all appropriate birthdays. It had to be something classical, too difficult and with show-off trills. And I still had to stand up to reach the pedals! Fräulein Liebmann loved Wagner. When I protested against that anti-semitic hooligan, she loftily informed me that, 'Poets are higher beings, warts and all'. (She had a wart on the side of her own nose.) For Papa's birthday we had to play the overture to *Tannhäuser,* for Mama's that to *Lohengrin.* As a reward, I was allowed to choose what I wanted to play for my own birthday. 'Nothing at all', I said. When she insisted, I opted for Mozart. 'Oh, Mozart – so dainty', she said dismissively. 'You're too grown-up now for such barococo bagatelles. As punishment you will play through Clementi's five-finger exercizes.' Then she tried to worm her way back into my affections with an arpeggio glissando. Before the next lesson I hid the music inside the piano. Fräulein Liebmann's arrival set off a desperate search, on top of the cupboards, underneath the carpets, behind the bookshelves, everywhere, until finally I opened up the piano and took out the music, a look of astonishment on my face. Fräulein Liebmann had been watching me through her steel-rimmed spectacles and remarked, without turning a hair of her moustache, 'That trick is as old as piano lessons. The pupil always finds the music in the piano after a quarter of an hour.'

In spite of all that, she did not succeed in destroying my love for music. It even grew with my first opera, Lortzing's *Zar und Zimmermann* at the Lortzing Theatre. Beside every seat there was a little electric lamp you could switch on and off (so you could read the programme in the dark), much more interesting than the music. At my second opera, *Fra Diavolo,* they had the same little lamps, thank God. By the time I went to see Baron von Flotow's *Marthamartha, where art thou?* the lamps were no longer a novelty, and I found opera boring and silly. Why did they have such ugly singers singing things that would be better left unsaid? Why did they all keep jabbering on at the same time and repeating things that no one could understand anyway? My first lampless opera, *Carmen* with la Destinn, was a disappointment. How could a bullfighter fall in love with such a fat cow? Lola Artot de Padilla as Cherubino was slimmer, and I fell in love with Mozart. I went straight home and composed my first (and only) opera,

Semiramis, in six acts. (Why always five?) I got as far as the fourth bar of the overture (strongly influenced by *Fra Diavolo*), plus the first verse of the Pharaoh's opening aria:

> *Bring on my dancing girls!*
> *Banished be sadness and sorrow.*
> *Let us carouse all night*
> *Nor give any thought to the morrow.*

At home I never heard any good music. I had to wait thirty years before I could quench my thirst for melody at the swollen breasts of radio and gramophone. At the beginning of the sixteenth century Papa Montaigne decreed that little *Que-sais-je?* should be woken daily by a bedchamber orchestra. At seven-thirty every morning my radio softly wakes me with baroque music, played *pianissimo* as never was heard before, and at any second of the day or night Mozart can be milked from the New York airwaves.

26   THEATRE

> *Bloody hell,*
> *Top of the bill,*
> *Some old tom*
> *With greasepaint on.*

Easy-going nursemaids first misguided my footsteps to the bock beer festival in Hasenheide Park where I laughed, cried and clapped at stuff I didn't understand performed by itinerant actors in makeshift booths. My parents took me to the circus as a reward for being good. There were two circuses, Busch's and Schuhmann's. There I could understand everything, especially the clowns, apart from what was said. The most exciting part was when the ring was flooded and crocodiles danced. Unfortunately I was only allowed to go to the children's performances where no one was eaten alive and no acrobats fell and broke their necks. But first and foremost Berlin was a city of the theatre. I fell completely under the spell of the stage, of which all the world is one, in the summer of 1905 after Max Reinhardt's *Midsummer Night's Dream* had whirled me into Shakespeare's enchanted woods where Gertrud Eysoldt with her watery-blue eyes as Puck and electric fireflies drifted through dreamy nights. I was determined to go on the revolving stage. I wanted to create my own little midsummer-night's dreamlets, to write plays in which I, in costumes of my own design and under my own direction, would act all the parts and then, as a sarcastic critic, pitilessly tear my own production to pieces. A rich life!

Classical plays I first saw at 'Afternoon Matinees at Reduced Prices for Secondary School Pupils'. The productions were models of mediocrity and the acting third-rate. Real theatre with famous actors was in the evenings, too late, too expensive – and I was too young. I had a good ploy for getting into first nights that were sold out: in my barmitzvah suit, with my school briefcase stuffed under my arm and my hair unkempt, I so convinced myself that I was an important critic that I could dash past the attendants without ever being stopped. I would spend the evening in the standing room (so-called 'standing seats'), compose a devastating review in the style of Alfred Kerr or Paul Schlenther at home in bed and pounce on the newspaper first thing in the morning to see whether I was right.

I was crazy about Reinhardt's leading man, Alexander Moissi, who stole everyone's heart with his lopsided curly head and his frantic, singsong delivery. I imitated him better than he did himself, stressed the lines even more wrongly, screwed up my youthful brow in theatrical furrows and painted black rings under my eyes with Leichner's greasepaints. Soon I could imitate other actors as well, even Kainz, Matkovsky and Sommerstorff, whom I had never seen. I went to great pains to learn monologues by heart and then pretended I had memorized Hamlet after just having leafed through the text. Woe to visitors if they did not force me, against my will, to give a demonstration of my acting talents. I courted applause while pretending to despise it. Nobody (not even I myself) understood, could possibly understand, what was going on in the depths of my artistic soul. To be misunderstood was one of the necessities of my youth, my life, my times.

27 THE MIRROR

My introduction to the fine arts took place at home. Among the innumerable keys in Mama's key-basket was an ornate brass one which kept us locked out of her mothballed drawing room. This holy of holies was only opened on very special occasions, and before the dust-covers could be removed from the silk-upholstered furniture, the room was given a thorough spring-cleaning, including a sauerkraut massage for the carpet. With that key I secretly locked myself into those sacred halls, my first museum. There, on almond-green wallpaper embossed to look like genuine moiré silk, hung a huge oil painting (which Papa, in his artistic wisdom, designated a 'daub'): *The Shepherd Boy* by Professor Franz von Lenbach, in an original copy made in the Pinakothek in Munich by Mama's best schoolfriend, Elise Mentzel from Stettin. (It was from her father that Grandpapa Henry had bought the wine-merchant's at an advantageous price.) A shepherd boy was lying down in the sun beneath a much-too-blue sky on much-too-green grass, large as life and tired of it. German pastoral Romanticism, circa 1900. Without ever having read Krafft-Ebing's collected fairy tales, I knew that this pan-German strength-through-joy-boy was a professional masturbator who had so overdone it with the rusty pocket knife lying on the ground beside him that he could flick his cock open and shut like a hot dog. A heavy gold frame only served to heighten the obscenity of it. To the right, a greyish-green copper engraving of Böcklin's unavoidable *Isle of the Dead* produced the intended deep impression. Between a twelve-colour print of Guido Reni's *Aurora* and a partly dressed sepia beauty by Henner (she it was, with her magnificent locks falling down over her breasts, who brushed me up into a hair fetishist), the grandfather clock solemnly struck the wrong hour with its double-cathedral-bell-chime. (The clockmaker, Gieritz, came every week to set it right; as soon as he had left I undid his good work.)

On the opposite wall, in gold frames and painted from photographs by the same Elise Mentzel, hung the anaemic portraits of my father's parents beside a copy, likewise by Elise Mentzel, of Achenbach's snow-covered Watzmann mirrored in an alpine lake. In front of a coyly disrobing Phryne and the brazenly grinning Hille Bobbe by Frans Hals were art-nouveau pedestals with bronze fittings on which stood a clutter of little statuettes: Michelangelo's *Moses* with verdigris (second prize at skittles), the drunken faun, *Antinous* (imitation marble), the *Spinario* (pink alabaster), a Mercury (plaster imitation of bronze), Meunier's *Sower* (from the employees on some anniversary of the founding of the business). Pasiphae and Iphigenia in Tauris/Aulis (engravings) aroused mythological questions to which the only answers were incomprehensible erections. On the coffee table lay Nietzsche's *Zarathustra*, unread.

The real, true marvel, however, was the huge mirror that dominated the wall. It hung between the two drawing-room windows, framed by elaborately gathered olive-green velvet curtains. Mother had taught me that the eye was the mirror of the soul, so I observed mine, eyeball to eyeball, sitting for hours in front of the drawing-room mirror on the genuine colourfast Saxon Turkish rug, pulling faces in order to mature, to look old, to discover my soul. Although by now I ought to have learnt the contrary, even today I remain convinced there is life in another world going on behind the transparent glass. We are doubles. Without a mirror I would never have become a human being. Only fools call it a Narcissus complex. No mirror – no art, no echo – no music.

When, at the age of eleven, I tried my hand at the joys of the flesh for the first time (after having given myself my most solemn promise I would carry out this metabolistical experiment only once, and that out of purely scientific interest), I knelt autovoyeuristically in front of the mirror in order to observe that important moment at which dark purple rings would appear under my eyes, unequivocally marking me out as a roué. Instead, my eyes closed and the meaning of the word *Liebestod* was revealed to me. Afterwards I was astonished to find the same old face in the world on the other side of the mirror. I had been afraid that everyone would be able to see my 'crime against the seeds of life' written all over my face. I had got these terrifying theories about the dangers of self-abuse from *The Greater Meyer's Encyclopaedia*, which lurked behind lock and key in Papa's bookcase, full of the apples of knowledge of good and, more interestingly, evil. Hidden under my bed, or by candlelight on the lavatory, I greedily extracted forbidden knowledge from the *Greater Meyer's*. Everything was written in such mystically garbled language that I took it as a pornographic religion: *credo quia absurdum*. Because it was nonsense, I believed that onanism, invented in the desert single-handedly by Onan the Jew, quickly led to septic *tabes dorsalis*, the dreaded galloping consumption of the spine, from which the totally debilitated boy would be released, after long and painful sufferings, by the mercy of a premature death. I took Meyer at its word. Whenever I was unhappy with my parents, life or myself, I willingly took my fate in my own hands and tried to put an end to my young life, using the technique outlined in the encyclopaedia. I never tired of putting this method to the test, without ever achieving the desired result. I merely fell into a deep sleep.

What drove me to the arts? Sex drove me. I drew my first visual stimulation from Papa's satirical magazines. My autoerotic programme was determined by the weekly appearance of the charms of the same *demi-mondaines* in lace panties. At the same time I was being prepared for my career in the women's garment trade:

> *You'll have to undo my bodice, dear,*
> *I can't reach the top button, I fear.*

Franz von Reznicek in *Simplicissimus* taught me how to undress a coy blonde expertly on the edge of the bed; from Ernst Heilemann in the *Lustige Blätter* I learnt how a well-stacked beauty cuckolds her old man over champagne with a cavalry lieutenant in the private room of a restaurant; in *Jugend* the perverted Beardsley imitator, Franz, Ritter von Bayros, gave me private coaching in the seduction of minors by cruelly corseted Messalinas in their ostrich-feather regalia, aided by obscene terriers. In those days every German boy went through the same school of onanism with these same love-goddesses, though with varying results.

Art and nature are one and the same. Starting with the dioramas (Passage and Kastans), where I stared in wonderment at the Siamese twins, Dr Agha, the floating maiden, midgets, Machnow the Giant, the entry to New York harbour, dusty waxwork figures in chambers of horrors, foetuses prematurely drowned in alcohol and other abnormalities, I progressed through the living-and-moving art of the theatre to the fossilized art of museums. Before that, in the Kaiser Panorama, I lived through all phases of the crucifixion of His Majesty the Saviour, done in three dimensions and multicoloured lighting, on Golgotha, that is the place of skulls. On another place of skulls nearby, that is the Commanders' Hill, Moltke, Bismarck and Roon enthusiastically hailed their wise Kaiser Wilhelm I and family, while in the foreground a grenadier just managed to raise himself from the ground and salute before bleeding to death.

My first real museum was the Postal Museum, where all the stamps in the world were exhibited in glass cases. Unfortunately I was too small and couldn't see anything. On Sundays, however, there was a special show in which X-rays revealed smuggled pocket watches in sealed parcels. Then the curtains were drawn. For a long time we stood there in the dark, until something fluttered far too quickly across a wet sheet, eliciting a general AAAAAHHH! Papa lifted me up so I could see better, but it was only later on, after they had explained it to me in detail, that I tearfully realized what I had seen: gulls in flight, my first movie. Just why it was shown in the Postal Museum I have never been able to understand. Nobody suspected they were witnessing the birth of a new art form.

Twice a year I had to accompany Papa to the *Great Berlin Art Exhibition*, with its stench of oil, where German anecdotal painting flaunted its tawdry wares. Cloying boudoir scenes alternated with imposing battle pictures, the harsh tumult of war with serene still lifes with fruit. I liked the genre paintings of Professor Eduard Grützner, the Master of the Lecherous Monk: a buxom dairymaid is serving a steaming roast goose to the obese prior, who is pinching her plump behind with a self-satisifed grin on his face. Underneath it, engraved on a gilt plate, 'A juicy morsel'.

From the *great* art galleries I expected undisturbed satisfaction of my sexual interests. My passion for museums took on such proportions that my parents were obliged to engage 'young Herr Drippe', the son of Papa's tailor. In return for a modest sum, this impecunious student with no feeling for art at all had to plod round a museum with me every Sunday. First we did the 'small' museums: the Museum of Ethnology with marvels of Peruvian featherwork and mummies, the Natural History Museum with giant fossilized trees, the Museum of Applied Art with tedious sets of china, the Imperial Stables with all coaches from all periods, the Armoury with all medals on all uniforms, the Hohenzollern Museum with stuffed monarchs, the Brandeburg Museum for Local History, the Urania Science Museum, where, for the fifty pfennigs entrance fee, you could experiment with valuable instruments until you broke them when nobody was looking. The most bore-ing was the Museum of the Mining and Metal Industry. With that my patience was exhausted; I insisted on the *great* museums.

Ignoring the marble fragments of the Old Museum, I plunged into the National Gallery where Mackart's gigantic orgies vainly tried to seduce me in the very entrance hall. I was looking for the intimacies of a more spiritual beauty. In the background of the smaller side-galleries shimmered French Impressionists, quivering, like warm air that could only be understood when viewed through the spectacles of a temperament: *Re Noir* = the Black Ray! I was thrilled to seek and find Daubigny's 'Red Spot', which I had found lacking in *Co Rot*. But it was the old masters in the Kaiser Friedrich Museum who provided the fulfilment of all my dreams. Completely unembarrassed, they displayed the naked beauty, rendered even more naked by their transparent veils, which my embarrassed parents had tried to keep from me: in innocent obscenity, Botticelli's Venus with her golden hair and Cranach's Lucretia with her dagger opened up to me the Mount of Venus of their eroticism. Though still a boy, with manly resolve I professed the fetishes of my life: eyes, hair, breasts, mouth. Following my theme, I mirrored myself in Cranach the Younger's *Fountain of Youth*, where on the left hideous old crones clamber into a square basin from which they emerge on the right as graceful young maidens, gallantly awaited by youths outside open crimson tents. A mixture of painting and literature: *avant et après*. Never have I marvelled at a young goddess without picturing to myself how time transforms these bewitching sirens into old witches. There is a medieval carving in the Louvre which I have often contemplated: *The Corpse of a Noblewoman, Partly Eaten by Worms* (Burgundian, thirteenth century). The piece of literature on this theme that has made the most profound impression on me is Villon's 'Les regrets de la belle Heaulmière'. My contribution to this chapter of the *Tragédie humaine* is a nude photograph of the eighty-year-old Carmen who, fifty years previously, had posed for Rodin's *The Kiss*. I was astonished to recognize the horrors of my own nights in the paintings of 'Hell' Brueghel: dance of death, witches' sabbath, inferno, murder; and from my very first glance I became a lifelong admirer of Hieronymus Bosch. I told myself stories which I read in Rembrandt's visionary look, and felt I was a poet.

28   POETRY AND PROSE

Eenie, meenie, mackeracka,
Hi, di, dominacka,
Stickeracka, roomeracka,
Om, pom, push.

Wordplayful counting-out rhymes appealed to me from an early age. Without rhyme meant without reason for me and blank verse left me blank. I adored poems that you could recite without understanding them. It was not until I was forty that I discovered François Villon, the poet of my life. But I never did manage to find out why France has no poetry of the grotesque, no Morgenstern, no Ringelnatz, not even a *Struwwelpeter* or a *Max und Moritz*. England does at least have that rhymed smut, those divine limericks.

By the time I reached puberty I had also reached – by way of fairy tales and sagas, Fenimore Cooper and the *Count of Monte Cristo* – the novel. I had been bitten by the reading bug. Minimum quota: one book per day. I devoured much, understood little, enjoyed everything. I did not even presume to imagine I could understand anything. Art sat enthroned on the Olympus of classical arrogance, too high to be understood by a mere third former. I did not dare skip a single word for fear that that might be the very word that contained the solution to the riddle of the universe. What the riddle of the universe was I could not even discover in Professor Ernst Haeckel's *Riddle of the Universe*. In the book department of the newly opened KDW store Edgar Allan Poe's *The Black Cat* (with illustrations by Alfred Kubin) leapt out at me from Franz Blei's anthology of horror stories and sent me rushing into the world of the necromantic short story. I raced home to write one myself: an eminent physician discovers the genius serum and injects it into the brain of his newborn son, who immediately turns into an incredible genius (prime numbers, Sanskrit, squaring the circle, the *Kamasutra*, the *Vedas*). The father is seized with jealousy. In a fit of madness, he kills the infant genius and jabs the same needle into his own cerebellum whereupon, with an endless cry, he gives up the ghost. I read this story to my friends, 'The Clique', by candlelight, cigarette smoke and cherry brandy, drawing out my cries of horror for so long that the jealous Brethren of the Clique immediately laid down a statute limiting the duration of any cry to no more than than one minute. In revenge I wrote a short story that contained five minutes of silence.

'What do I care about my thirteenth birthday', I wrote in my diary, 'as long as I can celebrate my thousandth!' I despised the books that Berlin devoured, was anti-bestsellers. A sure instinct, what used to be called a guardian angel, placed my intellectual development in the hands of Wedekind, Strindberg, Dostoyevsky.

Without them I would have been a different person, without them the world would have been different.

29 BARMITZVAH

When, at the age of thirteen, a lady librarian at the local public library refused to let me borrow Weininger's *Sex and Character* because, in her opinion, I was not sufficiently mature, I decided to start a library of my own, which would contain the complete works (not the 'collected works' that omitted the most important things) of all the classic authors, including all forbidden books. To get these as presents, I had to bow to the wishes of my parents and submit to the barmitzvah, which clashed with my ideas as a freethinker. *Paris vaut bien une messe.* This Jewish confirmation takes place at thirteen. Since, however, we were in the process of moving with the fashion and out to the west end of Berlin (postcode WW – like the sun, my life has gone from east to west) my barmitzvah was put off for a year. In a black grown-up suit, a black hat on my head, I had to rattle off prayers in Hebrew at top speed before the assembled congregation in the synagogue. When, in that large building, I could not hear my own voice, I got stage fright and broke down. Afterwards my aunts smothered me in kisses, telling me how marvellous I had been.

That evening there was a grown-up dinner, with evening dress and with printed menus *à la Kempe* (the smart restaurant, Kempinski's). Such orgies of ostentatious pretension were the culminating points of my parents' social life. For months beforehand the sole topics of irritated conversation were WHOM they HAD to invite and WHAT they had to serve up so that their dear guests (*chateissim* = pigs) would be suitably impressed. Papa declaimed with finality, 'Lobster, salmon and fresh bear ham.' Extra chairs were hired, extra crockery, coat racks, cooks, extra waiters, dish- and bottlewashers. Plus Herr Perls in white tie and tails, a comic, a singer of street ballads and a virtuoso of the piano. At the dress rehearsal the evening before, everyone who took part went off in a huff.

On the evening itself Herr Perls improvised an amusing pot-pourri of the Hohenfriedberg March, the Chanukkah chant, 'Pauline's off to the dance', and 'The Blue Danube' to accompany the entrance of the guests into the dining room, during which every gentleman escorted his lady with exaggerated stateliness to the place allotted in the seating plan. Once they were all seated, the party mood broke out, the room hummed like a beehive and grew unbearably hot. The feast began. Hors d'œuvres: gull's eggs in Cumberland sauce, Zeeland oysters, crayfish from the River Oder in dill, black caviar in crushed ice, beef marrow on toast, snails with herb butter, goose-liver paté. This was followed by an excellent consommé with matzo balls (hand-rolled with spit by Grandmama Lisette), then 'Rhine salmon' (*coregonus rhenanus* to be precise) with hollandaise sauce, Heligoland lobster with melted butter, and fresh, snow-white asparagus tips followed by the obligatory huge, bloody roast of beef with parsley potatoes from Malta tossed in butter, partridge with Mama's home-bottled cranberries or larded pheasants with morels and ceps in a sour-cream sauce, then the inevitable 'Prince Pückler bombe à la Henry Cohn', tutti frutti with fresh wild strawberries in maraschino with whipped cream, then a cheese board garni, with everything that stank and every kind of bread in the world, accompanied by bowls of fruit tastefully overloaded by Mama and featuring the first *German* bananas (from our colonies).

Every course was served with the appropriate wines, sparkling wines, liqueurs and French cognacs (all from Grandpapa's wine business in Stettin). White wine was served in the traditional rummers, cut-crystal goblets in hideously garish colours which Mama collected: 'In his hand the crystal tall, The shattered luck of Edenhall' – and immediately there were tears and everyone was blaming his neighbour and vice versa. Steaming black coffee came in tiny rococo cups with real gold-plated little coffee spoons in the form of a rose petal. The waiters served in white gloves. Now and again the guests were expected to refuse some dish or a second helping. Urging food on one's guests was a recognized ritual to which they always gave in. There was a little verse Mama could not repeat often enough, 'Better eat till you're fit to bust, rather than leave your host even a crust', but she herself was far too nervous to eat a single bite. There was also, unfortunately, a certain amount of vomiting, usually on the way to the lavatory, in the endless Berlin Corridor.

Once everyone had joined in the singing of the customary hymn to *Gemütlichkeit*, things really began to warm up. Entertainment Commissar Perls excelled himself at providing suitable piano accompaniments for everything. Printed song sheets with endless choruses were handed round and sung, as more and more delights were offered to our guests. Between the courses came momentous speeches. Grandmama Lisette's opening was known to everyone, 'Most esteemed subject of this celebration, ladies and gentlemen, honoured guests.' She never got any farther, the applause took over. Grandpapa Henry, on the other hand, was no speechmaker. When he made his celebrated toast to the ladies, 'Gentlemen – *and* gentlemen: the ladies!' he had to laugh so much – out of embarrassment – that everyone broke out into gales of laughter, until they all started singing, 'Hip-hip hurrah for Grandpapa, the greatest grandpapa by far.' When, however, my father tapped his glass, a tense, deathly hush broke out in the room, you could hear a pin drop, they hardly even dared to breathe. He savoured the mighty impression he was making to the full. Sweat beaded his philosopher's brow. He started to speak, incomprehensibly, in a whisper, but gradually, without anyone daring to shout 'Louder!', getting louder with every word. Aunt Philippina could not restrain a sneeze and Papa bellowed furiously, 'QUIET!' then started his speech all over again. After ten minutes they could hear, but still not understand him, he was too intellectual. He appeared to be giving a speech in the Upper House defending the rights of oppressed peoples. His eyes flashed. From human rights he progressed angrily through culture, religion, literature, ethics, economics or, *that is to say* (his favourite phrase in speeches) *umbrella politics*. After one breathtaking hour he triumphantly misplaced his Schiller quotation, 'Quick as the ravenous shark / tearing the waters apart!' to never-ending cheers and clapping. Hardly had this never-ending ovation died down than Papa rose again, to everyone's horror, tapped his glass and announced in stentorian tones, 'I now call upon my son and heir, barmitzvah boy and fourth former at the Askanisches Gymnasium, Erwin Blumenfeld to say a few words.' Oh dear! Hoping that they would forget me, I had had a little tipple. It was in a rather tipsy state, then, that I had to improvise the traditional barmitzvah speech which had been drummed into me over the last few months. I was forced to climb onto a chair so that they could see me better. I swayed. Two aunts supported me. 'Since time immemorial it has been the custom that every boy, on the occasion of his barmitzvah, expresses his feelings freely and openly. I do not intend to deviate from this fine old custom …' then I got stuck. I did manage to vow, amid a storm of applause, that I would be 'a worthy Blumenfeld to the power of Cohn squared', and rolled under the table, dead to the world. My most resounding success at the last big social gathering of my life.

These superhuman efforts brought in a disappointing harvest. Instead of the 360 books I was definitely counting on, I only received 237, including five copies of Büchmann's dictionary of quotations and three sets of Goethe. Mama donated a surplus kitchen cupboard and I huffily stuffed it full with my treasures: my own library.

30 THE JOYS OF DISCOVERY

I have been trying to resurrect a style from bygone years, but in vain. With the best will in the world I cannot today work out why, when I was fifteen, 'Rosa the beautiful policeman's wife' seemed the height of wit. The author was the neo-Kantian philosopher, Dr S. Friedländer, a fanatical specialist in polarities and excentric vision, who published these 'bonbons from the little spiritual sweetshop' which so delighted me in the Expressionist periodical *Der Sturm* under the pseudonym of Mynona. When I got to know him personally I found it almost beyond belief that he, a grown man of encyclopaedic erudition with published works to his name, should talk to me, a mere schoolboy. He resembled Hans Christian Andersen, played at being a man of the world and a libertine and cultivated an image of being 'original but malicious'; he was, in short, a stimulator. It was from his lips that I first heard the magic words 'psychoanalysis' and 'relativity' and the name of Montaigne. He showed me the emergency exit out of my parents' home through the 'Café Megalomania' (Café des Westens), where the geniuses spent hours playing at nirvana with an empty glass in front of them – whenever, that is, they didn't happen to be engaged in mutual insults. The bohemians acted either like madmen (Maupassant, Van Gogh, Nietzsche) or epileptics (Dostoyevsky, Flaubert). It was in the air. So I went out to seek my intellectual fortune in the café, but I never achieved the highest distinction, to be recognized by Richard, the red-haired, hunchbacked waiter in charge of the newspapers. He didn't even bother to ignore me.

At her little round marble table on the café terrace at the corner of Kurfürstendamm and Joachimsthalerstrasse, Else Lasker-Schüler, 'the black swan of Israel', sat in solitary splendour. She was the weaver of the 'Tibetan Rug':

My soul and yours, which loveth mine,
In the Tibetan rug are intertwined.

I sat down nearby and fixed my gaze on her. For hours. Until finally she, Yussuf, Prince of Thebes, Tino of Bagdad, the Malik, hissed at me in fury, 'Have you nothing better to do than stare at me, you insolent creature?' As always, my presence of mind was absent, and I blushed and stammered, 'No'. She obviously liked my answer. 'What class are you in, anyway?' she asked, with interest. 'In the lower fifth at the Askanisches Gymnasium', I whispered. I had broken the ice.

She invited me over to her table and raved on about her brilliant son, little Paul, who was at the Odenwald School and delighted everyone with his beauty. Before he was even a year old he had climbed out of his cot (she was watching through the keyhole) to scrape the plaster off the wall which contained the calcium he needed to build up his bones. I cleverly managed to get in a Strindberg quotation, 'Children are child prodigies', but she topped it with 'But little Pauls are geniuses'. (All dubious geniuses in my life have been called Paul.) I was beside myself with pride at having conquered, without outside help, through the force of my personality alone, 'the greatest living German poet.' (It was Karl Kraus who had awarded her that title, for which she raised him to the rank of cardinal.) I knew Lasker-Schüler and Lasker-Schüler knew me! *Gradus ad Parnassum*. It was her personality that fascinated me more than her poetry and her prose. Her hair was exciting in its unusual short page-boy cut. Copper half-moons dangled from her ears, round her neck were amber pearls, coloured glass and various items of cheap jewelry. She went round in her old sealskin jacket, beyond money and modes, poor, every inch a *malik*, always slightly bent forward, a tiger ready to pounce. It was only after she died that I learnt – I could hardly believe it – that she, who had treated me as someone of her own age, was as old as my mother. At the same time she demanded from everyone, friends and foes alike, a deferential respect which she regularly rewarded with the vicious outbursts of rage she wreaked upon her vassals totally out of the blue. I lacked the courage to address her as 'Prince' as so many did. Anyway, I thought it sounded ridiculous.

Soon we were old schoolfriends. 'Can you get really passionate about things? Die for an idea?? Throw bombs??? Blow this bourgeois metropolis to bits with a robber band of witty Blue Riders???? Dress rehearsal this evening in the Gnu. I will be reading some new poems and the ancient "Tibetan Rug", but first of all pay for my coffee. What do you think you are doing? Are you trying to insult me? With *my* money, you impudent young puppy! Only an hour ago I strangled an insanely rich philistine billionaire with my very own hands. His dying words, "Does it taste good?" Be there at Reuss & Pollack's book-bar, on the dot at any time between five and eight. Bring your pistols, we artists are sworn conspirators and we're going to have a revolution. Bloody slaughter with piles of corpses. They're terribly terrified of me! Password, "Dar es Salaam". I'm madly dying with eternal love for the greatest negro king's son from German-south-west-north-east-Africa, and for his favourite wife, Zuleika. They are living together in sinfullest sin, in a wigwam in the *Damuka* [acronym for the German Army, Navy and Colonial Exhibition]. He smokes a peace-pipe through heart-shaped lips and she smells like a gazelle – one from the jungle, not from a zoo. They are both wildly jealous of each other, of my love and of Kete Parsenow. Give me your oath to remain silent unto death and come, my Black-and-White Magician!' Secretly hoping that one day I might be allowed to photograph the great poet, I had gone into raptures about my camera, at which she had immediately dubbed me her Black-and-White Magician. Unfortunately I never did get to photograph her.

On the dot of seven I was standing outside the closed bookshop. No one there. An hour later I came back. After I had knocked for a long time a hawk-nosed gentleman appeared, said 'I am Curt Erich Glaser' and admitted me, speechless with admiration, to the dimly lit Aladdin's cave of books. Else Lasker-Schüler was sitting, fakir-like, cross-legged on the floor, shouting that she was not going to put up with any more of Höxter's slander, he had behaved like a pig, Herr Blumenfeld, the Black-and-White Magician, could vouch for it (I knew nothing about it). That was my introduction. I shook hands, bowed à la Moissi in an attempt to express my personality, and felt very grown-up as an up-and-coming artist. They were all squabbling about names that meant nothing to me, insults, flagrant injustices, plagiarism. The Prince screamed that as a matter of principle she had no intention of prostituting herself in the Gnu and dashed off in a rage, without having got round to reading the 'Tibetan Rug'.

One night, it must have been around 1915, I went in mellow mood to the urinal on Potsdamerplatz. A young dandy came in by the opposite entrance, stood beside me, fixed his monocle in his eye and in one fell swoop pissed my profile on the wall so masterfully that I could not but cry out in admiration. We became friends. He was the most brilliant man I ever met in all my life, a great raconteur and an immensely powerful draughtsman. It was George Grosz. Like Mynona, he belonged to the Lasker-Schüler circle; he was her Leatherstocking.

The few times after the First World War that I left Holland to go to Berlin I always stayed in the Hotel Koschel (later the Sachsenhof) on Nollendorfplatz, where Else Lasker-Schüler had a tiny attic room. (On my last visit in 1960 the hotel porter had never even heard of her name.) Once, some time around 1926, late at night and very drunk, Grosz accompanied me back to the hotel. As we were saying goodbye at the entrance the Prince of Thebes happened along and took us up to her garret. Actually our intention was to tease her a bit. Like a weather-beaten Indian witch she sat enthroned on her iron bed, wreathed in incense. Grosz was sitting on her wicker trunk, I was squatting on the floor. She was rambling on about Cabbalism and manifestations. We were unwilling to be taken in by her spiritualist claptrap, but she was stronger than both of us. Her eyes flashed with an eerie light and the laughter died in our throats. 'The bleeding, truncated hands of my mortal enemies will float through this room.' We sat, transfixed, as a few hands, dripping with blood, floated in through the closed skylight, stopped, then disappeared through the closed door. I saw that Grosz's hair was standing on end and asked whose hands they were. Instead of an answer came the hysterical announcement, 'And now the hands of Paul Cassirer will come, and those of his depraved Tilla [Tilla Durieux, Max Reinhardt's Princess Eboli, Judith, Jocasta]. My Black-and-White Magician, you must swear to avenge me!' Before our very eyes a woman's hand drove a dagger through a man's hand, drawing blood, then disappeared. The old sorceress pressed a child's dagger with a chased blade into my hand. 'The Cassirers have debauched my son, my wonderful Paul. They stuffed him full of morphine and cocaine to make him into a homosexual, they infected him with tuberculosis to hurt me, they let my books rot, broke every promise – their lives are forfeit. Next week Cassirer is travelling to America via Holland. In Kalverstraat in Amsterdam you will plunge this stiletto into his heart with the battle-cry of "Tino!" ' I did not know Cassirer, nor did I want to murder anyone, so I tried to use her prophetic tones to get out of this joke in bad taste, declaring, 'Cassirer will be badly received in New York. He will be discouraged and will break off his trip after a week to return to Berlin where Tilla will drive him to suicide. You will be avenged!' Grosz nodded, 'So be it', and we all solemnly shook hands, the two of us relieved to have this ghost sonata behind us. One month later

I received a letter in Amsterdam. 'My Black-and-White Magician, as you prophesied, Paul Cassirer has taken his own life. With thanks, Yussuf, Prince.'

Shortly before Hitler, she descended upon us for a few days in Zandvoort aan de Zee. An unbearable tyrant and trouble-maker. She died in Jerusalem in 1945, at the age of seventy-six.

Shortly before Hitler, George Grosz emigrated to New York, the city of his dreams, became an American and, like so many before him, lost his art. In 1959, before he returned to Berlin, we had one last drink together in a bar, and he complained that all he had to take with him was 65,000 dollars. Back in Berlin, he drank himself to death within a few weeks. The executor of his will, a mutual acquaintance, told me a few years later that the pictures and drawings Grosz had left to his two sons had brought in several million dollars.

31 MY OLYMPIANS

'Who would care to go out to an evening party to meet Tomkins, the friend of one's boyhood, when one can sit at home with Lucien de Rubempré? It is pleasanter to have the entrée to Balzac's society than to receive cards from all the duchesses in Mayfair.' (Oscar Wilde)

Shakespeare Greek Tragedy Marlowe
Molière Wedekind Strindberg
Mozart Monteverdi Purcell Bach Vivaldi Handel
Gluck Haydn Jazz
Bosch Brueghel Grünewald Cranach Holbein
Greco Rembrandt Vermeer Chardin Goya Daumier
Van Gogh Gauguin Cézanne Degas Toulouse-Lautrec
Seurat Douanier Rousseau
Futurists Cubists Dada George Grosz
Early Gothic Tapestries Unknown Masters
Villon Charles d'Orléans Scève Homer Ovid
La Fontaine Baudelaire Rimbaud Verlaine Apollinaire
Gryphius Claudius Heine Wilhelm Busch Morgenstern
Ringelnatz Struwwelpeter

Balzac Stendhal Flaubert Maupassant
Grimm's Fairy Tales Gogol Poe Dostoyevsky Kafka
Casanova Montaigne Diderot Voltaire Swift Sterne
Egon Friedell's Cultural History of the Modern Age
Lao tzu Schopenhauer Nietzsche Freud
Sourire de Reims Archaic Greek Sculpture (from the Cyclades to the sixth
century BC) Egypt Maya Negro Pre-Columbian
New York Paestum Laon Cathedral
George Melies Charlie Chaplin Buster Keaton Marx Brothers
Asta Nielsen

32 THE TURN OF THE CENTURY

Turn of the century: the happy days of my carefree childhood in Berlin. While I was almost dying with fear, my parents would rub it in daily, how idyllic my childhood was compared to others'. They doubted whether I would ever be able to take life seriously. The bourgeoisie prattled on about the inexorable march of progress thanks to the achievements of modern science, invented the concentration camp during the Boer War, but did not notice the world revolution set in motion by Nietzsche, Van Gogh, Rimbaud, Strindberg, Wedekind, Freud, Einstein, Curie, Cézanne. Because of the accelerated tempo of life, people believed they were living in a transitional period of epoch-making significance. Only the city railway remained true to an earlier age:

> *Berlin, you're in such a hurry!*
> *Now leisureliness is a crime;*
> *The least delay makes you worry,*
> *There's no time, no time, no time!*
> *Only the old city railway*
> *Keeps chugging through bustle and din.*
> *The last souvenir of the heyday*
> *Of dear old* gemütlich *Berlin.*

In those days one could still travel round central Europe without the medieval ignominy of a passport (except, that is, for the filthy east European Jews, who were expelled everywhere, and quite right too). The world was (still is) saddled with the Dreyfus affair. Zola's 'J'accuse' appeared on 13 January 1898. I suspected there was something obscene behind all the whispering. Obscenity was all the rage (Huysmans' *À rebours*, Oscar Wilde's *Dorian Gray*). Under the iron fist of our style-conscious 'Emperor of Peace' and his noble empress, Augusta Victoria, Berlin was well out in front in the ugliness stakes. After a transition from full beards to side-whiskers, moustaches disappeared entirely: nudism was just around the corner. People had no idea how soon they would be replaced by the machines they were just inventing. The horse, which for thousands of years had faithfully helped us build a civilization, could smell the *Decline of the West* with its more sensitive nostrils and declared itself out of the running. From the horse-drawn omnibus we slipped for a while onto the rails of the horse tramway, then via the electric tram to the motor-bus; from the hackney carriage we went via the BEVAG (Berliner Electrische Verkehrs-Aktien-Gesellschaft) to the taxicab; from candles and cosy oil-lamps via gaslight with gasmantles to the unaffordable luxury of the electric light-bulb and its sudden blown fuses. 'More light!' Only loos and churches were lit by paltry candles. Typewriters, operated by lady typists, could simulate printing. A new kind of autoeroticism made its appearance:

> *She loves to ride in my automobile,*
> *From Hamburg to Kiel*
> *With me at the wheel,*
> *She says it's ideal.*

The first automobile happenings. Lady to chauffeur taking a long time tinkering with the engine, 'Would you like a screwdriver?' 'I wouldn't mind, Madam, as soon as I've finished this.' No one had the least idea that the motor car, launched on an unsuspecting world as 'the perfect replacement for the horse', would grow up to be the greatest mass-murderer of all time. His Majesty the Emperor drove at the head of his army to a Valkyrie fanfare: 'Beep-*beep-beep*-BEEEP'. German dirigibles, rigid and semi-rigid, exploded spectacularly high in the sky to celebrate their superiority over the Gallic flying machines (*plus Lourdes que l'air*). Germany first in the air as well! From a specially erected grandstand

I watched with Grandpapa Henry as one of the Wright brothers (Orville or Wilbur?), wearing his cap the wrong way round, beat the 'Berliner Zeitung Midday Edition World Record': eleven minutes without landing at a height of over twenty metres. We got our first wrong numbers (Itsmewho'sthat?), courtesy of the telephone operator. We were rung up! Without being accused of oral sex, the telephonanist sang:

> *Hallo, central, tell me what to do!*
> *I keep on trying but I can't get through.*
> *I've got your number and you've got mine,*
> *So let me share your party line;*
> *If you reverse the charges I'll be blue.*
> *Why do you have to put me through such hell?*
> *Just put me through and let me ring your bell!*
> *I'd make a trunk call every day,*
> *Sundays I'd make two.*
> *I need a call, girl, why can't I connect with you?*

Gramophones with impressive horns scratched Signor Caruso's voice to pieces. We children even got chocolate phonograph cylinders which you could play, then eat. There were no loudspeakers or microphones yet. Even the Kaiser had to shout if he wanted to be heard. In those times everyone spoke louder and more emphatically, even silence sounded different. Mankind knew nothing of the waves which, with the help of little magic boxes (radio and television), can be resolved into pleasure, uproar, moving pictures of light and shade. Long before Asta Nielsen, Waldemar Psylander, Olaf Fönss, Lupu Pick, Sven Gade, Bébé Abélard, Henny Porten, Max Linder, Ernst Reiter, Harry Liedtke, Max Landa, Bunny, Prince Rigadin and Billy West (a forgotten predecessor of Charlie Chaplin) there were already minute-long kisses, hisses, misses flickering across the moistened sheets of all those motion-picture theatres, flick-houses, bioscopes, kinematographs that the Berliners called *Kientopp*. My birth coincided with the birth of photojournalism. Until then the events of the day had appeared, sketched with artistic overskill, weeks later in the *Woche*. Suddenly the *Illustrierte* printed an almost instantaneous photo of the Kaiser, blurred, out of focus but alive, eclipsing everything that had been seen before, including *Max und Moritz*.

The mark was still a solid currency, covered by 120 million in gold bars under military guard in the Julius Tower of the fortress at Spandau. Who could ever have dreamt that the mark, with its slogan of 'A mark will always be a mark', would be diluted to a trillion. Even more solid was the British pound. Prophets made fools of themselves, speculators made millions. Shortly after the European nations (larger than life in the colossal picture by Professor von Knackfuss after sketches by the Emperor) under Field Marshal von Waldersee, had defended their 'most sacred possessions' against the Yellow Peril in the Boxer Rebellion, there came the dress rehearsal for 1914: the Russo-Japanese War with Weihaiwei, Sakhalin, Mukden and Port Arthur. But that war was more than 6,000 miles and a whole month's travelling away; when the sun shone Papa sold more parasols and walking sticks, and more umbrellas when it rained, and no one could foresee that in a few years' time parasols, umbrellas, my dear old father and our dear old modern era would have disappeared. Only the umbrella is still with us, though seriously wounded by its rival the raincoat, the umbrella that I came to hate when, as a little child in the grip of Papa's powerful hand, I had to spend ages standing by umbrella-filled shop windows whilst he, snorting with rage, cursed the unfair competition of his rivals. Even the subconscious, though still in its infancy, began to stir, and pressed, too long repressed, for analysis. Nothing new under the sun. Juvenal (AD 90), *Satire VI*, '*Qualicumque voles Judaei somnia vendunt*' – 'Jews will sell you any dream you want.' The first slogans were let loose on an unsuspecting public: 'Take a bath at home'. A grotesque demand; even the Kaisers up in the palace only had one bathtub, though that of marble, of course.

Cook with gas! (Piss with bliss!) Odol is good for you!
Tired eyes? Try our brandy.
Keep a couple of bottles handy;
There's no need for an optician:
You'll see it all in double vision!
Try a little eastern magic:
Megabuzoli Oriental Pills for a fuller bosom.

All the men say 'Ooh là là'
When I wear my Forma bra.
First he sprays her
Then she sprays him:
Putex spray is
The rage in Berlin.
A fire's extinguished in a minute
If your house has a Minimax in it.
(If however I'm away,
What use is a Minimax, pray?)
For healthy children introduce
Them to Poetko's Apple Juice.
N-A-F-S-A-R: Nearly-Alcohol-Free-Sweet-Always-Refreshing!

Art was trying to liberate itself from representation, to become abstract, though Futurism and Cubism still had one foot firmly grounded in reality. The first Cubist landscapes of Juan Gris, Braque, Picasso and the self-propelling futurists Carlo Carrà, Severini, Boccioni, Balla all had a surrealist clarity. Kandinsky was starting his abstract flirtation with Expressionism.

Atoms were still almost indivisible – that's why they're called atoms, idiot! Although it was already known this was not true, it was still taught. Schoolbooks could not be revised quickly enough.

When the *Berliner Zeitung* reported that Marconi had telegraphed the letter S across the Atlantic without using the wire, Papa laughed at the hoax; only a nincompoop would fall for *that*, and certainly not he. 'How can you send a wireless wire?' he asked. Papa trusted to his common sense, just as I did when I declared in 1945 that the Hiroshima bomb was all a bluff. 'How can you murder eighty thousand innocent people with one single bomb, and that in the name of the Christ?' I asked.

33 BREAKDOWN

Shortly before his breakdown Papa dragged me off to see a sentimental French melodrama called *Damaged Goods* by Brieux with the idea that that would relieve him of the embarrassing task of acquainting me with the dangers of sexual intercourse. As an inducement, he first took me to Niquet's Wurstkeller, where they had the tastiest rump steaks and foaming Berlin beer. I hated melodramas in open-air theatres. In revenge I had sneaked a pair of Annie's lace panties out of the laundry basket, with the intention of masturbating like mad during the performance, which I would have done, had Papa not kept on interrupting. Why he took me to see the lousy play was unclear to me. Since the unmentionable disease was referred to only symbolically, I had no idea what it was all about. On the way home Papa pronounced with antediluvian grandiloquence, 'Only when medical science has crushed this terrible scourge of humanity will a better world commence!' I still did not know what he was talking about.

One year after that, on 26 June 1912, he jumped onto the table during my sister Annie's birthday tea, with the battlecry 'Caicus, Hermus, Caystrus, Maeander' (rivers of Asia Minor that flow into the Mediterranean). Then he flung himself wildly on the laughing Gerti, the fullest-bosomed of my sister's schoolfriends, and, to the amazement of the young girls, squeezed her breasts, for which I envied him. Thereupon he was confined to Dr Alexander's mental hospital in Westend, diagnosis: 'acute overwork'. Six weeks later he was discharged and sent home with rashes, erysipelas and shingles, incurably healthy.

When the family realized he had not long to live he was sent on one last holiday, to the Harz mountains in the care of Uncle Bruno. Meanwhile, back at home, a regular family council was held and I, without being asked, was unanimously designated breadwinner for my poor, aged mother (in those days old age began at forty-three). In keeping with the solemnity of the occasion, she laid the table with a home-made lace cloth, which hung down to the floor, and decorated it with silver-plated candelabra. As the pretensions of her life and our family were being snuffed out for good, she heroically, despite the first signs of tuberculosis (or even syphilis of the lung?), bit her lip when the wax dripping down from the candles threatened to ruin her needlework. The meeting was presided over by Papa's best friend, Uncle Willy Manes, a stinking-rich, stammering money grubber, uneducated, syphilitic and a judge in the commercial arbitration courts, which brought him much kudos. I found it all comically theatrical, and could not suppress my silly laughter, which infuriated all those present. They reproached me for not being ready for real life and for not even having chosen a profession. Consequently they immediately decided to put me into ladies' wear after I had finished that year's schooling at Easter 1913. I visualized myself as the Napoleon of crêpe de chine and burst out laughing, which infuriated the rest even more.

Uncle David Rothschild, a travelling salesman in coats and a repulsive dwarf who liked to brag about his impotence, much to the annoyance of his bearded wife, Aunt Emma, rose to announce that his friend, the undisputed blouse-king, Otto Moses of the Firm of Moses & Schlochauer (dresses, blouses, housecoats), with whom he had just spent two delightful weeks playing poker in Pontresina, had generously agreed to take me on as an apprentice, which was the equivalent of hitting the jackpot. Moses was a bachelor, ladies' man and the life and soul of the party wherever he went. On holiday he used the less Jewish-sounding name of Moser, joking 'nothing to add, nothing to take away'. (On holiday he was a different person.) After Moses & Schlochauer the whole garment trade would be open to me. The family council agreed, deeply moved. Then I was sent out, though not before I was made to thank Uncle David by planting a kiss on his bald pate; there were other, more important decisions on the agenda, for which I was too young. The family's good name was at stake. Money that had been entrusted to Papa was missing and the firm was close to bankruptcy.

In bed I started to think things over. It was only then that the clever answers occurred to me. I was caught, I had no choice but to accept my fate. Can one ever do anything to avoid one's fate? Instead of trying to get things changed in my favour, I became fatalistic and recalcitrant. At school we had been taught to look down on earning money. The noble Prince of Denmark as a huckster in the rag trade was an image that suited my outlook. I was also attracted by the prospect of getting away from that hated school. As a confirmed autodidact I had lost interest in learning on command. My best friend had left to do his military service; alone it was no fun any longer.

> *I've had enough of it allallall*
> *So I'll buy me a pistolololl.*
> *Without further ado*
> *I'll blow my head in two*
> *Three four five six seven eight nine ten*
> *jack-queen-king-ace!*

34 M & S

Contrary to all my expectations, the world did not come to an end when, punctually at eight on 1 April 1913, I started work as an apprentice with Moses & Schlochauer (nicknamed *Nochschlauer* – even smarter – by some, and *Arschlochauer* – arseholer – by less well-disposed tongues). As on my first day at school, there was a pain in my little heart and in my belly below. Nobody cared two hoots that my world was going up in flames. And not only mine; since then there has not been a single day with a cloudless sky. The same stormclouds that were gathering over my head scattered thunder and lightning throughout the world. After the nightmares of my youth, 'real life' appeared, embodied in the persons of Herr Otto Moses (along with his younger brother, Herr Leonhard Moses, 'Young Herr Moses') and Herr Sally Schlochauer.

Moses despised Schlochauer, looking down on him like silk on wool. Whenever Herr Moses made his dreaded morning rounds of the premises, the first person to see him had to shout out, 'Thirteen!' O eternity, thou thundrous word! Anyone who heard it had to pass it on immediately, and three seconds later everyone would be up to his ears in work. Even with his silent rubber soles, Thirteen never managed to catch an employee idling. He wore his grey-green flecked beard *à la* Henri IV (*le pervert galant*), and whenever he saw red, he would stick the yellowish points of his moustache into either corner of his mouth. At the same time two little horns would emerge from his noble but low brow, just as on Michelangelo's *Moses*. He very rarely spoke, but when he did, everyone trembled, apart from Fräulein Angrick, a model who belonged to him; she trembled in a quite different way. Even today Moses haunts my dreams at least twice a week. Herr Schlochauer, cautionary number seventeen, had thick, whitish-blue curls to match his whitish china-blue eyes. A handsome man in the blouse department. He expected to be idolized. With his engaging smile he would beguile every heart he desired once or twice a year. Apart from that, his rage was boundless. He always began his fits of screaming and shouting with, 'Now that's the limit', and ended them with foam all round his mouth which he would lick up greedily, growling, 'Damn and double damn!'

At ten minutes past eight Herr Schmidt II, the chief accountant, called me to his tall desk to give me my instructions from on high. He was a man who called a spade a spade – and worse – when it came to sex: 'No male employee of our firm is to maintain relations with any lady of our firm.' (After my first year there I knew that Herr Schlochauer [Seventeen] served all the ladies in the firm, while Herr Otto Moses [Thirteen] was more selective and concentrated on the models alone.) 'There are plenty of tarts in Berlin and we don't care what you get up to with ladies from other firms, apart from our direct competitors, Fraenkel & Roer, Fischbein & Mendel, Ball & Mueller, Mendelsohn, Meyerhof & Mamroth. Business secrets have to be kept at all costs, that's what they are there for. Our first business secret is our secret pricing code. Everything else that goes on within these walls is a business secret. Naturally! Everything that goes on in the world goes on naturally, apart from my trousers, they don't go on naturally, but that's a business secret too. I know a saucy little piece, Mietze Schmidt from Orgler & Fidelmann, well-stacked, very beddable, real class! Never says no to a bit of prick. She's got a cunt like a suction pump, when she comes it's there, when it's there, it's over. If I recommend you she'll let you stinky-finger her for free and if the shickse likes you she'll let you schtup her, but she's got catarrh in her passion-pipe. If you screw on Yom Kippur you'll have the clap by Sukkoth for sure. Clap costs money and makes you late, if you're late three times one mark'll be deducted from your salary, after six times you'll be shown the door, so you'd better stay healthy, but do enjoy yourself. Kiss them all while you're sweet and twenty but don't forget, youth's a stuff will not endure. How do those immortal lines go?

> 'What a pleasure it is to remember
> The days when my every member
> Was supple – apart from one.
> Those days are past and dim now,
> I'm stiff in every limb now –
> Apart from one.

'Your salary will, of course, be paid in gold. The apprenticeship lasts three years. On 31 March 1916 you will have completed your training. You will be a journeyman and the world will be your oyster. How do you like my new trousers? To be honest, I can't wait to get them off. In your first year you will be paid fifteen marks a month, that's a very decent salary, our competitors still make their apprentices pay a premium. Health insurance and social security will be deducted from your fifteen marks, of course; you'll get the benefit later, when you're seventy-five. We do not give advances, so you had better live within your means and not beyond them. You can get away with one cigarette a day now and then, but do not go to the lavatory too often during working hours, people notice. Have a good shit before and after. Working hours are from eight in the morning until eight in the evening, with one and a half hours for meals. If you want to get on in the world, stay on in the evening until your bosses have left, you can always make yourself useful and they like to see that. No eating during working hours, of course, anyway, there are no chairs. If no one happens to be looking you can lean against the wall from time to time, we're not monsters, we move with the times, but when I or any of the bosses come through the stockroom make sure you're working like mad, that's what you're paid for, after all. If we're satisfied with you there'll be a rise of two marks after a year, ten marks after two. And now hop along to your supervisor, Herr Schulz, you must obey him in all things. Everyone in this firm goes a little quicker than he can, even when there's nothing to do, 'cause there's always something to do, even during the off-season. And one last piece of good advice: it's grease that oils the wheels of industry. When a businessman's off his head is when he accepts shit instead of cash.'

I ran to Herr Schulz, the prototype of the shop-counter swell, a spotty-faced, slimy little lackey in a cutaway and pin-striped trousers, a few years older than I, much given to jiggling with his hand in his pocket. He took me round the premises like leading an animal to market and introduced me to every one of the forty-eight employees, 'This is the new apprentice, Herr Blumenfeld.' Each one said, 'Pleased to meet you', and gave my hand a nervous squeeze. Back in the storeroom Herr Schulz showed me a box filled with thousands of buttons, ordered me in surly tones to get them sorted out as quickly as possible, and sat down on the table to watch me work. When, a few hours later, I had finished this laborious task (only dashing off to the toilet twice to have a quick cry), he said contemptuously, 'You seem to be a real slow-coach. We'll soon knock that out of you here, you can start again straight after lunch', and threw the whole lot back into the box, giving me fifty pfennigs and the order to go out to the chemist's for a dozen *Neverrip* with double French ticklers and a couple of pills guaranteed to give a stag a hard-on. I found that beneath my dignity. Had I not, only two weeks previously, written my graduation essay on the subject of 'To what extent, in moral terms, should we find the Iphigenia of Aulis more admirable than the Iphigenia of Tauris?' So I did just the same (don't we spend our lives doing the same?) as I had done with the gas-filled balloons when I was a little boy: the sharp-needle treatment. That afternoon, after a terrible inner struggle, I refused to sort the buttons again, fully expecting to be shot. Instead Herr Schulz merely shrugged his shoulders. 'Don't then. Schmonzes maronzes.' He was a coward.

The next morning I had to go to the changing room at nine o'clock to assist Herr Wolfsberg to squeeze the firm's five models into their much-too-tight white drill smocks. It was not child's play; it demanded all the strength and dexterity of at least two robust men. In those days models did not starve themselves as they do today; there was no fashion photography and no slimming pills. 'The fuller figure!' was the rallying cry. The ladies had to be laced up in their corsets by brute force until the required wasp waists (19 or 20 inches) were achieved. This was supervised by Fräulein Mattausch, a former model herself, who sweated as she dragged her weight around with a smile of sweetest malice on her face. And did they sweat in those days! There were no daily baths, no deodorants, no female hygiene, but stench and vermin aplenty. Fräulein Mattausch was a dirty-minded old bitch, and as soon as she appeared everyone outdid themselves making smutty remarks. When we were introduced, Fräulein Angrick took exception to my chapped, rough winter hands, whining, 'I'm not letting my delicate little baby's bottom be manhandled by sandpaper like that.' With deep concern, she asked the other models whether they thought my hands needed treatment. Fräulein Mattausch announced that they had very considerately decided to help me. I had a feeling something nasty was about to happen, but I didn't want to be a spoil-sport. Mesmerized by the situation and flattered by the interest of these strange, half-naked, shameless young witches, I had no choice but to allow Herr Wolfsberg to blindfold me with a grubby petticoat. Then he led me round in a circle, while everyone sang the ritual Moses & Schlochauer hymn:

If thou canst drench a maid's dark crack
In floods of seed;
If thou canst satisfy, back to back,
A dozen widows in need;
Can screw until shit spurts from her arse,

Till her grapefruits clang
And thy rocks go bang —
Then lave thy hands in this full glass.

Fräulein Angrick dunked my rough, chapped hands in the warm witches' cauldron, a chamber pot freshly filled by the ladies. I shuddered at this contact with the mythical Earth Mothers. Edith, the nice one, gave me a smacking kiss, 'Now you're one of us.' Two days later my hands had healed. Not long afterwards an apprentice with the rival firm of Mendelsohn, Mamroth & Veilchenfeld told me he had been subjected to the same initiation ceremony. You don't have to travel to the other side of the world to study primitive customs. What does dear old Krause say? 'East, west, home is best', and Krause's right, of course.

Thus I became a businessman, but the next step, becoming a big-businessman, I never managed, even though my pride insisted I must be able to do anything I wanted to do. Potency is not a matter of will-power; money is potency, and I had none. I couldn't manage it. Sublimation is impotence.

The very second I joined the firm I knew that I was making a basic mistake. I should have been an actor. (That would have been another basic mistake.) Or a poet. Once, when I went to collect some blouses from a sweat-shop in Frankfurter Allee, I was duly overwhelmed by the whole misery of mankind. Until then I had never been in a working-class district, had never seen how 'the poor' lived, how seamstresses, crowded together in stinking rooms, sat working at their sewing machines. My despair drove me to imitate Heine:

Sewing, sewing, sewing,
Until you're dead.
Treadle always going,
Still no bread.
Sewing, sewing,
Lungs a-sobbing;
Treadle, treadle,
Heart a-throbbing.
Spasms – bleeding

> *Work is over*
> *Screaming – quiet*
> *Sleeping – death.*
> (3 May 1913)

I was better at suffering than at writing poetry.

The tone at Moses & Schlochauer was a mixture of the brash and the conventional: Freytag's nineteenth-century classic, *Debit and Credit*, combined with Lubitsch's first film success, *The Firm Gets Married*. At first I was in the woollen fabrics department with Mieke Tierfeller, a vicious hunchback, utterly charmless. I had to sort out the order forms, cut as per pattern book: 165 cms of navy blue voile no. 8103 each for five blouses no. 9626, find the right trimmings (buttons, braid, pads etc), and keep the stock in tip-top order. Herr Schulz, my supervisor, was soon given the sack because he kept on arriving late and spent most of the day in the lavatory because of his clap (my sharp needle?). I became head of wool. I would have preferred to go into silk, silk was more elegant, and, more importantly, that was the domain of an extremely alluring blonde with a laugh full of white teeth called Emmy Kussero. She liked to show her attractive legs, all the way up to her panties with the reinforced crotch that was adored by so many. She was the mistress of the head city salesman of Eisner & Ehrmann, wholesale materials; occasionally our Herr Schlochauer also enjoyed her favours. She had coquettish visiting cards printed with 'Emmy!', a carrier pigeon below, and below that:

> *Your eyes, so beautiful and mild,*
> *Are mortal, just like all before you.*
> *Won't you bequeath them to a child*
> *And let me bear that infant for you?*

On the back it read, 'Do it to me, baby!'

35 PAPA'S END

When I came home from my first day at work tear-stained and exhausted, my ailing father gave me such a guilty look that I vowed never again to show my despair. He suffered most of all from the fact that he could no longer afford to let me study economics. His business, his pride, his reputation and his health were all in the red. He developed megalomania, ordered ten thousand Chinese visiting cards, had tantrums, boxed my ears because I arrived ten minutes late at the inn in the zoo (The Nice Doctor called it 'euphoria'). On 15 September 1913 he had a stroke in his private office and was brought home in an ambulance, foaming at the mouth and paralysed down his left side. The Nice Doctor fed him morphine. He spent three days in his death throes, without ever regaining consciousness, and died on 19 September, mouth wide open. They tied up his jaw with a napkin and placed two candles at the head of his bed. The house stank.

Mama rushed home from the TB sanatorium, lit a memorial lamp (a Jewish oil-lamp for the dead), wept without tears and had her clothes dyed black. I had no idea what was expected of the son-and-heir in the event of death, so I retired sadly to my room and wrote bad poems in my diary about my poor father's death. It was only later that I discovered how poor he really was. There was no Horatio there to help that young Hamlet to discover the truth. I let the teardrops drip onto the poems I had just written and solemnly swore never to masturbate again and to look after my mother. I have broken both oaths. When I asked about the cause of Papa's death everyone lied and told me Papa had died from a particularly heavy dose of overwork.

This is the place to mention an ancient masonic custom of touching beauty that granted me a comforting insight into human kindness in those dark hours. When Ravel's sister Carola died an unknown man placed two leather caskets beside the bier, one empty, the other filled with gold. If the bereaved family is in need, they help themselves; if they are in more fortunate circumstances, they put generous amounts of gold into the empty casket. Since Papa had been a freemason all his life, and proud of it, I eagerly awaited the appearance of the black-clad Sarastro. In vain. Grandpapa explained to me that it was a custom that was only observed in the case of rich families. According to Papa's wishes, 'Sweet is the labourer's rest' (Georg Ludwig Hesekiel) was carved on his simple granite tombstone. His final resting place could be rented by the year or for all eternity. The latter seemed the better investment. That particular eternity was brought to an end by Hitler in 1938.

The only assets Papa left behind were liabilities: his family, his debts, no money. Agitated uncles liquidated the firm of Jordan & Blumenfeld with suspicious alacrity. They compounded with the creditors at forty-five per cent, in those days an unatonable disgrace. But at least it avoided the worst, going bust, *mechuleh*, insolvent, bankrupt.

It emerged that Papa had pledged shares entrusted to him by a business friend, using them to speculate on a fall in Wabash, and the operation had come unstuck. Rich Uncle Willy generously stepped into the breach with fifteen grand. We were impoverished. Thank God for the tie-pin with the whopping great diamond Papa had received as a wedding present from Grandpapa Henry. When they tried to sell it, it turned out to be glass. Papa had traded the real one in long ago. Grandfather cried piteously, teeth chattering, eyes red, not making a sound. Never since have I seen anyone cry so heartrendingly. The others found it difficult to conceal their *Schadenfreude*. Years later Aunt Ellinor, the mother of my best friend, was still boasting to her niece, my fiancée, 'In the days when nobody cared to mention the name of Blumenfeld, I still received Erwin in my home.'

The household was liquidated in dramatic fashion. Furniture was sold. We reduced our circumstances and moved into an apartment in the inferior rear part of a block. Mama took up poverty with gusto and introduced exemplary economies: old newspapers cut up for lavatory paper, a washable waxed tablecloth with paper napkins, no dessert with lunch, only one course for supper, stale crusts instead of fresh rolls, warmed-up coffee, margarine instead of butter. In order to save on lighting, the apartment was always in semidarkness. She anticipated the shortages of 1916. On the other hand she boasted how lovingly she kept Papa's grave decorated with fresh flowers. There was not one pfennig left from her dowry of a hundred thousand marks. Later I found out that she had kept forty-five thousand marks stashed away in a secret account for *even* harder times ('Put a little bit away for a rainy day'). That money was completely eaten up by the post-war inflation. In order to feed her hungry offspring and to set an example of the way a widow should fight to make ends meet, she tried to set herself up as an up-to-date *schnorrer* by peddling chocolate, tea and coffee at discount prices to relatives and acquaintances over the telephone.

Soon, however, she had to go back to the TB sanatorium. Heinz and I were sent to stay with the Jordans. By way of compensation they took our Ibach piano and Papa's walnut bookcases. Very Dickensian. Aunt Clara, a dumpy little sister of father's, had been made to marry a man thirty years older than herself, a so-called marriage of convenience. Uncle Moritz, known as *Möhrchen* (little carrot), once Papa's partner, despised slave and bookkeeper, was over eighty and at the height of his goat-bearded senility. Fifty-five per cent of his assets had gone down the drain in the collapse of the firm, and now the Jordans made the most of their opportunity to earn forty-five marks a month back from us as lodgers and to play the good Samaritans at the same time. I had hated Aunt Clara, an advocate of utilitarianism and chairwoman of numerous societies, ever since she had had the audacity to give me a pair of green woollen stockings with pink hoops for my fifth birthday. Useful presents are an insult. All that is now left of her three score years and ten (plus five for good measure) is her imperious *obiter dictum*, 'A chamber pot is for use during the night, NOT the evening.'

The moving spirit behind the vengeance that was visited upon us on Jordan's banks was Ada, Uncle Möhrchen's only daughter and the apple of his eye. She was in her thirties and of such exceptional ugliness that she felt we must be soul mates. She constantly insisted on having discussions (i.e., giving vent to her venom), in the course of which she would press her mammary protuberances up against me. Eventually, in the triumphant tones of a goddess of vengeance, she revealed to me the awful crime my father had committed against his innocent family, at the same time warning me against the dangers of sexual intercourse, 'Men who associate with loose women in their youth are punished by dying of siffelis in the prime of their manhood.' As she spoke, her eyes flashed as if she were declaiming her favourite poem, 'Deborah's Song of Victory'. I asked her when my father had 'associated'. 'At nineteen', she said. 'The mills of God grind slow.' This revelation opened my eyes to the madness of the world.

Herewith belongs an event that happened three months after Papa's death. One boring Sunday afternoon I was sitting in the Jordans' 'loggia' (a common-or-garden balcony) when I felt a draught from the right and my father's yellowish, transparent ghost came floating by, raised its hand as if it was going to say something, then disappeared stage left. Convinced of the reality of this apparition, I jumped up and had the courage to confide it to my diary, even though I knew every word was a lie.

Shortly afterwards I had to go to see Dr Grunewald, in connection with my Aquarius (Wassermann) constellation. He was chairman of a funeral concern and looked deadly earnest as he sat behind his desk, above which hung two copies of the same engraving, 'The Struggle with Death' in different gold frames, gifts from grateful patients. The Grim Reaper, armed with his scythe, is wrestling with the surgeon, armed with his scalpel, while the patient looks on with interest from the operating table. The Nice Doctor stared at me mournfully. 'There's not much to say about sex', he said, in tones that said much, a tear tumbling down into his grizzled beard. 'By the time you have an erection, Erwin, it's usually too late.' In the course of my life I have often remembered this piece of wisdom, usually too late.

Ehrlich Hata 606 arrived too late for Papa. With sulphonamide and penicillin syphilis is easier to get rid of than the common cold. The University of New York has difficulty finding a real case of the pox for teaching purposes. The doctors have won a decisive battle and lost a highly profitable business (that's why it took so long). As usual, a Jew and a Japanese were to blame. Auschwitz and Hiroshima compensated for it to a certain extent. In order to remain on good terms with his colleagues in the medical profession, God saw to it that they got the cancer business. Though not a public disgrace, cancer, with its endless treatments, radiation therapies and operations, provides a luxurious living for doctors.

The dark years of venereal disease saw the birth of that ugly symbol of the bourgeoisie, the contraceptive sheath (French letter, condom, rubber johnny, *capote anglaise*), preventing life and death at the same time. In men's lavatories there were machines where for fifty pfennigs you could get an ineffective disinfectant with long instructions for use. Mercury and arsenic were not sufficiently effective in either suppressing desire or preventing disease. Where medicine failed, religion hoped to triumph. In one ear it whispered, 'Be fruitful and multiply', while enjoining 'Continence!' in the other. Each nation reacted in its own specific way. *Comme toujours, la belle France se démerdait avec un certain sourire.* Latin temperaments can take nothing seriously. Casanova, volume 3, chapter 2: 'What halted my wild debauches was a disease a beautiful Hungarian whore gave me. My seventh dose. As always, I got rid of it after six weeks of treatment. I have spent my whole life doing nothing but make myself ill when I was healthy, and making myself well again when I was ill. I was always equally successful in both and today (at sixty-seven) I enjoy excellent health, which I would gladly ruin again, if age did not prevent me. The illness that we call the "French disease" does not shorten life, if you only know how to cure it. It leaves scars which you are quite happy to accept when you remember what pleasure it was to acquire them...'

The good honest Germans, on the other hand, were consumed with their usual remorse, and Protestantism dripped from inflamed prostates across the land; the Syphilis SS, the apocalyptic horseman of the god of vengeance unto the seventh generation of those who love one another. Religion as a venereal disease of Mother Venus. Lust was stifled by fear of shame. Life fought back, threw up barricades, created psychological antitoxins – antipsychotics. Disease either undermines your cognitive faculties or enhances them. The Germans went blind from their syphilis, in order not to see it. Cured much too suddenly, mankind – in the way mankinds do — immediately forgot the torments of four hundred years. Our reluctance to learn from our sufferings is one of the reasons why we are still retarded children. By the time syphilis was finally conquered, the Germans were ensconced behind their barricades in black uniforms and skull and crossbones, armed to the teeth against it: blindness, deaf-mute hypocrisy (not me guv, I don't know nothing about nothing), faith, lies and charity, *Deutschland, Deutschland über alles!* They could not live without syphilis any more, nor did they want to. The unleashed subhumans thirsted after new chains, new tortures. The German mind became feeble-minded, Germanness turned into Germadness. The German *Volk* became one stinking brown mass. Language predicted it from hearsay; since 1901 Rossignol's dictionary of Parisian slang has the entry: *avoir le nazi = être nazigué = avoir la syphe.*

To return to Wotan: he roared for human victims. Not one at a time in beech woods (*Buchenwälder*) but by the millions in Buchenwald. Wotan got his six million Jews, and the Deutsche Bank got their gold. The fact that Hitler was afflicted with a Jewish grandmother gives the whole thing – even if the Jews refuse to accept it – a certain piquancy. I like to imagine the Führer ending his days as a kind old rabbi in Brooklyn, having got one of his many doubles to commit doublicide with Eva Braun in the Wilhelmstrasse bunker.

One does not like having to feel grateful to diseases. For that reason we have always avoided following up the interaction between religion, syphilis, genius, madness and German nationalism. Modern European civilization is a spirochaete syphilization, the first souvenir brought back from the newly discovered New World. Will the sterilized world of tomorrow still be capable of having ideas? ('Non cogitunt, ergo non sunt' – 'they do not think, therefore they are not', Georg Christoph Lichtenberg.) An abhorrent vacuum! Where will we get the geniuses we need, that salt of the earth without which the idiots cannot vegetate? New plagues, new hope. Must we sink into a decline, waste away waiting for the revitalizing effects of atomic radiation (strontium 90 in your asparagus sandwich!)?

For the sake of self-preservation, let's be Epicureans, even if we have no idea what that means (I don't). If we don't want to be murdered by our children, we have to educate them. Yesterday's erotic pleasures were sex crimes the day before yesterday, and we should not forget it. 'Happy man, forget if you can.' Happiness plunges us into stupidity. Since the state has taken over our lives, like all authorities, the sex authorities have succeeded in merely interfering with sex. Sex education in the sense of the transmission of sexual knowledge from generation to generation, from father to son, is almost impossible without the help of brothels and whores. With the best will in the world, it can't all be left to the already overburdened mothers and their ladylike daughters, much as they might like it.

The envious regiments of frigid housewives' clubs keep on trying to suppress the sexual advances of the last millennia. A penny-pinching attitude to pleasure, cunt envy, Methodist puritanism are the most wretched, stupid, shortsighted of crimes against humanity. It is the Pilgrim Fathers who are to blame for the decline of America and, if we are not careful, the decline of the whole world. Where could Van Gogh take his freshly severed ear today? To his analyst? Don't let beggars play with Prometheus's fire. Fire can go out. Nietzsche and Wedekind hammered that point home long before me; my task is to repeat it.

Another far-reaching cure has been slowly taking place during my lifetime: religion, that Pascalian brain tumour, is withering away, after having corroded the world's brains for thousands of years. My great-grandchildren will not know what they missed; religion and syphilis will have become obsessions from classical antiquity – mythology.

36 PRINCIP(LE)

After a most refreshing summer Sunday morning at the recently opened Wannsee swimming pool, where we had smoked cigarettes while admiring the bathing beauties, my brother and I travelled back to the Zoo Station in the best of moods. Mama was in Davos with her lung trouble and the family was looking after us nicely. That day we had been invited to lunch at the house of a successful cousin, the bank director Georg Wolfson and, as usual, we arrived half an hour late. The food was always excellent at the Wolfsons'. Little Martha Wolfson was a cousin from Essen, provincial, young, socially overambitious and arrogant; to me, however, she was always flatteringly nice, regarding me as a paragon of modern metropolitan youth. Her young, smiling, sandy-haired husband had a permanent faraway look on his face, and because of his farsightedness he had just been made director of all deposit banks in the group of the three big German banks known as the D-banks. When we came in he was sitting there, pale with annoyance; he did not respond to our greeting, but just bit his lips in an offended manner. Martha was gazing into space, misty eyed, and did not say a word. Trying to be clever and show my younger brother how to talk your way out of such a situation, I made up a story, wittily told, about meeting Herr Otto Moses, my boss, who had been terribly nice and invited us to have a glass of beer with him, which it was simply impossible to refuse. (In fact the younger Herr Moses, Herr Leonhard, had seen me from a distance and immediately looked the other way.) My story fell flat; no one was listening. Banking looked down on the garment trade.

Georg had a faraway look on his face, and leapt up when the telephone rang in the next room. Martha disappeared with him without even a glance in our direction. Highly embarrassing. As punishment they left us on our own for a quarter of an hour. After our swim we were starving, and we were just conferring in a whisper as to whether we should not just leave, when the nanny appeared and in somewhat piqued tones asked the young gentlemen to make their way to the dining room. Herr and Frau Doktor (PhD in science), she added, would come later. The table setting was a model of perfection, like something from a shop window. Little Gerd was already sitting in his high chair screaming. Nanny subjected him to a little further torture and then sat down. The parents did not appear. We were served. With guilty feelings but healthy appetites, we ate beef marrow on toast, cold consommé with parsley, asparagus with morels and Rhine salmon with sauté potatoes, washed down with Piesporter Goldtröpfchen. (Martha's home town of Essen was in the Rhineland, though unfortunately not on the Rhine, the object of the German bourgeoisie's romantic longings, but in the industrial district of the Ruhr; by way of compensation the Wolfsons always served the choicest Rhine wines.) The offended couple finally joined us at table, deadly serious expressions on their faces. With ambiguous friendliness Martha said, 'I'm glad you boys haven't let all this spoil your appetite.'

Georg was staring into space, the epitome of a broken man. He had barely taken a mouthful when the telephone summoned him again into the adjoining room. Martha followed in his wake. Returning for dessert (meringues with whipped cream and wild strawberries) Georg asked, 'How's Mama?', ate one wild strawberry without listening to our answer and dashed back to the telephone. After dinner Heinz wanted to show *me* how to apologize properly, but Georg interrupted, announcing with great solemnity, 'At last I can speak freely, now that Wolf's telegraph service is carrying the news. Unfortunately – or perhaps I should say thank God – the stock exchange is closed on Sundays. Thanks to my direct line to Vienna – as director – I have received secret information first-hand: the heir to the Austrian throne, Franz Ferdinand, and his noble wife, Duchess Sophie von Hohenberg have just been assassinated in Sarajevo by a Serbian high-school student [he looked at me accusingly], Gavrilo Princip [did Kafka invent that name?]. Boys, a world war seems inevitable ...' My brother and I fell off our chairs and rolled about on the carpet in fits of helpless laughter. We had expected – and deserved – a good dressing-down for coming so late and could not believe that a managing director of deposit banks would make such a fuss about the assassination of some half-Slav archduke down in Serbia. Fortunately the telephone rang again, and again the offended couple disappeared into the next room. Still lying on the carpet, laughing, we wondered what to do next. It still seemed advisable to present our proper apologies. Coffee was served in the smoking room and my brother, with a convincing display of seriousness, said, 'Please forgive us for being late; please don't be angry, we promise on our honour not to do it again.' Georg had a faraway look on his face. 'Were you late?', he said, then the telephone rang again. This was the first war in which it had the chance to play a historic part. In 1815 Rothschild made his millions with the help of the optical telegraph; in 1870 the telegraph transmitted the Ems telegram; in 1940 it was the radio, and in the next war people will watch their sons getting killed on television. There is no stopping progress.

Never again did we have such a good laugh, nor did we ever go to the Wolfsons' again. My little brother Heinz had to give up his life for his country, and I had to give up my country for the rest of my life. All because of Princip(le).

37   THE FUTURE LOOKS BLACK FOR THIRTEEN

After only one year with Moses & Schlochauer my meteoric rise unexpectedly started when Herr Otto Moses (Thirteen) unmistakeably grunted 'Morning' at me during his morning round. Never before had he condescended to wish an employee good morning. The entire staff was plunged into speculation as to why I had been singled out for such an honour. I started to have a privileged position, and from now on I took to arriving six minutes late without Fräulein Schmidt III, who was positioned at the entrance for that purpose, adding my name to the list of latecomers. She thought I was a clandestine nephew of Schlochauer's and was allegedly the one who started the vague rumour that I was the product of a premarital indiscretion of Frau Schlochauer's. My fellow apprentices, Phillips, Diemel, Brasch and Wolfsberg, lacked the guts to come late, which was why no one thought they were secret nephews. Their only secret was Wolfsberg's secret clap, which everyone talked about, since he was always in the toilet, having his medication, a good drip and a good cry.

When I dashed into work at six minutes past eight on the Monday morning after Sarajevo, breathless and guiltridden as always, Fräulein Schmidt III told me I had to collect all the stock-books and go immediately to Herr Otto Moses's private office, the holy of holies to which people were only summoned for sackings and suchlike catastrophes.

In those days only millionaires could afford cars. Since Herr Moses wanted at all costs to avoid having people ask him for a rise, he had himself driven every morning by his servant Robert, disguised as a chauffeur in goggles and peaked cap, in his shiny black Audi limousine and deposited unobserved at a quarter past eight, a whole quarter of an hour after the official opening-time, on the corner of Leipzigerstrasse and Kommandantenstrasse, from where he walked the last two hundred yards to work. That allowed me to arrive late without risk.

That morning he was perfidiously punctual, had asked for me straight away and discovered that I was late. I put on a defiant face; I felt the end of my days with Moses & Schlochauer approaching. I had already worked my way up to head of stores and chief clerk for silk, wool, cotton and lace, leaving Wolfsberg with buttons and trimmings. I had the whole inventory of our stock in my head, no order was dispatched without my dynamic and totally illegible signature. My knowledge of the stock brought me recognition but no increase in pay. Instead I was rather flatteringly let in on some private confidences. Herr Schlochauer (Seventeen), for example, was having an affair with a real opera singer, Fräulein Sigrid Niklaus Kempner; she was small, but good things come in small packages, know what I mean? Her mother was a singing teacher, her brother a conductor, no less. Every evening she attended upon her Sally just before closing with the purpose of brightening up his life. Sally adored opera, consequently the place often didn't close until very late. One evening Herr Schlochauer in his affable way came to see me in the stock-room, offering me by way of a softener a peppermint he had been warming up in his hand for a while. 'As you are going to be here until closing time anyway, you could do me a very personal favour, nothing to do with business – business is business, as I'm sure you understand. You can just as well do your work in the entrance hall, the light is better out there, it'll be better for your eyes! And if my old woman should turn up – that's Frau Schlochauer to you, you understand – give two sharp taps on the window with the keys and tell her I'm waiting for her at the back in city dispatch, where I'm checking up on a shipment. Chat her up for as long as you can, talk to her about the weather and business, she's interested in both.'

From now on each evening I had to stand guard over my boss's merry chirruping, and with the aid of reflections, cracks and keyholes, I managed to enjoy the climaxes myself:

First came the coat and the dress,
Then petticoats one, two, three,
And then came lingerie, oh yes!
And then – oh, then came SHE!

One fine evening his old woman really did turn up. Fräulein Sigrid, pretty well undressed, legs wide apart and humming airs from Rigoletto, was seesawing on Herr Schlochauer's lap. I leapt up to block the way of three hundred pounds of lawful wedded spouse. There were several doors leading off from the vestibule, one to sales, to that heaven where Herr Schlochauer was having his singing lesson, another to hell, to city dispatch, whence I was to dispatch Mrs Seventeen. I was too flustered to find the key I was supposed to tap on the window with. I gabbled incoherently, said 'Herr Schlochauer is working on her in the dispatch city', flung open the door and Frau Schlochauer ran off to the back, shaking her head in disbelief. At the very last moment I dashed into the sales room at the front. Seventeen leapt to his feet, worried stiff. 'That's the absolute limit! Just now I'm not in at the moment!' he cried, buttoning his fly (the zip was still in its infancy). With my help he shoved the three-quarters-nude prima donna into an open wardrobe containing the silkiest of evening dresses and dashed off to meet his old woman in dispatch, crying, 'You just wait and it'll sort itself out!' From the wardrobe came cries of, 'I'm locked in!' (*La prima donna* was not very *mobile*.) I lost my head completely and jumped into the wardrobe and onto the divine diva. It was now or never! She was red hot! I was afraid her nerves might be suffering under the shock and wanted to comfort her. She slapped me above the belt, kicked me below and screeched hysterically, 'There goes your next rise, peasant! Help! My dress. Help! My shoes. Where are my panties, hurry, hurry, can't you get a move on? Help! My handbag!' After I had dashed round like a scalded cat, stuffed everything into the wardrobe and slammed the door, she was still whining for her parasol.

Hardly had I closed the door than Herr Sally and Frau Jenny Schlochauer appeared, arm in arm, the smiling image of the happily married couple. As if it were a matter of official business, I handed Seventeen the wardrobe key. He popped it in his waistcoat pocket and said, in rather more amiable fashion than usual, 'Bring the stock books right away, Herr Blumenfeld, we need to order more crepe georgette. We're going to have to work late tonight, perhaps it would be best if Herr Scharffenberg [the head porter] ordered a cab for my better half.' And with that he boldly sat down right in front of the wardrobe in which I had just locked the prima donna. It was better than *The Marriage of Figaro*!

Despite all that, it was not beyond the bounds of possibility that Otto Moses (Thirteen) might throw me out on my neck, to the jeers of the rest of the staff, who envied me my rapid rise. Then I would become an actor and, as the greatest Hamlet ever, 'drown the stage with tears, and cleave the general ear with horrid speech.' Resigned to my fate, I knocked on the door of the private office. The door was opened by a spittle-dribbling Herr Schlochauer (Seventeen), and once again it was 'the absolute limit!' He bolted the door behind me. What did they want? Before me stood Herr Otto Moses (Thirteen), gigantic, both ends of his moustache hand-twirled at the corners of his mouth, an indication of greater-than-normal agitation. I had played with the idea of flinging my scorn in his face as he pierced me with his green basilisk stare. Not long ago, through the hole made for the recently installed central heating, I had witnessed Frau Bernstein, the wife of his best friend, begging him tearfully for three hundred marks (more than I earned in a whole year!). She looked noble as she knelt before him. Only after a somewhat incomprehensible kiss did he grant her two hundred, and then insisted on her fishing the money out of his trousers pocket herself. But now I was tongue-tied. I would not even have been capable of saying that the Underground had been derailed at Hausvogtei Platz again. Herr Otto Moses was all the more voluble. He suddenly thundered, 'How much 7718 have we on order from Jarroson Fils?' Proud of my comprehensive knowlege of our whole stock, I answered promptly, 'Thirty-three rolls of tango [the fashionable orange colour] crepe on call in Lyon, and four here in the cutting room.' With conspiratorial gravity Moses turned to Schlochauer. 'Shall we wire?' In those days people only sent a telegram to announce a death, every word cost five pfennigs, double that abroad! Herr Schlochauer agreed: 'Leave it to me.' At that Herr Otto Moses took on heroic stature; the little horns sprouted on his brow and he grew taller and taller. He didn't bother to wait for Schlochauer's assent (Shlochauer was growing smaller and smaller). Divine wisdom poured from his lips. 'Ring Wolf [the agent for Jarronson Père & Fils] and tell him to wire Lyon that we are cancelling the thirty-three P-Ess [pièces] of tango crepe. Instead we are ordering two hundred rolls, same material, same quality, in natural, for express delivery within ten days.' Horrified, I whispered that we had ordered fifty rolls of white 7703 only three weeks ago. Was Herr Moses (Thirteen) suffering from overwork like Papa? From megalomania? Amnesia? Then something happened. He closed his left eye and fixed his right on the map of Germany that hung on the office wall, four inches above my head. Without even a glance in my direction with his open eye, he issued his command with crystal clarity. 'What is taking place here, today, in this private office is a business secret of historical importance. You mustn't breathe a single word of it to anyone at all. It's all or nothing. Walls have ears and –' here his open eye skewed round on me '– holes have eyes. I know my troops and have taken appropriate precautions. Robert Scharffenberg is on patrol. Although I know that discretion is always a matter of honour, this time I demand your solemn assurance that you can hold your tongue. Give me a clear Yes.' I was too shattered even to nod.

'War creates an undreamt-of boom in black. When the war breaks out', he said, baring his teeth in anticipation, 'we must be armed to the teeth in black. If this war turns into a thirty years war, as I anticipate, it will last from 1914 to 1944. Every German woman will marry several times and will need a corresponding number of widow's outfits. They'll be queuing up for black maternity dresses. The future looks black, blacker than black! As soon as the killing begins, mourning will be big business. And the more that get killed, the more desperate women will be to find another husband. If we strike while the iron's hot we can make a killing of our own. Verily I say unto you', he went on in prophetic tones, 'the women will be going round in black lingerie. Take this down: Peignoirs in black satin-stitch with detachable light-grey piping for half-mourning. Moses & Schlochauer's blue-black has conquered the world. Let the competition drown in brown-black! War means a moratorium: no one pays their debts. We should – no, we *must* – stockpile. Order for immediate delivery, with a cancellation clause, double last year's amounts of black velveteen, black zanella, black serge, black wool crepe, black cotton crepe, black marocain, black voile, black demi-voile, black wool voile, black cotton voile (for inexpensive transparent mourning blouses), black ninon, black Chappe voile, black marquisette, black taffeta, black cashmere, black silk cashmere, black wool corduroy, black damask, black silk tulle, black cotton tulle and black velours chiffon for low-cut evening gowns with black lace trimming. All orders to go off as express letters with the midday post. How much is your salary at the moment?' I was already beginning to see myself as a war profiteer. 'Twenty-five marks a month.' 'Better than a kick up the arse', said Herr Schlochauer. For the one and only time Herr Otto Moses placed his massive marble paw on my drooping shoulder. 'Herr Blumenfeld, when the war starts business will be very slow for weeks, if not months. I hereby promise, with Herr Schlochauer's full agreement [he nodded!], that your salary of twenty-five marks will not be cut during the first three months of the war. Time enough to worry about things then, if you're still alive.'

The day after the war broke out the following notice was posted in the entrance, 'Until further notice, the firm will only open half days. Accordingly all salaries will be reduced by fifty per cent. Moses & Schlochauer.' When, one month later, I made my timid attempt to call in their promise, I went to see Seventeen. (Thirteen would have annihilated me with scorn.) He said indignantly that he hadn't nodded in writing and that I should be ashamed to expect special treatment at times like the present. In wartime even written promises were nothing but scraps of paper; fifty per cent was better than nothing; it was the absolute limit.

Back to Moses. He was growing visibly more prophetic. 'In a seasonal business there are constant surprises, especially during world wars. Away with pink, away with *bleu ciel*, away with *eau de nil*, away with *champagne*! Cancel our current orders for pastel colours immediately, we only lose money on them anyway.' For the sake of his china-blue eyes, Schlochauer spoke up for *ciel*, but Moses would not be put off. 'Out of the question! We Germans are sick and tired of being fleeced twice a year by Paris. Poiret went too far when he demanded two grand per gown. It had to come to war, however rotten that is. Germany must be independent of the rest of the world, Berlin must liberate itself from the chicanery of Paris. If we have to have ideas we can obtain them via Switzerland.' (Twice a year Herr Moses bought ten fussy haute couture models in Paris which he had altered to create a chic German collection; that was Berlin ladies' fashion.) 'The future belongs to *noir* 7702! I can see the next fashion hit appearing over the horizon: field grey. We'll number it 7756. Before it's too late order colour samples of all available gris tones from France. There's even a chance artificial silk might make it. Not a minute to spare for lunch today, *victory must be ours!*'

As an accessory to vital business secrets, I returned to my desk head bowed beneath a burden of cares (*à la* Moissi). What will we do with all that crepe de chine if war doesn't break out? All eyes were fixed on me. I had spent almost an hour in the bosses' office. There was no one else who could say the same of themselves (apart from Emmy Kussero). From now on like her I arrived late with official sanction. Even Herr Moses did not dare object. My power came from the fact that I was obviously unfit for military service.

After the first big battles, sales of widow's outfits rose stupendously and the competition was nowhere. Only M & S could supply any desired quantity of first-rate mourning goods with immediate delivery. Victory all along the line!

38 WAR BREAKS OUT

In the following weeks there was a veritable torrent of revocations, ultimata, unsubstantiated stories (latrine-rumours), warmongering addresses to the populace and patriotic editorials which stacked their emotive phrases round the powder-keg until, on 3 August the thing really went up. And I can say: I was there when His Majesty the Kaiser roared forth his message of iron, down from his topmost battlements (well, the palace balcony), to the crowded masses, who had been waiting for hours down in the Pleasure Gardens, although despite the bull-horn that an equerry was holding in front of his snout, nobody could understand a word. Not until that evening could you read eagerly in the local papers what you had applauded so heartily during the day. There was also something that I had seen the evening before that wasn't in any of the papers: workers, lefties, 'unpatriotic rabble' were marching behind the Red Flag to demonstrate against the war. The police organized a hunt and shot down large numbers of them. Gradually it dawned on me that the Powers of Darkness were at work, and that it was goodbye to the freedoms, including the freedom of the press, that we had never had. There were no political parties any more, just Germans. The left was done for, a whole nation-in-arms started to sing for victory. 'Up and at 'em,' shouted the Crown Prince, standing up in his open Daimler in his favourite dressing-up-clothes, the uniform of a Hussar from the Death's Head Brigade.

The Kaiser – in his new field-grey Supreme Commander of the Forces uniform, overloaded with decorations and a beaver-collar, a riding-crop or, as it might be, a field-marshall's baton, and wearing leather topboots – the Kaiser called, and everyone, but everyone, came running:

Be a Prussian! Shoot a Russian,
Flog a Frog and hit a Brit!
Give a slap to Mr Jap!
Death to Serbia!
It's what they deserv-ia!

We love as one
We hate as one
We have one enemy alone
England!
(That was Ernst Lissauer's *Hymn of Hate*.)

But my old dad
Said these fine words:
'We'll keep the 'ome fires
Good an' stirred.'
'Long as our boys
'As got a gun,
We'll 'ave them buggers
On the run!

Don't fret, old girl,
You bet your bonnet,
There ain't no bullet
With my name on it!
We're all as 'appy as can be
In Number Fifteen company!

The happy games of childhood, how blithe they were, how sweet. But when we played at soldiers, my heart with pride would beat! We're gonna beat them, gonna defeat them, we've got the time, we've got the cash, we're the stronger, it's fine by us if it takes a bit longer! Stand fast, hooray, we'll not give way, bye-bye my sweet, we've an army to beat! Waldemar, Waldemar, my lovely Waldemar, it's lovely where we are, here in Galicia, Waldemar, Waldemar, Waldemar, give me a kiss you'll never miss, here in the swamp, here in the swamp, here in the swamp, true love is a romp, is a romp! I think, I think I heard, up there's a silver bird, she's one of our own, I hope she's not shot down! Marianne, Marianne of France, I know you're not going to advance! The Russkies drank your gasoline, now you can't get on to Berlin! Will he, little Willy, will he, won't he, get some wool? Every soldier-boy wants wool, and when there's a will for wool there's a way! (Poincaré, points and squares of French toast, we eat it for breakfast!) From the hills to the sea sounds this chorus: We must be German, German, German, as were our fathers before us. But above all: God save the Emperor, *Deutschland, Deutschland über alles!* And: Firm stands and true, the watch on the Rhine! A cry rings out like thunder's peal, the crash of waves, the sword of steel! But already after a few weeks we got: The morning sky is red above the young men dead, in the Argonne, the woods so fair, many a soldier-boy lies there, and death is marching by my side. In that same parade-march the flower of the schools, after taking emergency school-certificate exams (which were so easy that absolutely no one came a cropper or lost a mark), were marched off to fall like heroes in Langemarck in Flanders, singing patriotic songs and behaving as splendid examples to be put into future secondary-school textbooks. There's no finer death in the whole wide world! And for which an eternally grateful Fatherland nailed the Iron Cross, second class, onto the simple wooden crosses over the heroes' graves. And then they sang: The boys will all march home, when peace returns once more, we'll sing the same old songs, and drink and dance till four! And then a bit softer and in a sadder voice (Käthe Erlholzen's big hit): Not all the boys will be home again, the ones we used to know, myrtle and white lilac, on their graves they grow! Like every war since the Redeemer was crucified, this one was also lost in the sign of the Cross: the Iron Cross (Special Class, only worn by the Kaiser, the Grand Cross for Hindenburg and Ludendorff, then First Class and Second Class, just like on the railway), the Red Cross, the Cross of St John, the Maltese Cross, blue cross, yellow cross and green cross gas. And out of this unholy chaos of cross-hatching the most German cross of all was to crystallize itself: the hooked cross, the swastika. In this sign shalt thou conquer!

Alas, alas, 'tis war again
O angel of the Lord defend me
In God's holy name.
'Tis war alas!
Do thou commend me,
That mine be not the blame!
(Matthias Claudius)

A kind of mass degeneracy – new to me – now took over: one for all and all for one! In bombastic nastiness, Germany now marched arm-in-arm with his despised fellow-citizen, Comrade Sansculotte, in the general direction of Hell. That idol of the bourgeoisie, Thomas Mann, wrote: 'Now, in the war, I have heard that blinded soldiers are the most cheerful of all the patients in the military hospitals. They fool around, they throw their glass eyes at each other. And it isn't some kind of hell-ridden desperation, just ordinary high spirits.'

In the weeks leading up to the war I had smiled smugly at the childish worries of the grown-ups. Having imbibed with my mother's milk such prejudices as morality, progress, civilization, I knew with a rock-hard certainty unshakable until the very last minute that war was an impossibility. Twenty-five years later, in August 1939, I thought just as wrongly, in Paris, that war would leave me in peace, and now, half a century later in New York I still can't come to terms with the idea that any minute now a few H-bombs could wipe out all life on earth. The child is father of the man! I saw the war as a piece of tastelessness, as a conspiracy between resolute majorities of grown-up idiots against me – the representative of all the world's youth. I believed in the power of the slogan. It would have been beneath my dignity actually to raise a finger to do anything. Convinced that the youth of that precise moment would seize the reins, my money was on a worldwide spiritual revolution by the eminently comfortable means of passive resistance. Class warfare meant, as far as I was concerned, a snowball fight between the first form and the second form, a battle between dummies with – hopefully – the slightly less dumb winning. It was a good idea to stay out of it. For me, there were no such things as social conflicts. I had been muzzled too early and suffered injustice without so much as a bark, and anyway, I wasn't a dog. I would never have admitted to membership of the middle classes, and classified myself as belonging to an intellectual aristocracy. After the First World War I demanded in a manifesto that all those responsible for the war – everyone over forty, that is – should be shot at dawn. That manifesto ended up, like ninety per cent of my collected writings, in the wastepaper basket. And nowadays the one-time passive revolutionary himself wanders the world as a somewhat sheepish over-forty; and he hasn't been shot at dawn either.

At that time every German mother was all too ready to sacrifice all that was dearest to her on the altars of the fatherland: her golden wedding ring, her long blond tresses, her sons. In those great days of Our Country's Need, my own mother, already sorely tried, poor and consumptive, had no desire to leave her offspring to their own devices. In mortal danger and with all her worldy goods as hand-luggage she took the very last slow train, jam-packed with people, from Davos to Berlin. She arrived breathless at three in the morning, full of the most sensational eye-witness reports, and was most hurt that we hadn't met her at the station. While it was rattling through Southern Germany, she claimed, her train had – in contravention of all the rules of international law – been attacked by planes firing aluminium javelins. There had even been a bomb dropped on it – mercifully a dud. These *canards* were printed in every newspaper. Mama was also extremely cross that we had failed to lay in a supply of eggs; hoarding was the order of the day!

And all came to pass even as the prophet Otto Moses had foretold. After a brief transitional period, business was soon booming. In no time all the whores were running around in widow's weeds. My position went up a notch with every victory. Every battle was won, until after four years the war itself was lost and we, the unconquerable and unconquered heroes (those of us that were still alive), beat a retreat back across the Rhine and hobbled into our played-out homeland so that we could prepare to fight the next war for a republic that nobody believed in.

In that seductively beautiful autumn the melancholy scent of asters pervaded all of Berlin. Or were they autumn crocuses (things I had only heard of in poems)? In fact it was the new stink of benzol (ersatz petrol). I penned sad, bad poems about that autumn of my life and sent them to the magazine *Die weissen Blätter*. They weren't even returned. Another poetic creation of mine was more successful. Really as a joke, I had designed for Moses & Schlochauer a blouse in crepe (4848), battledress-grey, simple in cut and completely tasteless; it had an officer's collar, a recruit's piping, a general's epaulettes, a guardsman's lanyard, a discreet patterning based on the Iron Cross, and genuine military buttons. In a month we had sold four thousand of these battledress blouses. As a result, after the second battle of Ypres (when they introduced gas attacks) in June 1915, my salary was again paid in full, only from now on in paper money. I gave gold for our iron cause! The Iron Hindenburg was well-nailed. One morning Herr Otto Moses (Thirteen) appeared in the SPLENDID! in the LATEST! in the GREYEST OF FIELD-GREY! the new, beautiful, impeccably tailored made-to-measure service uniform of a deputy paymaster-sergeant in the supplementary battalion of the Army Service Corps. A week later Herr Schlochauer appeared, a mere half-rank lower, as an ordinary sergeant in the same division. Soon, both Thirteen and Seventeen wore with quiet pride the ribbon of the Iron Cross in their buttonholes. The motto of the Army Service Corps is, after all: Grease my Palm with Silver. The third accountant, Herr Laurinat, who had fiddled all this, still drew his full salary even after he had been called up, with a special bonus of thirteen per cent. Herr Moses was of the opinion that any more than that might have been interpreted as a bribe.

Soon Herr Wolfsberg and I were the last men at Moses & Schlochauer. While I was busy putting on nearly four ounces in weight and growing an eighth of an inch, Supreme Command obligingly lowered their minimum height requirements by a full two inches. Even dwarfs were called up, to serve as sappers. If things went on that way I could soon be passing my entrance exams for the mass grave with flying colours. And so I had to think up a few ways and means of undermining my health. 'Lie back and think of Germany, girls, the Kaiser needs more soldiers!' Maybe I could give myself a dicky heart by pursuing a programme of unbridled lust! I decided to debauch the nights away, to go down and join Orpheus in the Infernal Regions (the Orpheum was a dance-hall). I became a roué, dissipated my way through the black-out, frequented dubious nightclubs and clip-joints, went to dodgy shows from the Metropole to the Winter Gardens to the Follies. I went to the Amor dance-halls, the Stettin Singers, low-grade hops, all mostly on my own, a melancholy and bored shop-boy. I despised all the charm that I was exposing myself to: Fritzi Massary, Claire Waldoff, Joseph Giampietro, Tielscher, Bender, Curt and Ilse Bois, the child prodigies. I puffed at Brazilian cigars, drank black ersatz coffee – while it lasted, they were already sweetening it with saccharine – and I got experimentally drunk at Kantorowitz's on a range of exotic-sounding drinks; I went through the entire alphabet from absinthe, arrak, armagnac and anisette all the way down to amontillado. I felt sick even before I had my second glass. If one of the hostesses came near me I shook like a leaf; if she actually went so far as to fulfil my unspoken desires and spoke to me, I sank terrified into the earth. Would it not be more practical, after all, to fall like a hero on the field of matrimony, and thus avoid all danger of catching something? Marriage was the escape route, more specifically, a marriage of two minds. I was serious about this. My bosom pal Ravel shook his wise old head disapprovingly when I outlined to him my intentions, and gave me his hand in a mock-melancholic manner: 'He lived, he took himself a wife, and then he died. Say farewell to fame and immortality!'

You need cash for debauchery just as much as for waging wars. Money, money and more money. The Fatherland, sinking further and further into the mire, was taking everyone and everything down with it. I managed, somewhat oddly, to scrape a positively princely existence on my salary: you could still get ersatz breadrolls for nothing at Aschinger's if you bought a five-pfennig cup of acorn coffee. Conscientiously I gave my mother twenty marks a month for board and lodging. She thoroughly enjoyed bringing me up to be the breadwinner. For her, this meant making me petty-minded. Look after the millions and the billions will look after themselves. Earning money was demeaning. Earning money on the side was an insult. Being convinced that all trade was grubby, I promptly engaged in various grubby ventures without a qualm, supplied my aunts and their friends with blouses at less than the wholesale prices, reckoned up all the accessories at less than cost, and erred so much on the side of generosity to myself that I paid virtually nothing. The receipts were tiny, the deceits were enormous. I stole with self-contempt and contempt of the dangers. A thankless business. Thank God it was never discovered. If it had been, I would have had to do away with myself. My fellow apprentice, Brasch, had had a rather fine black dress in velours chiffon made up for his 'sweetie pie', inspired by Asta Nielsen and designed by us all. When it came out that he had put the ten yards of velours chiffon onto his own account at half cost-price, he got his cards. (His father, a buyer for the big department-store Wertheim had been patronizing Fischbein & Mendel for the past season instead of Moses & Schlochauer.) After that, Brasch was dressed up as a volunteer Uhlan and, looking dead smart and heroic, he was sent smartly out to a heroic death. I saw him one last time in the lovers' lane by the KDW store in the Tauentzienstrasse, arm in arm with Brunhilde Krause, who was wearing the velours chiffon number. From her black velvet hat, the size of a mill-wheel, drooped a melancholy ostrich-feather *pleureuse*. As soon as he saw me, Brasch took the monocle from his eye like a good lieutenant and looked the other way. Oh, but that one could die for Brunhilde!

Just after war broke out, Ravel was snatched away from me by his parents and sent to Holland. They really had worked things out in advance! The Dutch remained benevolently neutral, stood high above all the warring parties, and were indeed higher beings, their favours were sought by everyone, they were privileged, always knew better, and in consequence made a great deal of money: first on foreign exchange deals, then on foreign exchange deals de luxe. They had plenty to eat and impressed everyone. The word 'inflation' came along and inflation came to stay. I gathered that rats leave a sinking ship, and regretted that I was unable to join the rat-race. All alone in the still watches of the night I had to stay with mother in the Fatherland, as the law decreed. *Dum sanctis patriae legibus obsequimur*. I had grasped the deep significance of the passport.

39 LEENTJE

My fate was sealed on 26 June 1915, on the dullest, the warmest and also the most twentieth birthday of my favourite sister, Annie. It was on that despairing Saturday afternoon that the idea, which hadn't been too far from my mind, came to me to write a clever letter to the three little cousins that Ravel had described so enticingly from Amsterdam. Ravel belonged to that special breed of people who always meet special people, especially special female cousins. He was a cousin-fetishist. His stay in Amsterdam allowed for a practical exploitation of the Moses and Schlochauer postal arrangements, which became my ally in this hunt for happiness. Strict wartime censorship permitted only a one-page letter per envelope, and cut mercilessly anything that didn't suit it.

After countless closely-scribbled registered special deliveries, it was now the turn of the cousins. With black humour I requested that kindred spirits might give me solace in solitude. In those days a one-page letter flowed as easily from my pen as a many-sided page of writing is arduous for me nowadays. I considered myself the Don Juan of letter-writing. The younger sisters answered in a would-be witty way. The Dutch have a sense of humour that, to the uninitiated, is difficult to appreciate. Lena, the oldest of the cousins, with the melodious nickname Leentje, took me in the tragi-serious way I had dreamt of so longingly for my entire life. Nearly nineteen, and therefore two months more experienced than I was (something I have never been able to catch up with), she accepted me, the nail-biter, as man, as hero, as immortal lover. After three months of superheated correspondence, that was it for us! We signed off every letter with 'together for all eternity!' Suddenly her father died of septicaemia, and this reminded us of our own brief mortality. We drew the logical conclusions, and decided on marriage, without ever having met face to face. In our nineteen-year-old omniscience we decided, we ignorant romantics, to go through life hand in hand and soul to soul, unto the very end of the world, a point which now, half a century later, we have nearly reached as incorrigibly smart-ass grandparents. Tearful as ever, Leentje takes me, the world and herself just as ludicrously seriously as in that first letter. I object to her tears just as much as I did all those years ago. It's a wonder that it has worked so well.

Since future defenders of the Fatherland were no longer allowed to leave the country, she came to Berlin in May, against the will of her family, in the lovely Whitsuntide of 1916. I went to meet her in Hanover. After a microsecond of strangeness, the scrawny Napoleon of Crêpe-de-Chine embraced, there in the express train, his little, cuddly, bright-blue-eyed, owlish, golden-curled St Helena. After two blissful weeks she had to return to Holland: visa expired. My jealous mother gave her this as a parting gift: 'I hope that Erwin never ever gives you any reason to be jealous. Guard a fellow zealously or he'll make your life hell with jealousy.' The curse struck home: I ended up with a jealous wife.

40 A HERO'S LIFE

Soon I was to breathe my last as a civilian. In August I was still on the road as a travelling salesman, sent off to do the rounds in Magdeburg, Dessau, Brunswick and Halberstadt with a collection of mourning clothes: mourning dresses, mourning blouses and mourning peignoirs all packed up in seven suitcases, with two girls to model them all, and also Robert, one of the servants. My sales figures were great, and my experiences in a medieval alley full of brothels were also to my advantage. On 13 October 1916 the latest conscription board pronounced me fit for active service, and since I knew nothing about cars, I was assigned to be a truck driver. *Canis a non canendo* – 'if it barks like a dog, it must be a cat.' And so, in bitchy-cold November weather, I swapped the embattled gloom of home for the gloomy battlefield by way of the battledress-coloured gloom of a basic training hell in Zwickau in Saxony. Our battalion of recruits was quartered in a dancehall called 'Paradise', and that unheated paradise was worse than any hell. Away on the horizon you could already feel the first thunderous rumblings of the boundless German talent for concentration camps. In those days, parade-ground sadism gorged itself on us, the recruits. It is firmly rooted in the essence of human kindness to enjoy torturing the new boys.

'On yer feet and do yer beds!' (Your made-up bed was supposed to look like a child's coffin). In the bunk above me was a bloke who used to wet the bed, and every night there was that drip, dripping surely and slowly as in a limestone cave. At four in the morning the platoon-leader drove us with his rabid barking – 'Hands off cocks on with socks!' – out into the frosty winter's night to the washtub (for mess gear) down at the frozen pond (hack a hole in the ice), and with a pumice stone instead of soap. A hand-out of (ersatz) coffee, hours and hours of atten-SHUN! (livened up with knees-bend sessions) outside Paradise in the snow when it was forty below in the shade. Up! Down! Hit the ground! Up! Hands to your sides, eyes forward, chin down, chest out, belly in! Discipline! Orders is orders! When everything was frozen solid, out came the staff-bastard, Sergeant Peters, from the orderly-room and belched 'Flttt' (Fall out!), and we were off like greased lightning, and then came another 'SHUNNNN' and then pay-parade (at frozen rates of three marks thirty-three for ten days), and after that came 'any complaints'. 'Any complaints about the money, the bread, the food or any other relevant matter, fall out and report them now!' Icy silence. Never in the history of the German army has anyone ever come forward. 'Since no soldier has any complaints, this pay parade is over!'

Then he shouted to duty-corporal Brandy (known as 'shot-of-Brandy' because he once shot a recruit dead by mistake): 'Get the bastards to laugh', which, translated from bloody nonsense into a command, became: 'On the command two I want hay suckSINKT and hay milit-hary laugh: one, TWO', at which we all had to bray an abrupt 'Haha!' followed by deadly silence. Then the sarge gave a friendly snarl of: 'Polish their balls till their arses glow!' In other words, latrine duty, scrubbing the shithouse with a toothbrush! And in the afternoon, eighteen voices had to be raised in song to the sergeant about the love of his life:

Gold and silver, I love thee
Money, that's the stuff!

I wish I had an ocean-full,
That might be enough!

This was a friendly invitation to the better-off driver-recruits to grease the palm of the man who had the power of life or death over them. Singing another song – 'In the lo-o-ovely town of Zwickau, there lived a soldier-bo-o-oy' – at-the-double-quick-march shoulder-arms fast-as-you-like over to the other side of the town to the Rising Sun, another recruit depot. Junior MOs pumped shots of hold-steady-now benzol into your chest, to swell the courage of the German he-man: and all this turned pimply wimps into German Heroes ready for the front line. The oath of allegiance, administered in a snowstorm. The horribly itchy feeling of my new all-over sixteenth-of-an-inch haircut. Sentry duty at night! Rags wrapped round sore and sweaty feet run ragged and stuffed into rock-hard army knee-boots that had layers of filth on them dating from the Napoleonic wars (1813–1815). No deity could have cleansed their soles, but we had to. (For worker bees, work is work.) Grub: ersatz whalemeat paste in a cod-liver-oil vinaigrette with dried veg, and to follow, a good helping of the shits in horror latrines. Off duty, beer-swilling until the last post, buying drinks for the NCOs, chainsmoking to the point of zero visibility, pinching the barmaids' bottoms, being big men, pouring twenty glasses of rye down the old neck, puking as a company: what a bestial pack of shitheads! I came to hate the whole shitheap of them: shits to a man! A whole load of shit! Who gives a shit: from the shit-shave-and-shower on a shitty morning out to do your shitty duty in shit-awful weather in a war that was complete shit, then shitty grub that you shit away ten minutes later in the shithouse: everything you do is shit, and then they shit on you! Before you know where you are, you're used to the shit: and after a week or so you are as happy as a pig in shit, joking about the sh-sh-sugar and singing along with the best of them: 'The flames are licking all around the old shithouse door, hip hip hip hooray, but we'll stand firm together as ever before, hip hip hip hooray, it's a lovely life to be a soldier!' With some surprise we realized that we had left our worries behind us back home, Mama's daily sermonizing, Thirteen's anger and Seventeen's fury. Soon you couldn't remember what it was that you had been so afraid of when you were still a civilian. Now the barracks were home and what you were afraid of was the front, as the list of those killed or wounded got longer and longer. The safest place was the clink; you were only really free and protected when you were in jail, but nobody really had the guts for that.

I rented a little room where I could go when I was off duty and write love letters to my fiancée in the dim and distant peace of Holland. I couldn't even complain, on account of the censorship. In the Audi works I became a motor mechanic. Sitting at the wheel of an open car from the driving school and roaring at a maximum speed of twelve miles an hour through the snowy Saxon scenery of the Erzgebirge set you up as a superman. You weren't some ordinary footslogger, some poor bloody infantryman, no indeed – you were a gentleman driver. We learned to get drunk, and to shirk our duty. The worst threat they offered us: being demoted to the infantry! In the little town there were the attractions of non-alcoholic cider-shops, really bordellemporia. They had still lifes in the windows, cider jugs bathed in red light, drawing the eye of the beholder to the promised delights of a sofa behind them. Inside waited a selection of weary whores: 'Oh aye, oh aye, us Saxons knows about 'ow to 'ave a good time.'

Christmas leave (in uniform) to Bonn, where I met my Leentje, chaperoned by her Mama, a friendly little widow of forty, at the house of her ancient and diminutive grandmama. You don't only marry your beloved, you get her family as well. A week of blessedly exciting peace, a Christmas concert in Gürzenich, near Cologne, a farewell steak at Klein's in Honnef on the Rhine, a donkey-ride up the Drachenfels hill, goodbye forever, and back to Zwick-ow!

Three months later, in March, 1917, I was sent to the front as an ambulance driver, with a Red Cross armband, something which had the distinct drawback that if you were taken prisoner you were immediately exchanged again. Before we left we were fitted up in Berlin with splendid black leather uniforms and glorious long leather coats. We were taken in spanking-new Mercedes ambulances which were loaded with us onto a goods train at the Anhalt Station. My brother Heinz saw me off; I never saw him again. I soon noticed that we were on our way to the western front. Four days later we arrived in Montcornet, twenty miles north of Laon, and before we left the station we had to pack our beautiful uniforms into the Mercedes ambulances, which rolled homewards so that they could inspire a fresh lot of troops to leave for the front with fresh courage. For us, a new life in lice-ridden, tattered battledress had begun.

41 JADIS ET LA GUERRE

We were loaded like human livestock into freight trucks and taken to ambulance Depot 7, just outside Notre Dame de Liesse. The first days at the front were as bad as the first days as recruits in Zwickau. However, by now we had learned to get used to the worst. Double rations of schnapps, and also of the notorious make-it-droop-soup (laced with bromide!), helped us get over our initial homesickness. Roll-calls had lost their terrors. We soldiers had but one enemy alone: Officers! (Starting with the archfiend – the staff officer!) You only saluted your immediate superior. No more responsibility, you were free, and quite justifiably shit-scared of the very peace we all desired so much. Everyone's favourite fantasy was home leave. I wept hot tears over the first louse that I wormed out of my armpit. But it wasn't long before we were laughing in the Lice-eum, the delousing unit, where you failed to get rid of the dear little pets. Even the lice had their own little Iron Crosses, black on a white background. The ordinary lice looked down with disdain on the crab-lice. 'Carnal prostitution smiles gently down upon the prostitution of the soul' (Veit Kunz in Wedekind's play *Franziska*). The first Frenchwoman I saw squatting down without embarrassment in my presence in a public urinal to have a pee made my flesh creep. *C'est la guerre.* The first child's corpse I had to pull out of a bombed building (in Chivy-les-Etouvelles) made me throw up. *C'est la guerre.* Soon, fears of having to die a hero's death were supplanted by fears of life after the war, of the wretched existence of the middle classes. Looking back, nobody has ever had it as good as when they were on active duty, that's why there will always be wars. *C'est la guerre.*

Under a blazing July sun the twin battles on the Aisne and the Aillette raged in fiery confusion with the twin battles around Chemin des Dames near Soissons. The historians had a hard job to sort them out later on. In my life there was nothing but twin battles. I woke up in the mornings and shouted out: 'Holy shit and thunderstorms! Blumenfeld's here, let twin battles commence! In case of rain, the war will be held in the village hall.' I had been assigned to a field hospital of the Seventh Army (the Saxons) that was operating feverishly out of Ardon-sous-Laon. Defying death itself, two field ambulances had to be taken up to the line, under drum-fire and constant barrage, protected by the Red Cross on their trip through the heaviest shelling and all the noise of the Last Judgment, right to the front line, from which point full many a worthy warrior embarked for Valhalla.

And we drove, drove, drove through days that were too bright and nights that were too dark (with dimmed headlights) though Chauny, Craonne, Craonelle, Chevrigny, Chavignon, Chivy-les-Etouvelles, Coucy-les-Eppes, Coucy-le-Château, Cerny, Pargny, Filain, Vauxaillon, Bourguignon, Berry-au-Bac (*malheur du cack*), Nouvion-le-Vineux, Laval, Urcel, Château Presles. And the courage I never had became so tired, and the longing so great. Taking no account of materials or personnel, as GHQ ordered, I fell in love with the unforgettable names of these French villages, dotted around the landscape. I did not read *Le Grand Meaulnes* until much later.

Our field ambulances were equipped with four narrow stretchers. When business was booming, at least two seriously wounded men were tied onto each one (they were too narrow even for one man). Going like the wind (at a maximum speed of twelve miles per hour) we hurtled with our whimpering cargo first of all back to our hospital at Ardon, for unloading, sorting and labelling. Usually four of the eight were dead on arrival. I became a Corpse-Carrier. On one of the first nights, driving with neither lights nor experience, I tipped over the old bus full of wounded when I was taking a sharp bend. The dying soldiers yelled out in the overturned ambulance. Exhausted, I lay down to have a sleep. Only one person came out of it alive – me! The gymnasium of the village school served as the main ward, and when we got there the junior MO, von Schulzenburg, decided on the spot who was to be thrown into the cellar under the gym, where the coal went rumbling down in peacetime. 'You can't please the living, but a dying man is eternally grateful,' he would say, with a knowing medical smile. Screams of despair from the underworld gave the lie to this statement, whilst those who remained upstairs were tortured with anti-tetanus shots.

When the field hospital at Ardon was too full I had to peddle the 'malingerers' (who were making rapid progress towards becoming corpses) around in the little backwater villages, until I finally managed to get rid of them in some hinterland hospital, well behind the lines. It was splendid, dawdling along through this lovely world, safely out of danger. First of all zig-zagging up the steep hill through the Middle Ages, from the Porte d'Ardon to Laon cathedral, majestically dominating the landscape. That cathedral was my heavenly mistress in the First World War, just as the basilica of St Mary Magdalene at Vézelay would be in the second. Against the background music of drum-fire and the death rattle, the oxen who poked their heads out from the topmost windows of the great tower won me over for high Gothic. While the human resources were being unloaded and unwrapped under the supervision of a nurse at one of the side doors, we, the gentlemen ambulance drivers, did not so much as lift a finger. Meanwhile the seductively pale twenty-year-old Soeur Bonaventura would slip me a hunk of bread with a double-thick spread of liverwurst. To show my gratitude I used to smuggle – and this was high treason! – harmless little notes and religious packets into occupied territory, to a priest at the church of St Géry near Valenciennes, where I was also blessed with bread and sausage. Secret love inflames the heart, the way to a man's heart is through his stomach, and Bonaventura and I became friends. When it was quiet I read with her, hidden behind the great organ in the cool cathedral; the only French book I was able to seduce, sorry, produce, was Stendhal's *Le Rouge et le noir*. Reading it was a sin for her, and while I was trying to convert her to atheism, she was trying to turn me into a Jesuit. Converting someone is a sublimated form of seduction. If we hadn't both been so shy and, what's more, both betrothed (in her case, indeed, to a young chap called Lord Jesus), and if she hadn't been pursuing higher aims which were unknown to me, then we would have sinned with pleasure. Instead, she expressed her love through bread and liverwurst alone: 'Je suis Chrétien, je mange du pain, de la saucisse, c'est du boudin!' And in the course of all this I learned French the way one should learn French: *pour l'amour de Dieu.* Whenever I went back to the front, she would sprinkle me with holy water. I paid her back with a tiny bottle of eau de cologne, and was proud when my little nun dabbed some perfume behind her ears.

The summer got hotter and hotter. Ardon's gravedigger had given up. There wasn't enough quicklime and carbolic acid. In spite of tighter martial law, it was impossible to force the civilian population to bury our dear departed, who, in their own way, were screaming out for their eternal rest: they stank. To the delight of the flies up above, their cries stank to high heaven. The stench of a hundred bloody corpses crammed together in a cellar is a wonder of nature, especially in summer. We kept our gasmasks on all the time. Seriously wounded men suffocated because of the stench. Even wearing masks, the doctors found it impossible to carry out operations. The twin battles raged and rolled and roared. Got to keep the crazy war going! *Ultima ratio regum! Ad maiorem Dei gloriam!* The situation began to stink so much that even Supreme Command threatened to stick its nose in. We heard that one of the highest-ranking medical officers was on his way: that caused a bit of a stink! In spite of the heat we all came out in a cold sweat. The garrison commander ordered the people of Ardon to pay the burial costs of the deceased heroes – amongst them several *poilus* – currently in their school. His order did not, however, get the corpses out of the cellar and into a mass grave.

Chief Medical Officer Rosencrans was neither a Jew nor a professional soldier but a thoroughly decent vet from Königsberg, Immanuel Kant's home-town, a lively poker-player (also Old Maid and Beggar-my-Neighbour). He found it impossible to be definite about anything. He never ever looked at anyone. He always looked away, even when operating. He found responsibility suffocating. More from necessity than inclination he used to allow his ambulance drivers, Kuhlmai and Blumenfeld, into the operating room.

My good friend and comrade Gus Kuhlmai, salt-of-the-earth-if-you-know-what-I-mean, was square, as wide as he was tall, five-by-five, the merry, merry month of Cool-May has arrived. Twice my age – an old man. Even in the hottest days of that twin-battle summer he always wore under his heavy leather jacket a woollen cardigan knitted by Grandma Ladislawa Kuhlmai, legendary city midwife and abortionist. He stank half of 'half-and-half', and three times as much of sweat. He never slept without snoring. A polyphonic contest between a love-crazed tomcat and a raging bull-elephant would start up and would drown out even the fiercest battle-thunder from the Chemin des Dames. Beneath a heart of gold and in the right place he bore with pride a chronic bubo. Moreover, above his Berlin trap, he sported a straight and unkempt moustache, half Hindenburg, half Ludendorff. Before the war he had worked by turns as a removal man in Rixdorf and as a pig slaughterer in Pankow. He was the only soldier without a copy of Kant in his knapsack. Actually I never met anyone with Kant. We drivers never even had a knapsack, and nobody did any reading. Kuhlmai's motto was: 'No one fucks me, I fuck 'em all!' What was mine was his. Without a word he took everything from me. With fewer words he would have killed anyone else who dared swipe even the tiniest thing from me. When it came to unobtrusively cutting the money-pouch from dying soldiers and then going through their pockets, he was your trustworthy German monster.

One night he claimed to have carried a grand piano unaided on his back. To please him, I pretended not to believe him, at which I had to bet him the two marks he had left me in my money-pouch, which he always used to check while I was asleep. Whenever he'd had a few, that is, invariably, he was a man who insisted upon his honour. At midnight I had to go with him in his bum-ravager (his ambulance), on the sly (without a permit), to Crécy-sur-Serre, where he had tracked down a concert grand. Instruments like this were of strategic importance, since our Lieutenant Kotschote had discovered that their lids were ideal for displaying large-scale maps. You got a double ration of schnapps for every grand piano lid. Gus dragged the frightened civilians out of their beds at two in the morning for a house search. After many protestations of innocence and sundry shoutings, an Érard concert grand hovered through the double door and then wobbled down the village street in the moonlight as far as the bridge over the river Serre. From underneath it came a buffo bass, based on the 'Deutschmeistermarsch':

A cow shits more than a nightingale
You can hear it when it hits the pail
But the bull shits most of all
On the floors and up the wall!

Gus ripped the lid off expertly and heaved the piano into the Serre, where its concert career ended with a resounding full chord.

Once, when Kuhlmai and Blumenfeld reported in full field marching gear of immaculate leathers, clutching their rifles, the MO was trimming his nails with a scalpel and forgot to tell us to stand at ease. Without moving as much as a single eyelash, Kuhlmai stood to attention for ten minutes stiff as a statue. I just couldn't keep a straight face. Dr Rosencrans was too agitated, and he overlooked my unmilitary behaviour. In his command-voice (commanding is an art, much like yodelling) he gave us a direct official order first to pack up all the corpses in the cellar individually and then to get them out unobtrusively. The village was apparently going to provide a transport-cart with two horses, a driver and an assistant, to take all these packages off to a mass grave. The Pioneer Corps would do the shovelling. Behind the MO stood his orderly, Private Schpuhntz, armed with a lifesize bag made of brown wrapping-paper, from the front of which a big black cross grinned at us. The doctor did not have a horse, but to look more military he always wore spurs and carried a riding-crop, with which he now beat one of the crosses, and said disparagingly: 'Of course, the Jewish bags with the Star of David are late again.' Then he told his orderly to demonstrate the corpse-bag. Schpuhntz laid the bag, which opened along the side, on the ground and then lay down full length next to it. On the command 'IN!' Schpuhntz rolled in the prescribed manner into the open bag. Rosencrans told me to shut up, and to tie the three bands attached to the side in neat bows, and not to knot them. In the end he got a bit less formal. 'When you've done all that you've got to get the corpse-packages out of the cellar and loaded onto the cart. Should be child's play for a couple of heroes like you two. And to sweeten the pill a bit' – he lowered his voice – 'here's the good news. I've fixed it so that the people of Ardon have to come up with three marks compensation for every deceased hero in their schoolhouse. For every corpse you bring up, you'll get fifty pfennigs. The rest will be divided between the officers and the Red Cross. Dupont, the village schoolmaster, is in charge of counting the bags as they are loaded. I'd advise you to round the figures up whenever they are checked. Everyone knows that French schoolmasters are too mean to count beyond three. We're not going to be screwed by any Froggie. All clear? Just in case there was anything you didn't quite understand, I'll run over it again: ONE: corpses into corpse-bags. TWO: Get 'em up here! THREE: Get 'em away. Fifty pfennigs a bag. OK?' You could hardly hold Gus back. Everyone knows that a soldier who is in defiance of a direct military order during enemy action can be shot without question. That's why officers carry a service revolver. And besides, the bonus of half a mark demonstrated yet again the essential humanity of the way the Germans were conducting the war. A grateful Kuhlmai shouted at the top of his voice: 'Orders are orders! Shake a leg! Up the Fatherland!' The MO shouted 'Shut your trap' back at him, and Kuhlmai matched this with a 'At once, Senior Medical Officer, sir!' Even I couldn't control myself any longer, and snorted out one of the official Short Military Laughs. Kuhlmai's diabolical little piggy eyes twinkled, full of promise. The doctor dismissed us with a salute. 'Tonight at ten!' We shouted out: 'Yessir, Senior Medical Officer sir!' did a super-smart about-face and marched off in an orderly column, rifles on our shoulders, back to our ambulances. Kuhlmai roared out 'Come to me, my sweet, at ten, you won't want to go home again ...'

Before we could sort how we were going to divide up (I didn't suspect how accurate that phrase would be) the task, I got an order to go immediately to pick up some heavy casualties at the frontline casualty clearing station at Filain (Coffin Lid C.C.S.). Gus gave me a few final instructions: 'Don't leave a single bloody Saxon soldier hanging on the wire, every corpse is worth money, and don't bring them back if they're still alive – they can wait'. An hour later my ambulance was staggering along between the shell-holes of the Chemin des Dames on the way to the Coffinlid – Casualty Clearing Station No. 209. I'd been given a triple schnapps-ration because I was going into heavy fire, but Gus had guzzled it down, so I was standing there stone-cold sober in the middle of one of the bloodiest battles in the history of the world. Alone. Everything was exploding. Anything that had life had crept back into the ripped belly of Mother Nature, now violated for all time. Andreas Gryphius's vision of Hell: *Pain and misery! Murder! Death! Terror! Fear! Cross! Agony! Worms! Pestilence! – Black pitch! Tortures! Hangman! Flame! Stench! Ghosts! Cold! Trembling!* Shell-hole after shell-hole. The sun's rays on a stark and empty moonscape. Little cloudlets nailed to the sky and motionless, little puffs of shrapnel, little angels of death. A hand dangled on a bomb-burst-burnt tree-stump. A horse, split in two, whinnied its death-throes a whole day long at the edge of the road. Some joker had put a signpost round its neck. I was afraid of the night to come – here I was a fatalist. When I got to the dugout by the clearing station I left my heavy steel helmet and my gasmask hanging by the driver's seat and climbed down into the deep crater. While my ambulance was being filled up as rapidly as possible I daringly stuck my head over the edge of the crater to see if I could attract some beloved French soldier, challenging fate to provide me with a slight wound. I didn't yet know that fate can't be seduced.

Back to Ardon with a full load: no room inside. Up to Laon, where I swapped my cargo for some bread and blood-sausage. After that, off into a cul-de-sac, completely done in. I lay down on one of the blood-dripping stretchers in my ambulance and slept until I woke up dead tired and wondering if it was dawn or dusk. How I should have liked just to turn over and go back to sleep, but the sun was drowning in the far west, and I didn't dare leave good old Gus in the lurch. I freewheeled sans gas, sans gears, sans brakes, down to Ardon and then through the ruins of the Soissons gate. A steep path, where I had, a month or two earlier, broken with the Germans for ever. Reaching up to the heavens, Laon cathedral dominates the eastern arc of a horseshoe hill which rises steeply out of the plain. Flat on the western side is the ugly citadel. From there the road snakes down past the old church of St Martin into the Ardon valley. When I arrived at the front in March 1917 the first Russians had just been taken prisoner in the west, to everyone's fury. Did the Cossacks have to come and louse up the west as well? A hundred Russkie POWs had been crammed together behind barbed wire, waiting to be taken away, in a quarry a couple of dozen yards below the inner curve of the horseshoe. During my Easter walk down from the citadel, I saw groups of valiant lancers – territorials – sitting picturesquely on the edge of the wall. With one hand they were stuffing slices of bread and ersatz butter into their traps, whilst with the other hand they were, with true German *Gemütlichkeit*, chucking Easter eggs down onto the defenceless prisoners until all you could see was tomato sauce with vodka – Bloody Mary! The great German nation, Shall be the world's salvation! How exactly did the boxes of ready-to-use egg-shaped grenades come to be on that wall? In place of the German heroes, of whose Heroic Deeds I had heard so many uplifting tales at school, I found nothing but sadistic cowards.

Gus – of whom I was justifiably afraid – was snorting with fury when I presented myself in Ardon, and shouted at me for having left him to do all the preparations on his own. Meanwhile he had himself brought in twelve of the dead men in two loads, and they were already parcelled up, all proper and in good order, and were waiting in the schoolyard. To punish me for turning up empty-handed he said he wouldn't give me a brass farthing of the money earned so far. Besides, since no one had known if I would come back alive or not, he had drawn my rations and wolfed them down. My canteen stood there on the table, empty, dirty and smelly. Gus enjoyed my annoyance and shouted out – ''e got me full attention when 'e took his fist and hit me in the eye'. Then he hissed: 'Sarge wants you in the orderly room, double-quick! He's sent for you three times already, even the corporal's been here! Blumenfeld's sitting on his arse again. You'll probably get demoted to the pioneer corps for bunking off the whole bloody day! You can bury the dead heroes for nothing! But if my corpse-money goes up the spout, then you'll find out what's bloody what! They've probably got a right royal bollocking ready for you!' The sarge was a boot-fetishist. I pounded along to the orderly room with my boots polished and prepared for the worst. Drivers can always find their excuses lying about on the road: my artificial-ersatz-rubber tyres had had punctures. And may the Lord help me, Amen!

Staff sergeant Kunz Kranz looked down at me with unwontedly generous irony from the steps of the orderly-room (formerly the Café de la Paix). He had a profound hatred of the following: life and death, superiors and inferiors (principally the latter), Christians and Jews (principally the latter), and he used to stare at everyone's boots because they were never well enough polished. He was the one who decided who was to be given immediate promotion to kingdom come. On this occasion things were surprisingly unmilitary. When he saw me he came forward to meet me. As soon as I slammed my heels together in the prescribed manner and said, 'Driver Blumenfeld reporting, sir!', he gave me a very casual sort of command. 'At bloody ease. Want to get the Iron Cross for bravery in the face of the enemy?' A bolt from the blue! To my shame I thought that the black and white ribbon that nearly every soldier sported jauntily in his buttonhole was a desirable fashion accessory. If you are going to despise a cross, you have to get one first. Speechless, I said: 'Yessir!' and at that point the unthinkable became reality. God's reprobate on earth tore his glance away from my boots and looked me in the eye (his were a venomous green) and then he lost control. It's devastating to watch a real martinet turn into a whining beggar before your very eyes. I saw his inner struggle, his inability to keep a firm grasp on his emotions. This was too strong for him, and he underwent the full metamorphosis. His hands were pressed stiffly to the seams of his trousers, chin down, chest out, belly in, a staff officer standing to attention for me! Had I perhaps been killed in one of the double-strength battles and was this already the World Turned Upside Down with altered priorities, life, afterlife, halfway-house, up and down and we, the poor in spirit, suddenly exalted? Easily moved, I told the sarge to stand at ease. While he wiped a tear from his cheek with his sleeve I caught myself examining his highly-polished boots. With a voice like a whiny child he explained: 'The fact is, it's like this. Next month I'm going on home leave to Frankfurt. But when I get there I'm taking the Customs Officer exam, and for that I've got to know French, and I mean fluently. If you can teach me in a month I'll get you the cross and the ribbon, never mind that it isn't your turn.' 'Yessir Sar'nt Kranz sir!' I said, and my military tone turned him back into a sergeant again. 'Tomorrow morning at eight sharp you can give me my first French lesson. Any French clod can manage to speak it, so why shouldn't I? So that you can be fresh and well prepared you'll be excused driving duties for the teaching period. Hand your vehicle over to Driver Heubert in an orderly fashion. Any questions? Anything not clear?' Since I'm never quite on the ball at the crucial moment, but only afterwards, I didn't dare ask him to let me off the corpse-bagging detail. I've never been able to manage more to a superior than, 'Yessir! Right away, sir!' I about-faced, but he called me back in a genial manner. 'Don't worry! I'm still letting you pick up your corpse-money tonight, you Berlin Jews are all from the Tribe of Grabbit, dyed-in-the-wool businessmen! Dismiss, you Godforsaken bloody corpse-shagger!'

Back through the last glow of the summer night to Kuhlmai. The moon hadn't risen yet. In the sky across the Chemin des Dames there was a fireworks display of Magnesia-Super-Flashes. I could have found my way back with my eyes shut just following the stench of the corpses. In front of our door Kuhlmai gave off a blue aura. He had put on one of the asbestos uniforms they use against flame-throwers, and was carrying a shaded acetylene lamp: like a lemur, a spook, gibbering and twitching to get on with it all. 'We've been waiting for you, now let's get going! There's money in this! Get the old asbestos on, it's highly contagious, being dead!' Full of glee he pulled on his gas-mask and vanished. The haycart was waiting in the schoolyard with two horses, and Pascal, the hunchbacked village idiot, as the coachman. At a little desk by the school gate sat the teacher, Dupont, who was supposed to count the corpses, with a bottle in front of him. Beside the cellar entrance there was a gigantic crate with the top ripped off and the brown-paper corpse-bags falling out. Up from the cellar came the shimmering light of Gus's lamp. A rattle of drum-fire provided an accompaniment for the *danse macabre*. I pulled on my gas-mask hard, and climbed bravely down the twenty-two steps into the Underworld where three ready-filled bags were waiting impatiently for me by the bottom step. *C'est le premier papa qui coûte* – It's the first one that counts. (A good motto for the bloody-minded, and this was bloody as hell.) I tried honestly to get my first corpse up the stairs. The dead are a wilful lot, they refuse to pull their weight. Just breathing is hard with a gas-mask on, working even harder. I felt queasy, but under no circumstances did I want to look like a softy. A man of twenty has to be ready to cope with life and with death. Halfway up it got easier. Gus was pushing from below. We brought the rest of the bags up together, or in other words, Gus did it all. The first cartload of fifteen went off, leaving us alone in the schoolyard. Kuhlmai took a good long swig from his flask and started to nag at me: 'That's you all over, thought as much! But I'm so bloody sharp I could cut meself. A pleasure shared is a pleasure doubled!' He filled a sack with tools and staggered back down into the Infernal Regions. I foresaw calamity. I waited up above until the wagon with the tipsy village idiot – who was singing Lully's 'Au clair de la lune' – came back empty. Having a break had given me new energy, and the next bag seemed lighter; I brought it up over my shoulders on my own, and chucked it onto the cart with some vigour. The teacher counted conscientiously, fortifying himself at regular intervals. It wasn't until I went back down into the cellar that I found out what had made me so much stronger: in the blue light of his acetylene torch a blood-bespattered Gus was furiously chopping a corpse in half over a tree-stump, using a massive butcher's cleaver. With professional skill he carved the roast with a long knife, helping out when necessary with a hacksaw. Gus would have been delighted to hack me to pieces as well. A prophetically diabolical imbrueghelio: here Germany's future and my fate were being hacked to bits. Twenty-five years later and the world would be standing by watching, just as I was now, as millions of German Gusses butchered millions of people to keep the race of these stupid Gusses pure. Kuhlmai had hacked Germany, had hacked the world out of my life! As the next wagonload of twenty-five bags left the schoolyard, Gus came up for a breath of air and to get one down. ''Cos you're such a bloody nancy that you can't even lift a whole corpse, I reckoned I'd better mix business with pleasure and double our turnover! No sooner said than done!' And fortified, he rushed back to his labours in the shady Kingdom.

When, several hours later, the magical silhouette of Laon cathedral became visible against the morning sky, the cellar was empty as per orders and

179

disinfected with carbolic. The last bag contained (and was reckoned in as the last corpse) Kuhlmai's bloodied asbestos uniform. Flabbergasted, the village teacher made it 168 corpses. He'd been told there were under a hundred. Kuhlmai made it clear to me that I'd only get twenty marks. I never did see a brass farthing of that hard-earned blood-money: a grudging Fate decreed that I wasn't to have it.

42   LA PETITE VILLE DE VERRIÈRES

Dead tired, I reported to the sarge next morning on the dot of eight, and like a dutiful pupil he stood up when I entered the room. I came with the noble intent of putting into operation a modern language-teaching method of my own devising. To get me into a proper mood, the sarge produced a bottle of Courvoisier. We took turns swigging out of the bottle: there's a war on! (There's this girl who's just been raped by the Cossacks and she begs them to spare her old mother, but Mama comes out and says: 'What do you mean, spare her old mother! Don't you know there's a war on?') With some ceremony I laid the book on the table and said casually, 'Le guéridon de Madame Dubois est d'une élégance romantique.' The sarge stared helplessy at me, at the table, at the book. It was my copy of *Le Rouge et le noir*, of course. I pointed to the red bits of the cover and said 'rouge', then at the black and said 'noir'. He giggled and refused to repeat the words after me. 'Pourquoi?' I asked. He wanted to know what 'pourquoi' meant, and I said 'why'. 'Because I want to know', he said, crossly. Then he wanted to know why the book was called that. 'It's the binding – it was bound to be called that,' I said. He was a bit doubtful. He also found it weird that the author had the same name as a railway junction in Saxony. He knew a lot about railways. And that is how the French lessons started. He found everything completely and unbelievably nutty. I asked him to bear with me: you could make amazing progress in a foreign language if you applied yourself with an iron will to getting your tongue and ear used to it. In his case the easiest way would be to learn *Le Rouge et le noir* by heart. I opened up the magic volume: 'La petite ville de Verrières peut passer pour l'une des plus jolies de la Franche-Comté.' I translated it, and he asked with considerable intelligence what that had to do with scarlet and black. I said that would be a surprise at the end. He gave me a direct military order to tell him right now. I told him about symbols, but that only annoyed him. Humbly, and in all the different voices you would use for seduction, I read the first sentence over and over again until we were both so drunk that his servant had to drive me back to my quarters.

For the next few days I read that first sentence continuously. Suddenly and to my great pride and in an unmistakable Berlin accent, the sergeant began to venture a few French words. A major victory, to which we drank. When he was nearly able to repeat the sentence by heart, I made a fundamental error. I went on to the second sentence: 'Ses maisons blanches, avec leurs toits pointus des tuiles rouges, s'étendent sur la pente d'une colline, dont des tuffes des vigoureux châtaigniers marquent les moindres sinuosités'. Good old Stendhal! He ordered me to read the sentence again and again. On my final *sinuosité* he leapt up, had an hysterical screaming fit, accused me of sabotage, threatened me with a court martial and tried to brain me with the cognac bottle. He hurled the bottle through the window-pane and roared: 'Ten-SHUN! You traitor!' I stood to attention. 'Unfortunately your Iron Cross Second Class has already gone through, but I'm not going to be dragged through the shit by a Frenchman called Stendhal or a Jew called Blumenfeld. There's no room for malingerers like you in my unit, unnerstand? I'm transferring youse, I mean you, to the Rebekka West [the Reserve Eisenbahn Bau Kompanie West] where they're looking for a book-keeper. Early tomorrow morning after roll-call you'll be transported. Dismissed!' When I tried to object that I couldn't keep books, he foamed: 'You can't keep books? You can shut your trap! Or do you want me to have you going backwards and forwards day and night to the Chemin des Dames until I see you on the list of casualties? Now bloody fall out or you'll end up in one of the mass graves!'

At the morning roll-call the smart Iron Cross was nailed onto my heroic little chest. And because it was the birthday of King Gussie of the Saxons, I got the Saxon Medal for Valour as a bonus. On the other hand, the home leave I had been promised was withdrawn and given to someone else. Without deigning as much as to glance in my direction the sarge roared out in front of the whole company: 'Driver Blumenfeld, you reckon you're eddicated? Didicated? Educatered, that's what you are! Listen to this, you lot: *La petite ville de Verrières peut passer pour l'une des plus jolies de la Franche-Comté!* Eyes forrard! Atease! Three cheers for His Majesty the Kaiser, hip hip hooray! Dismiss!'

43 LUCILLE

I rushed back to my quarters in the house of the 'Garde champêtre', next door to the school, to get my bits and pieces together and say goodbye to Lucille, the lovely daughter of the household. Mademoiselle Lucille Féval, with her little nostrils that flared so nicely, her cheeky freckles and eyes full of curiosity, was three years older than I was, and if such a thing were possible, almost as bashful. She was primary school teacher, and could boast an uncle, Paul Féval, who had written the popular novel *Le Bossu*. I was flattered at how friendly the Févals seemed to be towards me, one of the enemy. Once they even invited me to supper, and I took an army-issue loaf of bread with me. Fraternization was strictly forbidden. Double-battles permitting, Lucille gave me French lessons in the little garden behind the house. We read Molière's *Les Femmes savantes*. I got my mother to send me a pair of black silk stockings for her in one of the parcels-for-the-troops. I made her a present of this rare treasure now that I was leaving. Instead of giving me the kiss I had hoped for, she giggled in a virginal manner and promised never to forget the stockings. She kept her word. Forty-seven years later, in 1964, on a wet Easter Sunday, our youngest son, Yorick, was driving us from Paris to the Laon area. You could still see in that pastoral scenery what it had been through; what's more, the landscape had been raped yet again in the Second World War. Back in my first World War I had had to pay such close attention to it that I was proud of being able to find, after forty-seven years, every path and byway of the Chemin des Dames again. The black silk stockings – now long since in shreds – came into my mind, and I told the story of Lucille, who by now must be seventy. Sons are always suspicious of their fathers' youthful experiences, and the very existence of Lucille was doubted. In a fit of enthusiasm we set off *à la recherche du temps perdu* to look for Lucille, in our excitement failing to take into account that she might have changed her name by marriage. The house next door to the school in Ardon was soon found. Some people had been living there for twenty-five years without ever having heard of the Févals. The postman, who happened to be cycling past, sent us off to a little house out in the fields. It was locked. We asked some farm-workers but they didn't answer. After an hour we had had enough of the hunt, but my son, who is a journalist, was beginning to relish the idea of proving to his father that he hadn't fought in the First World War at all. Around midday we found out in the bistro that on

Sundays Mademoiselle Féval dined at the Sestacs'. We crossed a courtyard surrounded by railings, knocked on a door and burst in on a French family contentedly sipping their pinard. A youngish couple, two children and a soldier were seated at a round table, the crowning glory of which was a fragrant *canard à l'orange*. In the place of honour, just behind the duck, was a young-looking old lady with little nostrils that flared nicely, cheeky freckles and eyes full of curiosity: Lucille Féval. After half a century she failed to recognize me as I would have failed to recognize her. I went up to her and said: 'Lucille!' The others stood up, shaking their heads. I introduced myself: '1917 ... première guerre ... chauffeur d'ambulance ... Boche ... Blumenfeld ... Berlin'. With old-maidenly modesty she lowered her eyes. 'Les bas noirs!' And then she bestowed on me the accolade that I had not received in the First World War. She confessed that only a few days before she had been talking – à propos of a new set of dentures – to her friend Yvonne about the little driver who had dubbed her 'la déesse aux dents blanches'. We were close to tears. My son was delighted that he had helped make the mythical Lucille a reality. I was beginning to have my doubts.

44 FIELD BROTHEL NUMBER 209

With sealed marching orders I was dispatched in a car known as a 'Wandererpuppchen' (an ancestor of the Volkswagen beetle), off to Rebekka-West, the local HQ for Valenciennes, from which I was sent on without a moment's hesitation to number 17, rue des Juifs. A knocked-out little backstreet. Closed shutters; an open house; *maison close*; army knocking-shop 209. Outside the closed door there was queue of clapped-out infantrymen standing in a line, dirty, louse-ridden and diseased. (Once, at a short-arm inspection of the ambulance unit in Montcornet the order was given for anyone who had ever had the pox to step forward. I was too embarrassed to draw attention to myself, so I stepped forward with the rest. The unit therefore reported one hundred per cent syphilitic.)

I was expected. My predecessor had been sent home with a chronic dose of the clap. And now I was to serve the Fatherland as army-brothel book-keeper, for serve one must, right down to the last man. My place in the sun was behind a large, open account book at a narrow desk in the entrance-hall. I was pretty narrow myself. Besides me, there were eighteen ladies working in the house, six of them reserved for officers, from warrant officer upwards. While the soldiers' girls had a minimum servicing quota set at thirty men per day, the daily turnover of the officers' ladies was only twenty-five. What's more, the officers had condom-privileges – these were much-sought-after rarities on account of the rubber shortage (and after use they were dried, blown up like balloons and hung on the washing-line so that they could be sold again as new). As one might imagine, the officers' ladies were proud of the fact that they had worked their way up by means of secret charms and secret arts. The industrious will inherit the demi-monde! They never tired of pointing this out to the others, and this led to unpleasant friction, biting, spitting, kicking, pulling of hair and triple twin-battles on this particular Chemin des Dames.

We didn't open for business until the pleasantly late hour of ten in the morning, and closed down at curfew. As an important front-line soldier miles behind the lines I got double combat rations here: double schnapps, ersatz honey and sausage. My work was simple, but, like everything else in this house, not fully satisfying. I was supposed to record in my running account ledger (which had 'May the Lord Be With Us' in decorative lettering on the front), after each numbered entry, the name and number of the girl, the room number, and the precise start and finish times. Next to that I had to note that I had received the unit price of four marks, then duly listed as divided on a debit and credit basis: one mark for the girl, one for the owner of the house, Madame Duval (*la taulière*), and the remaining two marks (noted in red ink!) for the Red Cross, which, for this payment, took upon itself the medico-moral responsibility for this particular military undertaking, to which end the fully qualified and state-approved pox-doctor, Junior Field-M.O. Hirschfeld, came in every morning and pinched the bottom of every girl. From time to time he also subjected the soldiers to a snappy short-arm inspection, in which he would willingly turn a blind eye. Every evening there was the cash equivalent of more than five hundred payments from satisfied customers in my till. I had to give a thousand marks to Madame Duval for further distribution, and the rest was collected by three soldiers from the local HQ, who turned up with fixed bayonets. Just like the manager of a department store I felt better when we had a good turnover. Luckily there weren't any quiet days. I was pleased that the ladies respected me. The soldiers were nice to me as well, hoping that I might put a particularly fiery girl their way, which actually it wasn't in my power to do, since the girls worked in strict rotation. I did make a little on the side by playing the first ten bars of Beethoven's *Egmont* overture for the lovers-in-waiting on a broken-stringed piano, followed by Walter Kollo's 'Pauline's off to the Dance.' Later on I learnt '*Toutes les femmes de rue des Juifs sont des grandes cocottes*' ('All the women on rue des Juifs are tarts') and '*Astebelief Mynheer, drink nog een pintje beer and as te vorbijgehst, da kannste mal rinnkomme, astebelief Mynheer!*' ('Please sir, have another little pint of beer, and if you're passing, you can come in, please sir!') And after that there were a few coins on the plate that happened to be there with a few coins in it on top of the piano. It was like living in Paradise. I was even amused by the constant plottings of the perpetually overworked, steaming harem-houris.

The fundamental question of towels (drawing by the French cartoonist Forain: 'Encore une serviette, Madame, Monsieur reste la nuit!' – 'Another towel, Madame, Monsieur's staying the night!') was Madame Duval's business. She charged the girls ten centimes per towel, and this made them thrifty. The remaining hygienic arrangements in this model business were in the experienced hands of the seventy-seven-year-old Madame Duranruelle, who had probably been one of the ladies of the night in Maupassant's *Mademoiselle Fifi*, set during the Franco-Prussian War. Nowadays it was only at short notice in case a man really was desperate, and when the sick girls simply couldn't go on, that she lowered herself to take for one last and positively final time a personal part in the business of love. She had a tongue the size of a dishcloth. Most of the time she ruled, firmly and justly, over brushes, brooms and buckets. There was no running water in the rue des Juifs. Instead, the indispensable Pascal, the village idiot, went back and forth at irregular intervals between the brothel and the pump. On the pump there was sign saying: 'Eau non potable!' – Not Drinking Water! Every girl got fresh water after the fifth act, the officers' ladies after the third! Old Duranruelle would empty the buckets of dirty water after use – 'whoops-a-daisy' – between the legs of the soldiers who were waiting at the door, and they seemed to enjoy this little diversion. You mustn't forget that these men had been looking for months directly at the face of Death, but never at anything female. They just stood there vegetating, with the fathomless melancholy of beasts.

In order to increase turnover, our business-oriented military authorities had transformed the once capacious rooms of the brothel into little love-nests by means of wooden partitions. These were not a lot bigger, but very much dirtier than dog-kennels. 'For a happy, loving couple, e'en the smallest cottage will suffice!' quoted the local commander, a high-school teacher from Kötzschenbroda. On the iron bedstead there lay a narrow and damp mattress half-stuffed with even damper sea-grass, and no sheets. The water bucket stood on an ammo crate that had to do duty as a bedside table. On this flickered a candle, forever in its last stages. On the wall was a nail, for hanging up uniforms, a holy picture (the girl's patron saint), a dirty postcard, or both. Behind the metal number-plate on the door was a spy-hole, through which you could check that everything was going according to regulations. Through this hole I learned more about the ins and outs of life than were dreamt of in our school philosophy. Always the same awkwardness in a love-life that had nothing to do with love and nothing to do with life. By and large the ordinary soldiers behaved better than the officers, who swilled champagne and played at being *bon-vivants*, which sometimes led to indignities. Where the men wanted to be on their own with their lovers, the sophisticated officers were partial to group sex. In extreme cases I had to raise the Military Police by using a secret bell-push. Of course, the officers always got away with it. After fifteen minutes of purest happiness, an alarm clock would shrill, and there was forever a bell going off somewhere in the house. The cathedral bells chimed in harmony and counterpoint with the in-house whorology. The holy trinity of church, barracks and whorehouse form a wholly flexible triangle. You put me down blindfold in front of a cathedral and I'll find my way to the knocking-shop without any trouble at all.

One day a truck turned up full of drivers, all dead drunk, on the way to Brussels, where they were supposed to be putting my old friend Kuhlmai onto a hospital train. On account of his chronic bubo he was being sent home, and he wanted one last thoroughgoing fuck. Gus refused to recognize me, afraid I might ask for my corpse-money. The assorted ambulance men hurled themselves in the waiting room onto the seventy-seven year old scrubber Duranruelle, hoisted her up by the feet so that her head hung low, and poured beer right down her horrible legs and into her snatch! As they did so, they roared from German hearts filled with the intoxication of the spirit, to the tune of the Radetzky March:

Get it in, get it in, get it in the hole,
Get it in, get it in, you can watch it roll,
Get it in the hole!
Titty-bum-titty-bum-titty bum bum bum
Titty-bum-titty-bum-titty-bum bum bum
Titty-bum-bum-bum,
Ass-HOLE, Ass-HOLE
A soldier's life for me!

And then finished off with the nostalgic lines:

From the woods there comes the lovely song
Of the linnet and the dove,
And back home in my own country,
I'll hold you again, my love.

Gus and his mates were thrown out when they started to set fire to Field Brothel Number 209.

My heart was spinning merrily for pure joy in the first days at my new job when a little girl of five in a little tulle shift decorated with an excessive amount of satin ribbon (*ciel* 860 at Moses & Schlochauer) climbed onto my lap and hugged me. The little love-child whispered lovingly in my ear: 'Soyons copains, je sais, que vous avez lu *Le Rouge et le noir* avec la bonne soeur Bonventura, mon petit parfumeur!' ('Let's be friends – I know you've read *Le Rouge et le noir* with Sister Bonaventura, my little *parfumeur!*') Arabella, in fact a forty-year-old dwarf, wouldn't reveal where she got this piece of information. I became curious. Her art was to turn every hero into a child-molester. She smelt of lily-of-the-valley and sin, and was the main attraction of our establishment. Because of her tactical importance, she worked with the men in the morning and officers in the afternoon and at night. It was said that a full field marshal once arranged to come by special train from the Eastern Front to Valenciennes just for her, to give a lift to his lust for battle. In full senile satisfaction, back he went, and battles were duly lost. The Clown Prince himself is supposed to have performed right royally with her. Even professional paedophiles found her more attractive than genuine children. She lisped to me some magnificently indecent stories about St

Joan (as if she had actually been present!). That's how I learnt to speak whorehouse Latin. Gradually the veil was lifted from my eyes and I began to understand how she knew so much. Suddenly, there I was in the middle of a really exciting bit of world history that could have cost me my young life. But Arabella remained discreet.

This hard-boiled dwarf was as pious as only people in provincial France can be, forever hanging onto the coat-tails of her father confessor. Before starting work in the morning, she never missed mass at St Géry, where she would collect little glass phials from the abbé in the confessional. Innocent carrier pigeons were supposed to have brought them (was I one of those carrier pigeons?). She distributed these phials, filled with cultures of *spirochaeta pallida*, to the whores, which seemed superfluous, since every one was pretty thoroughly infected anyway. Still, she guaranteed that every visitor to Field Brothel No. 209 would, with a probability that bordered on certainty, be infected when he left. One morning, Arabella was arrested coming out of the church, and incriminating material was found on her. Someone had spilled the beans. The priest had vanished. The woman from Alsace, *la taulière*, was found strangled in her bed. Even Pascal, the village idiot, came under suspicion. Field Brothel No. 209 was closed down. There were official cross-examinations. A lot of people were held on remand. I swore under oath that I had never ever noticed a thing. Arabella kept her little pink baby-mouth shut right to the bitter end, for which I still remember her with love. On 12 October, 1917, the sweet child Arabella, having been violated one last time by the officers of the Court Martial, though without losing her innocence, was shot under military law by a German firing squad. In accord with her last wish she was dressed in her little tulle shift decorated with sky-blue ribbons. She refused to be blindfolded and shouted: 'Merde aux Boches! Vive la France!' and ended up riddled with bullets in a ditch by the walls of Valenciennes prison.

45   SOME BORDELLO-BALLADS FROM THE RUE DES JUIFS
Letter from a trooper to his faithful wife back home:

If I were a jolly farmer,
Of hens you'd have a flock,

But while I'm here I'll have to find
Someone else to tend my cock.

And the good lady's reply:

You're not a jolly farmer,
You're a serving man, my dear,
And you can serve wherever you like
'Cos I'm getting serviced here.

Malheur la guerre
No pomme de terre
C'est la misère
Partoot!
Papa l'Afrique
Mama ficky-fick
Ma soeur machine
Kapoot!
You just watch out
Si ton mari de retour!
You just watch out
Si ton mari de retour!

46 FLANDERS

I was transferred to Army Motorized Column 268 at Bazuel près Le Cateau, not far from Cambrai, where on arrival (it was the birthday of the Empress) I was awarded the Worst-ever-berg Service Cross with a red and blue ribbon. Soon after that the frost made life for our chain-driven trucks with metal-rimmed wheels quite impossible. Our war had frozen up. The couple of miles from Bazuel to Le Cateau, where our convoy was loaded onto a train, took us three full days (going a steady sixty yards per hour). From there, a jolly little train rocked us gently into hibernation on the way to Flanders. Wrapped up in horse-blankets and lying in my two-tonner, I dreamt until next morning when the train stopped and I woke under heavy snow. The wind had blown away the cover of my truck and I was snowed in. From the loading-ramp I looked down at Brueghel-splendid Bruges in the snow. At my feet in a small yard, little old ladies in black dresses, *Beghintjes*, Béguines, were getting ready to go to church. It appeared to be a Sunday. Every single carillon in the innumerable pointed steeples started to chime the first couple of bars of half-familiar chorales in a minor key, mingled with the great bells in the belfry. In the distant blue a peaceful plume of smoke rose into the winter sky from a thatched roof; we couldn't have been far from the Dutch border. My Leentje's birthday was in a few days, and I decided that I would desert in her honour: to my beloved, to peace. To my horror I discovered that I did not have the strength to burst the chains which bound me to my past. Besides, there was a mandatory death sentence for desertion. They hadn't taught us anything as basic as desertion when I was at school. It was reckoned to be immoral to save your life by running away from lunacy. Nobody ever wrote *Desertion – a Primer*, which a lot of people would have found very useful. Nobody in my unit ever thought of clearing off – they were all war profiteers, of which more later. It was up to me alone to tear myself away from Germany.

Our Motorized Unit was quartered at the Fire Station in Ghentpoort West, in the Minderbroederstraat. You got out of bed and slid like Charlie Chaplin down poles and into your truck. I fell in love with *Bruges-la-morte*, with its canals, fed the swans on the Minnewater, had a look at the brightly coloured Memlings in the Hospital of St Jean, tried to learn Flemish and dreamed of being in Holland. The unit, under Lieutenant Feldmann, a grocer from Boms, specialized in shady deals: highway robbery. As a new arrival I didn't belong to his band of robbers. During the day we took it easy. At night, quite a lot got done. Selected tough guys used to take heavily snow-chained trucks to railway depots where food-supply trains were expected. Wagons were broken into and a rich haul was brought back. Motorized Unit 268 never went hungry.

One day at around noon, when we were sitting on our beds eating smoked ham with scrambled eggs and fried potatoes, Lieutenant Feldmann came in, elegantly and enviably attired in brown leather, accompanied by Horst, his great Dane; he put guards on the doors and then he addressed us: 'Comrades! For some unknown reason an investigative committee is coming this afternoon. Remember: we know nothing about anything! We're off duty, none of our motors has ever made a trip that wasn't kosher, and anyway none of them is roadworthy. The three carpenters will rip up the floorboards. We'll put the snow-chains under the floor, and the hams we picked up yesterday. How many were there?' Private Marquard said there were four hundred and ten. 'You bloody crook, there were four hundred and sixty', joked the lieutenant. 'Right. We don't know anything about anything!' There was an enthusiastic roar of 'Yessir!' from all sides. The great Dane was snapping at me. 'You, new boy, you've been working in a brothel and that's a point in your favour! You'll get your share of the profits. Now all of you get on with it and keep your traps shut for God, the Kaiser and the Fatherland!' Ham after ham was loaded off the trucks and disappeared, wrapped in blankets, beneath our floorboards. Once everything was well nailed down, we slept the afternoon nap of the just. The committee never got as far as us; Feldmann reached an understanding with them. That same night, Marquard drove over to the Military Law HQ in Ghent with fifty top-quality hams. The rest trundled homeward to Boms two days later in trucks that were still awaiting repairs. I formed my own plan: I reported to Lieutenant Feldmann (the man with the sable collar) and asked for a permit to visit Westkapelle, just opposite Sluis in Holland, for a 'small cross-border transaction', in which I was hoping to secure access to a thousand salamis. Feldmann taught me a lesson: 'They don't make salami in Holland.' I explained that this was a supply of pre-war Italian sausage and that the preliminary negotiations wouldn't take more than a morning. Even though he didn't trust me, I got the papers. He was obsessive about food deals, and wanted to take sixty per cent of all goods at cost. He warned me not to get caught on the electrified fence, nor to come back without the salami.

Letters from soldiers in the field to foreign countries were strictly forbidden, so the lively correspondence between me and my fiancée in Holland had to pass through an elderly maiden lady in Cologne whom neither of us knew, whose name was Clementine, Clem for short, a monocle-wearing lesbian. She got her well-earned reward just from being able to participate in our epistolary love-games. By using a code I was able to tell my fiancée about my plans to desert, so that there was the romantic possibility that I might even make my getaway under the admiring gaze of her blue eyes. And what's more, on a Sunday, since I had found out that border security was less tight then.

After a sleepless night I made my way to the little local station at seven in the morning, an hour before the train was due. I had imagined a Deserters' Special, crammed with hundreds of others like me, who just wanted to get out. There was only one train on a Sunday, which consisted of a little toy engine which ran on peat, a single goods wagon, and one wooden fourth-class passenger carriage. A crazy bell kept on ringing incessantly. The station superintendent with his red cap was a young railway soldier and he wore an armband with the words 'Railway Police'. Acting as ticket inspector, he punched my ticket and asked me idly what I wanted to go to Westkapelle for on a Sunday. 'Visiting a pal. Private Josephs in the Engineers, 217 Battalion.' (I'd found out what troops were stationed in Westkapelle and was proud of my instant response.) Without listening to me he nodded and said 'Yes, I know him', and I knew he was lying. I sat down in the chilly carriage on its wooden bench (which was far too narrow), and waited. I remained alone. At eight o'clock the ticket-man-cum-railway policeman-cum-guard, now wearing a battledress grey cap, joined me in the train, blew his whistle out of the glassless window, and the little toytown choo-choo set off. He was about three years older than I was, and he sat down opposite and stared at me. His front teeth were completely crooked, which made him look devious and crafty. Not knowing how to handle things, I took a drink from my flask and wished him a cheery 'Good luck'. He drank my brandy and asked jokingly if I was planning to desert to join my girl in Holland. 'You can tell me – don't worry, I'm military police – Corporal Haase, Railway Division. If I had a wartime sweetheart in Holland – mine's bored silly in Magdeburg – I'd have been off ages ago to the land of fat cows.' As he said that he sketched a huge bosom in the air with both hands. 'It'd be dead easy for someone like me, someone who knows when the 18,000 volts are on in the high tension fence and when it is turned off. Take today, for example, Sunday – permanent current day and night, because the frontier guards are off at church. You'd be amazed, the whole damned lot are in church. Every night a couple of unlucky buggers with more bravery than brains end up hanging on the wire. ZZZZsssssh...! Flash-bang, and what's left goes up in smoke! Smart-arses, all of them. One'll take a cat with him, another one a ladder, someone else'll throw chains over, to try and short-circuit it. The police-dogs are worse, they come bounding up to you all friendly and lick your hand. And the minute you make a move towards the wire they jump onto you from behind and bite through your neck. Phenomenal bit of training, it's a tremendous act to watch, I've often seen it. If you make it alive into Holland the first thing they do is lock you into a starvation camp – they've got a funny word for it, 'concentration camp'. The war's coming to an end anyway, everyone's had enough. The Froggies are clamouring for a separate peace-deal, we'll soon be back home with mum. There aren't any smugglers here, the greedy farmers wouldn't part with a single measly sausage. The smuggling all goes through the black market centre in Sass van Gent. I don't need to tell you about lucrative deals, your unit isn't called the Champagne Column for nothing – a bunch of rich crooks! I haven't got any official duties in Westkapelle until this damned rattlebox gets up steam to go home at six o'clock this evening. We could go out on the booze with your pal Josephs from the Sappers, and I know a damned good whore...'

While I was wondering whether this dreadful oaf, who had just wrecked every one of my plans, was a dangerous informer or just a bore, he offered me his schnapps, I gave him some of my brandy and by the time the train stopped in Westkapelle our flasks were empty and we slithered not without some difficulty over the icy platform to the exit. There he put on his tin hat and, having become a border guard, stamped my papers. In front of me hovered a large sign saying: 'Warning! This is a frontier zone! Any military personnel caught leaving the station without frontier authorization papers duly stamped with today's date face a mandatory death sentence! Signed: Frontier Commander.' Underneath was an additional notice: 'Foot and mouth disease! Meningitis! Typhoid Fever! Signed: The Mayor.' The fact that it was bloody cold, and the realization that I wouldn't dare make that leap for freedom today, sobered me up. And so, as the sun came up, we stamped our way through the crisp, fairy-tale covering of snow in this Flemish border village whose loneliness bordered on infinity, across to the estaminet on the other side of the road. Over the entrance was sign which said 'De reyse en is nog niet gedaen al ziet men kerk en toren staen' ('You can see the spires and towers of home/ but your journey is not yet done'). In the pub it was at least moderately warm. Haase made himself at home, shouted out, 'Menheer, Mewrau!' and when no one appeared, he went to the bar and fetched out a bottle and two glasses himself. I had decided that I wouldn't drink any more, so I just pretended I was drinking. Haase drank away furiously until he had guzzled the whole bottle and explained to me that Flanders would become German once again, and that the Flemings were brother Teutons. With my assistance he was just about capable of fetching a couple more bottles. After half an hour he stood in the middle of the room, mumbled, 'God damn the filthy Walloons', thrashed wildly about, threw up, and fell over onto the sawdust-strewn floor into his own puke, where he started to snore. Not another sound. The big clock had stopped. I was so alone that I felt that my very presence was superfluous. Would his greatcoat with the police arm-band help me get across the border? I tried it on. Both it and the danger of wearing it were too great for me. I got back into my own heavy leather coat, lined with lambswool, put on my ear muffs, ate my ham sandwich and crept out through a creaking door into the excessively bright light of a wintery Flemish world. Only a mile or so away behind the sand-dunes was the glow of the North Sea, and in front of me empty, flat terrain. A little bell from Holland tempted me towards freedom in Sluis. The bell of Westkapelle answered it loud and clear. The border was just behind the village. Right across the street was another threatening sign: 'Warning! High tension! 18,000 Volts! Dangerous dogs! Minefields! Military personnel not in possession of frontier papers will be shot on sight! Signed: Frontier Commander, General v. Stülpnagel'. 'Knife-rest' barricades with barbed-wire entanglements barred the way in the deep snow. To the right and left were unmanned pillboxes, and not a soul to be seen. A new placard, which said 'Death Zone', persuaded me to stop, while on the other side of the road a signpost with a pointing finger tempted me towards Sluis (³/₄ mile). Thirty yards further on a railway crossing barrier in imperial German colours blocked off the world. And there was another warning: 'Halt! 20,000 Volts, High tension!' Behind that there seemed to be a variation on the same theme, repeated under Dutch colours (*oranje-blanje-bleu*) in reverse order. Barriers, pillboxes, notices, and then the road disappeared into a white infinity. A medieval sound of barking dogs finished me off. As a precaution I had brought a juicy bone with meat still on it from the kitchen in Bruges, only at this decisive moment I couldn't lay my hands on it. Even the hound of the Baskervilles that was supposed to tear me to bits failed to materialize. A negative day. I did an about-turn, a coward defeated by fate for whom everything had gone wrong. I was still to learn that cruel twists of fate are the norm. If I had marched straight ahead I would either have walked uninterrupted into peaceful Holland, or sizzled my way to eternity on the electrified fence. Since then I have become aware that much-advertised threats are worthless, but I can still never sum up the courage to cross death zones.

Two o'clock struck. Still four hours to go before the embarrassing return journey. And first of all I had to report back to Corporal Haase, who had presumably come round by now. Even there I was wrong. He was still dead drunk and snoring, just as I had left him three hours earlier. I threw a log onto the dying fire and sat down at the table, tired after my Sunday morning constitutional. When he woke up, Haase asked what time it was, and seemed amazed that I hadn't cleared off in his uniform overcoat. He claimed that he had seen everything. I told him that I hadn't found the good Josephs at his company because he'd gone home on leave, and I complained that I hadn't seen a single living soul anywhere in this whole godforsaken dump. He jumped up and said: 'So the Josephs business was all lies, then, I thought it was. If you never met a single soul you couldn't have found out that he was on leave. I could have you court-martialled! But you're a good chap and anyway your papers are in order. Back in Bruges you can get me some eggs and some bacon and I'll keep my trap shut. But we won't get fat on that out here, so lets go foraging! I usually get my *pot-o-fur* at this place – where are the buggers hiding? Every Sunday it's a religious feast here. The sappers only get dried-up vegetables, the frontier police have an expensive canteen, but it's shut on Sundays. I don't fancy sitting here with my stomach rumbling. How do you fancy the whorehouse? I'll treat you'. I had eaten my ham sandwich and I was afraid of this empty village, so I pretended to be worn out, rolled myself into my greatcoat on a bench and fell sound asleep, a sleep in which I lived through all the horrors of this deserted world once again in my dreams. I couldn't run away, and all around me lurked wide-open hidden mantraps, ready to set off new and bloodier battles. At the slightest movement, dull bells boomed. When the station bell started to ring, Haase turned up, and hustled me back on the train for the return journey. It was night. On the way back he revealed that the high tension fence had been turned off for two days for repairs to the dynamo.

When I reported back, devoid of both courage and salami, Lieutenant Feldmann had me demoted as militarily useless and unreliable from the luxurious fleshpots of his unit to the transport centre in Ghent. Via Clem, I sent a telegram to my fiancée saying: 'Have found can't come', which arrived on her birthday with a minor misprint which made it read: 'Have wound can't come.'

47 FORCED MARCH

The hell-hole of a base camp at Ghent was even more infernal than Zwickau, because since then we had had a taste of front-line freedom. We rotted in the unheated misery of the barracks. Roll-call lasted from dawn to the last post. Down on our knees in the snow for church parades. You found yourself longing for the front. In the middle of January 1918 I joined the starvation column, Motorized Unit 209, the 'rumbling-guts-brigade' at Marcoing-près-Cambrai. At the first thaw, steel chains were welded onto our iron-rimmed wheels and we were supposed to shunt munitions and cannon-fodder backwards and forwards along impossible roads, 'without regard for men or materials', for the final and definitive spring offensive. We were finished. You lived on rumours heard in the latrines: French offers of a separate peace, mutiny, the Pope. No grub. The ersatz petrol was so bad that you had to warm it up over an open flame in tin-cans and then squirt it into the fuel pipe next to the sparking-plugs to get the motor started. They hadn't got round to automatic starters yet: three men had to turn and swing the crank-handle underneath the radiator in desperation before the motor would at last fire, only to stop again immediately. Then you had to try again. For hours. If you got any kickback from the handle it would break your arm. Healthy exercize for a cold morning. 'My old man said "crank up the van".'

When, after a week of deathly silence, our artillery suddenly let off a ferocious round of drum-fire 'without regard for men or materials' and not a single enemy gun bothered to respond, I set fire to my truck when it was fully loaded with ammunition (the day's password was 'self-detonation'), and watched the fireworks from a dugout. Unfortunately, I immediately got another truck, whose driver had decided to die of dysentery. I was so clapped out that I drove my truck with forty clapped out representatives of the poor bloody infantry right into a shell hole – the world was one big shell hole at that stage – and fell asleep until a tractor dragged me out with my cargo, wedged together like sardines, standing up. Without joining battle we chased an enemy who had been withdrawing strategically for months until we lost contact with our HQ. Earlier on, during the trench-warfare stage, fighting had gone on for days on end to take a single yard of ground, while in the last three days we had stormed forwards unresisted for sixty miles 'without regard for men or materials'; we had conquered ourselves to death. We crossed the cadaveresque Somme on pontoons. From Caix I looked through a folding telescope and got a shaky view of the buttresses of Amiens cathedral. In the ghostly cemetery of Rosières-en-Santerre, which had been churned up by the shelling and which put Andreas Gryphius's baroque sequence of graveyard-lyrics into the shade, I dispatched, with the only shot I fired during the First World War, a fat St Bernard dog that had a soldier's foot (still with the boot on it) in its mouth. One of my fellow-soldiers contributed two dead cats. In a dug-out that had belonged to the Tommies I found a bottle of vinegar and a little bottle of hair-oil. We didn't dare touch the tins of corned beef in case they had been poisoned. Thank goodness I didn't have to chop up the dog and the cats, but I was granted the honour of concocting a sour vinegar goulash. The water of the Somme stank of corpses. We fried a few half-rotten potatoes in hair-oil. Haute cuisine. Hunger is the best sauce, but we had been spoiled: the colour of the meat took away our appetites. The yellow flesh of the graveyard cats was not exactly in harmony with the light grey colour of the braised St Bernard. Funeral baked meats with a vengeance. Since that time I have never at any point in my life knowingly eaten roast cat or dog again.

After advancing by forced marches unopposed for some time, we were brought to a standstill by new trenches full of freshly arrived Yanks. Our brilliant Army High Command had fallen right into the trap. Making fun of the first tanks was no use at all, we were finished, our conquering days were at an end. This was certainly true of our column, which had to withdraw at the end of May, broken down and starving, to Vieux Condé sur l'Escaut.

48 ON LEAVE

On one of the first days there I was sent to the orderly-room, where, completely out of the blue, I was ordered to go and get deloused at once, so that I could begin home leave on 18 June, after which I would have to report back on 5 July. I firmly intended never to come back to this terminally dangerous German front, at the forefront of the most mindless stupidity. After my frontier experiences in Flanders it was quite clear to me that escape was perfectly possible with thorough preparations from the Dutch side. My fiancée had already taken the first steps towards these preparations.

How I managed to get eleventh-hour information to her at the last minute, when every letter sent via Cologne took at least a fortnight to arrive, is a mystery to me. One of the orderly-room big boys got me (on payment of two potatoes) a duplicate leave-pass with all the right rubber-stamps, onto which I typed, using the office machine, permission for myself to wear civvies. Under 'destination' I added beside Berlin also Herzogenrath, near Aachen and the border, with the proposed purpose of a visit to an uncle. Armed with this, I travelled through my broken-down homeland back to Mama. And, what's more, I used the duplicate leave-pass, which became valid by acquiring innumerable extra rubber-stamps whenever it was checked on the way. Everything depended upon whether my fiancée in Holland had succeeded in getting a German visa, and this was a question of Bribery and Corruption. Being on leave with just my mother would have made it absolute hell, worse than being at the front, and I'd have been longing to get back there.

After I had sat on my kitbag for two days and nights I got out at Zoo Station in pitch darkness and dragged myself and my luggage through a ravaged and savaged Berlin to our flat at 23 Leopoldstrasse. The dead city was ashen grey, and I was at a loss with the lost war in this lost world. What would become of our love? With no life? I hadn't slept in a bed for more than a year and I was tired out. At four in the morning, just as dawn was breaking, my by now cruelly eroded Mama wrapped her bony arms around me, delighted to have someone again that she could fall upon lovingly and criticize for turning up late, since 'you are not supposed to keep ladies waiting'. That was supposed to be a joke. Worry, war and TB had reduced her to the shadow of a skeleton. In her flannel dressing gown (which I could never stand, even as a child), held together, more or less, with safety-pins, she planted herself in front of me and overwhelmed me with coughing and interest. Was I still alive, was I healthy, had I grown at all, how much did I weigh, had I changed for the better, why wasn't I wearing my Iron Cross, had I, as the family provider, at least thought to stop at the station and ask for meat and grocery coupons, double allocation for men on leave from the front? When I was too tired to react, she decided 'the boy's living in cloud-cuckoo land, just like he always did', and, coughing furiously, fetched out of the patent hay-box (a wartime invention: in order to save on coal and gas, you hermetically seal the cooking pot with partially cooked food in a box full of straw, where it continues to simmer) some stinking turnip-flavoured sewage and told me off for not having turned up a day earlier, because then my Lena wouldn't have had to wait a whole day for me and 'you are not supposed to keep ladies waiting'. Hearing that, I embraced the skeleton, was shocked at the red blotches on her face, and swallowed the turnip soup as if it were a great delicacy. And while I did so, she confessed that unfortunately and through no fault of her own she had already had words with that defeatist, neutral and smug female who reckoned that Germany was to blame for everything, when everyone in the whole world knew that everyone was to blame for everything. Besides which, this female from the Netherlands reckoned that Germany had lost the war, which wasn't exactly tactful as far as she, Mama, was concerned, since she had been prepared to sacrifice two sons on the altar of the Fatherland. Maybe I should think this somewhat hasty arrangement through again a bit more thoroughly, she went on. Had I tried to find out a bit more about her by way of an agency, which is the right way of doing things? And those rings under her eyes! Was I sure she was healthy and of impeccable character? It wasn't enough that she was Ravel's cousin, in 1893 she, Mama, had had a dowry of a hundred thousand emmies – I was too young and too idealistic, she said, to have any idea of the importance of a sum like that – and whatever some neutral defeatist female might try and put about for entirely malicious reasons, a mark was still a mark, even if the cost of living was going up every day and soon you wouldn't be able to get a thing for your money. The queues and the under-the-counter selling were all the fault of the black marketeers, and had I made a list yet of where I was going to go and scrounge meals, when I'd visit the Jordans, the Rothschilds, Wolfsons, Manes, Mühlbergs and Lissenheims, better go without your girlfriend, first of all it isn't official or even unofficial and secondly it's difficult for everyone to get hold of food these days. Better wait until you've grown up properly, and anyway let's not forget Moses & Schlochauer, who proved they were interested in you by sending those food parcels. That lot could be useful to you after the war ... Whereupon I summoned my last remaining strength to kiss my mother goodnight. I wasn't used to listening to that kind of nonsense, although I was used to the lice, accompanied by whom I now threw myself unwashed (water rationing: supply turned on from seven till eight in the morning only) and wearing a nightshirt into a proper bed for the first time for fifteen months – my own bed. Brother Heinz's bed, next to mine, was empty. The poor little infantryman was in the trenches at Verdun, waiting to be sent up the line and slaughtered. I had been looking forward to this bed with its white sheets so much, but now a burning exhaustion made everything hurt. After three hours of dreamless sleep a telephone call from my fiancée brought me back to life. She was staying with her uncle and aunt, Ravel's parents.

Without asking permission from my mortally offended mother, I rushed out of the house in a blue civvy suit, straight into the arms of my darling fiancée, who was waiting for me, her eyes a little red. Aunt Nora, kindly as ever and wanting to preserve her from having a nervous breakdown or worse when she saw me again, had been telling her what a terrible shock she got every time she herself saw me in all my ugliness. 'The sooner you learn to get used to anything, my girl, the sooner you'll get used to anything!'

Trembling with emotion we fell into each other's arms and gazed at each other in rapturous wonderment, dissolved in sheer bliss, couldn't believe it was happening, found that we had aged beyond our years, matured, reached a new spiritual plane, had so much to say to each other that words failed us completely and we could only stare at each other with wan smiles of happiness before we even dared to kiss. We were almost blind to the horrors of the colourless streets when we strolled, arms round each other's waists along to the park. What did we care about the hell that was all around us, anyway? Ragged war-ghosts tussled with blind cripples in wheelchairs, as they queued, ration-cards clutched tightly in their hands, outside grocery shops that had already been plundered. We saw nothing but each other's eyes. Already the unholy stink of the coming November revolution was wafting in on the June air. We could only smell our love.

With the aid of my best friend, Ravel, Lena had got everything ready in Holland. On 26 June (three years after my first letter to her) a man would telephone us at the Roelofszs' at ten o'clock and ask us if we wanted to buy some books. If we said yes, I was to get off the train bareheaded at Herzogenrath on my way back to the front. A man carrying a dark green suitcase in his right hand and a brown one in the other would ask me on the platform when the next train to Aachen was leaving. I was to follow him to the gents, where I would swap my uniform for a farm-worker's jacket that he'd have in his suitcase. Then I was to go with him to an inn called the Kaiserstadt, from which I would be taken over the border to Holland that night. The people-smugglers had already been paid one hundred guilders, and as soon as I arrived over on the other side they'd have to be paid another three hundred. It was all clear and straightforward. My heart was pounding with fear. Of course it was dangerous, but it was far more dangerous at the front, so I had no choice. The man was due to ring in only three days time and there was only one answer: yes! Coward that I was, my throat tightened up completely. We swore not to discuss this plan of escape with anybody at all, and if anyone asked us, we would deny all knowledge of it.

The days flew past in the rapture of love, in melancholy and in family turbulence. On Sunday Mama served a festive meal in our honour, just for the three of us, as there wasn't any more food. Everything went wrong. The long-preserved chicken was now served, and found to be mouldy. Mother wept for shame, since she considered herself to be the great preserver. Since she was so upset she burned three potatoes, her monthly ration. Furious about that, she managed to break the last-but-one of our big wine goblets, a witness to past glories. The wedding-wine was cloudy and Mama hated the young bride and hated herself for hating her. All the clocks in the flat were wrong and one struck thirteen just as we were taking a demitasse of ersatz coffee at three, and Mama, just to make conversation, asked how I, as a notorious layabout, really pictured my own future. 'A rosy one', I said with annoyance, and then to my horror I heard myself go on, 'and the first letter you get from me after this leave will come from Holland. I'm not going back to the front.' Mama leapt up from her chair and shouted in a doom-laden voice, 'Better dead in the trenches than a traitor!' I said, 'Heinz, my poor brother!' My fiancée, tears clouding the blue skies of her eyes on account of my having broken my word so fatally, stood up and tried to get away from this family storm. When I got up to go with her my mother rose up like some terrifying skeleton at the feast and hurled at my poor little fiancée the classic line, 'You whore, you've stolen my son!' And out she went, spitting blood and slamming all the doors behind her until she locked herself, whimpering, in her bedroom in order to telephone around and tell people what I was up to. *Mea culpa! mea culpa! Mea maxima culpa!* I've never been able to forgive myself.

When I got home late that night Mama was still on the telephone. I didn't want to see her, and so I went to bed without kissing her goodnight, fearing the worst. I was paralysed with a fear that was as heavy as lead. Why was I so helpless in my struggles against tradition and against the state? This struggle, which bore no relation to the large-scale troop manoeuvres referred to as 'the world war', was *my* struggle; the struggle between my past and my future, and one that I had to win.

On the morning of 26 June at nine o'clock I went on an empty stomach to Derfflingerstrasse, where there had already been a call for us. Someone would be coming at half-past nine to talk to both of us. This wasn't the plan. Had we been betrayed by my mother or sold out by the people-smugglers? We had just realized with horror that it was impossible to escape from our fate when the doorbell rang. My fiancée went into the corridor to open the door and I watched through a crack. A tall blond-and-blue-eyed type with a smooth face (a primary school teacher) asked if she was Lena C., engaged to Driver Erwin Blumenfeld. I came out and stood beside her. He extracted a sheet of paper from his briefcase and read out, 'In the name of His Majesty the Kaiser, Emperor of Germany and King of Prussia blah blah blah both now under arrest'. (My middle class existence was destroyed once and for all at this point. In those days being arrested meant that you were a criminal. Respectable people didn't get arrested.) A little man who had been waiting halfway down the stairs now came up and gave the orders. 'You are both to put your coats on as quickly as possible and hand over all your papers to us. There will be no conversation between the two of you. At the slightest sign of resistance or attempt to escape you will be shot! Hurry up! Be quick!' I said, 'There must be some kind of mistake. I am a soldier on leave from the front, and my fiancée – as you can see from her passport – is from Holland!' He sniffed at the passport as if it were Dutch cheese and returned it with a respectful bow. He held my leave-pass (the one where I had made the addition giving me permission to wear civvies) up to the light like an expert, and then put it into his briefcase. I asked if I might have a look at the arrest-warrant. He shouted at me to shut my trap. 'You've bin arrested, got it? Another bloody word out of you and we'll take you right through town with the handcuffs on! Not you, my dear young lady, don't you worry, you're in good hands and we know how to respect neutrality, especially when it's young and blonde like you! Wouldn't we all like to live in

Holland, where there are lovely girls and butter and cheese.' He thought he could really take my fiancée from me. While Lena put on her straw hat very slowly – we were trying to gain time and stop fate in its tracks – the two heavies frisked me for hidden weapons. Slowly the four of us set off. I was sandwiched between the tall one and the short one, and the neutral lady was politely permitted to walk on the right. I was keen to get rid of the second leave-pass from my wallet and suggested that we should take a taxi at my expense (because of the upholstery!) The small one said no. 'Orders are orders. Petrol shortages. We'll take the subway from Nollendorfplatz.' Our captors were a couple of monumentally stupid corporals in shoddy suits that stank of sweat. Cushy jobs at home were far better than serving at the front. Bored by the silence, they asked us about the price of chocolate, cheese, coffee and soap in Holland and whether there was any chance of getting food parcels sent over from there. For an Edam cheese they'd have let me get away. I didn't have one on me, though Lena gave answers that were full of promise. Confidentially the two of them declared that they had had enough of this starvation war, and wanted to know what the neutrals thought about our final victory. A clumsy trick question, to which my fiancée gave a neutral reply. To give her some clue as to what I was going to say, I started muttering to myself that I understood it all now, that my poor consumptive mother, consumed by jealousy, and in a fit of temporary insanity after a perfectly normal family row, had denounced me in order to prevent my fiancée from taking her son and provider away from her. During the train journey I managed to tear up the other leave-permit, wrap it in my handkerchief and stuff it behind the padding of the second-class seat. In the entrance hall of the military HQ in Gendarmenstrasse, when no one could see, the two heavies allowed us to shake hands – they decided against a farewell kiss. I told my fiancée to be a man, an order I gave her later when, in May 1922, I took her to the Diakonessehuis hospital in Amsterdam to have our first baby. And again when she took me to the French concentration camp at Montbard-Marmagne in May 1940.

We were taken through dark corridors and passageways to an orderly room, where a sergeant permitted the lady – as soon as he had established that she was a neutral – to sit down. Then he set about taking down all my particulars. He was interrupted by the magic word 'Atten-shun!', which immediately hypnotizes all soldiers. In came a much-decorated Captain Blood, with a bushy moustache and a sword, who clicked his heels so hard in front of my fiancée that the whole building shook, saluted, and then bellowed at me, why wasn't I at attention? 'Because I'm out of uniform, sir.' 'Criminals are always in civvies! Nevertheless you can still stand to attention, you odious little bastard, what will the lady think of discipline in the German army?' I stood as rigidly to attention as I could, and shouted back: 'Yes SIR!' He snarled at the sergeant, 'Get this traitor and his fiancée out of here, keep them apart and take them to Kupfergraben and then the gallows! Atten-SHUN!' and with that he disappeared into the wings, leaving me standing attentively at attention, and waiting, waiting, waiting. War is a series of long waits, interrupted by brief periods of slaughter. Lena was led away by a sadistic-looking black-clad virago and the sergeant departed with his files. Left alone, I took a risk and jumped over the barrier in front of his desk and read in his day-book the following entry: 'writtn reprt. Corp. Cohn, Train. bat. 99 (Frankfurt/Oder) intention to desert by Drvr. Blumenfeld Erwin, on leave from mil. transp. unit 209 Western Front wt. Dutch fiancée Citroen Lena'. There was a note in red beside it saying, 'Hold on remand'. Oh my prophetic soul, my uncle! Corporal Cohn, Bruno, was my mother's youngest brother, a neurotic stickler for rules who had, twelve years earlier, stolen my beloved Tittimouse away from me, just so that he could marry her and make her unhappy. By the time the orderly sergeant came back I was in my place again.

After I'd been waiting for two hours my fiancée was hustled so quickly through the orderly room and past me by the black-clad prison-matron that we couldn't exchange a word. I made a stupid face by pressing my lips together, to tell her she should say nothing. Just after that they brought in a bearded infantryman who stank to high heaven, and handcuffed him to me. He grinned, I was shaking with anger. We were led away under guard, which consisted of a lance-corporal and two wretched home-guard soldiers with fixed bayonets. They took us by a circuitous route (so that we would avoid passing the imperial palace) to the court-martial division of City HQ in Kupfergraben. Nobody took the least bit of notice of us on the way, but I still felt ashamed. Whenever an officer came past the corporal in charge of us shouted out, 'Stand by!' and our legs would go straight into a high-stepping parade march, 'Ey-es LEFT!' It must have looked comical. Unfortunately, nobody took a photograph of me at the time, though I do have a photograph of myself being led away in a bathing-costume by the local constabulary at Zandvoort in 1930, because I had exposed a bare shoulder on the beach.

When we got to Kupfergraben our chains were taken off and we were each shut into a little cage in a dark corridor. Between the cages there were conversations going on in impenetrable dialects. After a long wait I was taken out and my particulars were taken down yet again and entered onto innumerable lists. There was a lot of discussion and head-shaking about my paybook, which I had left back where I had been based. Eventually I was taken into an adjacent room, and brought before a bald man with horn-rimmed glasses (the examining officer). At a desk there was a Jewish orderly-room clerk, who seemed familiar to me, and who was acting as if he was writing down every word that was uttered. The hearing began in a rather silly chatty tone: 'Your charming fiancée has made it all very easy for us by confessing to everything, and I mean everything! In recognition of this we have already released this most sensible young lady. This very evening she will according to her own wishes and at her own expense be on her way back to Holland. Who would not, these days, like to be on their way to Holland? I see you came in on the one-year registration scheme, which means you must come from the educated classes. What did you do before the war?' 'I was in the ladies' wear department at Moses & Schlochauer.' The orderly-room clerk laughed. Horn-rimmed glasses went on, 'Trust me now and tell me absolutely honestly how you were intending to desert, and I'll put in a plea of mitigating circumstances and get it carried through. You know there is a death penalty for desertion, just as there is for cowardice in the face of the enemy. With my help you'll get a life sentence and after we've won the war – which can't be long now – your sentence will be reduced to ten years in jail. That sounds worse than it is: with good behaviour you'll get out after nine years. How old will you be in nine years' time?' 'Thirty, Sir!' 'Congratulations! If you'd gone back to the front you'd have had cause to worry about the future! So why don't you just come out with it and stop making things so difficult for both of us, come on, tell us, what's a signature anyway, I want to go home. Are you prepared to sign a full confession of guilt?' I stood to attention, clicked my heels and shouted out: 'Lieutenant, sir! As a front-line soldier I would be proud to die for Germany, my Fatherland!' He gave an angry laugh. 'Idiot! You haven't been condemned to death yet! And anyway, you don't have to trot out any patriotic nonsense for my benefit, I'm the examining officer, and when I look at you I know what I'm seeing.' He looked at his watch. 'I'll tell you one thing: my willingness to help and my patience are both slowly running out and before long you'll see another side of me. We'll torture you, starve you, we'll break you down! Three days without bread and water and you'll soon be begging us to let you say what we want to hear. Just don't make me mad. You front-line bastards don't know what hunger is, it's back here at home where we're starving for victory!' And then, as if heaven-sent and without paying attention to anything that was going on, there stepped between me and my Grand Inquisitor a man who opened his attaché case with a ceremonial gesture and constructed before our eyes on the desk a still life of bread, butter and sugar, after which he took out of a shopping bag eggs, a chicken and several cuts of meat. My existence was pushed completely into the background by the appearance of the foodstuffs, and that gave me time to weigh up my situation. The prosecution had nothing except my uncle's denunciation to go on. I took comfort in the hope that I might be set free right after this hearing. The black-marketeer waxed enthusiastic about his wares. My stomach rumbled loudly. The officer tried to complain about the veal that had been delivered yesterday, licked his finger and tasted the sugar, slurped down a raw egg to see if they were fresh, put his glasses on and took them off again, tried to knock the prices down a bit, all this without the black-marketeer, who knew his business, reacting at all. The clerk tried without success to get in on the deal himself. After the black-marketeer had cleared off, with his purse bulging, the officer turned to me abruptly and shouted: 'What's *he* doing here?' He leapt up angrily, buckled on his gun-belt, swapped his horn-rimmed glasses for a monocle, went to the mirror and put his cap on at a jaunty angle (to look like the Crown Prince) and then instructed the clerk, 'Obviously guilty, a house-search is bound to turn up decisive evidence, then he can be court-martialled and shot, put the handcuffs back on him and get him off to the Alexanderplatz in the next paddy-wagon! Where's my orderly?' The orderly packed the grub into a briefcase and disappeared, three paces behind the lieutenant, whose spurs jingled as he left.

The clerk leapt up in delight and threw his arms around me. 'Bloody hell, Blumenfeld, ain't he done bloomin' well! That was fantastic, the way you didn't let them get to you, really impressive! Moses & Schlochauer ought to make you a partner, you're pretty good!' Only then did I remember that this same young chap had, not too long ago, worked some buttons off on me when he was the chief horn-button rep. at Treuherz & Fuss, on the floor above Moses & Schlochauer. Hence this display of customer service. With a twinkle in his eye he praised me for having such a beautifully dressed fiancée – he'd been particularly impressed by the little Parisian mother-of-pearl buttons on her summer frock – who had, moreover, confessed to nothing. He wanted to know what her dowry was, and whether there were any sisters still left and available for delivery from stock. When he found out that she was the niece of rich Uncle Fur-Dealer, he practically lost all control. Much moved by this entirely selfless display of friendship I asked him if I was really going to be sent to the notorious central jail on the Alexanderplatz. He laughed. It's much worse than you could imagine, he said, although not as bad as a Glorious Death on the battlefield. He said that he couldn't do anything about it, but what he could do without it being noticed was to forget about the house-search that the officer had ordered, and if necessary, lose the odd item from the file later on. I asked him when I might possibly be let out. 'Could be in three days, three months or three years, you can't tell! I promise you, word of honour, that if it all goes wrong I'll still remember you fondly as a valued customer. I told your fiancée that she might be able to catch sight of you again down by the door when you get into the paddy-wagon. From now on it's probably best if we don't know each other.' He took me past several guards, back to my cage in the dark corridor. I never saw this valuable friend – whose name I couldn't remember even then – again.

After half an hour, bells rang and a trumpet blared out a jolly version of the first few bars of the song about 'The dawn so red', stopping before it got to the bit about 'young men all dead'. Key-jangling guards fetched us, one after the other, doing their best to hurt us while they were at it. Everyone was glad that something was happening. Names were read out and we had to shout, 'Here!' They counted us from one end and then from the other, first there was one missing and then there were two too many. There were seven of us. Each of us was taken downstairs between two guards. Waiting for us there was the horse-drawn omnibus of my childhood memories, which had been transformed into a paddy-wagon by the addition of bars on the windows and some muddy-green camouflage. My fiancée was waiting there as well, and I was able to whisper to her to clear up well at home. She knew where a certain bundle of letters had been hidden away. Our eyes met in a kiss of eternal farewell. Not until after the war (a mere six months later) did we see each other again.

By every seat was a chain which was locked around your wrist. The guard detail, with ammunition pouches on their belts, rifles at the ready and steel helmets in the June sunshine, stood on the back platform of the bus. Everyone seemed to be happy enough with their lot and in good spirits. I, the youngest, was the only one to hang my head, and they laughed at me for being such a mummy's boy. A professional pickpocket was able to get his hand in and out of the handcuff with magical ease, and made even the guards laugh. Just before dark our bus stopped outside the prison doors. A little window was opened from inside, and our driver passed in an envelope and was given a key, with which he opened the large wooden doors. The omnibus drove into a gloomy courtyard and stopped in front of a second doorway. The first one was locked behind us, and the ceremony was repeated: again a hatch was opened, again a key was handed out for the doors to be opened, and the second one was locked behind us. We were prisoners. There was no question of escape. They unlocked our chains and hustled us with rifle-butts and the odd kick into the reception room, where we were frisked shamelessly by prisoners in prison garb. Our particulars were checked. Our possessions: money, watches, pencils and handkerchiefs were put into numbered bags. I never saw any of my stuff again. We were chased at-the-double-hup!-hup! into a stuffy room in which about a hundred men had to stand crammed together like sardines in stinking tropical heat with a searchlight trained on them until their numbers were called out. The low ceiling of this room was made of thick, transparent glass, and I could see feet trampling along just above my head. Every five minutes another number came up, someone shouted, 'Here!' and had to force a way through to the door. Armed sentries checked the numbers, and this took a bit of time since they couldn't read. More and more human resources were being crammed in all the time. I began to be captivated by these cage-dwellers, military and civilian, who were shouting incomprehensibly to each other, even though talking was forbidden. I felt sick and my stomach was empty, but if I'd puked they'd have trampled me to death. Like every known society, this prison also had its clowns, its tell-tales, opportunists who knew how to make themselves useful so that they could wriggle into their own place in the sun. They snooped for the guards, did some of their jobs for them, and enjoyed various disgusting liberties within the prison – much as the guards (Kapos) in the concentration camps would do later. For people like that there is no such thing as a locked door.

Since no one had a watch any more, time no longer existed. However, bells rang all the time. It seemed to be well after midnight when my number was called. They took my fingerprints in an office. Since I was accused of high treason, I got solitary. The office clock said three. The clerk called in a clown dressed in sackcloth and I was supposed to do what he told me. He grabbed me by the scruff of the neck and gave me a kick to get me moving, past cells, iron grids and peepholes up the glass stairs of the dimly lit solitary-confinement block. On the way he trotted out mechanically and maliciously a series of instructions: up at five – if you don't jump out of bed at the first bell your bed'll be taken away and you'll have to sleep on the stone floor. On the second bell you'll fold your bed back and on the third you'll be standing by the door with your slop-bucket in both hands. On the fourth bell the door will open and you'll be off double-quick and running with your slop-bucket down to the shit-house, where you'll slop out at the fifth bell, clean out the bucket and then half-fill it with water and give yourself a thorough wash in the next half-a-minute. On the sixth bell: double-quick back to your cell for morning prayers. You'll find a bible hanging from a chain from the window-bars, using it as bog-paper is blasphemy and that's a bread-and-water job! At half-past seven there'll be three rings; you hold your tin mug by the hatch for coffee-water. At eight there'll be four rings: exercize time, fast walking in a circle around the yard and you don't make a sound or any gestures. Anyone caught passing information gets three days in the punishment cells, no water, no ersatz bread and it's a cell where you have to stand up all the time. The rest of the day: complete clean-out of your cell with a broom and a washrag, there'd better not be a speck of dust, I have to check it because I'm the trusty here. If I'm not satisfied you won't even get your turnips for dinner. And this – he said – is your villa. He opened up the cell, which wasn't much bigger than a child's coffin. Hot and airless. No bed, no chair, the only item of furniture was the slop-bucket with a wooden lid to sit on. The cot was folded up against the wall and chained; you were only allowed to lower it at night. Then there wasn't anywhere to stand in the cell. He went out, bolted me in, opened the hatch from outside and whispered fiercely, 'If you've got any dough, hand it over,

I'll look after it for you! I've got a lot on offer, pal, and contact with the outside world. Just get one thing clear: if you don't give me everything you've got, you're finished, and I mean finished!' And with that, this friendly clown shut the peephole. I heard him shuffling away. Alone at last! I folded down the cot, peace, quiet, sleep. Only then did I hear the pipes banging away vigorously in code – tacktack, tick, tackettytack, continuous and sleep-destroying. In sheer desperation I masturbated.

The hour had come when rosy-fingered dawn did light upon the hatch above. Outside, there were owl-screechings of numbers and sounds with answers. Everyone had something important to say, matters of life and death. Crimes, greed, passion, the total fulfilment of the feverish nightmares of my childhood. The torments of hell. Most hellish of these pains was having to march along at the double in single file through the corridors down to the latrines for slopping out, in the course of which the court jester tripped me up. The so-called exercize in the prison yard was voluntary. It was enough for me just to hear from my cell the horrible trip-trap ONE-two, ONE-two. Since every landing trip-trapped at a different time, it trip-trapped all morning. I didn't touch my turnip soup. My mind was in a whirl, I was as completely conscious of my guilt as I was of my innocence. A day later a couple of plain-clothes policemen took me back to Kupfergraben for a second hearing, on foot and without the handcuffs. One of them bought some cherries and gave me one. It was my first bite to eat for three days. A man who did not evince the slightest interest in a confession cross-examined me. He was a stamp collector, and gave me his address so I could send him some stamps with Belgian occupation surcharges. He didn't treat me remotely like a criminal. Once you are in the hands of Justice, be it earthly or celestial, you never know if you are about to be set free or strung up. I was taken on the next bus in chains back to the Alexanderplatz prison, the last ride in a horse-drawn bus in my whole life. I was too hungry to eat, too tired to sleep and too weak to collapse.

At noon on the next day I was fetched out of my cell and hustled into signing several different papers in a great rush, and when I asked about my things the man said that I had already signed a confirmation that I had received them back in good order. If I wanted to make any claims whatsoever I would have to return at three that afternoon. I got my leave pass back and a set of orders for the front, which I had to present at ten-thirty that same night to the railway MPs at Friedrichstrasse Station. From there I would be sent back to my unit under military guard in a train leaving at one-thirty via Aachen and Brussels. I was taken by subterranean passages out of the prison and into the fresh air. So there I stood, a completely free man, in Alexanderplatz, alone, unshaven and unwashed, without a handkerchief, without a penny to my name, without knowing a soul in the area – indeed, without knowing the area, either. Done for. And without any idea of how I was going to make the long journey back home to Liutpoldstrasse in this barbaric heat. There were no taxis any more in that final year of the war. And I had to go home for a slice of humble pie and to fetch my uniform. I tried begging. That's something else I have never managed to learn in my whole life, even though I've always studied beggars carefully. When I asked an elderly widow for a few pence for a ticket on the underground, she kicked up a fuss. 'You get to the front where you belong, you shirker! My husband was killed, you join the army and you won't have to beg and pester respectable ladies! Yes! He's been pestering me!' She tried to raise a hue-and-cry, a policeman wandered over, and I took off. I drank a glass of water at Aschinger's. I fell asleep on a bench in the park off Löwenallee, where I used to play as a child. A park-keeper, whom I'd been afraid of even then, chased me away.

In Luitpoldstrasse Mama opened the door to the flat, having apparently been waiting behind it so that she could fall pathetically to her knees before me. With trembling lower lip and eyes red and bloodshot from weeping she swore that she was innocent of this whole catastrophe which had been brought down upon our family by my godforsaken fiancée. Even before she went away, she said, that intruder had come to the house and without so much as a by-your-leave had burned some family papers. 'What a relief that poor Papa didn't live to see this shame, he'd have died of it!' I just said 'I'm hungry, I've got to go back to the front tonight and give up my life for my motherland!' and went to my room. I gobbled down a pink *kwattareep* (Dutch chocolate) that I had hidden under the cupboard. I washed, shaved with a blunt razor. I greedily devoured a sausage made from turnip and oatmeal without saying a word. With it I drank a bottle of wine from Mama's wedding, of which we still had sixty bottles stored in the cellar. Then I fell asleep, and woke up at nine with a scream of terror. I nearly missed the train back. Mama sat in the next room, weeping. Completely worn out, I climbed wearily back into my hated battledress and packed my belongings into my kitbag. Mama would not be deprived of the chance to accompany her eldest son to the station. And so we reached the final scene. She capitulated and begged for forgiveness with even more pathos than before. 'You can't imagine', she sobbed, 'of what a Jewish mother is capable! I've forgiven you everything!' before forcing me to set the seal on this ceremony of reconciliation with a kiss of peace. And to give an ironic touch to this novelettish stuff, she added, 'Of what she is capable – interesting use of the genitive, that.' I forcefully tore myself away from her.

At the station they put rubber stamps all over my marching orders and then threw them into the wastepaper basket. So the war really was lost. We all had to stand jammed together in the overcrowded slow-train like herrings in a barrel, just like in prison, with everyone completely depressed and not a trace even of black humour, as if we were on our way to our own execution travelling from one delay to the next. At every station the endless train stopped endlessly. Red Cross ladies with joyless smiles offered us inedible stuff. Westwards, for a night and a day. At five in the morning we stopped at Herzogenrath. New hope gave me new vigour. I still don't know to this day what really happened then, and I didn't know at the time, either. I've been through and dreamed about this fantasy so often that the reality is no longer relevant. Anyway, doesn't our imagination distort even everyday happenings? I got out to try and find the man with a brown and a green suitcase. Wasn't he supposed to be waiting for every train? He wasn't on the platform. Without thinking I ran down the steps. Where was I heading? Holland, my fiancée, freedom, the world! And there he was in reality, standing by the exit, the man with the suitcases, and he said: 'You're too late! The border police are waiting for you in the Kaiserstadt, get back to the train as fast you can, it's every man for himself now!' I rushed obediently back up the steps and just managed to leap on to the train at the last minute when it was already moving.

On 5 July I reported to the orderly room of my unit in Vieux Condé, back from leave, present and correct. The duty sergeant looked me up and down in an ironic and knowing manner, as if he knew the whole story, then told me I was dismissed. He knew *nothing*.

On 19 July I wrote to my brother Heinz:

Dear Brother,

Back in Flanders. Just spending a day or two here at the base. A fortnight ago on Thursday arrested with Lena and put on remand thanks to Uncle Bruno. Lena deported, I was set free on the last day after innocence proven. Mama triumphant. Swears she knows nothing about whole thing. Mama says, 'Better dead in the trenches than a traitor', because she is scared of Aunt Minna.

Hope you're still alive!

Your brother Erwin.

Three weeks later when they distributed our letters I got this one back with a note written right across the address: Killed in battle, return to sender. The word 'return' was underlined in blue pencil. After mail parade I took myself off with this letter to the latrines, dropped my trousers and wept.

Behind some bushes just opposite, the German Popular Spirit was hiding. As I was staring at my letter to my dead brother, wretchedly and precariously balancing on the latrine-pole, a clod of earth thrown at me by a comrade-in-arms hit me in the chest. I lost my balance and hurtled down into the stinking depths of German filth.

49   PEACE WITHOUT HONOUR

Even though the history of the world records just as many defeats as victories, the military establishment tends to plan its advances more thoroughly than its withdrawals, and we had been involved in one of the latter since the beginning of October. The front had collapsed, and now our retreat was collapsing. In order to keep up the morale of the troops, the word was put out that our flight was actually a movement forward in the direction of home. We were drowning in lies. Nobody believed the one glorious truth, that the war would soon be over. Everyone had longed for the end, but nobody had imagined it, certainly not like this. On 10 November our column of trucks, loaded with food from depots that we were supposed to be 'put in reserve' was crawling across the Belgian border at Peruwels into Borinage, in the direction of Mons. In frost that made your teeth chatter we went at a snail's pace, step by step along roads that had become impassable because of the mud and snow, around ragged foot-sloggers and vehicles that had got stuck. The only thing that drove everyone on was the fear of being left behind. The night before peace broke out we parked in the market square in La Louvière. The field-kitchen cooked up pea soup with smoked bacon, while patrols stood guard to make sure that none of our stolen stuff got stolen. All the truck drivers had provided well for themselves: tomorrow's black-marketeers.

My truck was standing in front of an estaminet. Maybe there was still a last glass of bitter Belgian beer to be had. In a dark corner of the empty pub sat a student wearing a black velvet beret, in intimate conversation with my dream girl, the beautiful Guinevere with long, flowing blonde tresses, kitschy as a picture. Uninvited – after all, we were still the victorious army – I sat down at their table and invited them to have a glass of beer with me. Germaine, the owner's daughter, pretended to be amazed at my French and the fact that I was on their side. He, the student, then declaimed Rimbaud's 'Voyelles' with exaggerated pathos. Poems are for reading, not for being read aloud. Germaine listened in a trance, with eyes half shut and mouth half open, as girls from the provinces think appropriate when they are Enjoying an Artistic Experience. At the same time she was trying to catch my eye. After several glasses of beer and Rimbaud's interminable 'Bateau ivre' we hummed the national anthem, the *Brabançonne*, and shook hands. No woman's hand had touched me since July. I trembled and Germaine trembled back. The student was taken aback – it was eleven o'clock, long after curfew, he wasn't supposed to be out at that time and wanted to stay with her. We persuaded him to let me take him home in the truck. Before I did, he helped me to cart a large crate from my truck into the estaminet, ten thousand cigarettes, my tribute of love to the goddess. Gratefully she whispered in my ear that I should come back later. On the way back the student warned me: 'I know you're going back, *prenez garde, elle est une femme dangereuse!*' He made me wait for a moment outside his house so he could bring me out a typescript with the title *Le Génie français*, on which he scribbled a dedication: 'Le jour de gloire est arrivé, le dix Novembre 1918! Souvenir amical François Charlier.'

Alone I drove back to her. The door wasn't locked. I went through the estaminet into a little antechamber and a lighted candle showed me the way to the semi-darkness of her bedroom. She was sitting on the edge of a double bed wearing a chemise. Bedside her lay an old woman, who was snoring. Germaine reassured me. 'Mama is deaf and dumb, you can say anything you like!' I couldn't get a single word out. Bigoted nursemaids, aunts and schoolteachers had drummed into me that men are carnal, women chaste. I would never have dared to hope that a very goddess would feel the urge to spend a night of passion, let alone with me. 'Je sais bien, vous voulez faire l'amour', she said, as if it were the most natural thing in the world. Mind-reader that she was, she could see right through me! She was so far above me. I was lost in admiration. Before I was able to approach her with even a single word she sent me back to wait in the antechamber. 'Je vais vous initier!' I had no choice but to obey.

It was unbelievably dark. Midnight struck and the tenth of November became the eleventh. Then in she came, white with powder, in her nightdress, tall and slim in the glory of her long and golden hair, and lit up the whole room. She made strange preparations, as if for a séance, putting two chairs close together with a stool between them. My own inactivity was becoming embarrassing. She seemed to be sorry for me. We sat there and our knees touched lightly against one another. 'No need to tremble, *petit chauffeur*, I'm not a witch and I like you! Only a beginner would think he could conquer a love-goddess on the first night just with a case of stolen cigarettes.' Then she used a phrase I thought was original until I heard it, later on, from every whore in Paris. ' "Une Gauloise ne se vend pas, elle se donne!" After the war you will come back here as a man. So that you don't forget me I'll teach you how to lose yourself and plunge into the infernal depths of heaven (*dans l'enfer des cieux*). Let your eyes look into mine, deeper and deeper, deeper and deeper: the moment is all, life is nothing!' Entranced by the billowing bridal veil of her blondeness, I sank unresisting into her eyes until a torrent of ecstasy coursed through my veins. Paralysed by the magic of this paradisaical witches' sabbath I fell into a deep sleep. To enable me to come here and discover the secret of love, millions of men had had to lose their lives. A poetic kiss on the forehead awakened me before dawn on 11 November.

A cup of hot chicory coffee and the rattling of motors starting up just outside brought me back to reality. As I left, Germaine's shadow flickered behind the curtains. I've tried in vain in the intervening years to find her again. Anyone who has eyes to see can find her in every one of my portraits of women.

Germany had suffered a glorious defeat in the First World War. That was our first bit of fun; Soon we'll have another one! (Max and Moritz.) They kept the news of the armistice from us until midday, when every bell in every church tower rang out joyfully. The most unbelievable rumours circulated. Our own Kaiser had supposedly fled to Holland, Germany was supposed to have capitulated, whining for peace, and at home in *our* country they said there was a *revolution* going on, a *white* army fighting against a *red* one. None of us had the slightest idea of what this un-German word 'revolution' meant. So that we could find out, I was elected a member of the workers' and soldiers' council. The honour of driving to Brussels in the lieutenant's little car was bestowed upon me. I drove to the first barn I could find so that I could catch up on my sleep (my only deed as a member of the workers' and soldiers' council). When I got back I found out that I had only been elected so that my truck could be plundered without interference. On the following night the whores in the women's jail at Huy would have killed us if we hadn't run away drunk (my only hand-to-hand combat in the First World War). In the imperial glory of Aachen, the next night, our reception in the old-fashioned main hall of the brothel wasn't much warmer. Apparently we had been defeated. The following noon in Düsseldorf we saw a promising banner stretched across the beflagged Rhine bridge with the words 'Welcome home, our invincible heroes!' My truck limped along wretchedly on two cylinders through the icy streets of the German countryside until the petrol gave out and I flogged it to a farmer just outside Kassel for a hundred and fifty marks. My heart sinking by the minute, I jumped onto an overloaded freight train heading for Berlin. With sixty other men in an open cattle-transport wagon I reached my native city fourteen hours later, freezing to death, on 17 November, my fiancée's birthday. Almost two years before, and dressed in a new and splendid leather uniform, I had said goodbye to my little brother Heinz at this same place, the Anhalt Station. He was dead. Choked by this thought, I dragged myself and my kitbag through the dark city. A curse on this peace! On Hafenplatz, which had always stunk of murder, two zombies in ragged uniforms surrounded me and kindly offered to help me with my bag and with my destiny. It was useless trying to resist. They disappeared off into the darkest night of my entire existence with what was left of my belongings, love letters, Lao-tzu, *Hamlet*, *Le Rouge et le noir*, a couple of copies of the literary magazine *Die Fackel* and a waistcoat made of cats' fur.

There was nobody at home. I had no key and sat in the snow until daybreak, when the janitor let me into our deserted flat. Mama was in a TB clinic near Hanover, Annie was working as a police assistant in Hamburg. To keep warm and to get rid of my lice at the same time I burned my uniform, the Kaiser's stinking coat. Nothing to eat. The first thing I did was to sleep right through for several days, dead to the world, and then I woke up feverish and with a cough that sounded like a howling wolf. Because I had 'absented myself from my unit without official permission' they refused to give me any ration cards. There were skeletons scurrying around everywhere, on the very point of starvation even *with* ration cards. I went out foraging for food and got one potato, which cost me two silver candlesticks. Then I remembered the legendary wine from my parents' wedding, which had been in the cellar at Luitpoldstrasse for the past twenty-five years, under lock and key, just waiting to be drunk. Assisted by George Grosz I pushed about sixty bottles of it, hidden in sacks, on a handcart to his studio. There we roasted the potato, ate it together with a yellow beeswax candle, and sampled a couple of bottles of the noble liquid, as if it was a time of peace and plenty. Grosz painted a placard that said, 'Well-stacked young society ladies with potential film-star qualities are invited to a party at the studio of G. Grosz, Artist, 8 p.m., dress formal. 8, Olivaerplatz'. With this placard nailed to a broom-handle we paraded like sandwich-board men up and down the Kurfürstendamm. Eleven men came to the party: Mynona, Grosz, Piscator, Hülsenbeck, Mehring-the-Seven-Month-Old-Baby (later known as Wee-wee Dada), Benn, Gumperz, Yomar, Förste, Wieland and Helmut Herzfelde (who later became Monteur-Dada John Heartfield), plus me. When more than fifty ladies turned up we had to declare a full house and close the doors. Old Mynona (he was already over forty!) hinted that he had a pound of cocoa hidden in his trousers, and the hands of all the ladies were in his pockets. I envied the old roué! To get the party going we suggested that everyone should take their clothes off. We men withdrew into the kitchen and decided to keep our clothes on. When we came back into the studio the ladies were all stripped for action and the orgy began. Everyone got drunk and the empty bottles went flying through the glass of the studio windows and landed in the street. Splintering glass, screams, racket.

With everyone standing round, cheering and clapping, Grosz got a dose of the clap from Mascha Beethoven on a chaise-longue in the middle of the studio. Mynona immortalized this historical evening in a novel, the name of which now escapes me.

Two days later I woke up, freezing, in Grosz's bathtub, and my blue suit had been stolen. Next day, off to Holland via Hanover. Hail and farewell to my coughing mother, who wanted to go with me to Holland this time. To the border with two cardboard boxes, a border rigorously patrolled by Dutch soldiers who were not allowed to let any Germans in. First of all I tried to get over alone and at night, got caught, begged, wept, knelt and grovelled to my captors, who took me straight back to the German border checkpoint, where there wasn't a single living soul to take charge of me. A second attempt that same night was successful with the help of some smugglers, who took my last penny and my boxes. I've had plenty of luggage taken off me in my life. I'll set off on my final journey as *voyageur sans bagages*. At night, through fog, ice and snow, through rivers and swamps and with dogs at my heels, I at last reached, soaked to the skin just like in my worst nightmares, just before Christmas, the promised land of my fiancée, a land flowing with milk and honey. I had brought nothing with me from Germany except my Berlin youth, and I neither would nor could abandon that.

PART THREE

50 HOLLAND

My best friend, Ravel, whom I hadn't seen for three years, fetched me from the frontier hotel in Enschede. In spite of all the good-to-see-you-again bonhomie I realized in the first second that our eternal friendship was over. Feelings are decided in the first moments of meeting. Ravel wisely advised me to keep my mouth shut on the way to Amsterdam; I'd have been deported immediately as a *Mof* (a German). That very same evening I was able to throw my arms around my weeping fiancée in her mother's house. She had just come through a bout of pneumonia; the Spanish 'flu was attacking everyone who had survived the war. Leentje was a little bit miffed that I had wasted valuable days in Berlin, instead of getting there for her birthday, as promised. Birthdays mean more than life itself to the Dutch, and it is impossible to wish anyone 'happy birthday' a sufficient number of times. My battle against these middle-class demands ended in a complete rout on my part. In those days I used to think biologically rather than logically. I wanted to establish a livelihood as soon as possible, make money, get married, build a nest. I didn't even know where to start looking – no passport, no work permit, no ration books, no knowledge of the language and no desire to acquire one. I hadn't yet had much practice in emigrating, or acquired the taste for foreign languages. The Dutch are not best pleased when people take their language to be a species of Low German spoken by peasants, which is what it is. They are easily offended, and they also like to mock others. They gloated when they reminded me that I had lost the war. These profiteers were furious that the big business of the war had come to an end. When I tried to comfort them by telling them that Germany was only thinking about the next war, they laughed at me again. Nobody believed my war stories: I had no credit. Soon I was doubting myself whether I had really been there. People looked at me askance, as if I were an escaped convict. I had nothing to wear, was positively skeletal, and I spoke in too lively a manner. One egg cost a guilder, there are one hundred cents in a guilder, and I didn't have a single cent. My fiancée supported me generously from her small salary as a librarian in the Hague, and that hurt! It hurts to take. We only saw each other on Sundays. Love without a room and a bed is like a fish out of water, especially in winter. Together with Ravel, who was carrying on with Leentje's younger sister, I rented two miserable rooms with the Langenbergs in 'de tweede Helmerstraat' where the food was wretched. Seldom have I eaten so badly. They even counted the peppercorns. Pepper was expensive. A crappy version of the bohemian life.

Amstelodamum, city of my youthful dreams, the Venice of the north, turned out to be an impenetrable labyrinth of swamps, well below medieval sea-levels from beneath which sunken bells gave voice by day and night. Water and sewage stagnated in stinking canals, and even bacteria refused to start cultures in their filth. Once you had crossed the bridge over the Prinsengracht canal and threaded your way through a shambles of bicycles, people, barrel-organs, bicycles, hand-carts and more bicycles, keeping straight ahead through narrow lanes between crooked houses (brick-red, black, light ochre and shiny asphalt), after half an hour you cross, with some amazement, the very same Prinsengracht by way of a different bridge. You get lost, you get confused, you get laughed at. *Stommerd!* (Fool!) The canals run in a half-circle around the harbour, known as *het Y* (and pronounced 'eye'). A dazzling miracle: red windows, dreams of whores from Félicien Rops to Joachim Ringelnatz. The very same giant-pork-priestesses of Venus are still waiting behind the very same red windows on the Zeedijk or on the Oudezijdsachterburgwal for seamen or see-men, for me, for you. It was here, right at the start of my sojourn in Holland, that I experienced an unforgettable old Flemish witches' sabbath. Very late on *Sinterklaasavond*, the December night when St Nicholas delivers the presents, a horse-drawn sleigh came jingling along through the deep snow carrying Santa Claus and his helper, the *Pietermansknegt*, who was dressed up as a Venetian moor. It stopped right in the middle of the Oudekerksplein between the church and the ancient whorehouses. Santa and his pal, both of them already dead drunk, began toasting the ladies displaying their wares in the windows with bottles of gin. The latter rushed out into the icy-cold December night, covering their nakedness with woollen shawls, and performed an increasingly frenzied dance round the sleigh until in the end they tore Santa and his helper out of it, and rolled lustily with them in the snow while the bells in the tower of the Old Church played 'Here Comes the Steamboat from Spain'.

Out of pure pity a Calvinistic skinflint called Mynheer Swets, from the book-dealers Swets & Zeitlinger, took me into his service for fifteen guilders a month. My job was sorting out the mountains of books left by his predecessors, and in the rubbish I found some treasures. I stole some de luxe pornography, which Ravel sold, but that didn't help us much. After that we tried to set up an art business together. With the French I had learnt in the war I wrote to Famous Artists (unknown at the time) whose work we had heard of by way of the *Blauer Reiter*, *Sturm* and the *Erster Deutscher Herbstsalon* – Léger, Braque, Juan Gris, Gleizes, Metzinger, Severini and Carlo Carrà – and asked permission to act as their sole agents in Holland. They all sent us drawings on commission, for which we were unable to find customers. It was far too early. Grosz sent us his pictures as well. In that way I brought Ravel into the Dadaist movement, which was completely remote from his interests, and at the time he held it against me, although later he used it to prove to his disciples that he'd been part of the avant-garde and preened himself on it. I couldn't take his Dutch pettiness, the one virtue that a small country can be big in.

The mosquito *anopheles*, an import from the Dutch colonies, was thriving in the morass of Amsterdam, and I caught malaria. At about the same time I realized that it is impossible to impose cubism on peasants. Under the protection of some friends of my fiancée, who were as rich as they were questionable, I made the demeaning retreat into Dutch ladies' wear, a trade which showed an interest in 'young people' who had done their apprenticeship in Germany. I joined the Gerzon Brothers Fashion House (Amsterdam, Rotterdam, The Hague, Haarlem, Nijmegen, Breda, Groningen, Arnhem, Utrecht, Zutphen and Hertogenbosch). It was an antediluvian Jewish-German ready-made clothes organization, a provincial Moses & Schlochauer. Wholesale and retail: a department store. First they tried me out in the factory. I worked terrifically hard and proved myself, and was put in charge of a department in the main store, the one in Amsterdam. When I served my first lady customer – and every trick was permissible to sell her something – I died of shame. After all, I had learnt that there is nothing lower in the world than a shop-floor monkey, an unctuous sales creep. (Guards officers before the First World War weren't allowed to marry the daughters of anyone in trade, even if their name was Wertheim.) I was soon promoted to buyer in the novelties department for all the branches: made-up drapery, ruffles, dickeys, lace collar-trims, costume jewelry, leather goods, belts, bracelets, feather boas, shawls, sanitary wear and Directoire knickers. Business ethics: Betsy Stracke, my first salesgirl, was dismissed without notice because she had the audacity to wear transparent stockings. Gusta Berkemijer was booted out for wearing lipstick. I went as a buyer to Germany, and eventually I even conquered Paris. I didn't have a clue, wholesale or retail. I was even more clueless than the people I was acting for. Doing business doesn't need intelligence, it needs capital. Mallarmé to Degas: 'Ce n'est point avec des idées que l'on fait des vers. C'est avec des mots.' The Gerzons were uneducated and crafty. I, on the other hand, was stupid, other-worldly and inhibited. I was too inexperienced to express my gratitude to the management when I got a bonus – I was already making five hundred guilders a month – and this sank my chances of a future in department stores.

> The angels laugh with joy
> When a girl weds a boy,
> They all sing with delight
> When she's holding him tight.

And so it happened. On my twenty-fifth birthday I got married. I thought it was pretty late to have achieved my main aim in life. My wife had inherited 32,500 guilders from her father, which ought to have eased, at least temporarily, my fears of starvation. Not a chance. That fear has never left me for a second in my whole life. The 32,500 guilders *did* manage to leave me, however – a mere fourteen years later they had vanished without leaving a trace, or strictly speaking, without leaving any change. However, the monthly fear of a baby did recede a little. We had a honeymoon in Berlin, where there was wild inflation, moral as well as financial. A mark was still a mark, but for one Dutch guilder you got a million of them. The first evening there we were approached by a respectable widow in deep mourning, who invited us to the private showing of an artistic performance in her house in Knesebeckstrasse, in which, for a payment of fifty thousand marks per person one could watch her and her two daughters engaged in sexual activities with a whippet. It was too dark to see anything of this offering. What a rip-off! Refreshments were served – cocaine at twenty thousand marks a snort.

Zandvoort, 1929

Living Mummy, Amsterdam, 1932

Untitled portrait, Amsterdam, 1932

Untitled portrait, Amsterdam, 1932

9, rue Delambre, Paris, 1937

Death's Head in crystal, 1937

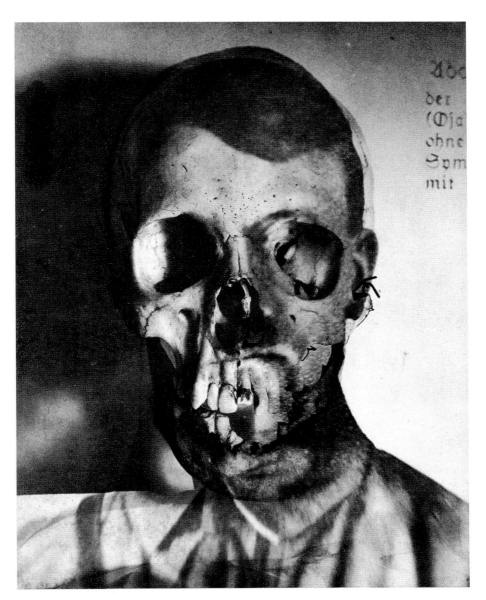

Hitler, 1933

May Kalf Kaptijn, Amsterdam, 1934

With Michel de Brunhoff,
Paris 1938

My favourite model, Paris, 1939

Der Augenblick (The Moment), Paris, 1937

Tara Twain from Hollywood, my first American girl, Amsterdam 1935

My 'kantoortje' in Amsterdam, 1923–32

Hotel Celtique, Paris, 1936

Our kitchen window, Catus, August 1940

Rouen cathedral, 1937

Carmen, the model for Rodin's *The Kiss*, Paris, 1937

Untitled nude, Paris, 1936

Mannequin, Amsterdam, *c.* 1932

Aristide Maillol's *The Three Graces*, photographed for *Verve*, Paris, 1937

Aristide Maillol, *Femme Assise*, Paris, 1937

Nude under Wet Silk, Paris 1936

Agen, France, winter 1940–41

Agen, France, spring 1941

Unpublished variant for 'Portfolio de Vogue: La Tour Eiffel', French *Vogue*, May 1939

This is how I slid into the *petits misères de la vie conjugale*. We set up home from the great Berlin end-of-season sale, middle-class, inexperienced, lurching from one cliché to the next and imagining that we were being 'original'. I had set my mind firmly on farmhouse rustic, and thank God we couldn't find anything in that line. We had to compromise with Queen Anne with a dash of Biedermeier. Upper-crust combinations of light-brown and dark green – the Goethe-house in Weimar that I visited in my youth set a mark on me for the rest of my life. We treated ourselves to a set of bedroom furniture in high gloss varnish, a dressing table, triptych mirror and two bedside tables. We had a bookcase built to our own specifications in walnut: the man is father of the child. We bought a black grand piano. We were in control of life. World problems were beneath our dignity. Communism was lunacy, democracy a fraud. We'd learnt nothing from the past and suspected nothing of the future. Our next aims: (a) children, begetting of; (b) commercial independence. Both of these aims were realized sooner than we expected. Much moved, I soon heard a new heart beating in my wife's belly. In May 1922, instead of the much-feared deformed monster (for which I had a padded suitcase ready to suffocate it in) the sweetest daughter, Lisette, came into the world. I was ready to do anything in the whole wide world for her!

The level of inflation in Germany had automatically elevated every do-it-yourself foreign-exchange-artist to a financial wizard. All any Dutch panhandler needed to do was stroll across the border and become a multi-millionaire. Like the Gerzons. I didn't understand a thing about this nonsense, and I didn't even suspect that I hadn't the slightest idea about business. When one of the Gerzon nephews refused to countersign a repeat order that I reckoned to be a matter of life-and-death – it was for twelve thousand celluloid snake-bracelets from Chavigny Frères in Paris – I was furious and handed in my resignation, which, to my horror, was accepted without a word. You mean maybe I *wasn't* indispensable?

With the financial support of the excessively crafty, leather-selling spivs, A. N. Schmidt and Co. from Offenbach, I set up on my own. I opened a handbag shop in the Kalverstraat in Amsterdam called 'The Fox Leather Company', in which I did everything wrong from the very start. This semi-stillborn child, begotten half by German credit and half by my wife's own money, was eaten up by expenses from the day of its birth and never ever learnt to stand on its own two feet. The premises themselves, adapted and rebuilt to my own designs, were the most miserable thirteen-and-a-half feet of shop-front anyone could imagine. I knew that you could make more by selling rubbish, but I believed in quality. I didn't want to sell the customers what their execrable taste demanded, but only things that *I* thought were beautiful. Turned on by the smell of leather, especially Russian calf, I was so deeply in love with my wonderful ladies' handbags that I couldn't bring myself to sell them to the haggling hyenas of Amsterdam. The stock grew, the stock got to be enormous. The Schmidts soon worked out that I was a no-hoper and skinned me alive: then they withdrew the promised credit. If the business had gone well, they'd have had the whole thing off me. I reckoned that I was hard-working enough to swim against any tide, worked like a lunatic at shopkeeping, changed the whole window-display twice a week on my own, during the night, so as not to interfere with the daytime trade. But a shop that was doing badly, in which I, three sales-ladies, two girl trainees and the errand-boy (*knegt*) Gerrit waited in vain for the next customer, wasn't a proper sphere of activity for an Angry Young Man like me. During these dark, Dutch, leathery years, desperation drove me towards art. During the day, sitting in my tiny private cubby-hole of an office, I wrote short stories and cultivated the merry little artistic souls of Amsterdam. If, around half past four in the afternoon, it got to be too unbearably quiet in the shop, I would flee to the Café Winkels, to engage in unrestrainedly smutty conversations with flabbynormous Dutch porkburghers over Dutch cocktails with names like *vorburgjes*, *slappe cats* and *oude klare*. At home at night I became a Sunday painter, with a genuine feel for colour and a spurious contempt for form. Since I couldn't draw, I didn't want to draw. My style: futuristic Dadaism. Three many-sided fine-art magazines (*Variétés* from Brussels, the Berlin *Querschnitt* and the Paris magazine *Minotaure*) kept alive my connection to the world of creativity. I thought that I was a modern, but I turned out to be classical. I have no idea what that really means, but people classified me that way so often that in the end it seemed plausible enough. A couple of my pictures from that period have survived, and they really do look to me as if I was on the right track. There is nothing harder than trying to assess youthful work, and one is blind to defects in one's own.

After Hitler took over Germany I got no more supplies. The stock I had decreased, the debts increased. With some embarrassment I got a three month loan extended, and after yet another month the creditors started to kick up a stink. I persuaded some of the ladies who wanted to buy handbags from me and couldn't, to let me photograph them instead. My little private office became my first studio. Half a century earlier another photographer had exercized his mysterious arts in the same building, and it still smelt of fixer. Behind a door that had been blocked off I discovered his former darkroom. Out of the body of my 'Fox', as it bled slowly to death, there blossomed a bellows-camera (a Voigtländer 'Bergheil') and above it glowed a lamp of ruby-red. I developed and printed all night long so that every morning a new and angelic face in 'high key' could shine forth in the shop window amongst what was left of the crocodile-tears-handbags. My first American lamb to the slaughter, Tara Twain from Hollywood, became my first publication, *mon premier pas* (my first step): *Arts et Métiers graphiques Paris, 1935*. And so I became, when there was really nothing left for me to do, a *photographer*. Everyone told me not to do it. Failed painters became window-dressers, failed window-dressers became photographers. The idea that you could get a hundred dollars for a photo in New York was dismissed as typical American hype; the top price in Holland was ten guilders and nobody paid the top price (they were pernickety, they haggled). And apart from that, there were (not unfounded) doubts about my talent. In 1932 I was allowed, after someone had recommended me, to spread my best photographic work before those infallible photo-mandarins Korf and Kroner, who worked for Ullstein in Berlin (who published the magazines *Querschnitt*, *Uhu*, *Illustrierte*). Unanimous judgment: no talent, waste of material, no hope, no use, no point! This death-sentence left me unmoved; I knew I was a photographer. I have encountered a similarly understanding attitude from plenty of editors and their like, even those who didn't have to worry about Hitler. The fact that in spite of everything thousands of pages of mine have appeared can be put down to a universal uncertainty of judgment. I got extra encouragement from doing the stills for Jacques Feyder's film *Pension Mimosa* and established how unsuited I am to collective artistic production.

But more than to anyone else, I owe a debt of gratitude to Schicklgruber, the Führer. Without him I would have slumped down into the Dutch swamps, and without him I would never have had the courage to become a photographer. He forced me out of my ivory tower (we called it our 'island of solitude') and into real life. As a gesture of thanks, on the night when he seized power, I did a photomontage superimposing his ghastly features onto a skull and ran with it through the night, drunk, for nearly sixteen miles from Amsterdam to Aerdenhout. In 1942 a million copies were dropped over Germany as American aerial propaganda leaflets. Heil Hitler!

51 MISÈRE NOIRE

The friends who had stood as guarantors for an overdraft of fifteen thousand guilders had to cough up, and then they fell like scales from my eyes. I lost not only my friends' money (which I paid back later) but also my friends (who wanted to come back later). My wife, my children and my worries all remained faithful to me. Shame, blame and threats to distraction were heaped onto my already ill-famed name, and I was starting to look down-at-heel and threadbare. The Plotskes brothers, Bible-Jewish loan-sharks, Shylocks of the kind that I knew about from antisemitic novels like Gustav Freytag's *Debit and Credit*, started to pop up like the Marx brothers out of trapdoors and cabin trunks, waving tempting bundles of banknotes under my nose. On one side I had my enemies smiling with hypocritical sympathy, on the other I was being threatened by blackmailers, lawyers were giving me bad advice, *deurwaarders* (the Dutch bailiffs) crept in on crepe soles and gave the corpse of my Fox, by now at the death-rattle stage, the last rites. Abandoned by all guiding spirits, good or bad, I flogged off the whole disaster *voor een appel en een ei*, 'for an apple and an egg,' for six thousand guilders, that is. While I was actually signing the deed of sale, the friendly expression on the faces of the sharks turned into one of ruthless nastiness. They threw me out of my own shop without further ado, and warned me never to show my face there again. I wasn't allowed to take so much as a single wallet with me as a souvenir. Even the embryo of a dearly beloved son, preserved in alcohol, that we had paid a thousand marks to a Professor Donner to have aborted two years before in Berlin and which lived out its life in a secret compartment of the safe, stayed in their hands. On the first day of this closing down sale the Plotskes got their six thousand guilders back. I would never have been able to part with my goods; I was a buyer, not a salesman. I settled on twenty per cent with my creditors, and there I was, *aan een wondermooie dag*, on a perfect day in September 1935, just as I had always feared, sitting on the edge of the sand-dunes with my wife and three lovely children without a cent to my name. *What now, my love?* When the gas and electricity had been cut off and the piano repossessed, I sent a registered letter *de profundis* to the Archbishop of Haarlem, offering to sell him my family's souls, all five of them, for five thousand Dutch guilders, which was way below the going rate. I never got an answer. As I said, I'm no salesman.

When my creditors began to assail me, so did violent stomach pains (*vreeslijke buikpijnen* in Dutch), which were immediately dismissed as a neurosis (this being the latest society fad). Consultant Charlatans (described as *onvol-preezen*, 'they who cannot be praised enough') and Know-Alls diagnosed a double-infected, down-the-diaphragm-to-the-duodenum tumour with diversely diverticulous diverticulitis, accompanied by severe financial impotence ('chronic dough deficiency'). Because of the last-named condition, they were unable to operate, and instead condemned me to water enemas, seventy pints of water a day, for a month. I was allowed one orange and a small bowl of almond pudding. Once I had lost a couple of stones and began bleeding, they gave me up, and I was saved. I fled without a passport, without money and without my family to Paris, so that I could become a photographer at last.

I finished off my seventeen years in the swamps-and-dykes with Voltaire's 'Adieu canaux, adieu canards, adieu canaille!' And just to say something nice about Holland as a farewell gesture: it has nice nursery rhymes, great Gouda, perfect prawns and potatoes, and as its finest delicacy, fresh *maatjes-haring*!

Anticipating future happiness I wrote this little prelude:

Sara, petite Negresse
If you seek Paradise, like me,
Then just like me you'll fetch up in Paree,
And anisette will be your usual drink,
But then you'll live on love and on absinthe.

Sara, the little black girl, strokes my hair
But stops – I don't know why or where.
Where does it end, when once you start to sink
Into the depths of absinthe.

And so I end, for she left me,
(She who was as sweet as anisette), there in Paree.
So now I stroke my own hair. Brother, think,
And never take up with Sara or with absinthe.

52 PARIS

You all know the one that I mean
The city that lies on the Seine.
(Friederike Kempner)

In the spring of 1935 fate had sent a blonde and bright-eyed Parisienne on her honeymoon into my moribund leather-shop. She wanted to be photographed in high key, like the photos in the window. Geneviève was the daughter of the painter Georges Rouault; she herself was a dentist, and she promised to exhibit my photographs in her waiting room in the Avenue de l'Opéra. Much taken with the idea, I had a vision of paradise waiting for me in the future, and named this particular St Geneviève to be my Parisian envoy. I imagined that, given my inclination towards alchemy, black and white magic, potassium cyanide and metaphysical nonsense, plus the professional experience gained with Moses & Schlochauer and Gerzon Brothers, I would be able to conquer the *ville de lumière* as a fashion photographer. Before 1920 all you ever saw in the fashion magazines were stiff and stylized drawings. At the most a model, posing with a smile, might sometimes be snapped at the races (Auteuil, Chantilly, Longchamps) by one of the track photographers. Suddenly, a Viennese Jew and fashion designer, Baron de Meyer, started taking fashion photos in a studio. A new art form. Right away this important new business was seized by the American sensationalist press and by the international homosexual community. In the beginning the fashion photographer was a genius, and he was paid and treated accordingly. It was expected that he would be arrogant, repulsively gifted, would behave in an extravagantly camp manner and would provide new material for the gossip columns on a daily basis. I very quickly grasped the artistic possibilities – and very slowly the difficulties – of this exclusive new enterprise.

What I really wanted to be was a photographer pure and simple, dedicated to his art for art's sake alone, a denizen of the new world, which the American Jew, Man Ray, had triumphantly discovered. Whether this would feed and clothe a family was another matter.

I had barely arrived in Paris when my inoperable cancer of the intestine left me, in the shape of twenty-five feet of agonizingly painful tapeworm. The first gleam of light in the *misère noire*. From then on, things got better. My Parisian career began in January 1936, in the Hotel Celtique in the rue d'Odessa in an attic room, *le numéro 69 au sixième, prix d'ami 100 frs* ($2.50) *par mois*. The only condition was that the room had to be made available for subletting between the hours of three and seven in the afternoon for amorous purposes. I could catch up on sleep in the mornings. When you are lying down you get less hungry, so I spent a lot of time lying down. On Saturdays you got clean bedlinen. The greatest source of inspiration for a budding artist was the sheer horror of Parisian hotel wallpaper: pale mauve cockatoos were intertwined with pale green harps against a pink-and-pale-blue-striped background, with an extra garnish of bright red tulips and chrome-yellow cornflowers. Anyone who can see that and not become an artist has no talent at all. The hotel proprietor, a boozy Belgian called Monsieur Maes, used to beat his wife, who was a little blonde dumpling. To get her own back on him she would quite often give me clean sheets as early as Wednesday. All the rooms in the Hotel Celtique were occupied by whores from the Gare Montparnasse district – hard-working girls, never beautiful, rarely young, often delightful. In their private lives they were chaste and reserved, taking love *au sérieux*. No personal affairs in the brothels, it was all reserved for their pimp, their *mec*. They only prostituted themselves professionally, just like the rest of us. All day and all night the bidets would gurgle their symphonies of love, Villon, Baudelaire, Rimbaud, Verlaine, Apollinaire. No Valéry, no Mallarmé.

While I was getting dressed in the morning I would look out of my dormer window across the narrow courtyard at little Nadja, a Romanian artist's model with long flowing black hair, as she performed her morning *toilette*. She used to wait for me, come to the window naked and smiling, and caress her little breasts with a rose in an inviting manner. In the street or in the Café du Dôme she would ignore me. Not until we met again twenty-five years later – when she was an old woman – did she confess that I had been the great window-love of her life in that *jeu de la rose*.

Ma voisine d'en face, my neighbour across the narrow corridor, was an elegant and serious blonde, always veiled in the black tulle of deepest mourning, with eyes downcast. The proprietor's wife, Madame Maes, let me know discreetly that my neighbour was the widow of a doctor, Madame Bellifontaine from Fontainebleau, who was staying here with her son (*garçon adorable*) so that she could sort out the details of a considerable inheritance. I rarely saw the retiring widow, and never saw her son. Then at about three o'clock one morning a clap of thunder woke me up, dripping wet, out of deep dreams. While I was establishing that a brimming porcelain chamberpot had smashed through the opaque glass panel on my door and landed on my bed, excited chattering ladies arrived on the scene and filled the place. With their quilted dressing-gowns buttoned to the chin these whores looked more like nuns (apart from a profusion of ribbons). Slowly the situation became clear. The doctor's widow wasn't a doctor's widow at all, but made a hard-earned living in the Sphinx (the most flourishing brothel on the boulevard Edgar Quinet, just round the corner from our hotel, run by Albert Sarraut, the Minister of the Interior, and his brother). The son wasn't her son at all, but her gigolo, whom she kept locked up in her room. That night he had been waiting for her behind the door with the full chamberpot in his hand so that when she came back he could chuck it at her and make a bid for freedom (in which he succeeded). Because the widow had ducked quickly the missile had missed its mark and landed on me. 'Les amants des prostituées sont heureux, dispos et repus …' Mademoiselle Cricri, the widow, invited everyone whose night's rest had been disturbed for a drink in her room. She came over to me in person to make a formal apology and to invite me, with a curtsey. I was still painfully involved with my tapeworm and tried to refuse, though without success, and anyway I was in fact quite keen to go.

This spicy little adventure with the smashed door, the soaked bed and all the chattering *poules* reminded me of short stories about artistic life, Murger's *La Vie de Bohème*, Maupassant's *La Maison Tellier*, Toulouse-Lautrec, Degas, Bubu de Montparnasse. And so Mademoiselle Cricri abducted me triumphantly to her now overcrowded double room. Like a defeated rooster I perched in an unbelievably unorgiastic manner on Cricri's double bed, where seven ladies were already sitting rather stiffly, taking synchronized sips of cognac, which had been a lover's gift from a wine-merchant. Each one of the love-goddesses addressed grave and stylized formulas of politeness in my direction: 'Grand artiste photographe', 'Monsieur Blondel' (the rue Blondel was the most notorious street of brothels near the Porte St Martin). They all wanted to have their photograph taken, not nude, as you might have expected, but dressed for their first communion. Even when they were all pretty tipsy there was nothing erotic in any of this. The streetwalkers' slang I had learnt in the First World War wasn't enough – nothing is up to Parisians rattling it out like a machine-gun ('il n'est bon bec que de Paris' – Villon). I camouflaged the fact that I couldn't understand a single bloody word of this twittering argot with the tired old émigré trick of staring intently at the lips of the woman speaking and either laughing or furrowing my brow as expectation demanded. The expression on my face was usually about three sentences ahead of the conversation. When the ladies began to complain about the *chaudepisse* of one of their younger colleagues, and started to sing 'Avec les pompoms, avec les pompoms, avec les pompiers', the glasses of cognac started to have a soporific effect on my empty stomach, and the assembled beauties deported me ever so gently fast asleep back into my drenched bed.

Three times now I have had imposed on me by fate the Herculean task of having to live my life in a new language. This is an indispensable form of brain-massage for anyone who wants to become a citizen of the world. Emigration keeps you young. For fifty years I've been unlearning my mother-tongue. In the absence of linguistic talent, I've never been able to find a stepmother-tongue. Although by nature I speak fast, I started to speak slowly so that I could think about my mistakes in advance; I avoided the *subjonctif conditionnel*, I became cautious and deliberate. It was worst in Holland, where everybody will have a spiteful laugh if a foreigner makes the slightest mistake. *En France on déteste les sales métèques –* bloody foreigners! *– mais on reste poli quand-même*. It's best in America, where everybody has been an immigrant at some time or other: zey simply adore ze foreign accents. Terrified of drawing attention to ourselves and getting ourselves deported, we émigrés whispered a lot, with our mouths meaningfully closed. After all, you were only being tolerated there. And you spoke quietly because your passport had long since expired, your *carte d'identité* was never *en règle*, you were working without a *permis de travail*, and you were ashamed of your mother-tongue. Only the aristocrats of the émigré community – diamond merchants and dealers in works of art or stamps, who had managed to get their dough out of the country in time – shouted even louder than they did at home, and even they had to admit that their fluent Berlin schoolboy French didn't actually flow all that freely. But they sat ostentatiously at open-air cafés scoffing chateaubriand steaks.

When I was making a start in Paris, Geneviève proved herself in a right royal fashion. None of the demanding customers that she sent my way ever paid, but every one of these customers introduced new customers who didn't pay either. And so I got myself talked about, started to build up a reputation. Paris doesn't pay you in hard currency: *on vous fait une réputation. Placé à Paris, placé dans l'univers.* I was crazy about my patron saint, Geneviève. Not that I would ever have gone further than kissing her hand, but my wife and I were often invited to dinner. For émigrés in Paris, this was a rare honour. When we were at table, her father, Maître Rouault, never let anyone get a word in, and complained unstoppably about his obsession, that *gangestère* (gangster) Vollard, his agent, exploited him. Rouault demanded homage, and in his turn he showed a mystic veneration for St Joan, which seemed grotesque to me, since I thought that a modern painter would be a modern man. Unfortunately I couldn't understand much of his excitedly witty diatribes. If you don't understand every single word, you don't understand any of it. On one of those evenings I asked Rouault to give me a few words to put on the invitation cards to my first exhibition of photographs (*chez Billiet, rue la Boëtie, vernissage le 2 mars 1936*). Rouault enjoyed refusing, and sent me instead to Valéry: 'il adore être embêté'. Valéry, whom I had come to overrate as the greatest mind in Paris from reading the *Nouvelle Revue Française*, received me, the young photographer, with the blasé amiability of the monocled genius and man of the world, and without interrupting his telephone conversations with the aristocracy. He knew how to impress, himself in particular. 'I am willing', he said in a patronizing voice, 'to glance through your portfolio, just so long as you don't ask me to write anything by way of introduction to your exhibition', and he flicked fleetingly through my pictures. Unfortunately I could sympathize with him. And when you understand someone, you can't scrounge very effectively. On the invitation cards I had printed a *bon mot* from Valéry's *Idée fixe*: 'Ce qu'il y a de plus profond dans l'homme, c'est la peau'. Underneath I wrote some crap of my own: 'On cherchait par la photographie psychologique le portrait definitif; on a découvert un nouvel aspect de la beauté'. I really thought I was brilliant. At that time I did 'definitive portraits' of Rouault and Matisse. Both bitched like primadonnas that I had made them look older than they were, and right after my photos were taken both of them did self-portraits that made them look a lot younger again. Masters of vanity. Rouault even wrote me a poem about his *tête de forçat*, his convict portrait.

Geneviève had a very tense relationship with her husband, Rapha, of the kind I knew all about from reading Balzac. They quarrelled over every word. When Rapha declared it to be a *choirée sarmante* for the tenth time in any given evening,

Geneviève would explode. There was a strange Judaeo-Jesuitical-French oppor-
tunism about the whole family. Maître Rouault was a royalist – *Action Française* —
while his son-in-law was a Moroccan Jew, a great dentist and a great boaster;
Geneviève, just finishing her medical studies, was one of the left-wing oriented
New Youth, *gauche sentimentale*. There were also mothers, sisters and a baby.

What appalled, delighted, and completely threw me was the fact that every
night, Geneviève was there soliciting passers-by on the whore-filled corner of the
boulevard Montparnasse and the rue Montparnasse. When I first saw her, in her
tight-fitting black satin dress, with her serious *sourire de Reims*, and with her
dimple, seducing a young matelot into the Hôtel des deux Maries (Mary Salome
and Mary the Mother of James), I was completely taken aback by the double life of
my patron saint. Was this the working-out of her famous father's erotic fantasies?
Once I did force myself to speak to her. While I was trying to find the words and
couldn't get further than 'pourquoi?', she turned contemptuously on her high
heels, left me standing, and took an older client into the hotel. Was she a doppel-
gänger or was it a secret life? Anyway, I was a stupid little libertine with double
standards. I idolized whores as saints, and took it amiss when my own saint
demeaned herself to the status of a houri. It wasn't until just before the war that the
puzzle was solved; I was sitting with Rapha and Geneviève outside the Coupole
when her double streetwalked past.

53 LA BELLE HÉLAINE – AVANT ET APRÈS

It soon became clear that the portrait business wasn't going to work. My fashion
hopes were left stranded outside the hermetically sealed doors of the fashion magazines. *Haute couture* also displayed an unexpected fear of my talent and a lack of
money for photos. So all that was left was the world of advertising, which I
despised. Every day I hurled myself at potential clients, clutching my portfolio of
photographs. To my amazement, it worked. People gave me commissions.
However, I had neither a studio, nor the money to buy the materials I needed.
Robert Guesclin was my first art director. The first time I heard that word, I
thought it was a joke. It wasn't. It seemed incomprehensible to me that my ideas,
my work, and my photos should be manipulated, castrated, denatured and prepared for press by somebody else, an art director. In Paris in those days people still
thought that art directors were concerned with art. Later on, in America, I came

face to face with the raw pathology of the arse-director: failed photographers, lashing out in all directions in revenge for the fact that they haven't got any talent. Their emblems are hourglasses, sunbursts, suppositories, and butterflies. An appalling lot. Robert Guesclin, however, was a Frenchman, with a flair for cosmetics ads, which he created for the biggest manufacturer of hair colouring in the world: revolutionary and tasteful posters, on which the whole cosmos of cosmetics has been vegetating ever since. Guesclin was a Parisian, a maliciously cultured introvert (Proust), who despised effort, particularly his own. He would let you work on a commission until you were bled white. Once you had delivered the work he would stare at it without a word, wrap himself in silence, and not be available to talk to you for weeks. He avoided conversations about payment as rigorously as he avoided payment itself. That's what I had to live on. His office, rue Volnay, faubourg St Honoré, was a journalist's junk room out of *Césare Birotteau*. A watch was kept on Guesclin from an ante-room by an old witch called Madame X, to whom he was somehow indebted. She wasn't an employee of the firm, but arranged on her own account and by judicious use of the evil eye that no younger women ever came near him. His lay-out-and-paste-up-as-a-page-boys (the assistants) kissed his hands and licked his boots, and were cheeky to newcomers like me. Later on they licked my boots as well. Once an artist has arrived, it's *cher maître* all the time. Guesclin never turned up before noon, never left anyone simmering gently in the waiting room for less than an hour, never kept appointments, disappeared for hours for lunch and staggered back to his office late in the afternoon so that the big boss would notice, and then dozed off. *Un philosophe.* We struck up an acquaintance fairly hesitantly, and started to become friends after a mere four years. Now that we no longer have anything to do with each other and never ever see each other, we have become real intimates, *des vieux copains*. He had a profile like Dante, with lips tight and thin, was a freethinker, a reactionary, a libertine, an antisemite and an epicurean – a combination treated favourably by the climate of Paris: *un combinard*. Tight-fisted, with taste and an eye for price, an exploiter, like all Frenchmen. Being exploited by him gave me a masochistic thrill. Often we would browse through the *marché aux puces*, looking for Sunday painters for his collection (fires and still-life paintings of red fruit). Afterwards we'd lounge around in the bistros of the Porte St Ouen. He always got me to pay, something I didn't find easy in those impecunious times. To pay me back he graciously afforded me the

honour (honour as in honorary, namely unpaid: *je vous autorise*) of photographing his divine young mistress, Hélaine de L., a *femme du monde*, the daughter of
some South American ambassador, *une grande dame d'autrefois*. I have a congeni-
tal weakness for that sort of magnificently perfumed luxurious creature, all
rustling silks and sophistication, giving them an appearance of soul. For one long
and wonderful afternoon I struggled with this magnificent being to try and take
her picture. It is far harder to capture the beauty of a real beauty than it is to make
a plain woman look beautiful. Hélaine was indescribably beautiful, although goddesses always want to be beautiful differently from the way I see them. It takes
decades for them to grow into their pictures. A good portrait has to mature. The
model gets older, the photo stays young.

Twenty years after this session, on a trip to Europe, I visited Guesclin – who
by now had become my best friend – in Aix-en-Provence, where he had mummified,
and was now playing Philemon and Baucis with his rich erstwhile Cerberus,
Madame X, who had conquered him at the start of the war (one of the few French
victories). She was eighty and looked sixty; he was sixty and looked ninety.
Cézanne's *Mont St Victoire*, pale blue, shone from another world into their little
olive grove. After a highly civilized lunch – just a little heavy on the garlic – the
ladies drove off into town to go shopping. Robert began to shake horribly, and took
me off to his study, clearly with a lot on his mind. Although we were alone in the
house, he locked the door carefully, rolled back some of the carpet and took a worn
envelope that seemed familiar to me out of a secret hiding-place, and lovingly
spread out before me the series of photos of *la belle Hélaine* taken in 1937. We were
both much moved by this glimpse of the snows of yesteryear. Squatting on the floor
amongst the photos, he looked at me with his white and flowing hair, like an old
woman with a bellyache, and he found it hard to speak. '*Cher ami*, you've probably
heard that I've been bound over for a year because of opium (the judge smokes it
too). I've got to be careful. When you take a pipe it really heightens the senses. But
I've got a toothache that's been nagging me for a long time, and you, *cher ami*, have
got to help me. Three weeks ago when I was in Paris I saw Hélaine again, in the
street, for the first time since our painful separation; she was more beautiful than
ever before, and I couldn't say a word to her, *j'étais avec Madame*. She didn't even
acknowledge my discreet salutation. My conscience won't let me rest. You see,
Hélaine still doesn't know to this day what entirely selfless motives I had for break-

ing up with her. *Cher ami*, you must go and see her on your way back through Paris and explain all this to her. In 1939 I was on my way to my beloved Hélaine when I broke a tooth, right outside the Théâtre Français (to prove he was telling the truth he pointed to his mouth). Instead of going to see her I had to go to the dentist, and while he was drilling away, it suddenly dawned on me that I was too old for a young goddess like her. *Cher ami*, you have to convince Hélaine that it was purely out of consideration for her that I dropped her' (*laisser tomber*, a constant theme in French morality).

My passion for *avant et après* seduced me into arranging to meet Hélaine again. She was a bit on the dismissive side when I rang her up. She'd be quite happy to see me again as an old acquaintance, so long as I did not let fall a word about the disgraced Robert. She also felt it necessary to prepare me for the fact that she had aged twenty-five years in the intervening period. At five in the afternoon I found her in Passy, in the rue Renouart, in a little maisonette near Balzac's villa, all very middle-class. It was a melancholy experience to discover in this rotund matron in her fifties faint shadows of her past beauty. We swapped experiences over a glass of wine. At the beginning of the German occupation she had fled to Lyons with her small daughter, on foot and without a penny to her name. To keep from starving she had worked in a *maison de rendezvous* there, and got to know the owner of a big concern, who had taken her under his wing. Since that time she had been his personal secretary and mistress. Unfortunately his ghastly wife refused to die, and *ça ne divorce pas*. I kept my own experiences to myself. In any case, the French never believe a word you say. If, on the other hand, you start to tell them about the horrors of French concentration camps (my favourite topic), they just don't listen. France is good at keeping its shame under wraps. And so I told her about New York, a topic which interests all Parisians in a spirit of malicious competitiveness, and then slipped abruptly into that cavity in Robert's tooth. As if she had been bitten by a tarantula she leapt up and said, 'That miser didn't drop me because he lost one of his toothy-pegs, it was because I'd lost all my money! As soon as the news broke about the collapse of the Argentina Insurancia, which is where my father had invested his millions, Robert let his old witch marry him. And to keep her claws on him, she's poisoned him, she's turned him into an old man, completely gaga, and she makes him dance to her opium pipe. You've seen how he trembles. I've had my revenge'. In her triumph she glowed with youth again. I'd have liked to spend the evening with her. Unfortunately I had to leave. She asked me to stay for another five minutes, so that she could give me a surprise, disappeared into the next room and allowed me to hear, through the half-opened door, that she was changing her clothes. Every item of clothing has its own music. After a quarter of an hour she posed, powdered and rouged, in a sky-blue taffeta dress that was far too tight, a formal ballgown by Poiret from 1912. When I had finished admiring her, she unrolled a roll of canvas that she had in her hand, a life-sized portrait of her mother in the very same ballgown, painted I think by Le Sidaner. When I left she asked me for one of the photos that I had taken. Robert hadn't given her a single print.

54   THE TALE OF GRIMM THE BEAUTIFUL

One summer evening in 1936 I ran into the photographer Landshoff on the boulevard Montparnasse, and told him with delight that I had been able – with the help of friends – to rent a wonderful studio, 9 rue Delambre, and that I was going to move in the next day. He promised to send me the most beautiful model, and he kept his word. The following afternoon the bluest of cerulean eyes shone into my still-empty atelier. Honey-blonde, heavily pregnant, and dead tired, Fräulein Grimm flopped onto the only piece of furniture, a worn out sofa left behind by the previous tenant. Grimm – who didn't have a first name – was only barely capable of trotting out the story of her life, and this was her sole topic of conversation, one she had learnt by heart. Born the daughter of the Professor of Classics at Frankfurt, she had committed a racial impropriety by taking up with a Hungarian Jew, Baron von Tillaly, had eloped with him to Prague, and landed in Paris by way of Vienna. Like ten thousand others she was penniless and without papers (if you had pennies, you got papers). On the other hand, she was the most beautiful woman in the world. Possibly also the dumbest. Reluctantly I had to admit that beauty and stupidity are closely related. My in-depth psychoanalysis was followed by depth of focus: some fantastic time-exposures. Grimm, sound asleep, was undisturbed by the heat of the lights or the heat of creativity. After a couple of hours she woke up with a scream of 'Tristan!' It was dark, and I helped her down the stairs into the street. By the door, her little Tristan was waiting, a repulsive would-be intellectual who immediately tried, without success, to bum five francs from me. Insulted, he exclaimed, 'Come, my dear Isolde, let us take our leave.

Another worthless individual!' Reluctantly I concluded that ugliness and intelligence are not necessarily closely related.

A few weeks later Isolde was safely delivered of a little daughter, called Tristania, the very image of her papa. My photos of the sleeping Grimm appeared soon after, a series that helped launch both our careers. Even in America. *Esquire* had bought fifty Blumenfeld photos for its new pocket magazine, *Coronet*, at the fantastic price of fifteen dollars each, and had even paid. France paid with promises, and even then *30 jours fin du mois 5% + 2% + 2%*. Thériade the Minotaur negotiated this one for me. In return I had to give him twenty-two photos for his new magazine, *Verve*, for nothing. *J'étais placé*. Things began to improve.

La Grimm became a sought-after model, and was in a position to support her husband and child, more or less. Wherever Isolde was modelling, Tristan would push the pram to the door, set up a little camp-stool and start knitting little things for baby while he waited for her eternal return. He let it be known that he was working at night on his *Isoldean Elegies*, which nobody ever laid eyes on. When I was starting at *Vogue* I made some beautiful pages with Grimm, until her German kitchen clap-trap started to nauseate me. If someone said 'Bonjour, Madame Grimm' she took offence at French superficiality. She soon became famous – models get famous faster than photographers – played the prima donna, and was soon expecting her third baby, which made things even more difficult. In June 1939 I photographed the unbearably beautiful Grimm for the last time, in the Bois de Boulogne, leaning against an ancient tree with a gigantic fur hat (Schiaparelli) on her (Botticelli) head. She grumbled and fussed so much throughout the whole session that I said we would never work together again. A fortnight later the Second World War broke out.

Fifteen years later, Madame Dillé – the fairy godmother for all photographers and models – asked me to have a look at a girl who needed some good photos to get started. I wasn't to ask too many questions, and she'd tell me all about it later. In came a browbeaten, uninteresting creature. *Tristania!* (No surname.) Touched, I told her that she had visited me in my studio eighteen years earlier in her mama's belly, just before she was born. She wasn't interested. She only wanted to know if and when I would take her photograph. I invited her to lunch. She refused, her father was waiting outside. I couldn't do a thing for her – she had too much Tristan and not enough Isolde. Later on, Madame Dillé told me the full story of what happened after August 1939.

Like all enemy aliens, Tristan was put into a French concentration camp. The fashion business had come to a halt, and Isolde wasn't any good at anything except being beautiful, the little ones were crying for bread. Trying to get Tristan released, Isolde appealed to the butcher, the baker and the candlestick-maker. They all promised to do their utmost if she would do the same. Isolde slept with the butcher, the baker and the candlestick-maker, without managing to get Tristan released. After the phoney war came the incredibly rapid collapse of France. The French concentration camps were handed over, as per the rules, to the victorious Germans, which made Grimm's negotiations that much easier, since she had always had a few problems with her French. Victors can promise more, no need to keep their promises. She went from officer to officer, got around and was soon the most sought after bacchante of the whole general staff. She was given a luxury villa in the Bois (abandoned by its Jewish owner), and a lot of her dreams came true – a governess and a pony for each child, genuine Rembrandts above the four-poster bed, diamonds, champagne, fantastic ball-gowns, liveried servants and luxurious lingerie. And she was doing it all for Tristan. Helpful as ever, the good old Gestapo took him up as a special case. Tristan the Jew was made into an honorary Aryan, taken out of Drancy and transferred to solitary confinement in a Paris jail, with partridge for breakfast. Through the bars of his cell he was allowed to wave to his children as they rode past. Isolde was optimistic. Just a few more formalities and he would be free. All she had to do was to wheedle this or that secret out of this or that general whilst engaged in amorous activities, and soon Tristan would be in her arms again, writing poetry and knitting. The dumbest woman in the world did her best as a Gestapo spy. Several generals who had enjoyed a little hanky-panky with la Grimm found themselves condemned to death. This went on until she became so besotted with a nordic god of a captain in the Luftwaffe that one night in bed she confessed to him her relationship with the Gestapo. The enraged airman kicked up a great fuss at Gestapo headquarters. The next morning, when the children came back from a ride in the Bois on their ponies in their little Scottish kilts they found their mama stone dead on the steps of their villa with a swastika nailed to her forehead.

55 EN VOGUE

Late one morning at the beginning of my Paris years I was woken from a deep sleep by Rosalie, the maid at the Hotel Celtique, knocking on my door to say there was a telephone call for me. Six floors down to the office in my tattered raincoat. An Anglo-Saxon siren voice started to sing my praises. Cecil Beaton, the Lord Byron of the camera, crown prince of Brilliantia, court photographer and *enfant gâté et terrible de 'Vogue'*, poured balm upon my wounded spirits. He said he thought my portraits of the daughters of the Vicomtesse Marie-Laure de Noailles were *divine*! Could I perhaps join him for afternoon tea at the Ritz that day? The doors to the drawing-room of the world – hitherto barred – seemed to be bursting open. In spite of first-class references and introductory visiting cards endorsed by the great and good I had never managed to get through to the editor-in-chief of *Vogue*. Between three and five on a Friday he used to receive artists. Every Friday I would wait, with a large group of fellow-sufferers. Around six he would come back, slightly overheated, from lunch, pass through the guard-of-honour of artists, as they rose politely at his entrance, without giving a single one the benefit of a glance. He would never receive more than one (either a man with particularly important connections or a woman with particularly attractive legs). His charming secretary, Lionne, would then put the rest off until the following Friday.

I knocked on Beaton's door at the Ritz, went in, and saw a lady in a lace negligée sitting in front of the mirror trying on a hat with a large ostrich feather. I assumed that this was Cecil's famous sister, Baba, and made my apologies. It was Cecil, who was in the process of selecting some clothes for a fashion photo. Laughing, he called out 'Erwaine!' In spite of our differences we quickly became good friends, and have stayed that way – *avec un certain sourire* – for a lifetime.

Under Cecil's wing I soon got into the *Vogue* establishment, and quickly learned to despise that philistine vanity fair, in which small-ad profiteers pretend to be arbiters of elegance. Illusions are there to be shattered. In that ants' nest of unrequited ambition, where *nouveautés* have to be pursued *à tout prix*, I remained – in spite of a thousand pages of published photos – an outsider, a foreign body. Michel de Brunhoff, *rédacteur-en-chef de Vogue* Paris, explained to me: '*Si vous étiez seulement né baron et devenu pédé, vous seriez le plus grand photographe du monde!*' ('If only you'd been born a baron and become homosexual, you'd be the greatest photographer in the world!') Only I had already discovered: *le monde n'existe plus.*

After a year I had had enough of *Vogue* and decided to go to New York and try my luck with *Harper's Bazaar*. The best decision of my life. The fastest and ugliest of the ocean-giants, the *Normandie*, got me from Le Havre to the steam-bath of New York in five days, where I disembarked on a hellishly hot morning in July. The 1939 World's Fair (*The World of Tomorrow*) had just opened. At that time the New World was still genuinely new. In Manhattan they were tearing things down and building things at a furious rate. The elevated train was going underground. The new skyscrapers were no longer trying to look like forty-storey barococo hot-dog stands and were daring to show a new and individual face to the world, thanks to Le Corbusier (Paris), Oud (Dutch neo-realism), Mies van der Rohe (the Weimar Bauhaus). What's new usually comes from outside. Air conditioning was starting to make life more bearable and the first radios that you could carry around like hand-luggage were shouting themselves hoarse on the streets. The New Deal had triumphed over the forces of reaction, nylon over silk, vitamins over human weaknesses. The world, which had been so big only yesterday, was shrinking. Air clippers were already flying a letter across the Atlantic in twenty-four hours. America had emerged from the depression as a superpower, and F.D.R. was conducting world politics from his wheelchair. The European intelligentsia found a safe refuge here, and by way of thanks invented the atomic bomb. *Happy days are here again!*

The tweed jacket that I had had made to measure in Paris to wear in New York was like being locked in a red-hot steam bath. I only spoke a few words of broken English and I didn't understand American at all. I settled in at the Gladstone Hotel on East Fifty-Second and took a day off, but decided to combine business with pleasure and get a fountain-pen repaired that I'd bought fifteen years earlier in Amsterdam. The lifetime guarantee that I'd kept for all those years in my wallet had the address on it: 10, Broadway. All I had to do was walk straight down Broadway. The desk-clerk at the hotel advised against it. I could do it on the subway in twenty minutes. According to the thermometer it was 103 degrees, but Fahrenheit didn't mean anything to me. And you only get to know a country and its people on foot (an essentially German idea!). Through the urban canyons of skyscrapers and low, old-fashioned houses I soon reached Broadway, and then I lost all sense of everything – distance, time and taste, and tumbled into the nearest bar, dying of thirst. Men in straw hats were standing around the counter, and I ordered a large glass of that freshly squeezed orange juice that I had heard so much about. They brought me a whisky highball, which I didn't have the self-confidence to refuse. They even admired me. By two o'clock I had already reached 1650 Broadway, only another 1,640 numbers to go. When I got to the famous Times Square, a conglomeration of shacks with billboards all over them, dirtier than the Place Pigalle and full of drunks, beggars, pickpockets and cops, my shoes got stuck in the soft asphalt. Had I drunk too much? After a few more highballs in a few more bars (every time I said 'orange juice' the bartender would laugh and bring me whisky; could it have had something to do with my pronunciation?) the buildings reached up and up, crying out to high heaven. When I got to Wall Street they overreached themselves and scraped the very skies. I, on the other hand, got smaller and smaller, like Gulliver in Brobdingnag, and started to run, and then, towards evening and gasping with effort, I reached number 10. It was closed. New York offices shut at five and anyway, Waterman had moved. I was suffering painfully from the absence of Paris-style *pissoirs*, and there weren't even any trees around, nor handy cafés. In Paris you would bump into some acquaintance at any time of the day, but here the people didn't even look at you. I was starving, but I didn't dare go into a restaurant. I'd heard that you could eat at a drugstore, but it seemed implausible that you might be able to get a meal in a pharmacy. So I just lurched from bar to bar until – around midnight – I got back to Fifty-Second Street, which had undergone a remarkable change. Coloured neon advertising signs, blacks kicking up a racket outside nightclubs where they were playing jazz, women dolled up to the nines and smoking, looking at themselves in handmirrors – night life straight out of the movies. Just before I got to the hotel I saw a sight which made my photographer's heart race: lying face down on the steps leading up to a brownstone was a man in a tuxedo but with no trousers, blood dripping from his naked backside. Above this floated a kind of halo. Passers-by were passing him by without a glance. It was just like in the pink *Police Gazette*. As always happens at crucial moments I didn't have my camera. I'm not a photojournalist. Forgetting how tired I was, I sprinted into the hotel and within fifteen minutes I was back there with my camera, just in time to see an ambulance drive away. Only a pool of blood was left of this vanished splendour.

Next morning I packed my hundred best photos into a briefcase, something which (though I didn't know it) would brand me as a German travelling salesman. I wanted to see Henry Luce, the publisher of *Life* magazine, to whom Lucien Vogel had given me a flattering letter of introduction when I left Paris. In the Rockefeller Center, faced with all those cathedral-like highrise buildings, I had a positively mystical feeling of awe for this world of tomorrow, just as the haunted stones of Chartres had on one occasion transported me mystically back into the world of yesterday. An express lift carried me to the thirty-fifth floor in twelve seconds. For the first time in my life I looked from an air-conditioned room on the top of the world down onto Babel in the burning July sunshine. The most genuinely lapidary expression of modern madness, a breathtaking heap of stones.

Luckily, Luce had left for Europe a day or so earlier. His secretary, visibly impressed by Vogel's recommendation, passed me – after a phone call – on to an androgynous creature of my own age, with a pink tie, reddish hair and a wolfish grin, fascinatingly unreliable, who now hurried along to take care of me – this was Alex King, alias Herr König from Vienna, alias Rosenberg from Budapest, an ideas man at *Life* who spoke, without a trace of accent or indeed a pause for breath, German, American, Yiddish and Mishmash. Although we had never seen each other in our lives he fell upon me as if I were an old friend. 'Of course we know each other, Irving, we met in Paris', he said, going straight onto first-name terms. Within ten minutes he had promoted me to being his cousin. The way he spoke reminded me so strongly of George Grosz that I asked whether he knew him. 'Do I know him??! George is my best friend, I let him work on my magazine *Americana* with me, fantastic graphic artist, too much of a genius for the Americans.' King wasn't only a somewhat suspect Grosz-imitator, he was a genuine one: everything he did was an imitation. In the chaos of his tiny office he explained his position. 'To become an editor for *Life* you have to be a chronic alcoholic. At the crucial moment, when a war breaks out or a president gets assassinated, they are all drunk. And so they need at least one Jew like me who's sober and can make the decisions.' While he was talking he looked at all my photos with an interest, an understanding and an enthusiasm that I have never found in the world of journalism before or since. He was possessed of a pathological urge to express himself. Shadowy faceless figures in shirtsleeves and with ties loosened kept coming into his office with photos or copy for him to look at. King dealt with everything with a virtuoso display of clowning, laughed at all of them and introduced me to every one of these nonentities as 'the greatest living photographer', to which every one of them replied 'Hello, Irving!' With the door wide open Alex took out a hypodermic, filled it with a milky fluid and quite unselfconsciously stuck the needle into his arm. 'Vitamin E!' This didn't arouse even the slightest suspicion in me. Only when King promised to give me a big feature in the next issue of *Life* as top photographer did it dawn on me that he was crazy. Clutching a handful of my photos he took me into a larger office next door to his. 'Wilson Hicks, Picture Editor.' A pair of glasses without a face, who stared at the photos without seeing them. King introduced me bombastically as a world-famous celebrity, which was embarrassing. He spread a series of my pictures out in front of Hicks and announced with a kind of suggestive formality: 'Speaking about pictures... Blumenfeld's are the tops!' Hicks nodded. 'OK.' I was strangely moved by the fact that you could do business in the Land of the Dollar without mentioning cash at all, until I realized later that '*Life* doesn't pay'. When he noticed that I was about to broach something prosaic, Hicks took my photo of Claus Sluter's *Death of Christ* and waxed lyrical: 'What an ad for Pepsodent!' King dragged me out into the corridor and whispered enthusiastically, 'Irving, you're made! What else can I do for you?' I asked him to show me the quintessence of the city of New York (I actually said 'the New Yorkiest'). King looked at his watch with a diabolical grin. 'In exactly twenty-five minutes, at twelve fifteen, your wish shall be granted! In the meantime if you like you can earn a quick five hundred dollars by picking ten of your photos that I can publish with an article about you in a little photographic magazine called *Minicam*!' So at last I had reached that blessed land which floweth with milk and dollars. While I was sorting out the pictures, Alex disappeared. A quarter of an hour later he took me up to the very top floor, to the penthouse, where there was telescope on a stand. A butler brought us drinks. Once again Alex introduced me as the greatest living photographer. The butler said 'Hello, Irving', too. This was democracy. In front of me a million windows were shimmering in the bright glow of midday. King let me look through the telescope, whilst he made do with binoculars. Through the lens I saw a window, away in the somewhat over-exposed blue distance but looking close enough to touch, and in the window a blonde girl was shimmering behind a typewriter, something which didn't seem to me to be especially American. Alex told me to be patient and in sixty seconds I would get the point. And indeed, in came a man, who stood behind the girl and kissed the back of her neck. She stopped typing and got up, he settled himself down and helped her out of her blouse. Like the commentator in a silent film, my mentor explained to me that the boss, a stockbroker, turned up every midday at exactly the same time, rain or shine, from the stock exchange to carry out this manoeuvre with absolute punctuality. American eroticism. As our observation post was higher than the love-nest we could look down into the room and share with vicarious enjoyment what other eyes didn't see or suspect. Where there are lots of windows there are lots of voyeurs.

In the Café du Dôme I thought of the Hungarian artist Tiyany, famous for his monocle and red waistcoat, a deaf and dumb raconteur who knew seven languages. His passion was lipreading the love-talk of Montmartre couples through a telescope from his balcony at Parc Montsouris, the highest point of Montparnasse.

After this successful morning we floated earthwards in the lift down into the breathtaking hell-heat of Rockefeller Plaza. I went to a meeting at *Harper's Bazaar*, where I got a contract, King went to lunch. As we were saying goodbye, he luckily discovered at the last moment that he had left his wallet upstairs, and I was happy to let him have twenty dollars, which I never saw again, much like many another time he managed to hypnotize twenty dollars out of my pocket, using a new ruse each time. A *schnorrer* of genius. However, my *Life* photos really did appear and so did the ten in *Minicam*, the five hundred dollars for which Alex pocketed himself at a time when I desperately needed the money, back in France. A coke habit is expensive, Alex needed a lot, and once again I never suspected a thing. A catalogue of his con-tricks would read like the tales of some New York Eulenspiegel.

I had developed a critical stance towards American sexual behaviour that was based upon those telescoperotic discoveries during my first few days in New York. Years later I found out that I had fallen for a one-act play that King used to get some students from the theatre school to perform whenever he had to show European greenhorns the quintessence of New York life.

A summary of America in 1939: the New World was even more utopian than in the novels we had laughed at when we were younger. The mass of humanity, computed from pills, pollen-count, polls and polio. Very confusingly, *homo technologicus* still uses the same old words, which leads to new misunderstandings. 'Loving care' has become a hair conditioner, 'Right' a ballpoint pen and 'Serutan' ('nature's' backwards!) a laxative.

The greatest experience: arriving in New York.

The best: Hellzapoppin, Olsen and Johnson's American *commedia dell'arte* at the Winter Gardens. I saw this Dadaesque slapstick burlesque every night for five evenings in a row. Orgies of disrespect, like Elsie, the Borden cow, which laughed as it allowed itself to be milked by a machine, to the strains of Beethoven's *Eroica*, at the World's Fair. The true style of New York is black, black, black: boogie-woogie in Harlem's Jitterbug Savoy. Concentrated cross-cultural comedy: the huge number of fake Rembrandts in the Metropolitan Museum. In that museum I was taken in, like everyone else, by two superb gigantic Etruscan warriors (500 BC), which also turned out twenty years later, alas, to be fakes. The minute you set foot on American soil you lose all sense of what is genuine.

The worst: the hothouse heat and humidity.

The very worst of all: the tasteless grub, and the even grubbier table-manners of those tasting it.

After seven weeks in the *World of Tomorrow* with cocktail parties, successes and deadlines, I sailed back to Europe, happy as could be, so that I could photograph the autumn fashions in Paris.

56 MADE IT!

After five seemingly endless days on the *Normandie*, I arrived safely back in Le Havre on 10 August 1939. The gigantic wreck of the *Paris* lay ominously in the harbour like a dead whale. She had been set on fire and sunk a few months earlier by unidentified saboteurs. The same thing was to happen to the *Normandie* itself a few years later in New York harbour. I was in a sentimental mood. Had there not been people watching and had my wife not been waiting for me on the quay I should probably have knelt down and kissed the soil of France. And what's more, I expected my love to be reciprocated. I hadn't just arrived, I had made it. I'd exchanged my *Vogue* contract for a much better one with *Harper's Bazaar*, *Life* had presented me to the world as a 'top photographer', I had been successful in the steam-bath of New York and now I wanted to live the life of Riley, in *la belle France*. At last, after years of *la vie de bohème*, moving on from one horrible furnished room to another and living out of suitcases, I could now think about having a proper place to live. I'd found a lovely apartment in the rue de Verneuil in the faubourg St-Germain, wood-panelled, with high windows, mirrors and fireplaces.

With a few alterations (for which I already had estimates) it would make an ideal studio-apartment. The lease was waiting for my signature after the holidays – so long as there *wasn't* a war.

Although I had been getting on everyone's nerves for twenty years with my permanent predictions of this very war, I counted once again, just as I had in September 1938 and August 1914, on a last-minute miracle, and I kept on saying very firmly that it was logically impossible for war to break out that year. My wife was of a completely different opinion, and ever since she has preened herself on her deeper insight at that time. At the very moment when I had begun to enjoy the sunshine of success, a world war was extremely inconvenient. I thought of France as a very clever chess-player, who would get Old Germany to walk into a trap, and then playfully wipe her out. Everyone knew that the Nazis were bluffing and that you had to out-bluff them. Every day you were reassured once again in the newspapers that France had the best and very probably (according to *Paris-Soir*) also the best-dressed army in the world, her billions in gold reserves (and a franc that was devalued daily), her Gamelins, her Giraudoux, and even her De Gaulles. We suspected that the unbreachable Maginot Line (and its intellectual counterpart) was only half in place, but at the same time we believed in it entirely. The proud Poles would show yet again what tradition means. Russia, the giant bear with paws of clay, would drop Germany and attack it from behind. France and Britain, the Entente cordiale, would forget their differences. Supported by their enormous empires, on which the sun very rarely set, and with the help of their stinking rich Uncle Sam, they would dictate terms for a lasting peace in an economically reorganized free Europe. There wasn't the slightest doubt that the democracies would have an easy victory over Hitler. Germany, half-starved and suffering from a lack of gold and genius, as well as from Goering and Goebbels, was on the point of collapse in moral and in military terms. What we were going to do with fifty million Nazis in the middle of Europe afterwards was another problem. Defeatist slogans pushed logic to one side. It was all the fault of Léon Blum, the Communists and the British, perfidious Albion. 'All France wants is to live peacably, everything is fine here. We hate war.' No Frenchman was willing to lift so much as a finger, let alone to fight, for his own freedom, and certainly not for something as remote as the freedom of the world. 'We've hardly got any idea where Poland is, and you expect us to die for Danzig?' All the air-waves were buzzing with bullshit: the Pope,

Mussolini and Roosevelt would all intervene at the last minute. Ciano had had thirty million pounds sterling paid into his personal account to keep Italy neutral. Censorship came in. You were no longer allowed to make telephone calls in a foreign language. I tried to look French and wore a beret so that I wouldn't be arrested as a spy, though anyone could see just by looking at me that I came from Berlin. Super-cautious *boulevardiers* started promenading with chic little over-the-shoulder gas-masks – who knows, maybe there would be an air-raid before war was actually declared? Foreigners hadn't been issued with any. The first gas-mask jokes appeared. Maurice Chevalier and Josephine Baker were already looking for big wartime hits (in vain: France didn't produce any in this war).

The war of nerves started: desperate optimism tried to scare away desperate fears. Housewives rushed around like headless chickens, stockpiling before the shops were emptied of goods. The buses were over-full, taxis not to be found, traffic impossible, shops and restaurants closed: *Clôture annuelle*. Paris is always empty in August and this time it looked as if it would stay that way for good. You could see cars leaving Paris with the family crammed inside, a mattress tied crazily to the roof and swaying about, and often a trailer behind as well. Newspapers had been reduced to a single page because of paper shortages (what, already?), and people would snatch them out of the hands of the news-vendors so that they could read what they had just heard on the radio. Conscripts headed for the railway stations as if they were heading for the slaughterhouse, without flowers, songs or enthusiasm. Like me they were all hoping that it was just a charade. The papers drivelled on about heroic determination. Paris was blacked out. The nights of *la ville lumière* lost their brilliance: it never came back. All the more feverish was the semi-darkness. People tried to avoid being on their own, argued in the cafés until dawn about possibilities and impossibilities, went home dead tired, and at seven in the morning were already trying to catch the first dove of peace on the radio.

I still could have fled to America and avoided many abominations, but I had to follow my destiny: *sequere deum*. Nowadays I can proudly remind people that when the old world collapsed, I was there, playing my own personal part in it all; it was ugly, stupid and life-threatening. It was only a matter of luck that I and my family managed to escape with nothing more than the fright of our lives.

When I was at school, professional patriots had drummed into us that it was sweet and honourable to die for the Fatherland. At home our parents had fed us pretentious ethics; 'to die for your ideals' and high-falutin clichés like that filled us with enthusiasm. This didn't turn us into heroes, but we came to expect the highest level of heroism from others. I was no novice at losing wars; I'd have been glad to rush theatrically (à la Delacroix) to man the barricades for *Paris et mon droit*. Together with a wretched handful of émigré intellectuals from the Café du Dôme I'd have met a noble end, to the amused laughter of the assembled *Parigots: 'Pauv' type.'* If it had been up to me at that time, the splendour of Paris would be in ruins today and I wouldn't even be alive to take photos of the debris. Instead, the streets are glowing with their old magnificence and stink of Gestapo-romanticism, chauvinism and the piss of German soldiers; *Pétain, pinard, patrie*: Hitler's playground. My big nose has retained its sense of smell, but without noticing it, the French have lost their fastidious olfactory sensitivity and every collaborator has become a post-factum *héros de la résistance. Qui perd, gagne* – the loser wins.

Having come back from New York to take photographs of the autumn fashions for *Harper's Bazaar*, I threw myself into the work so thoroughly that there was no time left over for what was going on in the real world. I was always wrapped up in illusions, never had time for the realities of life. I'd sent my wife – against her will – off on holiday with the children to the Haute Savoie, at the foot of Mont Blanc, where I was planning to join her at the beginning of September after the work had been done. I needed a holiday, I wanted to climb Mont Blanc, and I wanted to eat *marcassin au lait*, three more reasons for postponing the war for a bit longer. Anyway, if the worst came to the worst we'd be near the Swiss border – there was already talk, far, far too much talk about concentration camps having been set up for enemy aliens. But that sort of thing would hardly apply to me. I was an internationally known photographer, known to be anti-Hitler, had applied for naturalization a year ago, was working for the American Hearst press, and had made the romantic gesture of declaring myself ready to lay down my life to defend France against the barbarians. Every Frenchman to whom I sang this song just stared at me aghast. I'd committed an unforgivable *faux-pas*. As a precaution I had for some time been collecting testimonials of my loyalty from prominent people, something which was as embarrassing as it was indispensable. Only yesterday I had been with the fashion queen of the whole world, my editor Carmel Snow, to see the *haute couture* president of the whole universe, Lucien Lelong. He praised me to the skies and begged me to regard his house as my own. Unfortunately he moved just after the war broke out, and once he had settled into his new house he could no longer recall my name.

On the morning of Wednesday 29 August, I went to the Hôtel Westminster in rue de la Paix to say goodbye to Carmel before she sailed off back to New York on the *Queen Elizabeth*. We still had to decide whether the latest corset sensation by Mainbocher should be launched in America under the name of 'diabolo', 'wasp-waist' or 'hourglass'. Over the past weeks, days and nights we had worked together with a passionate fervour that had led to mutual admiration which was all the more intense in view of the fact that Edna Chase, Carmel's worthy counterpart at *Vogue*, had tried in vain to lure me back to her magazine by offering me three times the fee *Harper's Bazaar* was paying. Clair Boothe Luce had described Carmel, fifty-something, with pale blue-rinse hair and a drinker's snub nose, as one of the ugliest of the ugly career-women that are so plentiful in America. There was a ballet I never got round to writing called *The Four Graces*, to be danced by those midnight hags Carmel Snow, Edna Chase, Helena Rubinstein and her arch-enemy Elizabeth Arden – each one of them an arbiter of elegance and beauty to the world's youth. Any man who had to do business with these hideous specimens of American womanhood and managed it without turning homosexual had really passed the acid test. I had to work with all four of them, and also with a good number of even more hideous imitations, and it still didn't turn me into a woman-hater.

Carmel's spot-on instinct for fashion was based on a complete lack of cultural conditioning. The sharpest fashion journalist ever, her nastiness was stimulating. Totally tight-fisted whenever anyone wanted something; fantastically generous when she wanted something from you. Her secretary once assured me proudly that she would have murdered her old mother without a second thought to get a good spread in *Harper's Bazaar*.

Like every female fashion editor in every Hollywood film, she was sitting in regal splendour surrounded by carefully orchestrated 'I'm-just-about-to-leave-town' chaos, with huge bouquets of orchids, champagne on ice and telephones. Porters were forever carting the same suitcases in and out. Carmel was dictating letters and telegrams to three different secretaries at the same time, with precision, wit, an outrageous virtuosity and a total lack of soul. She acted as if she hadn't seen me arrive. Then all of a sudden she stretched out all three hands for me to kiss and assured me with an enormous smile that according to her latest top secret information, all dangers of war had disappeared. Peace in our time. Again.

She had just been on the phone to Bullitt, the US ambassador. He would be turning up at the *Harper's Bazaar* studio at twelve noon tomorrow, on the dot, with his daughter Ann, to pose for some colour shots, which he wouldn't have time for if there were any danger of war. While she was telling me this, she was dictating a cable to *Harper's* in New York: HOLD OCTOBERCOVER FOR DOUBLEBULLITTPIX BLU-MENFELD FULLCOLOR CARMEL, and told me with a laugh that in the hotel they had already started taking away pillows from the guest rooms to use in military hospitals, and replacing them with little notes of apology. At the same time she fired off a letter to 'Dear Ambassador Bullitt', confirming with thanks the photo-session that had been arranged, and to be on the safe side she dictated another to Bullitt's secretary, drawing his attention to the propaganda value of their publication for Bullitt, for the USA, and for Ann Bullitt, who was a debutante of marriageable age. Then she leapt up abruptly, looking as beautiful as only ugly American women know how, looked deep into my eyes with undying love and said with profound but phoney friendliness, getting ready as she did so to deal with the next farewell-wisher: 'Bloomie, 'twas divine. Never shall I forget it, never. It was divine!'

The next morning I got to the studio at exactly half-past eleven. Waiting for me, as I had ordered, was a gigantic globe against a green background. As stand-ins for Bullitt and his charming daughter I got my two assistants to pose under the lamps. While everybody turns up at least two hours late for a fashion photo-session in Paris, ambassadors are punctual to the minute. On the other hand they are hopeless as models. The sirens used to howl away every Thursday at twelve, just to test them. Today they didn't sound them, so as not to alarm the population unnecessarily. It struck twelve. I was called to the phone. The US Embassy. Bullitt's private secretary told me that the ambassador regretted that he would be unable to come today, since Miss Bullitt was already on her way back to America. Snap went the trap! Too late, mouse! War! Miss Bullitt would, however, be delighted to have her picture taken for *Harper's Bazaar* in Philadelphia, where she would be staying with relatives, whose address he also gave me. When I came away from the telephone I announced to the two stand-ins, who by now seemed frozen to the globe, that the Bullitt session would be postponed *sine die*. Both of them – one was a Russian, the other a Czech – grinned maliciously, pleased that I had been hit between the eyes. War! Late that afternoon I was booked to have my last photo-session before going on holiday: a young girl in a heavy brocade frock, posing on a chocolate-box swing garlanded with roses (Heim, *Jeunes filles*). My next Paris fashion photo was not to be until eight years later.

We were still at peace. Half an hour later I met an enchanting Parisian *grande dame*, Monique de Séreville, *éditeur de beauté* at *Vogue*, for a *déjeuner d'adieu* in the Tour d'Argent. We were both as entranced with Paris as with a lover, and sat as the only customers in a melancholy mood in one of the most beautiful roof-gardens in the city, overly conscious of a circle of waiters standing idly by. With the *canard pressé* we drank a heavy Châteauneuf du Pape. Monique wanted to know if I thought the Hun would violate anything as beautiful as this. Although I was convinced that several hours before any declaration of war – that is, quite possibly within the next few seconds – Paris would be reduced to a heap of burning rubble covered by noxious gases, I went to absurd lengths to prove to her the complete impossibility of any such thing. For example: if ten thousand German planes headed towards Paris, one of the fully automatic alarm systems on the Maginot line would ensure that at the self-same moment twenty thousand French heavy bombers would take off and be sent to Berlin. All German figures, I said, were wildly exaggerated, whereas the French were far stronger than people thought. (In fact there wasn't as much as a single hand-gun to be found anywhere on the Maginot line; these had been ordered from Germany, and the French were still waiting – in vain – to take delivery.) Monique admired my luminous intelligence, accompanied with *petites fraises du bois à la crème*, whilst with our coffees we indulged in huge balloons of armagnac. Our beloved city glowed in shades of grey and pink at our feet and the noble towers of Notre Dame, the sharp spire of the Sainte Chapelle, the lonely rock of St Jacques and all the famous belfries of St Eustache, St Gervais, St Germain of Auxerre danced a stately *gigue* for us. We decided unanimously to postpone the war for another year. It seemed to be the appropriate moment to tell a story with which Bébé Bérard used to do the rounds after the 1938 Munich business. At that time, when everyone was talking, as they were now, about world peace, the daughter of General Gamelin fell desperately in love with the lovely legs of Arletty, and hounded her with love letters that were never answered. On the morning after Munich she sent in desperation a telegram with the ultimatum, 'Rendezvous tonight or suicide.' Arletty didn't reply, and went that same evening to a fashionable party, where war was the only topic of discussion. Around midnight the doors were opened: his excellency the Generalissimo Gamelin comes in from a session of the Supreme War Council. Solemn silence. The fate of the world depends on what he has to say. He says nothing. Tension reaches fever pitch. Plucking up courage, Arletty goes up to him: 'Mon Général, est-ce que nous aurons la guerre ou la paix?' ('General, will we have war or peace?') After a theatrical pause (there is a French idiom for this: 'while an angel passes through the room') Gamelin answers without giving her as much as a glance: 'Mademoiselle, les affaires de ma fille ne me regardent pas!' ('Mademoiselle, my daughter's affairs don't concern me!')

When, after a few more armagnacs, the Arc de Triomphe was trying to climb up Montmartre so that it could flirt with the Sacré Coeur, I took Monique back to *Vogue*, 63 Champs Elysées. We never met again. At the Chase Bank on Avenue George V I took out enough money for a few months. I found the rose-garland I wanted for a final, joyless studio session; I knew that this picture would never appear. Eventually I managed to get through to my wife on the telephone. As a foreigner she had to take the children and leave Les Tines the next day, since it was in a national border area. We agreed to meet at the Auberge des Granges in Voutenay-sur-Cure, a hundred and twenty miles from Paris, near Vézelay in the Morvan. I didn't dare tell her on the phone what I really had in mind, which was to get from there via Bordeaux across the Pyrenees into Spain, and then disappear to the States.

That evening Michel de Brunhoff gave me a lavish dinner Chez Ledoyen. It was one of the greatest delights of my life in Paris to be able to enjoy the good life in the company of this epicure. Until I defected to *Harper's Bazaar* in June he had been my editor at *Vogue*. A gifted editor. With great magnanimity he filched every idea that came his way. Nothing was sacred to him, although he constantly maintained that he respected talent. As far as he was concerned, every issue of his magazine was the best ever, until the next came out. A vain, spoilt worshipper of success, especially his own. *Le combinard de la combine de Paris.* He knew everybody and everybody knew him. Influential because of his connections, but overcome by an abject terror of Condé Nast, *Vogue*'s New York owner, Michel was so deeply persuaded of his own charm that he tried to convince everyone he ever came into contact with of his unshakeable friendship for them. This included me, although I was sure that at some juncture he would drop me like a stone, even if only so as to pick me up again as soon as it seemed advantageous for him. He combined in his personality a whole range of Balzac's complexes and my own: Vautrin, Césare Birotteau, Rastignac, de Marsay, Finot, *le brave* Juge Popinot, le Cousin Pons, le Baron de Hulot, le Colonel Chabert, Nucingen, Lucien Rubempré, Guillaume Werbebrust, le Père Goriot: *un Parisien par excellence*. That evening his drooping melancholy upset me. As he greeted me he shook me warmly by the hand and looked into my eyes, like a rather cross dying swan. 'We've already lost this war, the future looks black, pretty black, *mon vieux*'. (Otto Moses, Number Thirteen at Moses & Schlochauer, had made a fortune in 1914 from things that looked pretty black.) Michel, still piqued about my desertion to *Harper's Bazaar*, told me how, during the last war, a German friend of his father's, a printer who had lived in France as a loyal citizen for fifteen years, was put into a concentration camp and they had only been able to prise him out with enormous difficulty two years after the war was over. He reckoned that as soon as things started to go wrong – and in a war everything always *does* go wrong – people would start to lose their heads, especially the authorities. Then the chauvinists would take over. Not a single Frenchman would fight in this war, they were too old for such childishness. He raised one finger prophetically. 'On aura une drôle de guerre!' For reasons of *Vogue*'s own internal politics, Michel, who was from Alsace, had me down as a Dutchman, and advised me to leave for Holland. I said no (and as soon as one did that he stopped listening) on the grounds that I had spent seventeen humiliating years vegetating in Holland, never wanted to go back, and anyway had an idea that this war, unlike the last, would be fought in the Netherlands. Besides, my hated brown passport had expired. Once again, Michel acted as if he were surprised, and once again I had to go through the whole rigmarole for his benefit, telling him how I had been arrested in August 1929 on the beach at Zandvoortbad because the left shoulder-strap of my bathing suit had slipped down; this counted as a crime against public decency, and I was fined fifteen guilders. After that, the Blumenfeld criminal record meant that I was refused citizenship when I applied for it. Michel, who had often laughed until he cried over that story, was simply not to be cheered up on this occasion. Not until we got to the calvados did he reassure me wholeheartedly that as long as I trusted in him, nothing would happen to me. The combined effect of his empty assurances and the calvados only served to depress me. I asked him for a character reference for my collection, attesting to my democratic and francophile attitudes. He said that he was sorry he couldn't do this on headed notepaper from *Vogue* now that I had deserted to *Harper's Bazaar*. His brother-in-law, Lucien Vogel, would do it on *Jardin des Modes* letterhead, they had already discussed it. Then he put his arm round my shoulder with winning amiability and asked me how the photo-session with Bullitt and his daughter had gone that day (there was an extensive espionage network between the two rival American fashion magazines). When I told him it had been cancelled he beamed with plain delight that *Harper's* had lost this journalistic coup. Pretending he had stomach-ache, he got up and went to cable New York about this (or possibly 'his') victory. He came back to the table, still exulting, a long quarter of an hour later. Only then did he realize that this meant there would be a war. He stared at me without saying a word, and shed a tear or two. 'Thank God my son is only fourteen and I'm already forty-five! Whether *Vogue* will continue to appear in France is debatable. What then?' His son was killed by a stray bullet the day Paris was liberated. Michel had never mentioned his family before. The French are afraid of the complications 'friends of the family' can cause.

To cheer us up he tried to seduce me away to a fantastic brothel near St Sulpice, where the girls ran around dressed as nuns. Despair always means a boomtime for whorehouses. Sadly I was too tired after the exertions of the day, so he took me in his run-down Peugeot back to my headquarters, the Café du Dôme in Montparnasse. After a farewell brandy on the terrace he wished me a peaceful holiday, and drove on alone to the brothel. Like Judas and his famous kiss: 'Good night boss, have a nice weekend.'

57 EXODUS

Long after midnight I dragged myself the hundred yards from the Dôme to the loneliness of my studio, 9 rue Delambre. It was never tidy, now it was filthy. For the last year I had been working mostly in other people's studios. While I had been in America my wife had gone to Brittany with the children and used it as a junk room. The floor was covered with a jumble of clothes, household goods, children's toys and photos. There were dusty lamps standing on the floor or hanging from the ceiling. Through the large, open window I could see down into the courtyard of the police station in the neighbouring building. I closed it as a precaution. On the walls were gigantic blow-ups: a six-foot picture of a female torso covered in wet silk that had detached itself from the wall and seemed to have become a three-dimensional figure floating in space; the Christ of Beauvais and that of Claus Suter from Dijon trying to outdo each other in sadness; a detail from the Gothic tapestry, *Le Bal des Sauvages* (Notre Dame de Nantilly, Saumur); a lifesize nude of the eighty-year-old Carmen, the model for Rodin's *The Kiss*; the cathedrals of Rouen (*en raccourci allongé*) and Laon; a calf's head on a draped torso of Venus: 'Dictator' (twenty years later I found a parallel from ancient Greece in the Athens Museum); the close-up of Manina's sleeping face, staring, eyes closed, into empty space. Every picture a short story, complete in itself. How seriously I take beauty! All my portraits are reflections caught in *my* eye. Every artist lives from variations on a single theme. Whether he writes by hand on paper or with his foot in the sand, the signature remains the same. That is why one can identify Mozart from one bar, Shakespeare from one line, El Greco from one brushstroke.

The telephone was on the stairs, with telephone numbers scribbled on the wall. The stairs led up to the bedroom, untidy, just as I had left it in the morning; beside the bed the portable radio, the latest novelty I had brought back from America. I fiddled with the knobs. Suddenly an ominous voice bellowed in German, 'German forces have crossed the Polish frontier. Siegheil!' followed by military music. Was it a radio play, a threat, a fait accompli? I could not tell where the broadcast came from, no one stuck to their assigned wavelengths and anyway, I wasn't used to the wireless yet. If Germany really had invaded Poland ... I tried hard to delude myself into thinking it wasn't true, saying goodbye to peace was too painful.

Outside, dawn was breaking. I felt sick. I was drawn back to the Dôme, which was open all night. Bleary-eyed whores were hanging round the bar while their pimps played the one-armed bandits. No one seemed interested in what was going on in the outside world. Perhaps I had dreamt it. I went back to the studio, carefully packed all my photographic plates in two boxes and fell into bed. When I woke up two hours later, the radio was announcing that Germany had invaded Poland. Now France had to intervene, if she was going to keep her word. If! No one kept their word here! I tried to find out train times – the telephone wasn't working. Conscientious idiot that I was, I actually went back to the *Bazaar* studios to examine the proofs of the Watteau girl. At midday general mobilization was announced. Only the previous day Marie-Louise Bousquet, society editor for *Bazaar* in Paris, a silly woman who was always going on about her important contacts, had heard from the Minister of the Interior himself, Alain Sarraut, that mobilization was the trump card in France's hand. There was no need to be alarmed. After France had mobilized there would be a world peace conference. Once, when my son was running away from a yapping dog and I reminded him of the phrase about its bark being worse than its bite he said, 'I know that expression, but does the *dog* know?'

The pace of life in the streets had speeded up again, just as in old films. People were devouring notices even while they were being pasted up. I had to go back to Montparnasse on foot. In the studio I packed two cheap suitcases, filling them to bursting. The telephone rang. I could receive calls, but not make any myself. An ingenious precaution. It was Guesclin, advising me to get out and go to Spain at once, he could get me a visa. I told him I had to meet my family in Voutenay first. After that I went next door to notify the police of my departure, according to regulations. I had to wait over an hour in a crowd of agitated foreigners before it was my turn, only to have a bureaucrat who had lost his head bellow at me in astonishingly menacing tones that no formalities were required if my papers were in order. After that I tried to send Monique a rose. The flower girl gave me a look of amazement; in wartime there are no roses. Not everything was against me, however. Outside the flower shop on the boulevard Montparnasse providence sent an acquaintance, a photographic model called Jo Regaldi. Together with her boyfriend Theo Bernard she was pushing a handcart full of paintings. I offered her my gramophone and all my records if she would look after my plates for the duration of the war. She took the two boxes, which were returned to me seven years later in perfect condition. No woman has ever done more for my ego. *Merci Jo.*

It was painful to have to say goodbye to my studio where, before I became a fashion photographer, I had immortalized many a goddess. I searched in vain for a taxi to take me and my luggage to the station. There was nothing for it but to go on foot to the Gare de Lyon, dragging my two suitcases along. With a last fat tip I took my leave of the concierge and set off with my belongings on the long, long trek. When I found I could not make any progress in the overcrowded streets, I went down to the Port Royal metro station where I ended up on a boiling-hot platform in the middle of an agitated, hostile crowd. Wedged in this inferno, I spent hours waiting for a train. Waiting is the real Medusa's face of war. Finally an over-crowded train came crawling along and stopped with a door right opposite me. People were pushed off, I was pushed on, and the train moved off amid bickering and squabbling. After several stops I was spewed out onto a not-too-full platform and clambered my way back up to the surface again. It was dark. The street lamps had been switched off, the city blacked out. A full moon illuminated the exodus with pitiless clarity. The bridge over the railway was blocked from parapet to parapet by a jam of cars packed with refugees; the pavement had disappeared. Deathly silence. A ghostly flight from Paris by moonlight. In an eerie symbol of a war that had not yet started (midnight was zero hour for the mobilization), the whole city had ground to a standstill. During the First World War it was on nights like this that air raids had taken place. A single direct hit on that bridge would have killed tens of thousands.

At about eleven o'clock I reached the Gare de Lyon. A cordon of militia in steel helmets, the *Garde mobile*, the French SS, seemed to be guarding the entrance without taking any kind of action. With my luggage I found it impossible to squeeze my way any farther into the station. I was stuck. I had long been enchanted by the innate aversion of every Frenchman to any kind of organization. In contrast to the German mania for organization that claims to be able to rule the world with dictatorial regulations, France was living proof of the artistic charm of *laisser aller*. Who cares about directives here, where every order is accompanied by a counter-order? The authorities had no doubt that at the decisive moment every Frenchman would know intuitively what he must do. It is only when improvising that the Frenchman displays his unique cultural greatness. The fact that in the critical days between peace and war this gift of improvisation failed to function was irrefutable proof of their peaceable nature. France failed to the very last man. If, in September 1939, Germany had invaded France instead of Poland, they could have taken it without a single shot.

From one of the announcements I learnt that there would be a train to Avallon at seven o'clock next morning. A taxi that happened to unload its passengers under my very nose took me back to the Dôme by a roundabout route. Completely worn out, I crumbled a few croissants and drank *une demie Vichy*. Back in my studio I didn't dare switch on the light for fear of the police. I also disconnected the doorbell, as I used to do during tense sittings. Couldn't take one last bath by moonlight: no hot water. After two hours of anxious sleep, I awoke with a start at half past four, taped my German passport, that I didn't want to use on the journey, under the bathtub, gave the place one last look, and in the cool of the street had no problem finding a taxi that took me quickly to the station through an unbelievably empty Paris. Where were the impenetrable crowds of the previous evening? Probably everything had sorted itself out on the very first day of mobilization; perhaps the demented disorder of yesterday had merely been the inevitable prelude to the French genius for order. I wanted to believe it so badly that I did end up believing it. The train left on time. I was sitting in a compartment with officers, mothers and children. Didn't dare switch on my radio for news of the war. Everyone was chatting; I slept because of my accent and arrived on schedule four hours later.

Voutenay-sur-Cure is a small and insignificant place in the Morvan. The area is said to have been the cradle of Gallic culture. In *Les Paysans*, a weak novel which he considered his best, Balzac described the region and its people: a handful of spiteful peasants vegetating in a romantic idyll of filthy, tumbledown houses. Babbling brooks meandering between low cliffs and wooded hills and through inviting meadows made me feel at peace. A refuge, far from danger, all the more so as within a radius of thirty miles there was nothing of any military significance whatsoever. Throughout the First World War the people here lived in unbroken peace. At the point where the *route nationale* 6 (Paris–Avallon–Dijon) enters the village stands the unpretentious two-storey Auberge des Granges. I was met at the door by the landlord, Monsieur Vanner, who was already going slightly gaga. In his German accent he gave me the equivocal assurance that I would be in safe keeping with them. He told me my wife was out in the woods with the children and suggested I should rest in my room until lunch. If it had not been for the 'What now? What next? What now? What next?' hammering in my head, I would have felt I was on holiday. In fact, I was already in prison.

I was woken by the lunch bell. The children, in excellent shape, came rushing into the room and kissed their father with anxious looks on their faces; my wife embraced me so reproachfully that I immediately accepted my war guilt. In the dining room the bloated Madame Vanner greeted me with an even stronger German accent than Monsieur. The few guests at the other tables displayed a patriotic hostility towards me which their provincial narrow-mindedness rendered grotesque. The food, though not bad, did not justify the exorbitantly high cost of full pension. My wife said it had been excellent until a few days ago when the cook was called up. The bus service, our lifeline to the outside world and food supplies, was being discontinued. We spent the whole day in endless discussions as to how we might get ourselves out of this situation. We still had freedom of movement, the frontiers were not yet closed, France was still at peace. It was our duty to try and save ourselves. The next morning we enquired at the station how we could get to the Spanish frontier. There were no regular trains running any more. They told us we would just have to head in the direction of Toulouse/Bordeaux and hope for the best. The journey would take several days. Not an encouraging prospect with children and luggage. Emigrating is not as straightforward as one might think.

By midday England had declared war. Bafflingly, France still had not. Monsieur Vanner swore there would be no war. His wife, without knowing what we were talking about, agreed with him. In the late afternoon the radio announced, in shamefully apologetic tones, that in accord with its international obligations France now regarded herself as being at war with Germany.

We took the last bus to Avallon, the nearest small town, to make one final attempt to hire a taxi to the Spanish frontier. On the way to the bus-stop we read a notice saying that all *ressortissants allemands* were to report within five days to an assembly point in Auxerre, bringing with them their luggage including a blanket, food and eating utensils. That meant internment, concentration camp, the realization of my youthful fears. I did not regard myself as a German national and decided not to obey this order, all the more so as my faith in French concentration camps was minimal. In order to provide unambiguous proof of my loyalty for my dossier, I wrote a patriotic letter (registered) to the *commissaire de police* in the rue Delambre, stating my willingness to serve France in any capacity she might think fit. Since I was ready to fight for the freedom of the world, it seemed logical to volunteer for the army. Above all, I needed my papers, and they were under the bathtub in my Paris studio. Since my passport had expired, my *carte d'identité* could not be renewed. Without papers one could not travel. Strict surveillance was kept on the roads and railways, the sole activity in which the French martial spirit expressed itself.

As we were going out of Voutenay on the bus we saw the ominous sight of two gendarmes cycling into the village. In Avallon we managed to find a car-owner who was prepared to drive us to Bordeaux and was not demanding too high a price. He could not leave until two days later; we had to make up our minds by tomorrow. When we returned to Voutenay we were met by three tearful children. Gendarmes had been to the hotel, asking for me. Of course. I had been enquiring far too openly about trains and connections, had attracted attention to myself, aroused suspicion, could be arrested any minute! That very evening from our bedroom window I saw dark shadows creeping up and down in the mist behind the trunks of the poplars lining the *route nationale*. They had to be keeping *me* under surveillance! (Later it came out that it wasn't me but our hosts who were under suspicion. At the end of the war both Vanners were shot as spies by the *maquis*.)

The next morning, after consulting Monsieur Vanner, I ventured out to put my problem to the mayor of Voutenay-sur-Cure. In order to counter as far as possible any suspicion that I was a spy, I went with my wife and children. Spies seldom operate *en famille*. The mayor, an old peasant, was sitting by the stove in a broad-brimmed straw hat (Van Gogh) reading Balzac (my very image of a French peasant!). When I told him how much I admired Balzac, he asked us with French courtesy to take a seat. He listened with interest to my story of how I had left Germany twenty years ago, that my wife and children had been born in Holland and that as Jews we hated Hitler. When I told him that out of love for France I wanted to join the army, he shook his head. Patriotism, he said, was for younger people who had no family to feed. Children could not live on sentimental clichés, they needed food to eat. Though, he added, he did understand the usefulness of a *beau geste*. Like a fellow conspirator he gave my hand a sympathetic shake. 'I cannot issue papers for you. The military authorities are keeping a close eye on us. You must go to Paris, you can get anything there. Many cars fill up with petrol next door to the *Mairie*. If I find a suitable one heading for Paris, I'll call you. *Bonne chance!*'

58 MY MOST HANDSOME MODEL

The next day, while we were comfortably ensconced in the leafy little hotel garden, struggling to down burnt *andouilles au Chambertin*, to the delight of the children, Pascal, the village idiot (France is blessed with many such), came hobbling breathlessly up to our table and indicated by gesture that I should go at once to the Mairie. I already had nightshirt, toothbrush and comb in my briefcase and ran, surrounded by the family, straight to the market square where an open Peugeot was filling up with petrol. The two men inside stank like escaped convicts. To make my gratitude perfectly clear, I insisted on paying for the petrol; they protested, but accepted it as a matter of course. I thanked the mayor most warmly, and he acted as if he had no idea why. I promised my wife and children I would return soon. As so often in my life my heavy heart told me I would never see them again.

Boldly I jumped into the rattletrap as it slowly began to pull away, Paris-bound. The driver turned round and stuck a bottle of kirsch in front of my nose. 'Me Maxime, him Philippe. Who you?' They made jokes in their argot about the name Erwin. Maxime asked, 'Toi Jupin [Yid]?' I nodded, to which he replied 'Tant mieux.' Maxime wanted to see my papers. When I asked why, he said, 'So we have something to show if we get stopped.' Cautiously, I inquired whether they hadn't told them at the Mairie that it was because of my papers that I was going to Paris, to volunteer. Maxime asked which prison I had been in and how tall I was. I didn't have the guts to answer the question about prison, but I did admit to five foot seven.

Maxime and Philippe were both fresh out of jail (burglary). Every prisoner who had less than a year of his sentence to run and was willing to volunteer for the army was being released. The two of them had found this car outside Perpignan prison and had set off to start a new life in night-time Paris, where rich pickings beckoned. In me they had found what they needed, a reliable accomplice, not too broad, not too tall, not too heavy, easy to lift through windows into apartments to open the front door for them. In addition he had to have a respectable home where they could sort out their loot undisturbed and store it safely. They were mainly interested in gold, jewelry and art, the value of which would rise during the war. Maxime laughed, 'You speak French *comme une vache espagnole*. If we get stopped you'd better hide under the blanket, we need to get you to Paris safe and sound.' We merrily drank kirsch and swore never to part. The moment anything suspicious came into view I slipped under the horse blanket on the floor of the car. When I re-emerged we would down another kirsch and the drive continued in ever more jaunty mood. In Auxerre we were stopped for the first and only time. Before the guard could put any questions, Maxime cut in, '*Nous crevons de faim*, where can we get a decent bite to eat round here?' The guards, eager to show off their gastronomic knowledge, recommended the Cerf Volant, accepted a kirsch and forgot all about papers. Maxime raved on about place Pigalle, the Bastille, St Ouen, rue de Lappe, the Eiffel Tower. He knew his Paris. Pépé, his shady companion, knew only Perpignan.

By nightfall we had reached the Porte d'Orléans without further alarms. In the deserted city my courage suddenly crumbled. I invited my two jailbirds to have a Pernod with me in the Café du Rond-Point d'Orléans, which I knew from better days. After the third cheerless round – each of us distrusted the other two – I gave Maxime my almost empty wallet as security (I always keep my money in my left back pocket) and descended to the *lavabo*, from where I knew a way out by the back stairs. Alone at last, dog-tired and full of alcoholic melancholy, I crept, a fugitive pursued by invisible bloodhounds, along the lightless rue d'Alésia. I lacked the courage to try and slip past the patrols to my studio, only a quarter of an hour away. Two minutes away was an elegantly deviant little alley where a good fairy from Holland, Mevrouw May K. K., lived in the Villa Seurat. That was where I hoped to spend the night. It was around ten when I rang at her door. No one answered, but the smell of her famous risotto, *spécialité de la maison*, wafting through the cracks gave her away: too much garlic and onions (she was a trendy pinko vegetarian) with chicken (only for guests, though she would take some when no one was looking). She was also hard of hearing, so I kept on pounding away at the door and window until she opened up, elegantly attired in tuxedo and monocle. (She was a transvestite and used to get very excited when I compared her to the German Crown Prince.) She claimed she was expecting me to supper (she was a spiritualist). We had met years ago in Holland, trying to save Else Lasker-Schüler from Hitler's clutches, and had remained close friends ever since. A real friend, ready to make any sacrifice, especially when it concerned young, unmarried girls who were pregnant. Her happiness reached its climax when, dressed as the father waiting impatiently in the hospital, she was given the good news, '*Monsieur, c'est un fils!*' ('Sir, you have a son!')

We had an excellent meal, drank pinard by candlelight and told each other our adventures. May believed in Stalin's genius and prophesied that the democracies would collapse. She advised me not to spend the night in her apartment, communists' homes had been subject to night raids, the *Deuxième Bureau* trying to counter the *cinquième colonne*. Too exhausted for any further decisions, I had a marvellous sleep on her sofa.

After a proper Dutch breakfast coffee, I started telephoning. None of the influential friends, who only a few days ago had sworn faithfully that I could always count on them, was available so early – it was ten o'clock. Their secretaries sounded distinctly cool. I decided to try again when I got to my studio.

Since earliest childhood I have had a phobia about being out in the streets and Paris the previous evening had been horrible. May advised me to avoid police round-ups by taking a taxi, but taxis were harder to find than ever. However, in the bright sunshine of an autumn morning Paris looked almost normal. Fewer people, more soldiers, fewer cars, more police. I watched two men stop a passer-by, demand his papers then lead him away. Dashing up the stairs to the studio, I ran straight into the concierge, who whispered that the police had come asking for me several times. I confided – one confidence deserved another – that I had just come *en vitesse* to get my papers so I could go off and join the army. At the same time I pressed a hundred francs into his palm for expenses, which made all the more impression as up to then he had always been very happy with my ten-franc *pour-boires*. With a knowing look, he said, 'Comme vous le désirez, Monsieur, je n'ai rien vu' ('As you wish, monsieur, I haven't seen a thing'). I asked him to see nothing the next day either, giving me two days to make my last-minute arrangements before he informed on me. For inform on me he would. Even when we were down to our last few francs, we refugees were forced to offer up regular tribute to concierges and waiters who bullied and harassed us, then informed on us. Fouché's system of informers is still alive in France today. Every report, untrue or false, gets a five-franc reward from the Commissaire de Police. From their headquarters on the terrace of the Café du Dôme, double agents Fréderic Drach (morphine addict and editor of *VU*) and Monsieur Lemoine (police *agent provocateur* with macabre cataracts on his eyes) organized consignments of human beings from Paris to Berlin. Gold doesn't burn.

In the dark corridor I tripped over a fire-bucket outside every door – in case of air raids. For the first time my studio looked tidy – it had been searched. My collection of pornographic photos from 1900 had gone. The telephone was cut. Why on earth had I come to Paris? The papers were just a pretext. The plain truth was that Paris was my mistress and she had run off with another man. While I was taking a shower I remembered the Laconic Telegram from the Spartan Fleet, 'Mindaros's had it. The old tubs are buggered. We're starving. What do we do now?'

The bell rang shrilly. My first reaction: jump naked out of the window. Into the yard of the police station?? The bell was still ringing. I had to open the door. My daughter's raincoat was lying around and I threw it over my shoulders, gave myself one last contemptuous look in the mirror, silently – I had practised it often

– slid back the safety chain and opened the door. There stood fate: a Maurice Chevalier boater, a scrawny waxed moustache and a suppressed smile, indicating cruelty. Under his arm was the briefcase containing the warrant for my arrest and the handcuffs. I was swimming in ice-cold sweat. My life stood still. I couldn't manage one final erection, nor even the strength to say *Bonjourmonsieur*. This ruthless arm of the law cleared his throat with an embarrassed cough, as if he were expecting a favour from me. 'Monsieur le célèbre photographe d'art Blumenfeld Erwin, 9 rue Delambre?' That was not the way your common-or-garden *flic* spoke. I was flattered at the 'célèbre'. Could they have sent an under-secretary from the ministry of the interior to arrest me? 'Oui, Monsieur', I replied, with all the *empressement* of a German émigré. 'Ressortissant allemand?' he asked, which I denied. As he came in he gave the furnishings a sharply appraising glance and checked the doors and windows. I pointed at the raincoat I was wearing to indicate my embarrassment, intending to withdraw to the bathroom where I would jump out of the window, after having first of all cut open my arteries with my razor blade. Better still would be to strike him down with the iron chair from the Jardin du Luxembourg and then make my escape. But where to?

He seemed to read my thoughts. He took me by the arm, sat me down in a chair, looked me straight in the eye and said, in resolute yet agitated tones, that he had to discuss a matter of life and death with me. With an urbanity worthy of the great French tradition, he offered me a *caporale grise*, the cheapest type of French cigarette. To show myself equally worthy of the occasion, I stood up and said in solemn tones, 'I beg you to allow me three minutes to write a final farewell to my wife and children. After that I will place myself entirely at your disposal.' He gave me a somewhat uneasy look. 'Couldn't you write to your wife later? *Je suis pressé.*' I could tell from the sly glint in his eye that this man had made a thorough study of Raskolnikov. He was playing a game of cat and mouse with me. He pretended to think hard, then said, 'If you really must write to your wife as a matter of the greatest urgency, permit me, *je vous en prie*, to withdraw to your bathroom for a moment. But you must promise not to run off, I don't like being alone in other people's studios.' I gave my *parole d'honneur*, he almost kissed me on both cheeks. Then, acting as if nothing were amiss, he disappeared into the bathroom, taking his briefcase with him. To give me the illusion that freedom was beckoning, he cunningly locked the door from inside. Fortunately I saw through his little game. He wanted me to make a run for it so that his guards outside on the stairs could shoot me trying to escape. A little *too* obvious.

I just could not think of anything to write to my wife, the ink in my fountain pen was as dried up as the marrow in my bones. Then I had an idea, the obvious idea for a photographer: I would take his picture. Vanity knows no limits. I would do a portrait of him and he would give me twenty-fours hours breathing space. A lot can happen in a day. Peace might even break out. I focused a few lamps on the bathroom door; strangely enough, the electricity had not been cut off yet. Mechanically I screwed the Linthof onto a tripod and set the aperture, intending to capture him forever standing in the doorway. Then there was the rattle of the key and something beyond my power of comprehension happened. Unfortunately I lack the literary skill to describe the scene adequately. The door opened and there, posing in the five thousand candle-power from my lamps, was the *tableau vivant* of my detective in all his miserable ugliness, wearing a bathing costume with a tight-fitting rubber cap: Nijinsky in *Le Spectre de la Rose, after* the leap. The current catch-phrase, 'Drôle de guerre' (phoney war), automatically came to his stupid lips. I was in no mood to appreciate the comic aspects of the situation. On the contrary, I felt insulted that they had sent a clown to arrest me. Dumbfounded, I fell to my knees, which is not something I normally do. Immediately ashamed of my weakness, I pretended I had to make some adjustments to the tripod. It was clear that the man was off his head, though that did not explain where he had found the bathing costume and the beach shoes. He stood there, motionless; I went behind my camera and said, 'Smile, please'. He stopped me with a wave of the hand. I could see he was going to be difficult. 'I'm not in the mood yet. To create a masterpiece you must understand the situation first. Sand, sun, Deauville!' He stretched out in a deck chair, one of the few pieces of furniture in the studio, played at being on the beach and told me his story.

'I'm a *notaire* from Sens. My name does not matter. For twenty-three years I have been more or less happily married. I have been in Paris since the day before yesterday, on my way to Deauville with my brother-in-law. My first holiday from married life. Every man has to cut loose once in his life. On my very first evening here I met my ideal woman. Cricri idolizes me; I love Cricri *à la folie*. A blonde with a fiery temperament. She works in the Sphinx (a high-class brothel). My wife is a brunette, from the Auvergne. Until the night before last I had no idea what blonde passion could be like. *O là là!* Since Cricri must stay in Paris because of her work, I have decided to spend my holidays here with her. Love demands sacrifices. We are ready to do anything. This evening my brother-in-law is going on to Deauville – alone. I want to give him a series of postcards to take with him: me on the beach, in my wet swimsuit, thinking of my wife, longing written all over my face. With a postmark and my signature they will give me an alibi which will nip any suspicion in the bud. My *dulcinée* recommended you as a great artist and first-class trick photographer, a real magician of the lens for whom nothing is impossible. She also warned me about your exorbitant prices. However, in exceptional circumstances such as these even an artist can justify his need to make a living. Everything must be ready by six o'clock this evening. A *père de famille nombreuse* is in your hands, take pity on him, and do not forget: the Second World War has started!'

I was seized with fury. Fate was using this clown to poke fun at me. I had lost my sense of humour, but my bank account was frozen so that I was reduced by necessity to playing beach photographer to this most philistine of philistines. Without thinking, I said, 'Five thousand, half payable in advance.' He offered 4200 francs, we agreed on 4655 francs. Grudgingly he counted out the down payment of 2325 francs and we got to work. Providence had deposited the necessary sand in the corridor outside; it was the only use anyone found for it during the whole of the war. That solved the problem of the beach. My *notaire* helped me empty the contents of all the buckets in the building over the studio floor and soon the deckchair was standing on the beach at Deauville. I suggested to my hero that he get into a bathtub filled with cold water, but since he suffered from chronic asthma, he was against bathing in cold seawater. While I was getting everything into position, he dashed over to the mirror, covered himself in brown powder, took his false teeth out to clean them, gargled ferociously, poked around between his toes, cut out corns, shaved himself underneath the armpits, plucked hairs out of his ears, applied some obnoxious perfume and at the end looked just the same as he had before. I wanted to talk about the war, but he refused; he was on holiday.

A well prepared session, when artist and model are working together in harmony, runs smoothly. After ten minutes and twelve shots I had what I needed. Since my victim had another half hour before he could go and pick up his lady love for lunch, I passed the time getting him to adopt pointless poses (without wasting film on them) which flattered his ego no end. He fancied himself the focus of the art world. When the session was over my notary dressed with meticulous care, wittily thanked me for the splendid time on the beach, shook the sand from his feet and promised to return at five to collect his goods. In the darkroom I suddenly realized that the development of this farce represented the conclusion of my Paris period (1936–1939). Hercules's final labour.

By five o'clock a dozen genuine postcards were sitting in a blue-green envelope, waiting for their purchaser, who did not appear until past seven, by which time we were both at the end of our respective tethers. He collapsed into the deckchair. 'A cognac, *s'il vous plaît.*' I was no bartender, had nothing to offer him and knew that he would start bitching to bring the price down. I had given myself my word of honour that I would stick to my price and to that end I had a thirteenth card in readiness. Proudly I handed my work to him. With ill-concealed enthusiasm he examined the masterpieces one by one through a magnifying glass several times. Suddenly he said, '*Non! Non! Non!*' and, exactly as I had foreseen, dropped all the cards into the sand. Swift as an arrow I bent down, and before he could stop me I had torn up one of his portraits and tossed the pieces away contemptuously. No client can stand being torn up like that before his very eyes. When I set about destroying the next one he whined for an armistice. Victory all along the line. I asked him what his *Non* meant. 'Madame n'aimerait voir mon rictus.' Without knowing what the word meant, I defended my art. 'A man of your age should be happy that he can still sport the traces of one.' He gave a forced smile and out of simple bloody-mindedness demanded some retouching, which I refused for artistic reasons (I can't retouch). After the usual French struggle with his miserly soul, he grudgingly paid over the remaining two thousand francs and left my studio, impoverished and immortalized.

59 DOWNHILL

The next morning none of my contacts functioned. Many of my friends were away, those who were still in Paris were not answering. Having accomplished nothing, I travelled back to Voutenay-sur-Cure with my well earned money and the same old infamous passport. When the innkeeper, Monsieur Vanner, had some business to attend to in Auxerre a few days later, I went with him. His car was ancient and I had to push on the uphill stretches. The recruiting office for volunteers was in the cathedral, which had been turned into a military hospital. A thousand empty beds. No doctor. One lone patient asleep in a bed. Exhausted, I lay down in the bed beside him. When I woke up several hours later he asked me what was wrong with me. When I told him, he laughed at me in amazement. He was the doctor and I was his first volunteer. He tried to talk me out of it on account of my age. I explained my precarious situation to him and without examining me he kindheartedly gave me a certificate saying I had registered as a volunteer. That was all I wanted.

Now began the most peaceful holidays of my life. A world war had to break out to bring peace to my soul! Every day in the most magnificent autumn weather we went for walks in an idyllic valley, our valley of sorrows: Roncesvalles. We picked berries (black and blue), looked for *escargots*, fished for trout, grabbed at lizards, killed snakes: we were happy. Until, that is, one evening when Monsieur Guignard, the head of the Gendarmerie in Vézelay, came asking for me. He was a country gendarme of peasant cunning (after the war he was sent to prison for collaborating with the Boches). We chatted, and over the Dubonnet it came out that he had been sent to find out whether I had anything worth confiscating, houses or diamonds, for example. After a few more glasses we were friends. Guignard was impressed by the paper certifying that I had volunteered. In a whisper he advised me to leave the inn as soon as possible, the Vanners were spies. We should go to Vézelay under his protection, he said, adding that there was a famous hotel there with two stars in the *Guide Michelin*. It was a relief to be allowed to change hotels, the Vanners were taking merciless advantage of our situation as prisoners of war. As the last remaining hotel guests we didn't need service (*c'est la guerre*), got meagre war rations, and everything at full, high-season prices (*c'est la guerre*).

When we arrived in Vézelay we were entranced by the medieval odour of wood fires. What a joy to live in this fairy-tale town. *Résidence forcée* in paradise. The marvellous Hôtel de la Poste et du Lion d'Or. Never have I eaten tastier *escargots*. It was blissful: first of all the foggy autumn amid the beauties of Burgundy with mystical clouds hanging over vineyards, then the quiet, snow-white winter followed by the budding miracle of spring. With the same delight every morning and every evening we went for a walk along the old wall round the little town from which Godfrey de Bouillon set forth on the crusade. We admired the beloved Basilique de la Madeleine from every angle. Once a week I had to report to the Gendarmerie, which was simply a harmless extension of my daily walk to buy the paper. Romain Rolland and Le Corbusier had to do the same.

The owners of the hotel, Monsieur and Madame Danguy, shrewd peasants who had worked their way up, saw to it that their few guests were looked after in an appropriate manner. We were discreetly placed in a dark corner of the dining room. The centre table was presided over by a terrifying giant in black widow's weeds, Madame la Générale Villemain. We called her *la grosse derrière*. Her companion piece was a puritan from Philadelphia, Pennsylvania, equally ancient but of lesbian leanness. As soon as the *grosse derrière* saw us she would spit in our direction, mostly at my wife and the children, less often, flatteringly, at me. She was a patriotic royalist republican; Pétain was her pet. Miss Sibeling, on the other hand, observed strict neutrality and ignored us.

These splendidly peaceful days lasted for six months, until the beginning of May when the French, without putting up the least resistance, allowed themselves to be overrun by the Huns. That reawakened the malice of the peasants with pitchforks in their hands. Madame la Générale's spit was replaced by the chamber pot. We could not go out for walks any more and were given poor rooms. Little Yorick, who was seven, was arrested after school by two gendarmes as a spy. The local paper, *L'Auxerrois*, carried a news item headlined 'Parachutiste Blumenfeld caché à Vézelay'. As the Germans were getting alarmingly close to Paris, my powerless gendarme decided I should go voluntarily to the nearest concentration camp, Montbard-Marmagne. Since there was no public transport, I would have to do the forty miles on foot, or hire a car at my own expense. Two policemen would take me. My wife was permitted to accompany me.

On a marvellous May morning, we set off downhill from heaven to hell, with heavy hearts and a grotesque taste in the mouth, which is presumably always there when you are being sent to the guillotine. In my briefcase I had a valuable recommendation from Général Georges, a big shot on the general staff, that my friend André Girard had got for me. I took two fully packed suitcases with photos, Linhof camera, books and typewriter. Unfortunately I left behind in Vézelay a volume of short stories and poems which I had written over the last twenty years. When my wife also had to flee, she hid it in a crevice in the wall of an abandoned house; we looked for it fifteen years later, but never found it. At the three-star Hôtel de la Poste in Avallon I was suddenly seized with a craving for one last decent meal before I went to meet my fate. I gave my guards a hundred francs and told them to have a drink on me and come and fetch me in two hours. The fare was princely:

écrevisses aux aromates, fondue de volaille à la crème, crêpes flambées. We had a bottle of '28 Hospice de Beaune with a Marc de Bourgogne as *digestif.* But our morale was too low to savour such culinary delights. A condemned man's last meal tastes lousy.

After the meal my wife and I had to walk up and down outside the restaurant for over an hour before the guards came reeling back, completely drunk. They had decided, in order to make a good impression, to deliver me to the camp bound, as a spy, and tried to put handcuffs on me. Fortunately the three of them were just sober enough to realize that they were incapable of driving, and let me take the wheel. Soon all three were snoring as I drove myself to the concentration camp. There was nothing to stop me getting out and running away. But where to? Murderers have problems getting rid of the body, how much more difficult it is to dispose of oneself! We passed the little railway station of Montbard and carried on a couple of miles to the small town of Marmagne. A sign outside the Mairie said 'Réception des étrangers'. In translation: concentration camp. The building looked like Van Gogh's *Mairie d'Auvers-sur-Oise le 14 juillet*, only without the flags. I felt it was bad taste to drive up with snoring guards, so I drove round the corner, picked up my luggage and walked, accompanied by my brave wife, up to the gates of hell, that were guarded by armed beggars.

Through the bars we observed a very encouraging scene: a giant dressed up as a general, his chest covered in medals, was wading back and forth through a swept-up pile of men's hair, giving little snorts of pleasure. Around fifty shorn unfortunates stood shivering in a military posture. Civilians in military formation always look ridiculous, especially when instead of uniforms they have uniformly shaven heads ('arses with ears'). In the left foreground two final victims were being given the bald-pate treatment. Thanks to my letter from the Chief of General Staff I would presumably be spared such an indignity. Or so I thought. At the barred gate I embraced my poor widow for the very very last time, told her to 'Be a man', asked her to take good care of the children and get happily remarried soon, tore myself away and acted as though I were descending to Hades, light of step but heavily loaded with suitcases – straight up to the Fiend Marshal, who, without interrupting his hair-wading, let my letter of recommendation flutter to the ground. At a wave of his hand I was thrust into a chair where a Luxemburger with clippers began to shear my head. I could see my wife watching my execution through the bars before she was taken away by our guards. We were both behind the same bars, but on opposite sides. In France at that time there were two categories, *les internés* and *les internables*, internees and those who were going to be interned.

My head was precisely half shaved when the barber was ordered to stop. The adjutant had saved my document by a hair's breadth and submitted it to the commandant as a matter of importance. I must have looked odd, the serried ranks of baldies were smirking, but I had won a battle, even if I had lost half my hair. The colossus was seething. In a German accent he asked whether there was anyone who could translate fluently from French to German. A bastard by the name of Stein stepped forward, said, '*Je*' and was made camp interpreter. The commandant planted himself before me, legs apart, and bellowed in barbaric French, '*T'es photographe, toi?*' When I replied, '*Oui, mon commandant*', he ordered me to stand beside him, shouted, 'Silence!' and issued the following order of the day: '*Ordre du jour.* I hereby appoint Blumenfeld, Erwin, camp doctor of the Montbard-Marmagne camp. Under my command he will take full responsibility for the hygienic ups and medical downs of the camp and its inmates. All inmates are to salute him in the proper manner and address him as *Monsieur le Docteur.*' Grins of fury among the ranks greeted my promotion. Our Führer continued, 'Be under no illusions. You filthy spies are here to work yourself to death for France. I'm going to show the Boches what a real concentration camp is like. Anyone who reports sick will automatically get twenty-four hours solitary in a pigsty, without bread or water. If that doesn't make him better, I'll get Professor Blumenfeld here to cure and castrate him. I have had your heads shaved not just to show your true faces to the world, but also to stop you getting any fancy ideas about escaping, since the convict's uniforms haven't come yet. They have been requisitioned from Dijon prison and should be arriving any day. If anyone has any questions he's to keep his trap shut. You can have a good sleep until three tomorrow morning; at four, before sunrise, it's off to work in the fields. Dismiss!'

Everyone did a smart military about-turn, we had all been soldiers some time or other. Last of all a doddery old man with flowing mane came hobbling into the yard on crutches. His letter of recommendation, which he handed over to the commandant with too low a bow was trampled on the ground unread. It was from André Gide, recommending his friend and translator, the writer Ferdinand Hardekopf, most warmly to the authorities. I made friends with this touchingly pathetic morphine addict, a *mensch*, one of the very few in that desert of concentration. It was through him that our family was later reunited.

Monsieur le Capitaine Carlé was, of course, not a general, but a plain Karl from Alsace, an ethnic German who, after twenty years in the Sahara with the Foreign Legion had been pensioned off to return to France with African fever and a brain tumour. Three weeks earlier, he had been mobilized and put in charge of this transit camp planned for two hundred *Allemands et Autres-chiens*. Carlé immediately realized there were unlimited business opportunities in slave labour and made sure that not a soul left the camp. Soon he had hired out fifteen hundred serfs to the surrounding farms at any price going. He never had enough people on offer. Since his guards consisted of six ancient militiamen, he armed every tenth prisoner with an antique, unloaded gun and had no qualms about leaving the prisoners in their charge. No German would ever dream of deserting. It was disgrace enough that a few shirkers kicked the bucket while at work. Their bodies were disposed of at night, without military honours. I had to make out the death certificates, in my best handwriting and in triplicate. That was my job.

In the very first minutes my meteoric medical career reached its zenith, which was some compensation for the fact that fate had not made me chief medical officer of a women's camp. Hardly had Hardekopf been dealt with than a worker from the Montbard munitions factory was dragged in by two gendarmes, bellowing with pain, blood streaming down his face. It was his own fault, they said, he had stepped too close to the blast furnace. The hospital had been quite right to refuse to admit the foreign worker. This hopeless case was handed over to me. Now was the time for me to show my skills as a doctor – and I didn't even know where the sick-bay was. So, without letting anyone see that I couldn't find it, I took his pulse. Whimpering, he pointed to his eyes. With a jolt of horror I realized that a photographer is not an ophthalmologist. Since I had no idea what to do next, I asked the man his name. 'Prestataire Späth.' *Prestataire* had nothing to do with prostate, nor was it a first name, but meant a military labourer attached to the French army, which, without knowing it, is what we all were. I ordered a stretcher to be brought and sent the others away. The courtyard emptied. It was beginning to get dark. Späth was quietly whimpering to himself. I fell into a trance such as I had never known before, and out of my mouth came the words, 'Verily I say unto thee, before the cock crows thrice, thou shalt see the Kingdom of Heaven with thine own eyes!' He whispered back, 'I know a better one about the miracle rabbi, you blithering idiot. If you help me get to the hospital in Dijon, I'll make you famous as a healer.' My medical reputation was saved!

The blood-covered malingerer was carried on a stretcher to the sick-bay, a pigsty with a thatched roof. I followed with my luggage. In the sick-room was an orange-box with a bottle of iodine and a broken thermometer on it. That was all. Not a drop of water. By the entrance, newly arrived from Paris, was a huge basket with the inscription 'Évacuation médicale'. It contained five thousand packets of neosalvarsan. In every packet, alongside the ampoule with the milky medicine, was a second ampoule with *aqua destillata*. Heaven-sent, if drop by drop. After consulting my patient, I cleaned the blood off him with the exception of his face, so that he made a gruesome sight as I led him through the streets of Montbard to the station next morning. People saw that the blind man had got his sight back and marvelled at my skill. I put him on the train for Dijon. On the way back an old woman gave me a little basket of wild strawberries, tried to kiss my hand and ushered me into her house. In it was an epileptic girl lying beside the radio that was just announcing that the Germans had reached Paris. I'd had enough healing for one day, so I roared at the patient, 'Get up, the Boches are at the door!' The sick girl obeyed, got up from the couch and collapsed on the floor. Dumbfounded, her grandmother cried, '*Vive Hitler!*'

Meanwhile the interned slaves were slaving away. Daily schedule: three hundred hours (before sunrise): reveille with a Wagnerian trumpet fanfare. Our trumpeter, Herr Fenster, was a negro who, although he had never been to Germany, was classified as a *ressortissant allemand*. He came from Dar-es-Salaam in German East Africa, where he had learnt German with a Jewish accent from a Jewish missionary. Until the war broke out he had been a much sought-after drummer and trumpeter in Paris nightclubs. Here in Montbard he was everybody's spoilt darling. With his wife, a chic, pert Parisienne, and his black-white-and-red-striped daughter he was the guiding star and guest of honour at the villa of the camp commandant and his wife. The latter, a provincial woman with several pasts, had taken it into her head to turn the dull little railway junction of Montbard-Marmagne into the meeting place of fashionable society of the Côte d'Or. For her, the evening gatherings *chez Carlé* were much more important than France's *défaite*, which was inevitable anyway. That was the time when people started calling out to each other, with a laugh, 'On nous a bien eu'('We really have been had this time').

Daily schedule (continued): after reveille, ablutions. (With what? It was strictly forbidden to wash oneself at the camp's only tap.) Collect liquid manure (otherwise known as coffee). Roll-call, assignment of duties, numbering off by fours to endless tirades from Carlé. Four hundred hours: departure, marching at the double at least ten miles to our place of work where we toiled away until night-fall. Food: animal fodder – scraps, Jerusalem artichokes, swedes, pigswill. Forced march back to the camp, singing the Marseillaise all the way (no one knew the words). Last post (beautifully played by Fenster), after which we were all locked up in pigsties. Horrible nights, one's sleep constantly disturbed by terrified, screaming nightmares in all possible dialects (Luxemburg was the worst). Three o'clock in the morning: the last trump waking us for another awful day.

The dull rumble of artillery came relentlessly closer – Hitler. Many who saw him as their saviour became increasingly arrogant. Communists wished they were back among the order and discipline of German concentration camps. Early on in our stay, a lorry arrived from Dijon with sacks full of tattered uniforms of the Grande Armée from 1870 to 1914. We were dressed up. I managed to get hold of some red trousers with a gold-braided officer's tunic. The whole camp was a fan-tastic collection of ragged, patched clowns. Hitler swept closer, preceded by an endless, crawling line of vehicles stuffed full of refugees and their belongings which, to Carlé's boundless fury, blocked the *route nationale* from Troyes, Langres, Nancy. He decided to bring some order to the flight and had a wooden throne set up at the entrance to the village where he sat in his general's uniform issuing orders through a loudhailer. *Prestataires* with German accents and uniforms from 1870 had to stop every car and ask for identification. If they were not satisfied, the driver was arrested, handcuffed and taken to the camp prison. Soon the town was too small for all the prisoners; fights broke out, shots were fired, the traffic came to a complete standstill. When, to crown it all, it started to pour with rain, Carlé aban-doned his throne to go for lunch and ordered all prisoners to be set free. For some inexplicable reason there was plenty to eat that evening. The next morning we were woken two hours later than usual. After coffee we were not sent off to work. Carlé appeared at roll-call in a plain sergeant's uniform, with very few decorations, and handed out cigarettes. There were rumours that peace had broken out.

All this was explained by the arrival of a group of young officers with packed briefcases: *La Commission de Criblage du Deuxième Bureau.* These intelligence officers were astonishingly well informed. Every one of us was interrogated. My interrogator was not only familiar with the work I had done for *Vogue*, he knew that I had recently been working for *Harper's Bazaar* and that I had just come back from America. He asked me whether I thought that, as in 1918, America would pull France out of the shit (*démerder la patrie*). We were separated into black and white sheep. The reliable elements were now officially made *prestataires*, military labourers in the French army, the unreliable ones and those without files became internees. As soon as the commission had left, Carlé donned his general's uniform again and we were all sent back to work as before. At the double, quick march!

Three days later, after the capture of Paris, Carlé went off what was left of his head, burnt all the papers so they would not fall into the hands of the Boches, gave the black sheep their freedom and dispatched the *prestataires* westwards, standing up in locked cattle trucks. On the door he wrote 'cinquième colonne' in chalk and climbed in beside the engine driver, dressed in his general's uniform and accompanied by the negro trumpeter, Fenster, to sound the retreat. The fifty miles to Dijon took one whole, long day. The whole, long night we stood in a siding in the overcrowded station of Dijon with air-raid sirens sounding continually, though no bombs fell. France was on its last legs and so, in our cramped cattle truck, were we. After two more days we stopped in Le Puy, almost dead with hunger and thirst. Special editions announced the truce. Maréchal Pétain had taken charge of the defeat: *Travail, Famille, Patrie!* Carlé had disappeared. With Fenster in charge, our train set off again, criss-crossing the countryside at a crawl, to stop two days later in Loriol-sur-Drôme, twenty miles south of Valence.

60 LORIOL

When we got out we were surrounded by a detachment of *spahis* (black soldiers from the colonies). Weighed down with our bundles, filthy and bedraggled after five days in the cattle trucks, we were hustled through the dusty little town at the double, *un-deux, un-deux,* march-march. Flower-pots, filth and abuse hailed down on the *sales métèques* who were to blame for France's *défaite*. *Un-deux, un-deux* for a couple of miles along the Rhône to our new concentration camp, the former aspirin depots of the Usines de Rhône. Passing through impenetrable barbed-wire fences we ended up in a huge factory shed with tables set for guests. Our starving eyes devoured enticing mirages: light-green grapes, red-cheeked peaches, carafes of pinard. The military bark of an immediate order to form ranks stopped us looking our fill: '*Attention! Garde à vous! Monsieur le Commandant!*' The large sliding door was pushed aside and, mounted on ponies, in galloped a most comical cavalcade of Tartarins dressed up *à l'algérienne* in flowing desert cloaks – the head and teaching staff of the high school in Valence. Too Offenbach to be true. For a whole hour this bearded philistine gave us a lecture à la Bossuet (*Oraisons funèbres*) on the duties and rights of captive traitors under the victorious régime of General Pétain (condemned himself for high treason a few years later). We found it difficult not to fall asleep on our feet. He prescribed silence as a cure for spies; no communication amongst ourselves except for essentials; not a word to our guards; newspapers and radio forbidden so we could not spread false rumours. On pain of death we were to keep away from the Viennese traitors imprisoned in Hut B. No work, apart from cleaning our rooms and kitchen fatigue (under the guidance of a hotel chef). As members of the *cinquième colonne* we were entitled to officer's rations: five meals a day and wall fruit with every one. For intellectual nourishment the classical library of the Lycée de Valence was at our disposal. Whilst this most humane of humanists, a veritable Brillat-Savarin in style, gave us a preview of culinary delights (*poule au pot, rôti de boeuf, friture de Rhône, spécialité de la région*), cannons thundered out a last trump in the not-so-far-off distance – the triumph of madness: Hitler!

We were all paralysed by nervous tension. The commandant seemed unmoved. When he ended with a cry of, '*Vive le Maréchal!*' we were unsure whether, despite the rule of silence, we should not join in, but we refrained. Only Schmidt from Leipzig, whom we had all assumed to be a firm believer in democracy (I had not yet learnt that such an animal does not exist) bellowed out, to our horror, 'Heil Hitler!' The silence became a deathly hush. We assumed Schmidt would be hauled out on the spot to face a firing squad. Scimitar drawn, the commandant strode up to him and ceremonially struck him on the shoulders with the flat of the blade. 'You are the only one of this rabble who has shown the courage of his convictions. For that you will immediately be given a double portion of peaches, grapes, wine and cake. Your comrades must wait until the morning. *Vive la famille!* The rest of you off to your quarters.'

There was a ramp running round the hall, and we went up it in twos to the immaculately clean rooms, beds with sheets on, electric light and running water – just like a hotel. With rumbling stomachs we watched Schmidt from Leipzig gorging himself on fruit at the table below. At the same time we felt helpless, convinced we were the prisoners of an idiot who would see it as a matter of honour to hand us over, nicely fattened up, to the Nazis. The distant gunfire was approaching *crescendo*. To judge by the sound of the heavy barrage, it was a battle for Valence, some twenty miles to the north. During the night we held a whispered council of war. The difficulty that each and every one of us had when it came to making a decision demonstrated just how hopeless our situation was. The guards, Senegalese who were armed to the teeth and with whom we were neither permitted nor able to speak, had been doubled. How could we break out of this cage? Whom could we trust? Where could we flee to? Nobody wanted to go to Switzerland, one hundred and twenty-five miles away. The fact that I had been in New York the previous year gave me a special position as resident expert in American matters. Everyone wanted to go to America; no one had a visa, which was almost impossible to obtain. First of all, we would have to swim across the raging waters of the Rhône, then make our way through the six hundred miles of the Massif Central to the Pyrenees, then cross fascist Spain before reaching Portugal and the Big Pond. That was too much. Having examined and discarded all possible and impossible alternatives, in a fit of black humour that visited us with the first grey light of dawn we delegated Fenster, the negro, to go and see the commandant and tell him that, even if our files had been lost, we were not spies, not fifth columnists, but *prestataires* of the French Army, enemies of the Nazis whose sole desire was to share victory or defeat with France. No one imagined this step would come to anything. As a last resort I had a Gillette blade in my trousers pocket, so that I could cut my wrists the moment the first Hun appeared at the camp gates.

During breakfast – peaches, grapes, coffee, croissants – a cloudburst came out of the blue, inundating everything in a few minutes. Fenster, the negro with the trumpet, was in his element, floating on his back and playing the blues. Ten thirty: consommé with egg. Twelve: *coquelet au pistou, pommes de terre maître d'hôtel*. When the *soufflé aux framboises* appeared Fenster blew a fanfare: the sliding door opened and in trotted the philistines dressed up as the Bengal lancers on their pretty ponies. Flourishing a piece of paper, the commandant bellowed, despite the deathly hush, 'Silence! Prestataires!' he went on, 'it is with profound emotion that I greet you as comrades in the victorious Grande Armée. Your papers appear to have been found and are on their way here. France has just inflicted a decisive defeat on the enemy in a battle that will go down in the annals of history as the *Bataille de Valence*. The Boches are fleeing in the direction of Chambéry!' (Turning to his adjutant, he added, 'An unforgettable *tournedos Beaugency* followed by *pêches cardinal* in the Hôtel aux Grands Ducs de Savoie!') 'On orders from the *Deuxième Bureau*, which seems to have great plans for you, you are to be dispatched to the Pyrenees, where you will form a new Maginot Line. Departure in twenty minutes with full baggage. The train leaves in one hour. For security reasons you will be taken to the station at the double by a roundabout route. Provisions for the march: two peaches, a bottle of pinard and ten aspirins per man. You are heading for great things! *Vive la patrie!*'

Everyone chimed in, including Schmidt from Leipzig. Saved! Ten minutes later, during roll-call in the courtyard, the most furious cloudburst I ever experienced in my life rained down upon us. Not a stitch was left dry. Wading in water up to the knees, we were rushed through the muddy swamps beside the Rhône to Loriol station. The *spahis* and their dogs knew no mercy. My carpet bag got too heavy and was left behind, stuck in the mire. By the time we reached the station we were at the end of our tether, kept going only by the certainty that we were saved. There the Viennese traitors were already waiting for the train. We eyed each other with distrust, not daring to talk. They looked no worse than we did, but then that would have been impossible.

There was a special train waiting for us, two carriages and a freight wagon behind an engine with its steam up. After being counted several times we were divided up and had to get in, completely soaked. Only then did we discover the incredible truth: we were travelling *first* class! Red velvet upholstery and white lace antimacassars embroidered with the initials P.L.M. (Paris–Lyon–Marseille – *Pour La Mort*). They did put twelve of us in each compartment that was only supposed to seat six, but it was still better than cattle trucks. As soon as we were safely inside, the carriage doors were carefully locked and sealed from outside. The windows did not open. We were shut in, but overjoyed to be travelling towards freedom, and in such luxury too. For most of us it was the first time we had ever travelled first class. One came back from the lavatory in raptures: there was a real towel!

It was not long before our first-class prison was transformed into a stinking pigsty. We spent the night standing in Avignon; the next morning in Nîmes; midday in Montpellier; that evening in Sète; that night in Narbonne. Slower and slower. The following morning in Carcassonne. At every station stones were thrown at the windows, which were unfortunately too thick to be broken. The train no longer stopped at stations, which were all overcrowded, but in the sidings. Miles of worrying stagnation. Every railway train in France had fled to Toulouse. All around the town families of refugees were camped in their thousands. After we had spent a whole feverishly hot day standing in Toulouse without water, air or food our journey eventually continued in the direction of Perpignan. Only to stop again once we were out in the country. *Gardes mobiles* flung open the doors. Air! Once we were out we discovered that again our carriages had had 'cinquième colonne' scrawled over them. Fenster, our negro and now our leader, returned to tell us he was sorry, but he had only been able to find quarters for half of us; the rest would have to look after themselves. To make it fair, he had us line up according to the alphabet: those whose name began with A to the right, those with B to the left, and so on. As a B, Blumenfeld was one of the lucky ones who were allotted the quarters at the foot of the Pyrenees. A holiday in the high mountains would do me good. We said farewell to those dejected comrades who were being left to fend for themselves and assumed that once again we were the ones who had all the luck. As the local train set off behind two puffing engines we had the comic sight of two *gardes mobiles*, revolvers drawn, posting themselves on the step outside each compartment door. Were they looking for a criminal or was it a military exercize? We laughed and waved at the guards. When we tried to open the window to ask what it was all about one shouted in not very friendly tones, 'Anyone who moves will be shot.' At the next station, with the unforgettable name of Saverdun, the corridors outside the compartments were completely packed with *gardes* in steel helmets who then practised aiming at us with their machine guns. Who was it who was suffering from persecution mania? No one dared make a sound. Puffing and panting, the little train dragged us up into the unknown until it stopped with a sudden jolt: Le Vernet d'Ariège.

61 LE VERNET D'ARIÈGE

I had never heard the name of this hell-hole before: Le Vernet. 'Everyone out!' During the whole of the First World War I never saw such a gathering of young

French soldiers. One by one we and our luggage were shoved out of the train with blows from rifle butts as if it might have occurred to some of us to resist. Beyond a football pitch beside the track the iron bars of the main gate with its bedraggled tricolor greeted us: 'Centre d'accueil des étrangers [Foreigner's reception centre] Le Vernet d'Ariège'. In broad daylight we all had to strip right there in the street and line up, naked, behind our things. Inhabitants of Le Vernet walked past without paying any attention to us. While we were each being frisked right down to the prostate for hidden treasures (money, weapons, drugs), a ragged horde of emaciated human monkeys hobbled back into the camp at the double: hollow-eyed skeletons from Brueghel's *Triumph of Death*. (Auschwitz Man had not yet been discovered.) We stared at them in disbelief. They, who knew that no one got out of there alive, grinned, 'Just you wait!' Fenster, the negro, had his trumpet taken away from him. A man who had earned the Croix de guerre fighting for France in the Foreign Legion had to hand it over. Towards evening, after hours of torture by roll-call, we were assigned to Hut 30, *groupement A* (criminals and men who had fought on the republican side in Spain). B was for political prisoners, C for suspects. My crime was that Blumenfeld begins with a B. Behind tangled thickets of barbed wire, with electrified fences and trenches stood wretched, windowless shacks, overcrowded with rotting corpses on shit-coloured mud with sharp stones. Everything stank of diarrhoea. In the background were the Pyrenees. It had already served as a prisoner-of-war camp in the 1914–1918 war.

In this place, under the new motto of *Travail Famille Patrie*, French bureaucretinism allowed men who were prepared to die for *Liberté Egalité Fraternité* to be tortured to death by sadistic peasant oafs (*Gardes mobiles, Pupilles de la Nation*). Out of fear of communism a grasping, menopausal Marianne had made eyes at Hitler, hoping to be ravished from stem to stern one more time by a virile Hun before it was too late. Now it was her pleasure to lie, legs wide apart and tongue busy, at the victor's side. Later, after her conqueror had been conquered, the little bourgeois whore, using the lessons of the brothel, managed to hush up her shame. Today, who ever talks about those who were beaten and starved to death in Le Vernet? I know of no book in which it is mentioned, apart from Koestler's *Scum of the Earth*, and that is out of print. Has anything at all ever been published about French concentration camps? Any list of the émigrés and Jews whom double-dealing France turned over to the Nazis for concentration-camp treatment in return for a modest reward (Laval accepted bribes)? Victors are not called to account. England, Russia and America defeated Hitler. France joined in when it came to gathering laurels. A few poor girls who had slept with German soldiers had their heads shaved, just as in the movies. The great whore Marianne, who had trampled all over the rights of man, was left untouched.

As we marched into this underworld, I imagined I would never be able to get used to the infernalities that went on in there. Hell is a body politic like any other with rich and poor, masters and slaves, people who are demeaned and humiliated. Here, where the French genius for disorder had squashed together 14,000 men deprived of their rights in 120 acres, the negative side was particularly conspicuous. Everyone and everything was full of venom. It is only in hell that human nastiness comes into full bloom. When he heard someone speak with compassion of the torments of the damned in hell, La Fontaine is said to have replied, 'Je me flatte qu'ils s'y accoutument, et qu'à la fin, ils sont là comme le poisson dans l'eau' ('I imagine that they become accustomed to it, and that in the end they take to it like fish to water'). After a while I had to admit that, like it or not, man does get used to everything.

Everybody had managed to smuggle some money through the body search. Anyone who had a thousand francs was a man of means and could go round puffing at his cigarette. Beggars had to search for dog-ends in the mire and then go begging for a light. Stinginess with matches has been a symbol of French pettiness since time immemorial. Here as in Paris there was a *marché aux mégots*, a market for fag-ends.

The lack of food put a damper on our love life. The lack of women left us with the agonizing choice between masturbation and homosexuality. The lack of a future meant we lived off retrospective mirages. Within a few days even the poorest amongst us began to realize that before the war he had been a millionaire, first of all just a plain millionaire, then a multi-millionaire, with cars, a castle, servants in livery, silk sheets and underwear, and governesses for his polyglot daughter. The more wretched we became, the richer we had been. At night steaming gold bathtubs flanked by roast breast of goose and asparagus tips floated through our pestilential hut, a mass grave for two hundred living corpses eighty foot long by fourteen foot wide by eight foot high, not unlike a couchette car and with a corrugated-iron roof on which the raindrops clattered like stones. The doors at either end were bolted from the outside at night so that we could not use the latrine outside, though we could still smell it. A narrow passage ran between the two-tiered bunks made of unplaned wood on which we attempted to sleep, fully clothed and wedged in between two hostile comrades, feet towards the passage, without straw or blankets, hard and cold, just as in a coffin, but without the splendid isolation of eternal peace. I was on the upper level with my head beside an opening which let in the icy night wind. No stove. By day it was scorching hot. During the first night there were horrible screams outside. From above I watched three drunken *gardes* send a man tied up in a bunker to eternal rest with blows to the back of his neck. *Vive la grande nation!*

When we arrived the camp was already in its death throes. Since the administration expected Hitler to arrive any day, all the interned Nazis were given better treatment. There was nothing to eat: pale-brown chicory-water for breakfast, one ounce of bread to last the whole day, and for our main meal *cassoulet de Toulouse*, maggots stewed in lukewarm dishwater. People fell sick. Anyone who reported sick was given three days solitary without water, bread or light. We stayed healthy. I lost a pound every day. Out of our group, four died within a month from diarrhoea and vomiting.

The French militia was recruited from outcasts, who were trained like dogs to attack civilians. They were used to suppress workers' revolts. In Le Vernet they worked off their anger on us. The first morning I was put on shit-shifting duties. I could have bought myself out for five francs, but I lacked the determination to avoid the worst. Nor did I know what I was in for. In pairs we had to carry a crap-container the height of a man, filled to the brim and weighing a ton, for miles before emptying it into the Ariège. *Gardes* with dogs and leather whips kept the column of a hundred huge tubs moving. With every step the stinking diarrhoea slopped into my face, the same as in the Alexanderplatz jail in Berlin in 1918. *Les histoires se répètent* – history repeats itself. Schwarz, a member of the anti-Hitler Confessional Church who had had his nose smashed in in Dachau, thought it was worse here. At least German cruelty operated in punctual and orderly fashion. (The gas ovens were still in their infancy.) Here there were hardly any washing facilities at all, no hygiene. Everyone went round dressed as they liked. Some old hands came to roll call barefoot with only a towel round them, flaunting their rags. One Oriental, whose sole crime was that he did not speak a language for which they could find an interpreter in Paris, had spent months sitting mutely in his kimono on the same spot in the mud, unmoving, gazing at the snow-covered peaks of the Pyrenees.

We were totally cut off from help from the outside world, from an outside world which – with the exception of our families, who heard as little of us as we of them – had other worries than bothering about the fate of a few thousand miserable émigrés. If things are bad enough, even the devil will turn to prayer. I had read enough Balzac to have romantic illusions about being rescued by a priest. On the first Sunday I went to mass in the church, a hut with a cross on it. There was a queue to get a word with the father confessor. In the confessional I immediately confessed that I was a Jew, which gave him a good laugh. Then I whispered that our group in the criminals' section consisted of *prestataires*, to which he replied, '*Cela ne fait rien, le bon Dieu vous pardonnera*' ('That doesn't matter, God will forgive you'). My plan was to use religious and humanitarian arguments to persuade him to smuggle a petition I intended to write to the authorities out of the camp. He reeked of wine and told me how much he could do for the poor of the diocese, if only he had the means. The next Sunday I gave him the letter to the prefect in Pamiers, together with ten francs. Since it was an official letter he asked for a further ten francs, for which he gave me his blessing. I discovered that the confessional was a posting box. Everyone gave the servant of God money and letters, and everyone received his blessing.

It was forbidden to shout across the barbed-wire barricade between Group A and Group B. We could speak to anyone we liked in our own group, which meant that at last we could chat to the Viennese traitors. One of them did actually come from Vienna, a certain Fechner, a would-be intellectual, a wine salesman in flowing cloak and beret, a jesuitical show-off and poseur, a baptised Jew obsessed with the ambition of becoming senior resident in our room, in short a *Viennese*. The others were Rhineland Jews who had emigrated to Belgium and who all introduced themselves as industrialists. When Hitler marched in they fled to Paris from where they had been transported as fifth columnists to Le Vernet. A keen rivalry for intellectual leadership broke out between these captains of industry and us *prestataires*. The *quatorze juillet* was the day on which all would be decided. The whole camp forgot hunger, hell and Hitler; nothing mattered apart from the preparations for the festivities.

One evening a middle-aged mandarin with a jaundiced complexion crept up to me from behind, bowed and introduced himself. 'Guido Stern from Pforzheim, lavatory manufacturer. I have a reputation for being a decent chap with a social conscience, don'tyerknow? During the inflation I didn't pay my workers with worthless paper money, but with lavatories, half a lavatory a week, don'tyerknow? I married my secretary, even though she isn't Jewish, a butcher's daughter as strong and true as a man, don'tyerknow? Furthermore, I'm the biggest stamp collector in the state of Baden, and I have no children. My wife Adèlche can't take a bath. I've put the "Virginia Green" in a little rubber bag and stuck it underneath her bosom. Not the easiest place to get at, no one will find it there before we reach the land of the free, don'tyerknow? And that brings me to my request. Everybody here is convinced I'm a great authority on America just because I happened to mention that I have two brothers over there, millionaires who don't do anything for me because I didn't do anything for them when they were down on their luck, the usual way it is in families, don'tyerknow? So they've given me, a man who has never been to the United States, the honour of making a speech on the "New World" during the 14 July celebrations. Even the camp commandant has said he will attend. Who could refuse? There's great interest in the subject since everyone here, from the commandant to the internees, wants to get to New York. Even the guards want to go. That's why this talk must have a solid foundation, must be authentic, authoritative, don'tyerknow? I'm not the kind of person to try to pull the wool over these people's eyes. Since you have just come back from over there I wanted to ask you to assist me with my lecture. You scratch my back, I'll scratch yours. When the war is over I'll show my appreciation with a few lavatories. Or do you perhaps collect stamps too?'

I lacked the art to wriggle out of the persuasive net spun by this slitty-eyed lavatory maker and promised to supply a speech. How often in my life have I allowed myself to be taken for a ride by a sanctimonious lavatory maker! It was not my fault that this lecture on America came to nothing. The cantankerous old eunuch with his grotesque demands tore up my schoolboy effort in scorn and ordered me to deliver, within twenty-four hours, a better composition containing the three guiding principles of American democracy, namely:

'1. *Service to the Community:* Immediately upon arrival every immigrant has to don blue jeans and spend a week scrubbing the chewing gum off Times Square with a specially made brush, for which he is paid 20 cents per hour. Democracy, don'tyerknow?

'2. *Habituation to the customs of one's new Fatherland:* Anyone who dares to appear in the street after 1 May wearing a felt hat instead of the official straw boater will have the latter knocked off his noddle and trampled on by Uncle Sam in person.

'3. *Training in hygienic responsibility:* Anyone spitting on the sidewalk will be arrested on the spot and sent without further ado to Sing-Sing for three days. Democracy, don'tyerknow?'

My reaction was 'Heil Hitler!' Guido thought that any decent person would have to admit that Hitler had his good points. I suddenly realized that if Adolf had had the patience to keep his racialist madness at least until after the war he would never have needed to go to war. If Hitler, the idol of lavatory manufacturers the world over, had concentrated on uniting the poor in spirit of all countries, with stupidity as the lowest common denominator, the world would have simply fallen into his lap without a single shot being fired.

We had been put in Hut 30 with the Spaniards, who had made themselves at home there for a year. They cold-shouldered us as newcomers and hated us as Germans. I never managed to get a conversation going with any of them. Each of the bearded hidalgos had a beardless youth as his lover. At one of our first morning roll-calls (four roll-calls per day with endless standing to attention) a young Spaniard was missing. After the roll-call he was found hanged in our hut – unhappy in love. Immediately a furious struggle started for the rope; hundreds of short pieces were sold as talismans. It was the specialists of Hut 31 who cornered that particular piece of lucrative business.

At the outbreak of the war all the former inhabitants of Devil's Island, who had been allowed to settle in *villes ouvertes* (towns that still get second-class treatment because of tax evasion in the seventeenth century), were taken into custody again as a precautionary measure and sent to Le Vernet. Thanks to their superior criminal skills, Hut 31 quickly became a legend and the centre of *Groupement A*. The camp administration was no match for these seasoned criminals, the *gardes* were soon bought over and no one dared issue orders to the *bagnards*. They were an autonomous kingdom. Their leader, the 'Prince of Andorra', a one-eyed dandy *sans peur et sans reproche*, every inch a murderer, wore his panama hat at a rakish angle and, beneath it, a black monocle in his sunburnt, scar-slashed face. His tennis shirt, unbuttoned and tied provocatively above his navel, revealed a luminous crown tattooed in blue, white and red on his chest. Without having to say a word, he would conduct the roll-call of his robber band with elegant thwacks of his riding crop on his high-heeled, pointed, patent-leather shoes. Like Edward VII of England, he never wore the same pair of trousers twice. Nothing could faze him. During one roll-call I saw his young catamite, known as El Greco, step out of line, slit open his belly with a kitchen knife and collapse without the Prince of Andorra taking the slightest notice. Immediately afterwards he was in his usual deckchair, sunbathing and having a manipedicure and massage from his bondslaves.

I wanted to get to know him and sent him a copy of *Harper's Bazaar* which had some of my photos. The very same day he granted me an audience during which, without deigning to address as single word to me, he graciously allowed me to autograph the magazine. His aide-de-camp then condescendingly informed me that I had been admitted to membership of the exclusive gambling club. I thought it was a joke; a casino in a concentration camp was beyond even my wildest imaginings. It was impressed upon me what an honour it was to be included in the mysterious nightlife of the camp. This was the only genuine success I had from my work for fashion magazines. Nothing was impossible for these galley slaves. On their orders Hut 32 had been left empty. That was where they spent the nights gambling: baccarat, chemin de fer, dice. The Prince's footmen had pass-keys to all the huts from which they fetched the gamblers at night. They could get you through the electrified fence to the brothel in Tarbes, smuggle letters in and out (in order to save the cost of censoring internees' mail, the camp office had it all burnt every day) and buy things for you, from cocaine to pâté de foie gras and silk panties, all at fixed but fancy prices.

To fulfil 'certain formalities' (probably to give me a financial once-over) the Prince had sent me to see the great Simon Simonovitch Seidenschleim, alias Weiszager, business manager to the all-powerful pawnbroker and black-marketeer, Haiman Heiman, who each week bought the entire supply of canteen provisions from the camp administration at double price and sold them to the camp inmates at four times the price. Heiman had spent (was to spend?) four years in prison for spying. In August 1940 he returned to Germany in his official capacity as an 'economically valuable Jew'. The *shammes* immediately showed me into

Seidenschleim's counting-house, jumping a long queue of anxious supplicants. This medieval usurer received me sitting on his bed in his kaftan, bent over his account books. He asked me about my bank account in New York and granted me, if I should need it, an open-ended credit of up to three hundred dollars at the preferential interest rate of one per cent per week. I found 52 per cent per annum rather high, and asked what would happen if someone should forget to repay. 'That doesn't happen with me and anyway, you can afford to repay so why brag?'

The casino was an empty hut with gaming tables. It was an underworld dimly lit by candles. Threepenny-opera beggars sold beer straight from the bottle, one franc per swig. Anyone bold enough to take an unpaid-for swig got an uppercut on his Adam's apple. The casino was packed, but everyone spoke in barely audible whispers. You heard the gambling, not the gamblers.

From an elevated throne the Prince, panama at an angle, black monocle and open silk shirt, dominated the tables. Below his silk shorts two eyes tattooed on his knees gleamed menacingly in the smoke-filled darkness of the gambling den. The lighting must have been arranged by a theatre designer. The Prince's knee movements signified life or death for all those present. In the background stood knife-throwing henchmen who never missed and for whom the slightest wink of one of those eyes was a command. Everyone here was a master cardsharp, but nobody dared use his tricks. Only the Prince, who held the bank, was allowed to win. Wooden chips of a thousand francs were used. Unfortunately I only went to the casino once. The greedy camp commandant demanded a bigger cut so the Prince simply closed down the casino from one night to the next. Under his leadership all the Devil's Islanders set fire to their hut, then formed up in ranks and marched out of the camp, taking all their baggage with them. No one dared stop them. They went underground, became *maquisards*, plundered the countryside and ended up as heroes of the Resistance, like all the rest of the French.

We lily-livered scaredy cats, lacking the will, the courage and a Prince of Andorra, stayed imprisoned in the camp. We could, however, pride ourselves on a particularly impressive *quatorze juillet*, culminating in a jubilant eight-part *Chanson des Prestataires*. It started optimistically with 'We the brave *prestataires*', and ended with a resigned 'as sinks the tearful sun, in the blood-stained Garonne'. (It had to sink in the Garonne because we couldn't find a rhyme for Ariège.)

The abandoned gambling den was filled with two hundred wild hooligans from a Belgian juvenile prison, who immediately started beating each other to death (three dead in two days). The *gardes* were incapable of coping with them either, they were only trained to deal with defenceless civilians. They tried to put me in charge of the hut because of my knowledge of Dutch. It was only the fact that I could not speak Flemish that saved my life.

After the fourteenth of July the days grew hotter and hotter, the nights colder and colder. There were hailstones the size of duck's eggs and the same *canards* produced the latrine rumours that Hitler was going to take over the camp the next day. There was no hope any more, only fear. Next stop Auschwitz. On the afternoon of 2 August I was taken to a shed beside the football pitch where, totally unexpectedly, I found my wife and children. It was an interpreter who was staying in the same inn as my wife in Le Vernet who brought about this undreamt-of, unallowed family visit. The miraculous reunion had been made possible by Hardekopf. His lover, the actress Sitta Staub – so beautiful in her younger years; in my Dada days I had kissed her hand when she had played Wedekind's naked Franziska – was in the women's concentration camp at Gurs in the Pyrenees. He had passed on my greetings to her. My daughter, Lisette, was sent to the same camp where she slept beside the old morphine addict, and that was how she had discovered where I was. My wife, who had fled from Vézelay with the boys at the very last minute, had lost a lot of weight. The children stared in timid wonder at my bald head, but chattered excitedly about the gigantic hailstones of the previous night. I, a skeleton once more puffed up with hope, suggested to my wife she try her luck with the prefect in Pamiers.

After this reunion our sleep was interrupted at four in the morning by roars of, 'Special roll-call in five minutes!' Shivering with cold and agitation, we waited in the grey light of dawn. After a while the commandant, Pernod fils, arrived with his staff and started laying into us, 'You, who call yourselves *prestataires* of the Grande Armee, are unworthy of the humane treatment afforded by this camp. Revolutionary elements among you have been pestering the government with petitions. For that you are being transferred to the dreaded punishment camp of Catus. There you'll be buried up to your navels. Speaking is forbidden. At the first word one of your eyes will be gouged out. At five-thirty you will board the train with your baggage, under strict security, after each one of you has signed a statement that he has been well treated here and has no claims to make on the camp. *Mes félicitations, Messieurs*. Fall out!'

Could this have been the result of my interference? None of the *prestataires* spoke a word to me. I felt in my trouser pocket for my only friend, my Gillette blade, and swore not to let anyone bury me up to the navel alive. When we were ready for our transport – one *garde* armed with rifle, revolver and whip to every four *prestataires* – we were joined by three unknown men with carefree laughter. They had hair on their heads, too, so they must have been from the political section. There was a tall one, a short one and an older one; I dubbed them the Three Horsemen of the Apocalypse. They were having an animated conversation about politics and ignored us. Even the fact that before we got on the train we were handcuffed two by two did not seem to bother them. Slowly the train puffed its way downhill on side-tracks until late that night we were deposited in a siding that served the Toulouse abattoir where we were put into a pigsty without food and the door nailed up. I would have liked to get to know the Three Horsemen, who continued happily talking politics, but the nineteen-year-old classical scholar, a neurotic from Breslau, to whom I was handcuffed, was sleeping like a log, and snoring like someone sawing one. Before daybreak – so that no one would see us – we were crammed into two cattle trucks attached to a train which crawled its way through Cahors and across Gascony towards nemesis.

62 CATUS

An avenue of poplars led from the station to the village of Catus. For the time being we were made to lie in the ditch beside the road and were not allowed to speak. I clung to my razor blade. The *gardes*, leaning against tree trunks, kept their rifles pointed at us. Nothing happened.

Towards noon a small open sports car came roaring up. A good-looking young man in a pink pullover casually asked for the leader of the transport. When no one answered, he shouted angrily, 'I am Capitaine Schlosser, commandant of Catus camp!' Startled shouts of '*Garde à vous.*' Handcuffed as we were, we leapt to our feet. With much military clicking of heels a folder full of papers was handed over to the young man. The new commandant, astonished to see us manacled, ordered the bloodhounds, who stood there, open-mouthed, to release us immediately and then to get the hell out of Catus as fast as they could. When they had undone our chains, the *gardes* formed up and beat a pathetic retreat to the station.

After they had gone, Schlosser stood up in his car and asked us to come closer.

'I must beg your forgiveness', he said in a somewhat piping voice, 'for keeping you waiting. There was no petrol in Catus. I've read your files. You were sent to a concentration camp by mistake, and to the worst one at that. Something like Le Vernet should not exist in France. *Je vous demande pardon.* You look starved. I will see to it that you get double rations and the arrears in your pay. At the moment France has lost everything. In your own interest you will help us drive Hitler out. We will discuss that later. Your quarters are not great, but I think you will find them interesting. Anyone with a family can look for lodgings in Catus. First of all, though, have a few days rest. I will send a bus to collect you. *Vive de Gaulle!*'

And off he went. Too dazed to comprehend this incredible turn of events, we dragged ourselves back to the ditch as if we were still in chains. As the sun was setting I had to be shaken out of a deep sleep to join the last batch going to the camp in the disused Paris omnibus, route Q. We passed through the old village and drove along a heroic valley painted by Joachim Patinir (the landscape of my dreams) to a grand medieval castle in a fantastical state of ruin. Trembling with hunger, sentimentality and weakness at the romantic nature of our new concentration camp, I flopped down on an empty bed and slept until I was woken by a dream that I was wearing the stinging shirt of Nessus. Not conscious of where I was, my burning body tossed and turned on the sea-grass mattress until morning, when I discovered that I was covered with black, jumping dots – fleas. I ran out into the morning mist, rolled in the wet grass like a mangy dog and went back to sleep. I woke up to find myself lying among crumbling gravestones in the castle graveyard, eyeball to eyeball with a skull. I laughed. Life itself was a grotesque flea circus.

None of our predecessors was still living in the castle, and not just because of the fleas. We were told that a neurotic nudist in the camp had managed to convince his companions in misfortune that the only thing that could save the world was vegetarian exhibitionism. The countless caves in the hills around the castle provided ideal homes for the *Neobaldurites*, as the community called itself. On the first walk I took I could not believe my eyes when, outside a cleft in the rock not five minutes from the castle, a long-haired Teuton, barefoot right up to the neck and with a babe at her breast, raised her arm and greeted me with, 'Heil Baldur!' while a giant of a man beside her dressed only in steel-rimmed spectacles was furiously trying to coax a spark from two stones. When I offered him a match he rejected it with disdain.

The next morning I was called to the office, which mostly left us in peace. Capitaine Schlosser was magnificent, perhaps too magnificent. He never wore uniform, played tennis and spent all his energies trying to build up a new army in Africa, at the same time organizing the *maquis* in unoccupied France. He had decided I was too old for his purposes. He informed me that my family was arriving that afternoon and advised me to look for a small apartment in Catus. He offered me money and sent a telegram to Carmel Snow at *Harper's Bazaar*, New York, to which she never replied. As I set out to meet my family off the train I realized that I was at the end of my tether. In my six weeks at Le Vernet I had lost forty-five pounds. Happily we were all together again. We rented two rooms and a kitchen full of spider's webs in the village and arranged a peace treaty with the fleas.

63   THE THREE HORSEMEN OF THE APOCALYPSE

Right from the beginning I made it my business to get to know the mysterious Three Horsemen. They knew everything. They also knew too much and they talked too much, and that was to be their undoing. It wasn't long before they were telling me too, under the seven seals of secrecy, that they had worked for the counter-espionage section of the *Deuxième Bureau*. Since that now came under the jurisdiction of Vichy they had started spying for an independent parallel organization called, I think, *La Surveillance du Territoire*.

Their story was that we *prestataires* had only been moved out of Vernet to camouflage *their* disappearance from the camp. According to them, the whole sadistic farewell parade, together with Commandant Pernod fils' speech, was nothing but a subtle trick on the part of the French secret service since they, the Three Horsemen of the Apocalypse, were high up on the Gestapo shopping list. (The Gestapo did in fact turn up in Vernet on the day we left, hoping to get them. Incidentally, I was on that list as well; I read in a book by Thomas Kernan that on the first day of the occupation of Paris a Gestapo unit turned up at the *Vogue* offices to arrest me.) Each one of the three was in pursuit of a quarry. The tall one, Ewald Zweig, alias Yves Rameau, a political journalist with a lively temperament and a provocative laugh, was hunting for Monsieur Lemoine. The short one, Berthold Jacob, a military journalist and a typically neurotic Jew, was famous as the hero of *The Jacob Case*: the Nazis abducted him from Switzerland and had been forced to send him back after enormous international protest. He was on the trail of

Frédéric Drach. The third, the older one with dyed hair, was Herr Oliver, the opera singer; he was less prominent, although he considered himself the most important. He was looking for an opera house that would let him sing Don José in *Carmen*.

Drach and Lemoine. I knew both of them from Paris: Alsatians, informers, scum. Lemoine, a speechless, faceless monk with hideous cataracts, was the *dernière incarnation de Vautrin*. In 1914 he had murdered the mayor of Barcelona, having previously been deported from the United States for counterfeiting. He got to know Drach in the Spartakus uprising in Berlin in 1919, in the course of which they betrayed and sold both sides. These were the talents Lemoine used to work his way up to head of the French secret service. Frédéric Drach, on the other hand, was made editor in 1932 of the illustrated magazine *VU* (a precursor of *Life*), which belonged to the dandy Lucien Vogel. When *VU* brought out a sensational pro-Soviet number, Drach denounced his boss, who had been bribed by Russia to publish it. There was a great scandal and Vogel was forced to sell *VU* to Laval. After that Drach was dropped and went down in the world. I used to see him, growing increasingly bloated by the day, slouching along in his felt slippers to the cafés of Montparnasse. His wife, a lesbian heroine out of a De Sade novel, kept the family going with small heroin deals. Suddenly Drach was back on top again. He was working for Lemoine as a confidential agent of the aliens branch of the police. This was all the more profitable as the two of them were paid by both the French secret service and the Gestapo, who used them to check up on German émigrés in Paris. No immigrant was granted his *permis de séjour* from the *préfecture de police* without a report from Drach. In that way every opponent of Hitler could be taken care of most efficiently. At the same time forged documents relating to German armaments could be passed on to the French general staff by emigrants, via Drach. Even Marshal Pétain and General Gamelin were said to owe a debt of gratitude to the Lemoine-Drach outfit. When Madame de Gaulle visited Pétain in Vichy on a secret mission, Drach was allegedly sent out to North Africa, with the approval of the Gestapo, to act as her escort and aide. Later Drach, who was, incidentally, the spitting image of that scoundrel, Whittaker Chambers, an editor of *Time* and denouncer of Alger Hiss, was strangled in his hotel in Marseilles.

We listened to the amusing *blagues* of the three braggarts with enthusiastic scepticism and came to the conclusion they were not to be taken seriously. Their fate, however, showed how ignorant we were.

Oliver, the opera singer, found the nudist caves of Catus too much to his liking for his own good. He fell in love with one of the Teutonesses and moved into a back-to-nature cave with her. One fine day both he and the young lady, who worked for the Gestapo, vanished completely. Ewald Zweig was found hanging from a lamppost in Toulouse. Berthold Jacob went farthest. The international writers' association, PEN, got him a visa for America. He went with his wife (we used to call her 'Fibroma') to Lisbon where they were to take the ship. On the way to the harbour the car broke down. Frau Jacob went on ahead in another car while Berthold stayed behind with the luggage. Never to be seen again.

Back to Catus. A wonderful autumn soon healed the wounds of Le Vernet and the horrors became amusing anecdotes. Anyone who comes out of a concentration camp alive thinks he is going to be healthy ever after. But soon new worries arrived. A horrendous famine. The rationing system broke down and we had no money to buy on the black market. Worse than the hunger, however, was the increasing insecurity. France was now divided into occupied and unoccupied zones. Being in the unoccupied zone, we counted on a degree of security from Vichy, but Laval, Mephistopheles to Pétain's Faust, was selling people to the Gestapo. I had to concentrate all my energies on the hunt for visas. First of all I tried to re-establish my contacts with the outside world, which had been disrupted by the collapse of France, and visited my friend André Girard in Toulouse. He told me that an American visa could only be got in Marseilles, and then only with the very best connections.

When I arrived back from Toulouse there was great agitation in Catus. The dreaded German manhunt commission was expected. Capitaine Schlosser had already sent the Three Horsemen of the Apocalypse, disguised as peasants, in his own car to the nearest village, Puy-l'Évêque. He advised us to take to the hills and put a dozen unendangered *prestataires* to sawing wood in the castle courtyard. The Gestapo kicked up a fuss about this attempt to pull the wool over their eyes, and Capitaine Schlosser disappeared to Africa. The Catus camp was closed down. The vacation was over. We were transferred to Agen, between Bordeaux and Toulouse. The cave-dwellers regarded themselves as demilitarized and stayed where they were, as unclothed as ever.

Le Capitaine Lacroix, Commandant, *la 308e Comp. de Travailleurs Étrangers à Agen*, an admirer of De Gaulle, was soon replaced by an admirer of Pétain,

Capitaine Leroy who, with money and empty promises, recruited mercenaries to fight in the German army against Russia, for which he was executed by firing squad after the war. He was also an amateur photographer, therefore well disposed towards me, whom he appointed *photographe attitré de la famille Leroy*. I was relieved of all duties, allowed to live outside the camp with my family ('à Segond' was the name of the small farm), and wear civilian clothes. I was even given a pair of shoes, a *laisser-passer* and freedom to travel anywhere in unoccupied France. My first commission as photographer to the family was to photograph his mother-in-law, who was paralysed and lived in Nice. I could not have asked for more, since my route passed through Marseilles.

Nice was one huge emigrant camp. Because of the heavy police raids the value of the dollar on the black market had just fallen, while an American visa had become prohibitively expensive. For that reason Mr Engelking, the greatest living visa-dealer, had gone in for Venezuelan visas, which he sold for a thousand dollars, though only if the buyer was willing to sign a legally binding declaration that he would never in his life set foot on Venezuelan soil. After I had photographed the paralysed mother-in-law between two ravishing St Bernards, I went to Marseilles.

P.S. It is possible that, after twenty-five years, I may have confused Captains Leroy and Lacroix; even at the time it was difficult to distinguish between them.

64 HOW TO GET YOUR AMERICAN VISA

At eight in the morning I went along to the American Consulate where there was already a mile-long queue of visa-hungry émigrés. You could tell from the looks on their faces that they had already been waiting for days. Before taking my place at the back I counted to see how many there were before it was my turn: two thousand four hundred. In the first hour ten were dealt with, therefore I would have to wait two hundred and forty hours or, since the consulate was open eight hours a day, thirty days. The people in the queue, many of whom had folding chairs, took turns with other members of the family. I was on my own; the most hopeless situation I have seen in all my life. I strolled down the Canebière to the Vieux Port, where, in the Loup de Mer brasserie, I found a whole gang from the Café du Dôme. I had a pastis and a hearty bouillabaisse and listened to variations on one theme: *visas*. Someone mentioned that one of the vice-consuls, Oliver

Hiss, was a passionate amateur photographer. As I was paying, fate had it that an American press card fell out of my wallet; *Life* in New York had obtained it for me when I was photographing the World's Fair. I was even impressed myself at how official it looked, with passport photo, stamps and signatures. With that my war was won.

Late that afternoon, after closing time, I flashed my press card and went unchallenged past the guards into the American Consulate. There was no one there I could ask where to find Consul Hiss, so I went from door to door until I found his name on the second floor: Oliver Hiss, Vice-Consul. I knocked. I could hear voices, but no one answered. I knocked again, again without success, so I opened the door to find an empty office with a huge desk strewn with papers, a model of disorder. On the wall behind hung the American flag, 'Old Faithful'. Noises that were hard to define were coming through a half-open door to the adjoining room, evoking memories of the Hôtel Celtique in Paris. For the first time in my life I felt the thrill of a religious vision: God was taking a hand in my fate. I glanced through the door. At this point any other visa-seeker would have discreetly withdrawn. As a confirmed voyeur I stared, spellbound. What first caught my eye was a bottle of champagne (Mumm Cordon Rouge Extra Brut) between two half-filled flutes. Behind that still life was a woman kneeling who seemed to have her head jammed between the thighs of a man squatting on a sofa. The man looked just the way little Morry Cohen might imagine an American consul: grey flannel trousers and a Harris tweed jacket. The picture was completed by a Dunhill pipe on the floor and a sourly smiling Franklin D. Roosevelt on the wall. All that was visible of the lady was a mop of dark curls held by two male hands. And yet – at this point the whole affair took on a surrealist tinge – I recognized her. In the weeks before the outbreak of the war I had found myself in precisely the same position with her in Paris. Unless I was very much mistaken, this was my charming friend, Sissy M. from Vienna, for whom this was the sole form of happiness in life. Prescribed by a stomach specialist, she claimed.

When the consul finally noticed my presence he vainly tried to extricate himself from the lady's grip, then asked me in a typically American businesslike way, 'What can I do for you, sir?' At my answer – 'I want a *visum*' – the lady finally turned round, recognized me, jumped up and kissed me with moist lips. 'Of course Erwin will get his visa. We were talking about you only half an hour ago. Oliver greatly admires your nude under wet silk.' The Vice-Consul hadn't much choice. He zipped up his trousers, stood up and shook my hand. 'Glad to meet you Erwin, in spite of the hardships – I mean the war. Couldn't you come back tomorrow at a more convenient time, say about eleven, to pick up the application forms? Hope you don't mind, we still have a job to finish here.' My lady friend winked and threw me a kiss. Discreetly – and highly satisfied – I left the Consulate of the United States of America in Marseilles.

I travelled back to Agen in triumph, laden with forms. We spent a cold and hungry winter with the Pyrenees in the background and the Gestapo in the foreground. They were coming closer with every day, sniffing around for Jews; there were already direct transports from Agen to Auschwitz. At the end of March to our relief word finally came from Marseilles: the Blumenfeld family had to present itself on such-and-such a date in April at the American Consulate to finalize arrangements for their visas, armed with fifteen dollars per head plus certificates of health from the Consulate doctor, Dr Rodecanacci. Without even bothering to glance at me, this humanitarian gentleman made out my certificate of health for America for one hundred francs. For the certificate of *illness*, without which I would not get an exit visa from France, he demanded a thousand. For that I could choose between cancer of the kidneys and tuberculosis of the brain. When I protested at the high cost of these diseases, he said, 'I dislike telling lies.'

At the consulate we were given written confirmation that our visas would be handed over if we presented tickets for the Atlantic crossing within six weeks. The shipping companies, however, would only put you on their waiting lists if you already had your visa. All the ships were fully booked. There was a rumour that Germany would not let any ships out after 1 June, since England was seizing them on the high seas and using them as troop transports. The trade in tickets was entirely in the hands of the Marseilles underworld. One impossibility seemed to lead to another. Now the Gestapo was beginning to mount raids here too; manhunts in blocked-off streets, hotels being searched at five in the morning. Everyone was living in mortal fear.

In the Loup de Mer I happened to run into the brother of my friend Laure d'O. from Paris. He was an eighteen-year-old tough operating on the black market. I knew him only slightly. He got interested in sorting out my difficulties and took me to see a friend, a director of the *Messageries Maritimes*, who wanted to be photographed and who promised to get me passages to Martinique on the *Mont Viso* for 10 May for 10,000 francs (I still had 13,000 left). Since, so he said, he could not deal with me directly, young d'O. would act as intermediary. With the help of the aforementioned Sissy (a skilful tongue can achieve more than a thousand wise words) I managed to persuade my consul to hand over our visas, contrary to regulations. At six in the morning on 9 May young d'O. came to our hotel to collect the money and our passports. He said he would bring everything to the Loup de Mer at eleven that morning and asked me to be on time, since he had an important appointment afterwards. I felt very uneasy. I was at the Loup dead on time and waited and waited like I have never waited before or since. Noon, afternoon, evening. Still he hadn't come. Passport gone, money gone, everything gone. I was done for. I had neither the courage to get up, nor the strength to get drunk. I talked to no one, I waited and waited. Then, suddenly, at eight in the evening young d'O. came charging in, flung an envelope onto the table and said, as if he had been through something awful, 'Don't ask me why I'm late, it was terrible. Here's what you've been waiting for, tickets and passports.' I was so grateful I tried to press my last thousand francs into his hand, but he refused. 'I don't accept money from a friend, only from enemies. *Bon voyage.*' And off he ran.

65   THE MONT VISO

The rickety freighter *Mont Viso* had cabins for twelve passengers at most. Four hundred and forty emigrants were crammed into two holds of this death ship. A floating Vernet. Bows: *Hommes*, stern: *Femmes*. We were not even out of the harbour of Marseilles, safe from Hitler's clutches, when an unholy battle broke out between the eastern Jews (the filthy Polacks) and the German Jews (the filthy assimilated Jews). Only the vigorous intervention of the crew – the boat was manned by jungle gorillas – prevented them all from throwing each other overboard.

We were already well out on the Mediterranean when, staring out at me from the front page of a neighbour's newspaper, I saw young d'O., his head bleeding and bandaged, flanked by two policemen. Below in bold type was ROBBER ARRESTED IN SHOOTOUT ON CANEBIÈRE. First he had gone to fetch my papers from the *Messageries Maritimes*, then he had murdered a jeweller, with the papers still in his pocket, before dashing off to the Loup de Mer, where he delivered them to me without asking for a single centime. They caught him the next day.

Two mornings later they unloaded a cargo of sulphur in Algiers, covering us all in a film of greenish-yellow powder. Then we went, much too quickly, past Oran, through the Straits of Gibraltar and along the coast of Africa to Casablanca, where no one was allowed on land: quarantine. An order from Hitler via Vichy. For weeks they left us to fry like eggs on the red-hot iron ship in the boiling harbour during which, as in the concentration camp, the social classes crystallized into different layers. As the heat increased daily, both people and food became increasingly odious. As the rations decreased, the shits increased. Our menu of *soupe forestière, ragoût Impérial, légumes printaniers* was just dried vegetables under various guises. The water stank, you could hardly even wash in it. The captain did not deign to speak a single word to any one of us. As captain of a freighter he hated passengers. Kassy, a Red Cross driver who vividly imagined she was Bismarck's granddaughter, slept with the captain, allegedly to find out why we were stuck in the port. He whipped her, but still didn't utter a syllable (some passengers eavesdropped at the cabin door).

On 22 June (Hitler's invasion of Russia), without anyone saying a word to us, the *Mont Viso* steamed out of Casablanca harbour with an escort of French torpedo boats, heading for America. Passengers sobbed and embraced – SAVED! I didn't feel like spending he night in the boiling-hot cargo-hold, so I stayed up on deck, hoping to see the Southern Cross at last. What I did see around midnight, to my horror, was the Pole Star doing a 180 degree turn. We were going back! In despair I ran to the captain, who motioned me off the bridge with a wave of his hand. The next morning the *Mont Viso* once more lay at anchor in the very same spot in the hell of Casablanca harbour. A few days later the Alcina, a larger emigrant ship which had just spent six weeks stewing off Dakar, anchored alongside us. The exchange of ideas between ships began with Kaluschek bellowing, 'Got any Swiss cheese?'

After almost two months in the harbour there was a threat of plague, and to prevent it the order came to move us within two hours to Moroccan concentration camps, adults to Kasbah Tadla in the Atlas Mountains, invalids and people with small children to Sidi-el-Ajachi, sixty miles south of Casablanca. Amid the scorching sirocco heat of the desert in that July of 1941, behind barbed wire in miserable mud huts, plagued by stable-flies and watched over by Senegalese guards (much more humane than the *gardes mobiles* in Vernet) we groaned as if our end was nigh. My youngest son had head-lice and constant fever, they were threatening to send him to the typhus sheds in Magazan. My daughter, without a word of complaint, endured swollen lips and eyelids caused by scurvy, while I spent my time poking around with my pocket knife in a nasty festering abscess on my wife's breast.

When, however, we had overcome the initial shock, and had also got used to the stable-flies, Sidi turned out to be almost a romantic idyll. One morning there was even a boa that incautiously raised its head out of a privy and was shot and carried through the camp accompanied by a triumphal procession of cheering children. The camp commandant, another German ex-foreign legionnaire, invited me to drink peppermint tea in his harem. He made the ladies of his seraglio kneel before me and commanded an eleven-year-old Scheherezade to beat the oldest woman of the harem (a twenty-eight year old) with a feather duster while we smoked a hookah. The guards could not read, but they were happy to accept a Paris metro ticket as a *laisser-passer* (they liked the hole), and would present arms and give us a broad grin as they opened the gate to fairyland. On a black rock high above the chocolate-brown river we discovered Azemour, a gleaming white dream-town straight out of the *Arabian Nights* with caliphs, storks, veiled houris, dervishes and miracle rabbis. We ran through cactus groves where camels, with their young beside them, walked round in circles turning idyllic water-mills, then through gentle green dunes to the warm ocean. While we were swimming Arab boys ran off with our last pairs of shoes.

On the *Mont Viso* we had made friends with a Spanish grandee and his beautiful wife Gesussa, who were on their way to Mexico. He was a distinguished surgeon (specializing in operating on goitres) and a morphine addict. When camp life got too much for him he took a substantial dose of his favourite substance, which put him at death's door, in a coma and in Magazan hospital. Two days later he was already medical superintendent there and inviting us to an elegant *homard flambé* with champagne.

Our American visas automatically ran out after three months. At the last moment, the end of July, an efficient commission of the HIAS (Hebrew Immigration Aid Society) appeared, Jewish civilians who examined our papers without fuss and despatched telegrams. Totally unexpectedly we found ourselves on 2 August 1941, nothing but skin and bones, steaming out of the sweltering heat of Casablanca to freedom as steerage passengers on the Portuguese luxury liner, the *SS Nyassa*. At the first dinner on board my youngest son polished off a whole pound of sugar. I would spend hours at my favourite spot in the bows of the ship, staring down at the waves we made as we ploughed our way through the ocean – and towards new problems. In order to keep up my courage I remembered how, two years ago, I had conquered New York in less than no time at all, imagining that meant I knew and loved America. Now that I was arriving as a ghost from a concentration camp would it even receive me? As an insignificant émigré I really had no choice but to embrace my illusions with blind abandon, unencumbered by factual knowledge.

The contributions the New World had made to culture so far were very much in my line, the grotesque. (Edgar Allan Poe, jazz, burlesque, striptease, slapstick, and film comedy from Charlie Chaplin to the Marx Brothers.) I resolved to smuggle culture into my new country by way of thanks for accepting me.

On the seventh day, after passing the Ambrose lightship, the steamer slowed down. Seagulls screeched, passport officials, pilots and reporters clambered on board. For the second time I watched excited passengers jostle each other impatiently with their binoculars on the rails, each wanting to be the first to spot the first skyscraper. As the veils of Gulf stream mist thinned, a strip of land emerged, silvery green in the distance, a line of dunes rising from the Atlantic: the New World! Roofs on disappointingly pretty-pretty toy houses began to appear, one beside the next in childish old lady's colours: pink, mauve, light blue, beige, all alike. Behind them rose pointless iron constructions from some gigantic Meccano set: Coney Island, New York's amusement park. Slowly we glided along among the busy tooting of little tugboats, past an ancient Mouse Tower (Fort Hamilton) into the Narrows. Only at the very last, under the watchful eye of the verdigris Miss Liberty, did the immense backdrop of the Manhattan skyscrapers with their greyish-mauve glaze (every city has its own colour, New York has a purplish tinge) rise up into the inhuman August sky, eliciting from Kulaschek the compliment, 'Is that it?'

New York received us with open arms and empty hands. My Chase Bank account had been blocked (it was unblocked after a few days without any difficulties); friends who had promised me money to help me get started reneged. The next morning I borrowed some money, bought a tropical suit for nineteen dollars seventy-five cents, and went to *Harper's Bazaar*. Shoes off, feet up on her photo-strewn desk, surrounded by arse-licking editors and her arsehole of an art director Brodovitch, Carmel Snow dominated the tiny, boiling-hot private office. Without getting up, without looking up, she delightedly gave me her orders as if we had never been separated by two years of world war. 'Blumenfeld! Talk of the devil! Two of Huene's pages are impossible and he's gone off on holiday again. We have to have the September issue finalized by tomorrow. Run up to the studio right away and do some fabulous retakes. I'm right in the middle of the autumn collections at the moment, we'll have lunch together some time in the next few weeks and then you can tell me all your war stories. You look splendid! But quick, do me a few genuine Blumenfeld pages, sensational masterpieces. We have to keep to deadlines! So long!' It sounded devastatingly encouraging.

The *Bazaar* studio was high under the roof and as torrid as the notorious leads of Venice where Casanova sweltered during his imprisonment. Without air-conditioning, at a temperature of a hundred degrees and a thousand per cent humidity, I sweated out eight pages until, well after midnight, I fell asleep in a chair. When I woke up next morning a letter was thrust into my hand:

My dear Blum,
We're all delighted that you and your family have made it safely to the USA, to work for Harper's Bazaar again. Since the eight photos you took yesterday were done in our studio using our equipment we'll have to deduct $100 per page towards our overheads so this time, as I'm sure you understand, you'll only get $150 per photo.
Love Carmel

'Love' at $800 for the first night – that's America for you!

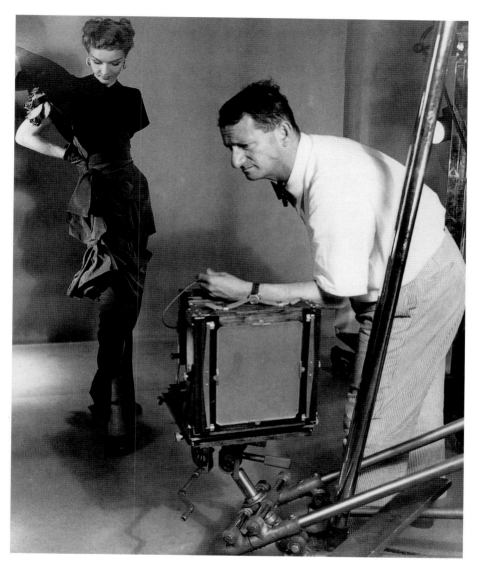

New York studio, 1948

New York, 1942

Untitled fashion photograph, New York, 1945

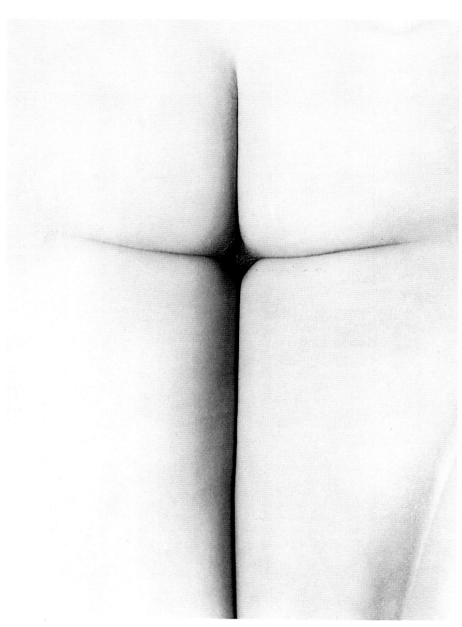

'In hoc signo vinces.' New York, 1967

Plaster cast, New York, 1943

Untitled nudes, New York, 1950

Untitled nude, New York, 1948

Elizabeth Nightingale Graham (Elizabeth Arden),
New York, 1960

New York City, 1950

Marua Motherwell, New York, 1944

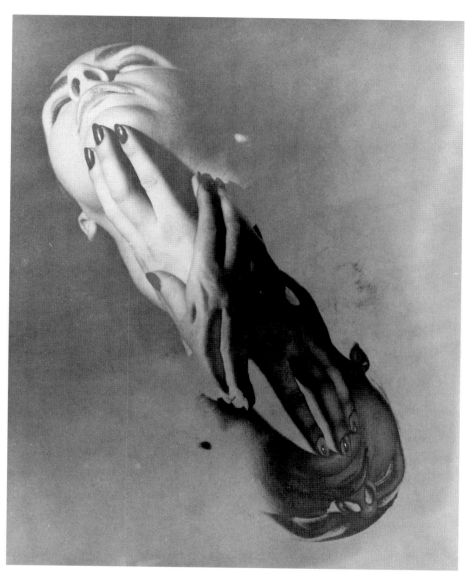

Half-solarized hands and face, New York, 1948

Portrait, 1940s

Solarized portrait, 1947

VOGUE

1950

MID-CENTURY
FASHIONS
FACES
IDEAS

TRAVEL
HANDBOOK

Doe Eye, cover for *Vogue,* 1950

Over 100 Blumenfeld covers

Evelyn Tripp, New York, 1955

Fashion photograph for Dayton Company, Minneapolis. New York, 1955

Fashion photograph for Dayton Company, Minneapolis. New York, 1955

Fashion photograph for Dayton Company, Minneapolis. New York, 1955

Cadillac for *Vogue*, New York, 1956

Portrait à la Greco, New York, 1950

New York, 1930s

Window, New York, 1939

Erwin Blumenfeld in New York, 1960s

66 BLUMENFELD STUDIO INC.

What one desires in one's youth, one has aplenty in old age.
(Goethe, *Dichtung und Wahrheit*)

I hit the Fifties together with the rest of the world. Blumenfeld Studio Inc., 222 Central Park, South Midtown Manhattan. On my nose the hated glasses I had to put up with, like them or not. Dreams of my youth came so extravagantly true they threatened to overwhelm me. Gadgets (an American word for devices that are supposed to make life easier, but just make it impossible): any number of photographic gizmos and gimmicks and assorted focus-pocus, intrigues all around, implausibly painted beauties (models), powder, make-up, nylon underwear, nylon eyelashes, artificial light, phony shadows, real falsies, false teeth, synthetic tears, feigned smiles, dyed hair, plastic fingernails, tempestuous petticoats, waistcinches by the inches, an inextricable excess of everything – everything is always too much for everybody.

Here I am, the chaotic disorganizer, in the midst of all these distractions, searching for the magic word to transform nonsense into sense while a gramophone record scratches out Don Giovanni's end. Terrifying strobe lights (shock treatment, 1/10,000 second flash) – eclipsing a thousand suns – stare at me blankly as I, the photographer who never produces enough, struggle with bloody-minded equipment, with form, with time – that is, with the deadline. No lunch, but always ready for the last supper, a last shot in the dark, the happy ending. Inside, a record distemperature, outside a record snowfall. All for the record. Damn the telephone! The tax man wants his take, *Vogue* wants a retake, the mailman always rings twice, the vermin exterminator is enquiring about termites, the bells! The bells! And when they don't ring, you feel you've been forgotten. You hang up, you're left hanging. Rembrandt was living on the breadline by the time he was fifty – I'm fifty-eight and no Rembrandt. Here I'm labelled a 'commercial photographer', as insulting as when the Germans used to refer to 'art-photographers'. 'Old fashioned', that's me and very few drinks. No smoking. The occasional Havana (Upmann) followed by a hang-over that feels like cancer of the brain. No dope, no dough, no carnival: unAmerican forever.

Like a scourge, a cloud of alcohol descended – by prior arrangement – on the studio. From it emerged a gang of cigarette-smoking robots in grey flannel and light-grey stetsons, well-fed, six-foot, provincial executives: The Corporate Image USA (the very embodiment of lack of imagination). Each of these spitting images had the same green-and-violet striped tie hanging down its front, fastened to its shirt with the same gold clip, on which was engraved the legend, Green & Violet, Kalamazoo (Mich.); all their belts had the same whopping big silver buckle, since Geo. Green (pronounced GeeGee), Chairman of the Board and President of Green & Violet, the biggest calendar manufacturers in the world, was proud of his 250,000-acre farm deep in the heart of Texas. The uniformity of the horde was voluntary. Americans are exhibitionists when it comes to costumes and parades, but anyone who dared to show individual taste would be thrown out as a Commie. (The Americans have no idea how conformist they are.)

They all stared vacantly round the studio until one of them, who was a head taller than all the rest, started to speak. He spoke just like a tape recording, over-emphasizing each letter so much that the monotony almost sent me to sleep. 'Mister B. – or may I call you Eugene? Eugene, I am Duane Stewart, Senior Vice-President and Supervising Head Art Director at Gee & Vee. To put it briefly, Andy Armstrong, the indisputable Leonardo of calendar art, the Raphael of the air-brush, the greatest living illustrator (illustration is an American art that paints from photos and aims to be truer to nature than nature itself), lives in the same building as you and has told GeeGee about you. Are you interested in making a million dollars a year for the rest of your life?' I had never heard of my benefactor, A. A. (I had only been living at 1 West Sixty-Seventh Street for ten years; in New York no one knows their neighbours.) An offer of a million dollars a year was also something new. I tried to give a blasé nod. 'Andy', he went on, 'is committed to us one hundred per cent. For a minimum of 100,000 dollars per calendar, guaranteed by contract for life, he has to deliver a calendar to us on the first of every month. He is punctual; he is a genius. He is just as much a genius with pin-up girls licking ice-cream in a Turkish bath as with cows grazing in the snow on the edge of the Grand Canyon. A genius is a genius in everything, and Andy is the completest genius we have at Gee & Vee. Since he has hinted that he suspects you might have ability, we have come to find out if you have the necessary flexibility. To give you an example of Andy's elasticity: in the grazing-cows picture GeeGee quite rightly took objection to the fact that all four teats were quite unnecessarily visible on several of the udders of several of the cows. Without a word of argument, Andy went away and satisfied him within twenty-four hours simply by taking his airbrush and spraying over one teat on every cow. For a million a year people don't mind making little concessions. Concessions make the artist. Except when it comes to morality. GeeGee doesn't make any concession there. We're puritans. As you probably know, the Postmaster General keeps a strict eye on morality in the United States of America. Sending by mail the representation of a female person with more than one nipple showing is a punishable misdemeanour. GeeGee goes one step further. He allows one nipple on our calendars, but *only* if the impact is softened by transparent fabrics. The Postmaster forbids armpit hair. GeeGee will not even allow head hair unless it is kept in check by a hat, or at least a ribbon. One further example of our moral tolerance. GeeGee allows pictures of ladies in a state of partial undress to have bare feet, provided no more than four toes on any one foot are visible. Why would a woman need five when she can be seductive with four? In our opinion polls (we have taken 18,000 random samples) all the states, with the regrettable exception of New York, came out in favour of four toes. As servants of public opinion, we at Gee & Vee are famous for never having published a single foot with more than four toes in all our fifty-five calendar years – it's our trademark! "Art should *be* sexy and *look* moral" is GeeGee's favourite slogan. We have over a billion calendar customers to please, from Kalamazoo to Calcutta. Whether you are the kind of man to help us in this, Eric, we can only judge after we have been through your portfolio together' (*togetherness* was the in-word).

I lack the urbane manner to rid myself of such vermin elegantly. Just as during religious instruction at school, my sense of humour sent me rolling round the floor in a paroxysm of laughter. Scarcely, however, had the bleating flock followed its indignant leader out of the studio, than I began to regret the lost millions; even more, though, I regretted the barbarization humanity has undergone in America. In the short span of a single generation the cultural heritage brought from Europe has been watered down to a tasteless soft drink, which is now being sucked up by the Old World as a psycho-delicacy.

Hurrah for America! Today, a mere fifteen years after the above encounter with the puritanical calendar clowns, you can buy the *Story of O.*, which even in Paris is banned as immoral, for a dollar twenty-five at any news-stand, while the

New York Times, true to its motto of 'All the News That's Fit to Print', carries a lubriciously earnest review of *My Secret Life*, the memoirs of a master sex-merchant of the Victorian age. In Greenwich 'Village', in the heart of the city, there are countless underground cinemas where you can see naked lesbians playing with each other and half-naked beatniks playing with themselves, and the police and the Postmaster, who were overreacting only yesterday, now see to it that they turn two blind eyes. However, as long as American boys' hair grows longer in proportion as women's skirts get shorter, America is not yet lost!

67 ADAILE

On 3 January 1951, after spending Christmas in Florida, we were whizzing back to New York at ninety miles per hour. I was sitting in the death-seat, the one next to my son who was driving the open car. One of the rear tyres burst, and in slow motion I saw the convertible spin out of control and head for nirvana. A blissfully painless end, had I not been pulled out of the wreck one hour later, covered in blood. Son: unharmed; mama: two broken ribs. As she proudly kept on pointing out, she was the only one who had remained conscious; however, she still could not say precisely what had happened. With nine stitches in my head – none of my more vital organs had been affected – I dreamdanced the night away with a black nurse through the wards of St Joseph's Hospital, Charleston, South Carolina, just as I had all those years ago in the Rotonde in Paris. And the next morning, back to New York, where some freelance sessions were scheduled.

One Saturday morning a month later, I collapsed onto the living-room carpet with concussion. Four weeks of whimpering sleep and once again I was ready to take up my old life, a doddering corpse. On 22 May, my first session back in the studio: a full-bleed colour spread for Beautiful Bryans – 'Walk in red-carpet resplendence wearing beautiful Bryans "frost and fire fantastics"... It's the new lambent glow for legs! Always a shade ahead!' Sally Plummer, the mentally deranged head-copywriter, had spent the last six months concocting this rubbish, and was now in a trance, reading it out loud for the thirtieth time, overemphasizing every word and not realizing that no one was listening to her. In one corner of the studio, with his back to everyone including himself, sat the art director, Ed Turner, a stuttering pansy half-way through analysis, who lisped because he thought it sounded British. In black chalk on black paper, he was drawing invisible, sundial-like butterflies, while his bushy eyebrows, which year after year achieved fame on Christmas cards, quivered irresistibly. In the opposite corner Guiness McGuinnec, the account executive, was having an attack of hurt feelings. After a business lunch with eight well-shaken, extra dry Beefeater Gibson Martini highballs, complete with silverskin onions on a stick, he felt he had lost his grip on life. Account executives don't have a purpose in life. He was gnawing at a crumpled newspaper out of the wastebin. *Delirium clemens.* Fortunately, the agency people were not on speaking terms.

Still somewhat weak at the knees myself, and looking down from the top step of a none-too-stable ladder, I was doing my best to get the session going. In front of me, on a stand that looked like a guillotine, the big camera was pointing downward. Beside me, a 5,000-watt bulb was blazing down on three improbably long, nylon-clad legs. The three bodies belonging to these splendours were squashed together under an ermine cape on a hard mattress, each unexposed leg tucked up beneath its owner's charming behind. According to the lay-out, six stockinged legs 'in the new lambent glow' were to descend the double spread from right to left. My desire to give value for money meant that the complexity of any photo session increased in direct proportion to the fee.

It was the first day for my assistant, Evelinde, a charmless, middle-sized dwarf, who was running everywhere at once like a headless chicken. The studio was a madhouse. The first twelve takes for the right-hand side went according to programme. As I was doing the second take for the left side, *Bang! Hiroshima mon Amour!* red-hot splinters of glass, screaming women, the end of the world, blood, fire, conflagration, short circuit, blackest night with fireflies flitting about. Before I had even realized: the big lamp had exploded, the apocalyptic prophets from the advertising agency had disappeared from the scene for fear of claims for compensation. In the darkness below, Evelinde was rushing round pouring one bucket of water after another over the bleeding models, who were rolling about on the filthy studio floor, whimpering as they calculated how much they could sue me for. I could stand it no longer at the top of my ladder. I climbed down and completed the ruin of a $15,000 ermine cape that was smouldering in places by pouring a bottle of Coca Cola over it.

The light went back on and my first post-mortem session proceeded to develop in a satisfactorily harmonious way. Whilst Evelinde was fetching a young doctor who lived next door (in NYC the house next door always houses a ready supply of doctors) to administer first aid (which was not really necessary), I told the three goddesses, who listened with disinterested interest, that I was insured for up to $10,000 per lovely head and promised to do what I could. Apart from some serious holes in the ermine cape, each of the models had a few less serious scratches high up on her legs, which the young doctor treated with loving care. Finally he filled in the social security forms, exaggerating everything as much as possible in order to blow himself up in the eyes of the girls and ingratiate himself with them. After he had left they stayed sitting on the floor, where they had made themselves comfortable, since they had been booked for the whole afternoon anyway.

Doddy Goddy, a platinum-blond cowgirl from Arizona, where the longest legs come from, was whining for gin in a baby voice. At fourteen she had been a rodeo queen in the Wild West. Now, depending on what was required, she was sixteen, twenty-six or thirty-six. She was a dike (finger in the hole, lesbian) and a fagmoll who had thrown all moderation overboard. One month she was stinking rich, the next she was stony broke. A few years ago she had gone through the million-dollar inheritance of one of her boyfriends in nine happy months, filling a garage in Los Angeles with twenty-six white Jaguars and twenty-six liveried black chauffeurs. When the money was gone, she got by as a waitress and banjo player's girlfriend in a junkjoint in Frisco. There she was discovered by a talent scout for 'Latin Quarters' in New York, where she sparkled as a big-bosomed showgirl on Broadway until a photographer tempted her with the vision of a brilliant career as a high-fashion model at $60 per hour, providing she managed to lose forty pounds. Immediately she began starving herself and swallowing pills. For six weeks she lost ten pounds per week until she was a walking skeleton. Vitamin injections soon brought her back up to her original weight. Pills made her thin as a rake again. Eventually both her metabolism and her mind cracked up, and she ended up in a lunatic asylum, from which she was discharged as cured, though not before she had slept with all the doctors, nurses and patients. Now she consoled herself with marijuana and a form of double analysis of her own invention. She went to two shrinks at the same time, letting neither know about the other, and slept with both of them (Hanns von Neurosenthal and Doctor Nini Spermakård) – 'lay analysis'. Finally she got Hanns and Nini together and they had a threesome. She came to me for new dreams.

Adaile Allmay, daughter of the Cosa Nostra Don Adolfo 'Four Fingers' Allemanno, was 'a good trooper' with two healthy lungs. She was quite unflappable. With a gold lighter she lit herself a corona and ordered a rye on the rocks as if she were in a bar. As a symbol of her intense desire for independence, she carried a loaded revolver, wrapped up in a lace handkerchief, in her bra. She liked to keep things close to her chest. When I was starting out in New York, which was the same time as she was, she would not rest until I did some test shots of her. She wanted to become a fashion model, but never did; she had other, greater successes. In return, she initiated me into the local ways and customs, and we became friends. Years later she asked me to teach her all the secrets of colour photography in two weeks. She refused to believe me when I told here there were no secrets in photography and spent a few weeks getting in my way in the darkroom, for which she promised me eternal gratitude.

I knew least about snub-nosed Barbara Codik, the only model I have ever discovered in the street. With her naked aggressiveness I imagined I had found in her the woman of tomorrow and used her immediately for a *Vogue* cover. Sitting on the floor, she gave me an inscrutable stare, ordered a vodka martini and fell, creaking like an adding machine in its death throes, into a promising swoon, from which she didn't wake up until the drinks arrived.

The pix were 'glorious', the agency 'tickled pink'. Three weeks later a highly satisfied Doddy rang me up to say the insurance had settled with her for $2,500. Adaile passed up the compensation because nothing had happened and because she didn't need the money. From the Woman of Tomorrow, eloquent silence. She had been unobtainable the day after the accident because she was posing as a 'bathing beauty' for Macy's, so her wounds couldn't have been that bad.

Six months later a bailiff served the writ in the Codik vs. Blumenfeld suit for $300,000 compensation. Twenty times more than I possessed. Co-defendants were the manufacturers of the lamp, General Electric, a billion-dollar concern. It was followed by an additional suit: Barbara's husband was demanding $100,000 compensation for the fact that for six weeks he had not had full, unimpaired use of his wife. Apart from the sharp lawyers of Katsch, A. S. Katsch & Kann, who had a fifty-fifty share in Barbara's misfortune, Barbara also had two shapely legs. If she had the opportunity to show them to the jury, I was lost.

The nice thing about democratic red-tape justice is its snail's pace. Perhaps Barbara's legs would have gone downhill a little by the time the case came up. Almost four years after the accident, the telephone rang: my lawyer, a *schlemiel* (I hate competent lawyers), telling me we had to be at the offices of the lawyers of the opposing party at four p.m. the day after tomorrow for the 'pre-trial examination' in the matter of Codik vs. Blumenfeld. I asked whether we couldn't get another postponement. He said we couldn't, since we'd already had it postponed four times. To my suggestion that he go by himself he replied, 'They don't want to examine me, but you.' So I went with him to see the uninterested lawyer of G. E. who had not yet even glanced at the papers and whose sole concern was not to miss the five past twelve from Grand Central Station. When he heard I was a photographer he proudly showed me the picture of an armless boy in a wheelchair with a little hand growing out of his forehead. I congratulated him on his Dada photomontage (Pop art had not been invented yet). He modestly waved my praise away, saying that he was just an amateur and in fact his son was much better-looking than that.

Americans are cripple fetishists. During my first visit to New York I had been *shocked* to see, in Olsen & Johnson's slapstick show, *Hellzapoppin*, a one-legged pegleg doing a masterly tap-dance. Later, on TV, I marvelled as two thousand paraplegic-club ladies danced Paderewski's minuet in red-white-and-blue wheelchairs in honour of the paralysed jazz heeby-jeeby Connie, of the Boswell Sisters.

We had a lively reception at Katsch's. With customary American impertinence, the lawyers immediately called me by my first name which – 'time is money' – they reduced to 'Erf'. They thanked me for devoting my valuable time to a case which was as good as lost anyway, did not allow me to get a word in edgeways and completely disregarded my lawyers. To show me that they represented all the top models, they dropped first names all over the place: Arpi, Avonne, Bibbes, Bobo, Bubbles, Ceemee, Ceepee, Clitoria, Charmione, Daphnia, Dildo, Doddy, Dodda, Dotti, Evonne, Ethic, Fren, Fuck, Fussell, Gill (with three 'l's), Hernia, Huri, Inkitinki, Jinx, Janx, Junx, Kay, Key, Kee, Lippy, Misty, Mips, Mops, Mistory, Nups, Nips, Nippel, Omfaly, Onnany, Pad, Pud, Pod, Poxie, Penelopia, Peenis, Peeppee, Phart, Queenie, Razbree, Sueme, Tipsy, Titty, Twaddell, Undee, Vance, Vademecca, Waffy, Xenia, Xix, Yvenne and Zaza. During the cross-examination my three lawyers kept clumsily prodding my foot, without making it any clearer to me what I was supposed to say. Katsch said he regretted he hadn't sued me for a million; since there were no witnesses for the defence, negligence was proven. I heard myself saying in a flat voice, 'But I do have witnesses.' All the others leapt to their feet. 'WHO?' I was silent. Furious lawyers stuffed papers into their briefcases and left the room in arrogant indignation. It was high train for the General Electric lawyer to catch his time. In the lift my unholy trinity kept asking me, 'Who is our witness?' I could only shake my head sadly. We parted without shaking hands. In America you never know when you're supposed to shake someone's hand anyway.

All alone, I waded through the filthy black slush of Madison Avenue back to the studio. In what passes for nature, between Forty-Second and Fifty-Seventh Street where America produces the inanities with which they flood the world (advertising headquarters), I sometimes get ideas as well. The carbon monoxide exhaust fumes do for me what sulphurous vapours did for the Sybil at Delphi. In front of me a plump beauty with a bobbing super-bosom was wiggling her Monroe Doctrine behind, bringing back memories of Adaile ... Eureka! My witness!!!

Finding Adaile after four years was not easy. Her name was not in the telephone book and none of the modelling agencies remembered her. I finally found her social security number on a model release form and was soon speaking to her on the telephone. (For the last two years she had been the wife of Dr O'Higgins, East Sixty-Third Street, a good neighbourhood.) She was helpfulness itself. The next morning she came to pick me up for lunch, covered from head to toe in white mink: simple, expensive and tasteless – Hollywood. *A Lady Never Wears Mink* (not even to a football game). A childish question, 'Daddy, how do minks get babies?' Answer, 'The same way a babe gets her mink.' Adaile's hairdo: piled high, waved, blue-black, lacquered. In honour of my *Vogue* cover of January 1950, she had doe-eyes (a way of doing eye make-up invented by Blumenfeld) with extra-long mink eyelashes. Her make-up must have taken her all morning. When I kissed her hand she responded with the stereotype American woman's smile. She observed that I had changed as little as my studio, then submitted the tokens of her progress to my gaze: a many-carat diamond cross with a dazzling blue light round her neck and smaller diamond crucifixes on platinum chains round her wrist and ankle: *in hoc signo vinces.*

Triple-parked outside the studio was her white Jaguar. No cop would have given her a ticket: there was a card stuck to the windscreen: 'OK. The Mayor'.

I asked her how she came to enjoy such protection. 'New York has the best police force money can buy.' When I brought up my $400,000 problem she just shrugged a mink shoulder. 'Baloney. *We* aren't going to let anyone blackmail *us*. No one was hurt.' I asked her if she would appear as a witness for me. She was unperturbed. '*We* won't let it get that far. There's a lot of things going to happen before Thursday. Babs hasn't just got a past, she's got a present too. That call-girl's only small fry, we'll soon sort her out!'

'Ché Parée' is an expense-account joint, expensive, arrogant, tax deductible. Even the hat-check girl patronizes you in pidgin French. VIPs and agency presidents show off in front of their clients there and drown their stupidity in drink. As we were arriving late, I expected a rather acid reception. Instead, as soon as he saw Adaile the normally unapproachable M'sieu Victooor, supreme champion maître d', fell to his knees, licked her mink gloves, turned into the dog he always had been and crawled, foam dripping from his chops, between the legs of the other customers waiting impatiently for a table, to reappear, a few seconds later wagging his tail and bearing the owner himself, Monsieur Louis, in his jaws. That great man bowed reverently, and I pulled away my hand in embarrassment as, stammering words of gratitude, he attempted to kiss it. It was all a mystery to me.

Completely unmoved by all this red-carpet treatment, Adaile posed imperiously for non-existent photographers, until she had all eyes upon her. Meanwhile the maître d' had deported eight peacefully masticating customers from the oval *pièce de milieu* to smoke-filled nooks and crannies. Before you could say Jacques Robinson, slaves had reset the table with all the trimmings, including perfumed artificial flowers. With an indignant twitch of her index finger Adaile registered her objection to the floodlighting on our table whereupon we were immediately plunged into deepest semi-darkness. As we sipped our Bloody Marys I tried to discover what was the reason for this reception. Adaile said, 'Shut up', and ordered black caviar with French fries, Dom Perignon 1948 and South American cherries with whipped cream. She was on a diet. Further Bloody Marys intermixed with the champagne and black coffee raised her spirits and put me out of action. When, however, she spread mustard over her caviar, my *vagus* started to twitch. In order to cheer me up she took a gold twenty-dollar coin out of her mink handbag and prodded around at it with her repulsively long fingernails until a wafer-thin watch slipped out. She popped the toy into my hand and told me I had to learn to do the trick with the watch myself – it was important! I began to doubt her sanity. Adaile stood up. According to American etiquette I had to jump up as quickly and as noisily as possible to let the whole world know that a lady was going to have a pee. Same performance on her return. Instead of manners the Pilgrim Fathers brought a ponderous formality with them from the Old World. The American upper crust is nothing but a gang of criminals who have made money and are trying to play at café society.

While Adaile was away I tried to fiddle out the watch. Impossible without fingernails. Only when I used a fruit-knife did I manage it. As a reward Adaile planted her freshly painted lips greasily on my cheek when she returned. She had found out over the phone who was dealing with my case. She was a master of the American art of speaking without facial expression. 'Tomorrow afternoon you're going downtown to the courthouse. Ask for Judge Agelli and show him our gold coin.' Effortlessly she conjured the watch out of the coin again and held it under my nose. 'As soon as His Honor sees the diamond monogram F. C. on the back all your troubles are over.' Adaile was hurt that I didn't know who F. C. was. As she slipped the coin into my trousers pocket, she whispered lovingly, 'F. C. is Frankie, my sugar daddy. He's in the pen, poor old soul. He's sixty. Youth had to take over, so now I'm the head of the boys. And now you know all my secrets, and if you can't keep your trap shut you'll have an automobile accident tomorrow. That reminds me. I've saved your life once before. D'you remember when I was your Gal Friday and you were furious when I ruined a whole color run at the studio? After work I ran down to the street crying. Frankie was waiting for me. He's allergic to tears and he yelled, "Did that slob hurt you? If he did I'll waste him with the car tonight." It wasn't easy to stop him; he was jealous because I thought you were a genius. This restaurant was his first present when we got to know each other. A gold mine in the speakeasy days. It's losing money now. I keep it for sentimental reasons. Now you're coming home with me. I'll show you my etchings. Unfortunately my husband has had a coronary and is in an oxygen tent. O'Higgins is a really dedicated plastic surgeon. He'd give you some new fingernails right away (he gets them from the morgue) or fit you up with a new face to make you look more like an artist. You look too modest. It's not good for business. Art's getting to be a bigger racket every day. We have a bank-note specialist under contract to paint us two guaranteed genuine Cézannes per year; we sell them at colossal prices to German museums, via Zurich. The most important thing in the art business is the provenance, and he conjures that up with impeccable stamps, verification by experts and letters. You could get a nice cut as artistic consultant.'

Dreams come true – a double-edged sword. On the one hand, as the protégé of a gangster's moll I had had decent service in a restaurant for the first time in my life; on the other I could already see my bullet-riddled corpse swirling through Hell's Kitchen down the East River. Headline: FASHION PHOTOG'S FINAL FLOP! It gave me the creeps. I wanted to get out of it, so I pretended I had a post-lunch session. 'Coward!' she said, and she was right. I couldn't afford to chicken out, so dashing down another drink to bolster up my courage, I went with her. No question of paying, everything on the house, even the tip. Monsieur Louis conducted us personally to the huge, black, chauffeur-driven bullet-proof funeral limousine waiting for us. The Jag had been taken away. We only had five blocks to go, but babes in NYC never walk a single step, they have a massage instead. No one goes on foot in the USA, apart from German immigrants.

Dr O'Higgins' waiting-room was full of men wearing hats: hoodlums, henchmen, gangsters, bodyguards, underworld mobsters who rose respectfully when Adaile entered, but gave me suspicious looks out of the corner of their eyes. Sadly I was a bit high and my power of judgment was correspondingly low. An elevator took us to the holy of holies, her boudoir. Adaile threw her mink over a chair, kicked off her shoes, put her feet on the table and under my nose (a horrid local custom) and started switching on lamps: superduper Cecil B. DeMille Hollywood-Dali-window-display-kitsch. In the middle, behind transparent black lace curtains, a huge circular bed. Two one-armed bandits beside it grabbed me. My first nickel was lucky: lemon – lemon – lemon and eighteen nickels came tumbling out. While I was wasting my money, Adaile was not wasting her time. She was telephoning her stockbroker about some enormous transactions and pressing buttons at the same time. The room went dark, and in glowing colours high on the wall above us appeared the *divinité du Styx*, the Lord of the Underworld, F. C. himself, fresh out of the swimming pool, in a wrestler's pose, with a short, thick neck and a hairy gorilla chest with a diamond cross on a thin chain dangling down over it. Without realizing it, I stood up and exclaimed, stunned, 'Excellent portrait!' 'Rollei Tripan X with yellow filter, available light, 1/250 sec, f:16. Howard Chandler Christie hand-coloured the enlargement himself', Adaile answered modestly. Galvanized into action by my applause, she manipulated various levers, giving F. C. a greenish, bluish, reddish, yellowish glow, while music of the spheres by Sibelius thundered from the loudspeakers. Adaile commanded me to turn round to where floodlights illuminated a gigantic abstrosity by Jackson Pollock. 'Nonsense, promoted by Republican lesbian Jews who know what they're doing. A triumph of the American art trade. My investment of ten grand will have quadrupled in three years' time.' (It did!) Now she threw on a black ostrich-feather negligee and suggested we let our hair down. Scared to death, I said, 'I have to go now.' Fortunately she was ready for her afternoon nap anyway and flopped onto the bed. She made F. C. give one final appearance in a sunset glow and got a bodyguard to return me to the December night, still alive. Another afternoon frittered away!

The next day I went to Foley Square. Court buildings make me even sicker than hospitals: hours waiting in a hostile atmosphere until Judge Agelli emerged from his case, still wearing his gown, a pockmarked Daumier figure in a skyscraper. I barred the way to his office door and thrust the watch, which I had taken out well in advance, under his nose. He assumed I was an escapee from a lunatic asylum and called for help. I stuttered, 'I'm only Blumenfeld from the Codik versus Blumenfeld case. A lady friend of mine asked me to show you this…' Unimpressed, he looked at the monogram. His face swelled in fury. Strange navy-blue blotches appeared on his puffy cheeks and I heard the word 'crackpot'. He called an usher. 'Show this imbecile the quickest way out. If he ever has the audacity to come back, have him arrested.' The man pushed me along in front of him until we came to the flight of steps at the entrance. One word of protest, and I would have been sent flying down the twenty-two steps. That word remained unspoken. Once again I was standing in the wet snow, and downtown at that, all thanks to the influential underworld connections of a little adventuress who wanted to play big. Furious, I went to my flower shop on Fifty-Eighth Street and had the precious watch sent to the Queen of the Mafia, giftwrapped with twenty-four long-stemmed, dark-red roses. On the enclosed card, 'Thanks! E.'

The next morning Adaile rang me with a bedroom voice to thank me for the roses. She had meant me to keep the watch as a present. She acted surprised that her influence had worked so quickly. That was too much for me. 'Worked?? They threw me out!' All she wanted to know was whether Agelli had seen the monogram. She thought I was pretty naive. 'What did you expect him to do? Give you a kiss?? The judge will do what *we* want him to, nincompoop.' Annoyed, I hung up. An hour later my lawyer phoned to tell me, in a voice quivering with scarcely suppressed pride, that he had reached an out-of-court settlement in Codik vs. Blumenfeld for a payment of $750. It had, he said, been an incredibly difficult case. The fact was reflected in his bill.

It wasn't until five years after the happy end to that nightmare that I heard Adaile's siren singsong rasping out of the receiver again. 'Good news and bad news. Last week my dear husband passed away, and I've been a blonde since yesterday.' I made my condolences and asked how the slot-machines and F. C. were getting on. 'The machines are longing for you in my brand-new Louie Sayze bedroom, lavishly redecorated by French and Co. F. C. is a goner, poor man. I'm holding the youngest Senator now, a first-grade ladykiller. He calls me his Italian princess. You'll like his sophisticated guts. He comes from a family of rum-runners as well, and he loves dames, dope and dollars. We'll make a president out of him and then I guarantee there'll be sex orgies in the White House.' One more promise Adaile kept.

68 WESTWARD HO!

The metropolis of New York, the only living wonder of the world, is, like the pyramids, not a work of art but a gigantic manifestation of power. It still has one foot in Europe, glancing back over both shoulders on its desperate look-out for new attractions. America only begins where New York ends. Westward Ho! All the way to L. A., the symbol of modern ugliness, in search of culture: three thousand miles of unbelievably splendid highways through almost virgin land sullied only by filling stations with garish billboards, weeks without edible food, not a single expression of the human spirit far and wide. On the other hand, every motel does have Vincent's (pronounced Vango, to rhyme with dough) *Sunflowers* in assorted fashion colours beside the TV. Motorized human riffraff vegetating at top speed towards its end. Popcorn, hot dogs in cellophane and ice-cold Coca Cola dispensers – what they call 'gracious living'. Everywhere visibly multiplying crowds of insufferable children pour out of overcrowded 'station wagons'. Raving 'fags' complete with poodle in open sports cars recklessly overtake pairs of small-town witches pottering along in old Fords with the windows full of clothes on hangers, gossiping and holding up the traffic. *Memento mori!*

This middle-class, middlebrow, middle-American technocracy drove me onto by-roads and to the wonders of yesterday's world, unfortunately already degraded to the status of national parks: an eagle's eyrie mysteriously hidden in clefts in the rock almost eight thousand feet up in Colorado's Rocky Mountains: Mesa Verde, an Indian town abandoned five hundred years ago, a stage-set for eternity, interlocking Giotto towers, an early Cubist sketch for New York's Rockefeller Center; 3,500-year-old sequoias growing on the slopes of California's Sierra Nevada, giant red trees older – and more alive – than we Jews. They too need the occasional pogrom in the form of a forest fire, from which they emerge with vigour renewed. But what makes you feel really young are the tree trunks in Arizona's Petrified Forest, fossilized for two hundred million years.

69 O'HOLE

High above suspicion, in the starry firmament of history shines the constellation of homosexual geniuses: Socrates, Jesus, Michelangelo, Leonardo da Vinci, Shakespeare, Castor and Pollux. Deep down in the city mire hang out the hordes of Horst Wessels: arse-bandits, breech-loaders, shirt-lifters, cocksuckers and nancy boys. As a turn-of-the-century brat I was taught to run away from the 175-boys (paragraph 175 of the German criminal code laid down prison sentences for homosexual acts between men; lesbians were unmolested). Later – from Oscar Wilde, Gide, Genet – I came to understand something of the problems of those who are different from the rest. Throughout my professional life I've had to spend too much time and effort coping with the effeminately unpredictable prima-donna moods of homosexuals, an international freemasonry of arse-directors, hairdressers, psycho-analists, designers, couturiers, window-dressers, fashion photographers and other such arse-and-craftsmen, over-obliging friends who helped and harmed me in equal measure. Their charm can all too easily blind you to their depravity. You have to be on your guard against their intriguing tongues. Here is a profile of the absolute prototype of this species.

For more than three decades Dorian O'Hole, Esq., had reigned as the prettiest queen of New York City. At forty-five – if pushed he would admit to thirty-five at most – he remained, even if showing slight signs of wear, the darling of the maturer ladies of old Womanhattan. Beneath his made-to-measure suits the experienced eye could detect the lines of lacy underwear, bra and girdle. He made a habit of wearing sanitary towels every month. His suede shoes had highish heels. His permanently waved hair had Irish-red highlights. Since the hair dye made by the firm he worked for gave his hair a greenish tinge, he used a competitor's product, though with a bad conscience.

Dorian O'Hole, born in New York, but having enjoyed a British/cosmopolitan upbringing in Oxford, had learnt the art of the brazenly courteous insult. As a young lieutenant in the Irish Guards at the beginning of the World War II he had conquered London with his busby, his smiling cat's eyes and his freckles, at the same time dispelling all doubts in ultimate victory over the Hun. At a cocktail party in the French Embassy at the beginning of the blitz the air-raid siren sent all the guests flying down to the cellars. After a terrible bombardment Dorian came to in one of the WCs, underneath the not-so-young ambassadress, but only after she had robbed him of his virginity and crumpled his nice new officer's uniform. Dorian claimed that since that baptism of fire he could love only men.

After the war he became advertising director, private secretary and Girl Friday to the ninety-year-old beauty queen, Aphrodite Karbunkelstein Inc. This emancipated Jewess from Kiev had married, on favourable terms, a bankrupt king and backgammon player as her second husband, and had declared herself queen. She considered it a great *metsieh*, a bargain. Ethel Boredom, equally nonagenarian and her great rival, beauty queen of the Puritans, had only managed to make it to the rank of divorced princess. These two harpies, dripping with ugliness and kept alive by Swiss monkey glands mixed with cocaine, had made youth their business and went round in little-girl dresses. They never remembered the names of their friends – they had none – but never forgot the formulas of the thousands of products from which they made millions.

In all his years of parasitic bondage to Aphrodite Karbunkelstein, O'Hole had achieved nothing. So in thrall to his old queen was this gerontomane that he had no energy to pursue his own interests, something she was constantly throwing in his face. What made it doubly annoying to her was the fact that he had no need to. His money came from the leftovers of his maternal grandfather, an Irish immigrant who had struck oil in Texas around the turn of the century. There was even a town with his name. Just before the great crash of 1929 (which has left a far deeper impression on America than the two world wars combined) Grandpa and his millions remigrated to Europe, bought a villa by the Bois de Boulogne, bricked his gold up in an alcove there, married a red-haired demimondaine known as 'la Juive Jacob', and died. The widow, according to French law, inherited all the gold and valuables in the house.

Although four times a year Dorian acted as courier to his Aphrodite on her trips to Paris (a wheelchair in a jet plane), he had never yet met his step-mother, and that was something that bothered him. In the spring of 1964 he plucked up his courage and, behind the 'Queen's' back, went to see la Juive Jacob. She, in her mid-seventies, received him in a very low-cut, purple velvet dress with dignified charm and bright-red hair. This good-looking grandson from America was her dream. As they sipped their cognac, she beguiled him with anecdotes. Attending on his 'Queen' had taught him to listen open-mouthed. After an hour step-grandmama and step-grandson were gaily holding hands. He became weak at the knees, and even weaker when she casually mentioned that of his grandfather's twenty-nine million, more than one million dollars was extant. Dorian felt he had met someone who understood him and, stammering with excitement, attempted to establish his credentials as heir. Grandmama gave a sensuous laugh and offered her startled grandson her hand in marriage, adding that she expected his answer within three days. This flabbergasted fairy already had visions of himself walking down the aisle of Notre Dame, a chrysanthemum in his buttonhole and his grandmama on his arm, to the strains of Eric von Stroheim's Wedding March. Ecstatic, he dashed straight off to the 'Queen' to apprise her of his good fortune. She gave him a box round the ears and feigned a stroke. Dorian had to undress the seemingly lifeless body, put it to bed and hold its hand day and night. The whole time the 'Queen' did not address a single word to him. She just lay there, totting up her accounts, while the old necrophiliac was already visualizing her corpse decked out with peach blossom for a colour spread in *Vogue*. Only in the third night did the old crone's withered lips move, and they babbled, 'If you really must get married, you stupid *goy*, then you will marry *me*. As dowry you will get a rise of 15 per cent on your monthly salary, guaranteed. If, however, you should dare to see that whore, your grandmother, ever again, you will be thrown head over heels out of Karbunkelstein Inc. and Karbunkelstein International and you'll land up in the gutter without a penny. *Her* or *me*! Make your choice.'

Just like every other American in despair, Dorian's response was to pick up the phone. He rang me in New York – from Paris, reversing the charges – to ask my advice. Oh, I almost forgot the main point: Dorian was a client of mine. From time to time, after the pettiest of wrangling, countless lunches and stupid meetings, I had to produce ads for the various Karbunkelstein concerns. He liked to play the part of an artistic commander-in-chief and, without having anything to say, would disrupt the work with a constant stream of drivel. Even before a picture was taken, he would be demanding retakes. Dorian was very generous in letting others pick up the tab. Once, though, even he felt it was necessary to reciprocate. In his sap-green boudoir with orange satin upholstery he served me fresh-frozen urine in a champagne glass, claiming it was Vouvray nature; I poured it down the side of the seat-cushion. Even his pink poodle – fags keep poodles because they're good at learning tricks – turned up its nose in disgust. There was an acrid smell in the apartment and pictures by queer B-painters on the walls, Bébé Bérard, Bernard Buffet; above the bidet was a Beardsley bishop in lace vestments as part of a photo-montage advert for sanitary towels ... because!

Over the telephone Dorian begged me to choose for him between his seventy-five-year-old step-grandmother with a million and a half, and his ninety-year-old Beauty Queen Aphrodite with her two hundred and fifty million. He didn't care, he said, about the money. I advised him to stick to grandma since he wouldn't get a cent out of old Ma Karbunkelstein. But Dorian, incapable of tearing himself free from the queen of his life, cast doubts on his grandmama's virginity and financial soundness. After the call had been going on for half an hour (= $100), during which he had been buttering me up by calling me 'Herr Professor', he started to get cantankerous, as if it were I who had called him up. He told me he was much too busy to waste his time talking to me on the phone. There was an important fashion show the next day, a must, then he had to take himself off to the American Hospital in Neuilly for his annual nervous breakdown, after which he was going to descend upon a young Berber stallion in Tangiers by way of convalescence and be back in New York in precisely one month's time to celebrate his father's eightieth birthday.

Unfortunately that joyous celebration was not to pass off without a hitch. The evening before, all necessary sacraments having been administered, Dorian's mother set about departing this life. After a long vigil, the doctor retired toward midnight, as did the aged birthday boy, leaving the suntanned son alone with his dying mother. If the need arose, the doctor said, he could consult him over the phone. Dorian was in his element. The apartment was filled with birthday bouquets, some still in their gift-wrapping. When his mother in her death throes no longer responded to his caresses, he had an inspiration. In his heart of hearts every homo is a window dresser and it is but a short step from the cult of beauty to mortuary beautician. Flowers seemed to leap into Dorian's hand to adorn his dying mother. His passion for lay-out took over. With every final breath she drew he decked her with a flower, one here, one there, one on her forehead, one in her hair, a bud on her breast. He could not resist stuffing a purple orchid (the symbol of the right-wing Daughters of the Revolution) into the mouth from which the last gasps were emanating. When a pot of yellow chrysanthemums fell onto her legs it all became too much for him. He rushed over to the telephone. In spite of the ungodly hour – it was around four in the morning – he met with complete professional understanding from his dear friend Boob, a window dresser at Bonwit's. He described to him the position of every last leaf and flower, the folds of the lace on her shroud, her hair-do (*l'auréole*), the family jewels, aquamarines and moonstones, all the while putting a cross immortelle in its place. When, in her very last breath, Mama bit off the orchid with her new dentures (two weeks old, $4,000) and complied rather too literally with her son's request to lie still, Dorian realized that he was now semi-orphaned. Kneeling beside his mother's death-bed, he asked Boob to listen to him weeping, stopwatch in hand, for ten minutes, while he strewed the corpse with rose-leaves in assorted fashion colours. He had learnt from his 'Queen' always to do at least two things at once. The marathon phone-call ended with the litany, *In nomine patris et filii et spiritus sancti, requiescat in pace*, while he quickly distributed two dozen candles round the room. The birthday boy, hard of hearing, slept through it all. Mama's funeral turned into the most-talked-about cocktail party of the season.

Soon after, the Beauty Queen followed her to the happy hunting grounds. In her will she left $150 to her 'left hand', as she often called Dorian. In addition, the mocking heirs allowed him to choose a memento. His choice fell upon the purple velvet chair with the marks on the seat from which his late lamented boss had done her business. The museum piece was handed over to him for $25. 'A great *metsieh* – A bargain already'.

Dorian still has not got married. So that the noble line of O'Hole will not die out, he has adopted a slim, eleven-year-old Chinese boy from Hong Kong, Pee Wee O'Hole.

70 RETAKE

I was waiting for a green light at the corner of Fifth Avenue and Fifty-Seventh Street, the place where, between twelve and four, you can see the most beautiful women in the world, when I was suddenly accosted by a bent, middle-aged crone. (You also meet the most unlikely women on Fifty-Seventh Street.) 'What about my pix?' When you've photographed thousands of women, who change all the time to remain themselves, you give up trying to remember. She gave me a clue: 'La Comtesse!' The title was all that this American woman had left from a marriage to a French playboy – apart from an idiot son she had to support. More than twenty years ago she had breezed, drunk and with a beau she introduced as her brother, into my Paris studio. She was editor of *Town and Country*. At that time I was impressed by anything American, I had no idea then how insignificant she was. She promised me pages in her magazine, I had to photograph her. She gave me no work, I gave her no pictures. Her beau, a department-store tycoon, drove blind drunk into a tree, killing himself and leaving her with a broken spine. That was all he left her. Stupidly I told the Comtesse that I had happened to come across those pictures only a few days earlier. To show them to her now seemed too cruel. Back at the studio I laid them out on the sofa one last time in order to indulge in my favourite game of avant et après before the auto-da-fé. There was a ring at the door. The Comtesse, impatient to see her past again. I was afraid I might break her heart, but she didn't have one. She scrutinized them print by print with American matter-of-factness, occasionally picking out one or the other, as editors do to pretend they know something about the art. She stood in front of a mirror, holding a photo next to her face. 'How silly, how empty I was in those days! Only now am I an interesting woman.' Disdainfully she proceeded to tear up her portraits, one after the other. When she had finished she limped over the shreds in triumph to the door – 'You owe me a retake for my son. When?' – and was never to be seen again.

POSTSCRIPT

The following lines were found among Erwin Blumenfeld's papers after his death. They describe in prophetic terms a heart attack from which Blumenfeld was to die a few days later.

My blood was prickling, full of needles.

My eyes were staring, my breath croaking, I felt I was suffocating. Cold beads of sweat broke out all over my body, my bones were crumbling away, my will no longer controlled my movements, I was shrivelling up, my teeth were falling out and sticking in my throat like bad jokes, my guts were leaving me, I was still suffering from life.

My eyes were stinging, my teeth were stuck in my throat like rotten jokes, my bones were crumbling, my breath stopped, I felt I was suffocating, beads of sweat were dripping onto the floor, pearls before swine, I was shrivelling up, my will no longer controlled my movements, my guts were leaving me alone. Heading for that bordello from which no traveller returns.

My stinging eyes were staring into nirvana, my bones cracked, my breath rained hammerblows on my heart, my teeth were stuck in my throat, threatening to suffocate me, pearls of sweat were dripping before swine, my mucus-filled guts were leaving me revoltingly. With time my will-power had evaporated in space. I was still hanging on to life by a thread.

My stinging eyes stared into nirvanas, my bones were crumbling, cold, wet breath rained hammerblows on my heart, my teeth threatened to stick in my throat, pearls of sweat fell before swine, my mucus-filled guts left me revoltingly. My will-power had evaporated with time. I was only hanging on by a thread to this pointless life. The present was the past. The past: I was just so much rubbish.

Wet breath rained hammerblows on my heart, teeth threatened to stick in my throat, bones crumbled, pearls of sweat fell before swine, mucus-filled guts left me revoltingly, eyes stared impotently into nirvanas, the thread broke, everything was past: I was dead.

CHRONOLOGY

BIOGRAPHICAL NOTES

INDEX

CHRONOLOGY

1897
Born on 26 January in Berlin, to Emma (née Cohn) and Albert Blumenfeld; second of three children (Annie, b. 1894 and Heinz, b. 1900).

1903–13
Attends Askanisches Gymnasium, Berlin.

1907
Receives his first camera as a gift; experiments with a chemistry set and a magic lantern.

1913
Death of his father; starts a three-year apprenticeship at Moses & Schlochauer, Berlin.

1915
With Paul Citroen, his best friend from school, begins to frequent the Café des Westens, favourite meeting place of the Expressionists; meets the poet Else Lasker-Schüler and the artist George Grosz, who will become a lifelong friend.

1916
Meets Paul Citroen's cousin Lena, with whom he has already conducted a lengthy correspondence; they become engaged soon after.

1917
Sent to the Western Front as an ambulance driver. Also serves briefly as book-keeper at Field Brothel 209 near the Belgian border. Awarded the Iron Cross (Second Class).

1918
Plans to desert and flee to Holland but is arrested and imprisoned, before being released and returned to his unit at the Front. Learns of the death of his brother Heinz near Verdun. After the war ends returns briefly to Berlin; then leaves for Holland to join Lena.

1919–21

Undertakes various short-lived jobs, including a partnership with Paul Citroen who has set himself up as an art dealer. Participates in the Dada movement. Makes collages, paintings and drawings; continues to write poetry and short stories; photographs family and friends.

1921

Marries Lena Citroen in Berlin.

1922

Birth of his daughter Lisette.

1923

Opens leather goods shop, the Fox Leather Company, in Amsterdam.

1925

Birth of his son Heinz (Henry).

1929

Arrested on the beach at Zandvoort for allowing a strap of his bathing suit to slip; this dashes his chances of Dutch citizenship, for which he has applied.

1932

Birth of his son Yorick. Moves to new business premises and discovers an operational darkroom there. Begins to photograph female customers (portraits and some nudes). Exhibits at the art gallery Kunstzaal van Lier, Amsterdam.

1934

Second exhibition at the Kunstzaal van Lier, Amsterdam. Still photographer on Jacques Feydeau's *Pension Mimosa*.

1935

Bankruptcy of his leather goods business, the Fox Leather Company. Publication of three of his photographs in French magazine *Photographie*. Exhibits at the

Esher Surrey art gallery, The Hague. Included in a group show organized by Paul Citroen at the Nieuwe Kunstschool (New Art School), Amsterdam with Grosz, Umbo, Man Ray, Moholy-Nagy, Arp, Delaunay, Léger, Mondrian, Schwitters and others. Meets the daughter of French painter Georges Rouault, Geneviève, a dentist, who arranges to exhibit his work in her waiting room near the Opéra, Paris.

1936

Leaves Holland and settles in Paris with the aim of becoming a professional photographer. Geneviève Rouault helps him secure clients for portraits. Photographs (among others) Georges Rouault and Henri Matisse. Takes on advertising work. Exhibits his work at Galerie Billiet, Paris. Rents a studio at 9, rue Delambre.

1937

First magazine cover, for *Votre Beauté*. Photographs published in *Verve* (Winter 1937 and Spring 1938), *Photographie* (also 1938 and 1939), some 50 photographs sold to US magazine *Coronet*. Photographs several of Aristide Maillol's sculptures, including *The Three Graces*. Photographs Carmen, Rodin's model for *The Kiss*. His photocollage of Hitler (1933) is withdrawn from a group show in Berlin after official protests.

1938

Meets British photographer Cecil Beaton, who helps him to secure work at French *Vogue*.

1939

Contract with *Vogue* not renewed; sails to New York and is taken on by *Harper's Bazaar*. Returns to Paris on the eve of war, but fails to make plans to flee. Interned in a series of camps (Montbard-Marmagne, Vernet d'Ariège, Catus) as an alien.

1941

Flees to New York. Signs contract with *Harper's Bazaar*. Finds an apartment at the Hotel des Artistes, 1 West 67th Street, where he remains for the rest of his life. Shares studio with Martin Munkacsi.

1943

Opens his own studio at 222 Central Park South. His 1933 photocollage of Hitler is used as an Allied propaganda leaflet, of which thousands are dropped over Germany by the US Air Force. His work by now appears in many publications, including *Vogue*, *Harper's Bazaar*, *Life*, *Look*, *Cosmopolitan*, *Popular Photography*, *Coronet*, *Lilliput*, *Picture Post* and *Graphis*. Now rated among the world's highest paid fashion photographers.

1944

Leaves *Harper's Bazaar* and works freelance for *Vogue*. Begins to build a lucrative career in advertising, with such clients as Helena Rubinstein and Elizabeth Arden.

1944–55

Produces dozens of cover images for *Condé Nast* and for other magazines.

1955

Relationship with *Vogue* ends (although he works sporadically for them after this date). Starts work on his autobiography.

From 1964

Offers manuscript of his autobiography to several publishers, without success.

1969

Completes his autobiography. Makes the final picture selection for *My One Hundred Best Photos* (of which only four are fashion shots). Suffers fatal heart attack while in Rome; he is buried there.

BIOGRAPHICAL NOTES

Beaton, Cecil (1904–1980)
British photographer, friend and correspondent of Blumenfeld's. He began to take photographs for society magazines in 1925; during the 1930s and 1940s he was a fashion photographer for *Vogue* and *Vanity Fair* and an official photographer during the Second World War. The world shown in his best-known photographs seems almost entirely social and theatrical, where appearance matters above all else.

Cassirer, Paul
Prominent Berlin art dealer. Exhibited (among others) Van Gogh, Cézanne, Matisse, Kokoschka.

Citroen, Paul
Cousin of Blumenfeld's wife Lena. Manager of *Der Sturm*'s bookshop in Berlin. He and Blumenfeld later appointed themselves sole representatives of the Berlin Dadaists in Amsterdam, where Blumenfeld briefly joined Citroen selling art after the First World War.

Grosz, George (1893–1959)
German graphic artist. After his early involvement in the Dada group, his satirical depictions of Weimar Germany record fierce caricatures of soldiers, policemen, prostitutes and businessmen at the time of Hitler's rise to power.

Lasker-Schüler, Else (1869–1945)
German poet, dramatist, short story writer and essayist. She led an eccentric and bohemian lifestyle in Berlin, where she was briefly married to Herwarth Walden, owner-editor of the Expressionist journal *Der Sturm*.

Max and Moritz
Two horrible and mischief-making children, created by Wilhelm Busch
(1832–1908), artist and extremely popular comic/satirical poet.

Mehring, Walter
Poet and habitué of Berlin's Café des Westens, meeting place for artists
and bohemians.

Mynona
Pseudonym of Dr Salamo Friedländer, used for his contributions to the
Expressionist journal *Der Sturm*.

Reinhardt, Max (1873–1943)
Austrian impresario and theatre director, who worked at the Deutsches Theater
in Berlin 1905–33; he started the Salzburg Festival in 1920 with Richard Strauss
and Hugo von Hofmannsthal. He was responsible for introducing Strindberg,
Shaw and Pirandello to German audiences.

Rouault, Georges (1871–1958)
French painter and printmaker. Although he never belonged to a group, he
exhibited in 1905 with the Fauves (he was a friend of Henri Matisse). His use of
the grotesque and his dark-toned expressionistic style were considered shocking.

Strindberg, August (1849–1912)
Swedish dramatist, novelist and critic. His use of historical drama and
naturalistic experimentation were widely influential, and his work anticipates
many innovations in twentieth-century theatre.

Valéry, Paul (1871–1945)

French poet and essayist. Elected to the Académie Française in 1925, he became a kind of official man of letters, whose public opinion on the widest range of subjects was often sought, and nearly always given.

Vogel, Lucien

Publisher of *Vu* magazine; championed innovative photographers.

Wedekind, Frank (1864–1918)

German dramatist. His use of parody and the grotesque, and especially his expressionistic depiction of sexuality, was often considered offensive – his work was the subject of frequent censorship. His plays include *Spring's Awakening*, *Earth Spirit* and *Pandora's Box*.

INDEX

Figures in italics indicate illustrations.